/10 Neil.

Keep on Keeping on. — !

Izabella —

April 2019.

Once Upon a Cook - Food Wisdom, Better Living

Reclaim your kitchen - Take back your health

Produced in the United Kingdom.

First Edition: 2019

ISBN: 978-1-9993426-0-9

Published by Better Living Press

www.izabellanatrins.com

welcome@izabellanatrins.com

ACKNOWLEDGEMENTS

Knowing with whom and where to begin to thank all those who have inspired, encouraged, motivated and helped me get *Once Upon a Cook - Food Wisdom, Better Living* into your hands is no easy task.

So, let me start at the beginning…

My dad, who gave me confidence, self-esteem and an enquiring mind and worked relentlessly to create a new life, in a new country we could truly call our home.

My mum, who worked so hard to put real home-cooked food on our table every single day and who gave me my love of food and the skill to cook it from scratch, creatively and with passion. My parents left this world too young - but what a legacy they left behind in their two daughters.

My family and friends, for the pleasure I've had in seeing them enjoy the food I've cooked over the years.

My (erstwhile) doctors, consultants and surgeons, whose conventional tools were not able to help me or heal me, but whose failings drove me to discover food-as-medicine and restore my health.

My teachers: **Darina Allen** who instilled in me the passion and wisdom for fresh, organic whole foods and time-honoured, but forgotten methods of its preparation; **Sally Fallon Morell**, whose work taught me about the universal importance of nutrient-dense traditional foods for optimum nutrition; and **Dr Natasha Campbell-McBride**, who introduced me to the fundamental wisdom of the gut, its pre-eminent importance to every single aspect of our health and taught me how to heal it.

My clients, whose healing journey and successes have confirmed everything I've learned and driven me to learn and do more.

My partner Geoff, who has stood at hand with encouragement, unwavering patience and practical support throughout the whole process of writing this book.

My son Al, whose moral support, encouragement and teasing has spurred me on.

Anne Thorn, whose intelligent critique and editorial skills have helped to make this book better.

A very, very special and heart-felt thank you to **my son Ben**, who has walked the long, often frustrating and sometimes difficult of path of *Once Upon a Cook - Food Wisdom Better Living* with me every single step of the way - learning new skills and rising to each and every challenge that we've encountered. If not for him, then quite simply, this book would not be in your hands. Thank you so much, Ben.

I'm grateful for the comments and encouragement from the many subject experts who gave their time to read earlier versions of the manuscript - **Darina Allen, Sally Fallon Morell, Dr Natasha Campbell-McBride, Dr Chris Masterjohn, Dr James DiNicolantonio, Andrew Jackson** and **Joanna Blythman**. Thank you all.

And I thank you too, **dear reader**. Thank you for responding to my call to action to reclaim your kitchen and restore your health and for embarking on the journey toward more conscious food choices and much better health.

Thank you for making the task of writing this book worth the while!

"One thing that [Izabella's] programme has done - probably the best thing - is that it's given me the tools to be able to recognise patterns in my health and behaviour and most of the time, it all links to what I eat. But there's a lot more to the programme than sorting out your diet. With help, guidance and a really personal service I felt like I was chatting to a best friend. It was really helpful to know that someone else was on my wave length. I'd really wanted to lose weight, but that's no longer a priority; I want to be healthy, not thin. I want to (and do) love myself - something which I never thought I'd say!"

- Charley

"[Izabella] helped me to understand what my body will tolerate, what it won't and why! The regular Skype calls kept me on the straight and narrow; Izabella didn't let me off the hook… in fact I could often hear her voice in my head! The health benefits are enormous, I feel so much better - a lot more energy and feel much less tired and much less stressed. My sleep pattern is a lot better too. People are passing comment on how well I look - and I like it! I feel like I've got ME back!"

- Sue

"Izabella's support, knowledge, empathy and recommendations have helped me achieve an incredible turn around in my health. Now, 6 months down-the-line, I am not only playing with my children, I am not taking any medication, I am walking every day, doing yoga every day and I sometimes try a little jog - far from where I was just 6 months ago!"

***12-MONTH UPDATE*: "I just wanted to let you know that I had my routine consultant's appointment at hospital yesterday and my Psoriatic Arthritis seems to be inactive! My bloods are great, everything is within normal range! I am ecstatic! It seems as though my arthritis has gone into remission!! I never thought I would say those words - so, so pleased! I thought you would be interested to hear this, especially as you played such a huge part in helping me get here."**

- Sara

"At the stage of reaching out to Izabella I was drained, exhausted and just doing a days' work was an achievement. The advice and support that I received was second to none - throughout the programme Izabella was extremely supportive with very quick responses to my emails when I had questions between our scheduled calls, sending advice and suggestions, often substantiated by articles or blogs that helped make sense of everything. I feel like a completely different person, full of energy, with a passion for wellbeing, healthy eating and committed to feeling the absolute best I can. Without question, working with Izabella certainly has changed my life for the better."

- Julie

"As a single 60-something woman, this book has really opened my eyes and made me completely rethink my diet. I lived on ready meals, but since reading Izzy's book I have switched to high quality meat, organic produce and now read all labels. I have found local farm shops and butchers and have a new awareness about the most basic things we eat like bread, milk and eggs. This book is a must for anyone who wants to become a more informed consumer and who wants to make better choices and learn how food cooked by our parents and grandparents was really good for us; real unprocessed food. When we understand how our body is a finely tuned machine that needs the right nutrition to keep it running at optimum health, the results can be life changing."

- Anne

I'm here to inform, inspire and support you to hear your body's whispers before it starts to scream; to make food and lifestyle choices for much better health; and to help you put the traditional foods that kept generations healthy back onto your table.

- Izabella Natrins (2019)

CONTENTS

WELCOME

If you've bought this book, it's because you care.

I suspect you care because you worry that the 'food' we are eating now isn't what it once was and still should be - delicious, nutritious, whole food, produced in sympathy with this planet and the wisdom of Mother Nature.

Perhaps you care because you (or someone close to you) isn't enjoying the energy, vitality and good health that is a birth-right. Instead, life is a struggle, with little energy, poor sleep, constant tiredness and generally feeling unwell or suffering from chronic disease.

I wrote this book because I care about those things too and decided to take action.

I care that people are getting sick and staying sick, because I know from experience that our food is our first and our best medicine. I care that people around me - family, friends and clients - no longer know what to buy or where to shop. It matters that people are losing the skills to cook food at home. I care that as a nation, we are becoming more and more reliant on industrially manufactured, ultra-processed and chemically-laden 'fake' foods, which our body cannot recognise and certainly cannot process.

It's distressing that we in the UK are now leading the global race to the bottom of international league tables for health and disease through our consumption of these ultra-processed foods. These cheap, manufactured food-like substances offer us little or no nutrition and, even worse, are sending us down the road to the diseases that are sabotaging our health, destroying our health and quality of life, bankrupting our healthcare systems, shortening our lifespan and that of our children.

When we look around, more and more of us becoming sicker than ever before. Many of us will know someone with diabetes, obesity, cardiovascular disease, degenerative, digestive or autoimmune disorders or who has been diagnosed with cancer.

Worldwide, chronic diseases are escalating out of control. The World Health Organisation's (WHO) statistics report that 1.9 billion adults were overweight in 2016 and of these, over 650 million were obese. Obesity is preventable.

The WHO's *Global Report on Diabetes* (2016) calculated that over 422 million adults were living with diabetes in 2014, compared with 108 million in 1980. Type 2 diabetes is preventable.

Millions of our children are stricken with obesity, diabetes, autism and other distressing health conditions in epidemic numbers. The WHO statistics for 2016 reported that 41 million children under the age of 5 were overweight or obese, as were over 340 million children and adolescents (aged 5 - 19).

Our existing healthcare system in the UK is no longer sustainable; we're spending trillions yet we're still getting sicker and our life expectancies are getting lower. In my view, the crisis in healthcare will not be solved by money, but by education about getting the right nutrition from high quality, nutrient-dense foods and by lifestyle changes and support for all. It's reassuring to see that many people are now becoming better informed about the problems with industrial-scale intensive farming systems, processed food and failing healthcare systems and are passionate about finding out how to feed themselves with healthy, nutritious food.

Many chronic diseases can be impacted by changes in diet and lifestyle. Not only have I reversed my own autoimmune disease, but I have helped many of my clients reverse theirs and witnessed my colleagues' successes with their clients.

If you are tired of struggling with confusing eating trends, of filling your fridge with faddy and expensive 'super-foods' in the hope of feeling better, or if you are despondent about losing your excess weight, then this book is for you. Your path to good health starts in the kitchen with home-cooked foods made from real, whole ingredients (plant or animal) that are grown or raised in clean, healthy, chemical-free soils.

Food is much more than a filling fuel for our body; it's data for the body. Real, whole ingredients carry life- and health-giving molecules of information that tell our cells how and when to work. The ultra-processed, chemically-damaged, pseudo-substances that we have all come to call 'food' carry misinformation which our body can't recognise and it responds in the only way it knows how, with inflammation that harms our digestive and immune systems.

I care deeply that the traditional, time-honoured foods, the powerful medicine that kept generations before us fit and free of chronic disease, are incorrectly demonised and side-lined by poorly-designed, biased and misinterpreted science and often, no science at all.

As you will see as you read on, I am deeply troubled that so many people are unaware of what is happening in our conventional broken farming, food and healthcare systems and are confused by the plethora of conflicting misinformation about food.

I care about our future generations and I care about you. This book is a call to action to reclaim your kitchen and take back your health.

What you will learn from this book

The pages of this book will take you back to the future, to learn about real food and how it leads to your good health.

Once Upon a Cook - Food Wisdom, Better Living isn't a book that teaches you how to cook, nor is it just another cook book with recipes. It's not another health book featuring the latest fad diets, nor is it a comprehensive book on nutrition.

In this book, you will find traditional food wisdom, supported by sound, independent science. You will learn about forgotten culinary skills and you will discover simple, delicious, nutritious recipes for better energy, vitality and health.

Everything you will read in these pages is well-researched and evidence-based. You will find key research and links to a library of references and sources of reliable information. Some of the evidence I will present is historical or has been buried and forgotten, but it's just as valid and relevant as the new and emerging science being discovered every day.

All the evidence I have found is pointing us in one direction: Granny knew best! The time-honoured, traditional foods of our grandparents (and theirs) are the ones we must put back onto our dining tables if we are to halt the race to the bottom which is endangering our health.

This book will equip you to ask questions, to make demands and to get rewards and I hope it will inspire, support and motivate you to take action on a journey towards a healthier, more energetic and better quality of life.

So, let us start by rewinding.

Once upon a time...

Our lives have changed more over the last 100 years than at any other time in human history. Things have changed so much that our grandparents (and theirs) would probably recognise very little in the modern world.

Today, life gives people access to awesome technologies, global communications, travel opportunities, a vast array of 'push-the-button' home and mobile entertainment gadgets and gizmos. And we have access to any kind of food, from any part of the world, with nothing more for us to do but heat and serve. There is so much choice we can have anything we desire and we call that progress.

But is it?

Once upon a time, we knew our local farmers, butchers and bakers and could trust the integrity and quality of the food they produced. We cooked from scratch and with the seasons and knew what to do with a chicken, a piece of brisket or a whole fish. Meals were planned, shopped for with a list and cooked ahead.

We saved money by making meals go further and used delicious left-overs creatively. We knew how to choose good fruit and vegetables and what to do with them. It was a priority to nourish ourselves and our family with delicious home-cooked meals. Apple pies and special treats were saved for Sunday teatime. Our food was good, we respected and enjoyed it and we certainly didn't waste it!

Today we eat for convenience and speed, not for flavour and well-being. Our staples are ultra-processed, food-like products, made with unpronounceable ingredients, by people we don't know. With each food scandal we increasingly scrutinise labels, trying (and often failing), to understand what is in our food.

As time goes on, even though we now eat a greater variety of food, it does not provide our bodies with the nourishment needed to keep healthy. In fact, as a population, we are actually *mal*nourished.

If this is progress, it has come at a price:

"As consumers, we opt for convenience, but the trade-off is that we know almost nothing about how our food is grown, where it comes from, or whether it's good for us.

If we are what we eat, then our bodies and souls are largely at the mercy of agribusiness, commodity traders and advertising executives thousands of miles from our homes and a world away from our real needs."

- Sandor Katz
The Art of Fermentation

Disconnection

Just as we are rapidly losing the ties that once bound us together in supportive, caring families and communities, we seem to have lost connection with how real food is farmed and grown and with the alchemy of cooking. We have forgotten the sheer fun of sitting down to eat together as families, friends or as a community.

Once upon a time, our food wisdom, so fundamental to good nutrition, was handed down through tradition, experience, observation and teaching. Everyone had special 'taste memories' of home.

The ancient science of Ayurveda teaches that the cook's energy profoundly affects the quality of the food. It teaches that we should prepare our food calmly, in a happy frame of mind, with a focused, positive and loving intent towards those for whom we are cooking.

This makes complete sense to me. However good it seems, restaurant food never quite has the same flavours of nourishing energy as a meal cooked by someone who knows, loves and cares for you. From this perspective, it's especially important to make the time to cook for ourselves and for our family. Nothing can replace the special ingredient of a parent's love in a child's food.

Confusion

Today, we look to professionals, 'eat well' plates, 'traffic lights' and all kinds of diet gurus to tell us what to eat. Depending on which way the wind blows, each tells us something different. How many of us have been seduced into confusion by the promise (and treadmill) of a high/low/no fat diet vs a high/low/no carb diet, yet still struggle to achieve and maintain a healthy weight, or increase our energy, vitality and regain our health?

If you are sick and fed up with being drawn into the latest diet trend, faddy foods, or just want to lose a little excess weight, then you need to get healthy first. You don't always get healthy by losing weight, you just get thinner! [1,2]

Loss of skills

Modern life can be overwhelming, we are all too busy, stressed-out and distracted to reach for a saucepan when there is always something more important to be done. Instead, we reach for convenience and vow to make it up at the weekend. Sadly, each successive generation is losing the ability, the confidence and the will to cook real food from scratch.

Food manufacturing and retail food industries are just that - industries. It's their job (and legal requirement) to ensure shareholder value, not to keep us healthy!

My mum worked full-time in a tiring factory job, but she cooked every day and always put something delicious and nourishing on the table. In her day, there were few refrigerators, no convenience foods, no ready meals, no takeaways and eating out was a treat reserved for special occasions or holidays.

Thinking ahead, planning and preparation were the order of her day and they can be ours too, with a little food wisdom and the will for better living for ourselves and our families.

As I watched my mum, I absorbed her techniques and methods, and saw how she treated ingredients and constantly tasted and seasoned each dish. From her I learned to recognise the flavours of food cooked with love and I carried on this tradition with my family and my boys, now men, are both great cooks!

STOP THE CLOCK!

We haven't changed

The process of evolution is SLOW! Although our man-made environment has changed drastically, our human physiology and digestive system has barely evolved from that of our ancestors. Whilst our intellect has harnessed technologies to create a brave new world, our physiology is struggling (and failing) to cope with an environment it cannot compute.

Food carries information that directs whether and how our cells should grow. Real food carries trillions of information molecules (nutrients) with which we have co-evolved. These delicious messengers instruct our genes to switch on or off, tell our cells how to work and determine which hormones we need to produce, where they need to go and when.[3]

To continue the computer analogy, it's a simple matter of 'garbage-in, garbage out'. When our body's computer doesn't recognise the codes, it can't compute them. Eventually our computer says "NO!" and starts breaking down.

Unlike a computer, we can't upgrade to the latest model, so health services across the world struggle, and fail to cope with the growing numbers of broken human hardware.

I was just such a body, struggling with a rapidly advancing autoimmune disorder, enduring one surgery after another and taking more and more medications. I decided to stop the clock and embark on a journey of personal and then professional education, to regain my energy, vitality and health naturally. What I learned for myself changed my life.

I learned how the damaged, processed, chemical concoctions that we have all come to call food, as well as the commercially-produced personal and household products I was using daily, were destroying my body's microbiome, my gut flora and my digestive and immune systems, paving the way for chronic autoimmune disease.

I rediscovered the forgotten food wisdom of Granny and her fore-bearers and I learned that no matter where we live on this planet, Mother Nature has provided us with nutrient-dense, healing foods that are powerful medicines if they are grown and farmed in traditional, time-honoured ways in healthy, unsprayed soils.[4]

I learned how real food, properly prepared, cooked with love and eaten together, reconnects us with ourselves, with each other and with our planet.

Food-and-lifestyle as medicine

As we've seen from the WHO data above, despite huge advances in medical research, more of us are becoming sicker than at any time in our entire history with an escalating catalogue of chronic, degenerative and autoimmune diseases. I believe the key to good health starts with the food we eat.

Dr Max Gerson, a German-born American physician who developed a dietary-based alternative treatment for cancer and most chronic, degenerative diseases, held that there are only two root causes of disease: deficiency and toxicity. Like Hippocrates, the father of modern medicine, before him, and ancient medical systems even before that, Gerson believed that food is our first and best medicine.[5]

Every single one of our cells needs to produce enough energy to fuel not only itself, but the organ to which it belongs and all our bodily processes, including our cognitive and emotional processes. How we feed our body determines the strength of our metabolism, our overall energy, vitality and health and even how quickly we age.

But achieving true health means much more than eating a metabolically supportive diet. In my work I take a holistic 'food-and-lifestyle-as-medicine' approach, which puts a whole person at the centre of the complex and interconnected web that is a whole life.

Although food is absolutely our first and best medicine, it is by no means our only medicine. No amount of perfect-for-you, nutritious, healing foods will mend a broken lifestyle and the impact of a toxic environment.

"When diet is wrong, medicine is of no use; when diet is correct, medicine is of no need."

- Ayurvedic proverb

In addition to a nutrient-dense diet, achieving true health means becoming much more aware of how:

- restful sleep
- reducing stress
- taking regular breaks in nature to move your body
- clearing out toxins from our home and our personal care products
- fostering inner and outer connectedness

will create a truly whole and healthy lifestyle for you and your family.

Toxic lifestyles

Our modern lifestyles are deeply and chronically stressing our bodies and at worst, are causing life-threatening and chronic diseases:

- electromagnetic field and light pollution from devices and screens
- air and water pollution
- agricultural chemicals
- reliance on pharmaceuticals
- toxic and endocrine-disrupting household and personal care products.

Undoubtedly our environment is poorly regulated and contributes heavily to increasing the number and complexity of toxins our body has to deal with. Understanding and educating ourselves on these issues and their impact on our health is critical.[6]

Addressing these issues is a huge area and outside the scope of this book, but if you are struggling with feeling well, or with niggling or diagnosed health issues, then you might consider whether nutrition and lifestyle health coaching might be beneficial for you. You will find more information about this in the concluding chapter.

About me

Formerly a health research psychologist at the University of Birmingham Medical School, and an NHS Programme Manager and Management Consultant, I left academia and the corporate world behind to train as a chef with Darina Allen at the Ballymaloe Cookery School, set on a 100-acre organic farm in Cork, Ireland.

The experience of learning about the value of real, whole, organic food, the alchemy of artisan food production and classic culinary skills changed the course of my life and helped me win my battle with a progressing autoimmune disease.

It led me to research and study food and nutrition. I became a Certified GAPS (Digestive Healing) Practitioner and a qualified Nutrition and Lifestyle Health Coach. I helped myself and knew I could to help others struggling with chronic and autoimmune disorders.

Now I spend my days coaching, researching and developing coaching programmes and writing for my health education website. My health coaching practice focuses on women and particularly women in midlife. It's not because the guys don't need help - I choose to focus on women because I truly believe that women hold the family, the community and world in the palm of our hand, and it's a very heavy responsibility.

Historically, in many traditional and tribal societies, women played a significant role in the existence, structure and administration of tribal nations, where they were respected and deferred to for their innate ability to reason, dispense wisdom and the teaching of children. While women have lost that role and their due respect in modern society, I believe we retain the 'genetic memory' of our natural being.

Modern life can be increasingly overwhelming and exhausting for both men and women, but for women particularly, the feeling that we need to do more, be more and care more haunts us daily, and our health and happiness is suffering. Our ability to hold it together is suffering too.

At the Vancouver Peace Summit in 2009, the Dalai Lama said something which rocked the globe:

"The world will be saved by the Western woman."

But, in this book, my focus is on us all and on our context: men, women, children, grandparents, family, community, environment and planet, because we are all deeply and inextricably interconnected.

My research and my learning helped me and now I want it to inspire and help you too. On that note, as you read on please remember:

I offer well researched, science-backed and fully referenced information to inform, educate and inspire you to make better choices when selecting, sourcing and cooking the foods that you put into your body to create more energy, vitality and enjoy better health.

I'm not a registered dietician or doctor. I am a Nutrition and Lifestyle Health Coach, nutritional chef, and a Certified GAPS (Digestive Health) Practitioner. The contents of this book may help health conditions but are not intended as health advice regarding any acute or chronic medical condition, or to replace any treatment or medication prescribed by a qualified health professional.

If you have a health condition, please consult a qualified health professional alongside the advice given in this book.

So, without further ado, let us begin our journey back to the future…

ABOUT THE RECIPES

While the focus of this book is on putting 'traditional' foods back on the table for much better health, the recipes I offer here aren't traditional in the sense that they hark back to the days of 'plain ol' biddles'. Rather, they're an eclectic selection of recipes showcasing traditional foods in a modern context and embracing a range of cuisines, flavoursome herbs and spices and a sprinkling of creativity.

Do try to be creative: most recipes aren't written in stone and nothing terrible will happen (unless you're baking!) if you swap ingredients or use different amounts from those stated. Every time I make a particular dish, I'll often change the recipe slightly according to what ingredients I have to hand.

I hope you enjoy my selection, and please feel free to browse for more recipes and traditional food inspiration on my website: www.izabellanatrins.com.

Tips on cooking without tears

- Always read the recipe through before you shop for ingredients
- Read the recipe through again before you start to cook
- Prepare a 'mis-en-place': i.e. get everything ready and set out (washed, peeled, measured, chopped, whisked, greased, lined) **before** you start
- Invest in a couple of decent knives (at the very least a chef's knife and a utility knife for preparing vegetables) and keep them sharp. Also, make sure you have a good-quality wooden chopping board available (natural wood is anti-bacterial)
- For baking, always use the precise quantities and tins of the specified dimensions
- When seasoning, just go with your palate, but please don't be afraid to season well - it makes all the difference between an OK meal and a great meal
- Always use good quality oven gloves and never use a damp tea towel (ouch!)

Oven temperatures

Please be aware that the actual temperatures of ovens vary, depending on brand, fuel, age and… its own foibles!

The temperatures given here are based on a multi-function, fan-assisted electric oven. Food cooked in a fan-assisted oven will cook more efficiently than that cooked a convection oven, so the temperature will need to be reduced (by around 20°) to take account of this. For example, if a recipe gives a temperature of 200°C, lower it to 180°C in a fan-assisted oven.

The oven temperature table below is taken from Dove's Farm UK:

Gas	**°F**	**°C**	**Fan**
1	275	140	120
2	300	150	130
3	325	170	150
4	350	180	160
5	375	190	170
6	400	200	180
7	425	220	200
8	450	230	210
9	475	240	220

Sourcing

A plea here for sourcing as locally as possible, whenever possible. When sourcing online, search for ethical suppliers who offer good product information and producers who sell direct to the public and consider using an online local foods portal like Big Barn to find suppliers near you.

Safe cooking equipment and utensils

Whenever possible, choose pots and pans made from safe, non-toxic materials like carbon steel, ceramic, lava rock, porcelain enamel, or tempered glass. Cast iron and stainless steel are generally safe, but when cooking acidic tomato-based foods or slow cooking, they can leach heavy metals into the food.

The Organic Authority caution against two materials, however, that should be avoided whenever possible:

- Aluminium (and aluminium foil) has been linked to central nervous system problems like Alzheimer's, ALS, and autism spectrum disorders
- Teflon is used in most non-stick cookware, but studies show that heating the coating polytetrafluoroethylene (PTFE) creates perfluorooctanoic acid (PFOA) - dangerous both for the cook and for diners.

A note about provenance

Your health is your wealth - please invest in yours and try your best to source your ingredients as well as you are able, even if this means making sacrifices elsewhere. As we shall see, pasture-raised and finished organic meats, dairy, eggs and wild-caught fish have a vastly superior nutritional profile, as do organic or cleanly-raised and grown fruits, vegetables and herbs.

CHAPTER ONE

NOURISHING TRADITIONALLY for ENERGY, VITALITY and HEALTH

"A journey of a thousand miles begins with the Satnav taking you the wrong way."

- Huffington Post

Confusion reigns supreme

It seems that every time we open any newspaper or magazine, turn on the radio or TV, we're bombarded with guidance about what we should be eating, when we should be eating it and how various foods will severely damage us if we indulge.

With online research, the confusion becomes greater. In this information-rich age, a certain amount of disagreement is to be expected. But when experts, doctors, nutritionists and dieticians (not to mention the millions of health bloggers) have completely differing viewpoints, how can we tell what's true and what's not? It's no wonder that we're left in a state of utter confusion.

Milk is a perfect example. Once upon a time, milk was a valued medicine and as we shall see, was used by doctors to restore health. Milk was prized by bodybuilders and school milk was free. Fast-forward to the present day and we find that milk is vilified as a food unfit for human consumption - you'll hear more about this later.

Dairy intolerance is rife, and more and more people are blaming their health conditions such as eczema, asthma, and allergies on the consumption of dairy products. Milk substitutes made with soya, almonds, coconuts and oats are now abundant on supermarket shelves.

Around five million diet books are sold every year in the US and fad diets abound. We've had *The South Beach Diet, Weight Watchers Diet, The Zone Diet, The Akins Diet, Volumetrics, The Raw Food Diet, The Cabbage Soup Diet, The Macrobiotic Diet, The Vegan Diet, The Green Juice Diet, The Grapefruit Diet, The Banana Diet, The Clean Diet, The Ketogenic Diet, The Low Carb, High Fat Diet... and The List Goes on Diet!*

Essentially, each is a version of no-fat/low-fat/eat-as-much-as-you-can-fat diet, or a no-carbs/low-carbs/good-carbs diet. Many diets give conflicting advice and are based on restricting or removing whole food groups, combining foods in very specific ways, or eating at specific times. The advice given can be complex and confusing, and much of it is just plain wrong. For many of us, the impact of cutting out major food groups, like carbohydrates, can be detrimental to our long-term health.

If these diets work at all, they offer only short-term gains. Most popular diets are aimed at weight loss which cannot be sustained when returning to normal eating, often leading to an unhealthy process of 'yo-yo' dieting. As we shall see, it's perfectly possible to lose weight, maintain a healthy weight and support optimum health by eating traditional, whole foods.

How is the 'traditional food' approach better?

For far too long, the relationship between what we're eating and the state of our health has been refuted and ignored. Hippocrates (born around 460 BC on the island of Kos, Greece) became known as the 'Father of Medicine' and was regarded as the greatest physician of his time. He based his medical practice on observations and the study of the human body and held the belief that:

"All disease begins in the gut."

Hippocrates' centuries-old wisdom has stood the test of time. The tremendous advances in research on the human microbiome, particularly on the nature and function of our gut microbiota, are showing us how profoundly the gut bacteria in our digestive tract, as well as the integrity of our gut lining, can lead to disease. We are learning that many chronic, autoimmune and metabolic diseases do actually begin in the gut and we'll hear much more about this as we read on.

One of the main reasons dietary advice is so conflicting is that there is so much we've yet to discover about how our human physiology works and particularly how the nutrients (or lack thereof!) in our food affect our body and ultimately our health. It's also a harsh truth that much nutritional and medical research relies on funding from bodies who are not completely independent and often have vested interests in the results. In this context we might consider the role and influence of the pharmaceutical, agrichemical, biotechnology, food processing and retail food industries.

What's more, the pressure to inform clinical practice with data from randomised controlled trials (RCTs) is problematic. A RCT is the 'gold standard' of research design, in which people are randomly allocated to receive one of several clinical interventions (or no intervention at all) and the results are then statistically compared. These kinds of trials are expensive to run, difficult to fund and often not feasible on ethical grounds. For example, no research body would be allowed to set up a methodology where volunteers are asked to consume suspect foods to the point of harming themselves or developing a disease.

Bearing this in mind, can we do better than to keep reacting to whatever the latest dietary fad, or contradictory advice based on questionable research, seems to be telling us? I say: "Yes, we most certainly can!"

Back to the future: studying what worked

Some 80 years ago, a prominent American research dentist, Dr Weston A. Price (subsequently to become the founder and first director of the American Dental Association's Research Institute) noticed something worrying in his day-to-day practice:

> **"Price was disturbed by what he found when he looked into the mouths of his patients. Rarely did an examination of an adult client reveal anything but rampant decay, often accompanied by serious problems elsewhere in the body such as arthritis, osteoporosis, diabetes, intestinal complaints and chronic fatigue. They called it neurasthenia in Price's day.**
>
> **But it was the dentition of younger patients that gave him most cause for concern. He observed that crowded, crooked teeth were becoming more and more common, along with what Price called "facial deformities"- overbites, narrowed faces, underdevelopment of the nose, lack of well-defined cheekbones and pinched nostrils.**
>
> **Such children invariably suffered from one or more complaints that sound all too familiar to mothers of the 1990s: frequent infections, allergies, anaemia, asthma, poor vision, lack of coordination, fatigue and behavioural problems."**

- Sally Fallon Morrell
Founder and President, Weston A. Price Foundation

Dr Price set about finding why. His ground-breaking and meticulous research took him far and wide across the world, studying the diets and lifestyles of 14 isolated (but healthy) societies living entirely on traditional, local, 'whole' foods that were far removed from what was, even then, an increasingly industrially-processed American diet.

From the Swiss to the Irish, the Eskimos to the Africans, these people enjoyed almost perfect health. Free from chronic disease, dental decay and mental illness, they were strong, robust and produced generation after generation of healthy children.

While their geography and diet differed in many respects, there were important dietary commonalities. Dr Price's seminal work established him as a pioneer in nutritional anthropology. Not only did his findings fill an entire volume (*Nutrition and Physical Degeneration*), his work started two nutrition research and education movements - The Price-Pottenger Nutrition Foundation and The Weston A. Price Foundation, where Sally Fallon Morrell works tirelessly to promote traditional foods. It also seeded the growth of The Ancestral Health Movement.

"Almost without exception, the groups he studied ate liberally of seafood or other animal proteins or fats in the form of organ meats and dairy products; they valued animal fats as absolutely necessary to good health; they ate fats, meats, fruits, vegetables, legumes, nuts, sees and whole grains in their whole, unrefined state (and) contained some raw foods, of both animal and vegetable origin."

- Sally Fallon Morrell

All these disparate peoples' diets had the same thing in common: they were based on ancient food wisdom and they have stood the test of time, to be validated by modern scientific research.

Dr Price compared the health of those who remained true to their traditional foods and time-honoured food preparation techniques, with those who became influenced to consume the Western, industrially-processed diet of refined grains, canned foods, pasteurised milk, excess sugar and devitalised, industrially-produced oils. In every case, Dr Price found that the longer the exposure to the Western diet, the greater the incidence of tooth decay, infectious and degenerative diseases and infertility.

The evolution of medicine: symptom control vs root-cause resolution

The practise of medicine is evolving in our lifetime. The many millions of us locked into a relentless struggle with our health, and the crisis in health care across the developed West, is testament to a worrying fact: the conventional medical model - which treats symptoms as causes, shoe-horning clinical symptoms to fit diagnostic categories and then prescribing suppressive drug-based or surgical interventions - is well and truly broken.

Root-cause resolution, on the other hand, is a functional approach which systematically uncovers the underlying causes of presenting symptoms and intervenes to correct dysfunction in associated body systems. It goes way beyond asking "What is causing the issue?" to ask: "What are the issues that are *causing* that issue?" and then: "What needs to be done to resolve these issues?" This new medicine has no prescribed solutions and no 'one-size-fits-all' approach because each of us has a unique constitution and each is in a very different place in our journey towards true health. It follows that each of us will need a different approach and here is where the synergy of functional food-and-lifestyle-medicine comes into its own.

Evolution of nutrition: a synergy of approaches

My own approach is based on bringing together traditional food wisdom and forgotten knowledge from historical medical sources and - crucially - it's evidence-based and supported by sound, independent evidence from established and respected experts and emerging science.

I believe we owe a great debt to the work of:

- Dr Weston A. Price
- Sally Fallon Morrell
- Dr Natasha Campbell-McBride
- Darina Allen
- Chris Kresser MS L.AC
- Chris Masterjohn PhD
- Dr Kelly Brogan MD
- Dr Rangan Chatterjee
- Dr Tim Spector
- Dr Ray Peat PhD
- Dr Broda Barnes MD
- Drs Paul and Shou-Ching Jaminet
- Dr Todd Caldecott Dip. Cl.H., RH(AHG), CAP(NAMA)
- Dr John Douillard DC

and other well-qualified and well-researched authorities and practitioners who speak to the truth of traditional foods and functional food-and-lifestyle-as-medicine and whose work is referenced extensively throughout this book.

While the above approaches differ in their detail, some widely, all are physiologically sound and well-argued. Each broadly agrees that for optimum nutrition we require certain basic building blocks and that each has its place in an optimally nutritious diet:

- **macronutrients** - the structural and energy-giving components of our foods - carbohydrates, fats and protein from animal and plant sources, in the right balance for each of us
- **micronutrients** - the water- and fat-soluble vitamins, minerals, trace elements, phytochemicals, and antioxidants that are essential for good health. We need these in much smaller quantities, but they're nevertheless essential for our health.

From the seminal work of Dr Price and the huge contributions from the others mentioned, we can tease out a group of key traditional foods that make up a nutrient-dense, easy-to-digest and metabolically-supportive diet. Not surprisingly, it's a diet with which our grandparents (and theirs) would have been very familiar.

Granny's Larder

Eggs - the humble egg - organic, genuinely free-range or pasture-fed - is an all-round superfood with proteins, fats, vitamins A, B, D, E and K and other key micronutrients. Our grandparents' encouragement to "Go to work on an egg!" was sound advice!

Seafood - although oily fish like salmon have been very much in vogue, the benefits of the humble sardine, white fish and seafood such as mussels, crab and oysters are once again coming into their own.

Dairy - dairy and its products have been prized throughout history and were widely used as a medicine before industrialised, pasteurised dairy products came along. We are witnessing a renaissance of organic, non-homogenised milk; grass-fed, free-range milk; full-fat raw milk from certified producers; full-fat and raw cheeses, supporting our gut health and immune system function. Raw dairy is rich in fat-soluble vitamins A, K and E - 50% more than in pasteurised - and in vitamin C which is not present at all in pasteurised dairy products.

Bone broths - straight out of Granny's kitchen come bone broths and stocks. Chicken and beef bone broths and stocks from pasture-fed animals are a nutritional powerhouse. They are incredibly healing for the digestive tract, aid liver detoxification and support the immune system and heart health. Among its many other nutrients, bone broths contain a magical ingredient: gelatin…

Gelatin - is not just for jelly. Gelatin is a good source of protein, containing important amino acids not found in lean muscle meat. It supports skin, hair and nail growth; is good for joints and can help joint recovery; can help tighten loose skin and improve digestion since it naturally binds to water; and helps food move more easily though the digestive tract.

By the way, this is the ultimate 'beauty' food, as it's not only rumoured to help improve cellulite but is a great source of dietary collagen. Forget collagen creams and make broth instead!

Bone-in and 'slow-cook' cuts from grass-fed animals - back in the day, lean meat was cast aside in favour of what we now call 'cheap' cuts. But very lean meat is tough on our digestion and lacks important nutrients like gelatin. Granny's slow-cooked casseroles and braises used the old-fashioned cheaper cuts on the bone, containing lots of connective tissue which melds down its precious gelatin into the gravy, greatly helping digestion.

Organ meats - before you run for the hills, think: chicken liver pâté with bacon, pâté de campagne, pork and herb terrine, meatloaf, steak and kidney casserole - all delicious! All liver is beneficial, especially liver from pasture-fed animals; good for all vitamins and packed with minerals. Beef liver, although strong in taste, is particularly nutritious and there are tricks that even liver-haters will like to make it more palatable. Thankfully, 'nose-to-tail' eating is encouraging more of us to enjoy these organ meats.

Cultured and fermented foods - every civilisation throughout history has known about the power of cultured dairy - home-made yoghurts, labneh, raw-milk kefir, cultured butter - and fermented vegetables such as kimchi, sauerkraut, carrots. They are incredibly efficient chelators (detoxifiers) and contain more nutrients than before fermentation.

Grains - properly prepared and in moderation! Grains and their products are complex carbohydrates which release their energy slowly, but they need to be well broken down into simpler sugars in our digestive tract before they can enter the blood stream. Although organically-grown wheat, spelt, oats, barley, cornmeal, rice - and grain-based products like flour and cereals - can play a part in a varied, nutrient-dense diet, they are hugely problematic for our digestive (and other) systems.

Grains need to be prepared by traditional, time-honoured methods to ensure they can be well-digested and don't pave the way for nutritional deficiencies by binding minerals. As we shall see, with grains, it's not just a gluten issue, but has become a serious public health and environmental issue too.

Roots, shoots, tubers and squashes - these starchy carbs get broken down to glucose in the digestive system to deliver energy efficiently to our cells. Although starches have become demonised lately (too much sugar), for many of us, these undervalued, below-the-ground vegetables - carrots, beetroot, parsnips, swedes, celeriac, the varieties of squash and potatoes - are much easier to digest (and therefore can meet our energy needs) than the fibrous and very difficult to digest leafy greens that we obsessively whizz into that healthy green smoothie every morning.

Leafy green and sulphur-rich vegetables - we eat first with our eyes, so green vegetables are a colourful addition to any meal. Reasonable helpings of organically-grown kale, spinach, broccoli, pak choi, cabbage, cauliflower, brussels sprouts and sulphur-rich onions and garlic are fine. They supply much-needed fibre in our diet, but they can be problematic for many of us if eaten to excess, and they need to be cooked well - and served with butter or olive oil - to support digestion and nutrient absorption.

Fruit - evolutionarily, we're hard-wired for sweet foods. For our ancestors, fruit was an indicator and important source of vitamins. Although we now must recognise that modern fruit has been hybridized to be sweeter than the sharper fruits our ancestors enjoyed, it still plays an important part in a traditional, nutrient-dense diet.

The real issue isn't in eating whole fruit - where the fibre slows down the absorption of fructose - but that we are now so used to eating ultra-processed foods, chock-full of hidden sugars. Our dependency on these kinds of 'foods' has led us down the sticky path of over-consuming vast amounts of added and manufactured sugars, such as high-fructose corn syrup.

Sugar - there is no doubt that we in the developed world now consume horrifying amounts of sugar. However, Mother Nature has given us natural, simple sugars in the form of honey, maple syrup, molasses, and fresh, ripe fruits. These sugars are built from glucose, fructose and galactose. They require little or no digestion, so are quickly absorbed into our blood stream to provide rapid energy to our cells when we need it. Natural sugars have a rightful place in a well-balanced, metabolically-supportive diet. The isolated, added and synthetic sugars which abound in processed foods do not.

Carbohydrates - grains and their products, starchy and green vegetables, fruits and sugar are carbohydrates. Despite the current backlash against carbs (see below) which is gripping diet-gurus and media alike, these dietary carbohydrates provide our bodies with energy to use and to store for fuelling our cells. They provide structure, feed beneficial gut bacteria and bulk out our stools, as well as supporting our immune, digestive and cardiovascular systems.

Ultimately, our body breaks down carbohydrates into simpler sugars - mono- and diglycerides - which it can readily use for energy. One such sugar - glucose - is particularly important and too little can be just as bad as too much. In fact, if we don't get it, our body resorts to breaking down our muscles and fat stores to make it.

A heads up on a new food phobia

Our over-consumption of processed carbohydrates has tipped the proper balance of other macronutrients - proteins and fats, for example - and spawned 'carb-phobia', with disastrous results for our health. Carb-phobia is fast replacing fat-phobia as the new dietary demon on the block, with any and all carbs vilified as the cause of all mankind's ailments.

There's no denying that as a food group, carbohydrates have become highly controversial. Whether we even need to eat carbs at all is currently at the centre of a huge debate within nutritional science. While this mighty subject can't adequately be covered within the confines of this book, in the context of the current fashion for carb-bashing, there are some important things to understand about how they work in our body. I've highlighted some key issues and provided additional notes in Appendix 1 - A Deeper Dive into Carbs.

Not in Granny's pantry! Added sugars - devils in disguise

Ultra-processed and convenience foods are full of excessive and carefully hidden amounts of sugar, far more than we would ever use in our own kitchen. Because we've come to rely so heavily on these products, we drastically over-consume sugar, displacing other important nutrients from our diet. Although we tend to think that 'added' sugar is only found in desserts, cakes, biscuits and other sweet treats, it's widely found in *savoury* processed foods, such as bread, pasta and pasta sauce. To make matters worse, many foods promoted as 'natural' or 'healthy' are laden with these added sugars. The food industry uses a dizzying array of names to conceal the frightening amounts of added sugar contained in these super-sweet foods.

Fat - is our healthy friend, particularly if it's saturated or monounsaturated. For decades, fat-phobia ruled the day. Thankfully, both buried and emerging science is now proving what Granny always knew: that saturated fats like coconut oil and animal fats like butter and cream (grass-fed, raw if possible) or beef tallow (from pastured and grass-fed and finished animals), are all high in fat-soluble vitamins A, D and E. Mainly monounsaturated fats like lard (from pastured pigs), avocado oil and extra virgin olive oil are highly beneficial too. We'll learn why we should put these healthful fats back on the table and why we should banish damaged and rancid polyunsaturated fats such as vegetable, sunflower, soya, rapeseed and other oils from our kitchens and from our plates.

Salt - is most definitely the victim of misplaced blame and takes the rap for a variety of serious health conditions. Salt plays a complex role in the body and we need it to keep our metabolism high and manage our body's stress response - anything that chronically stresses our system will lead to a health issue.

But not all salt is created equal. We need to understand the difference between healthful, unrefined salts like Maldon or Cornish sea salt or Himalayan salt and the free-flowing, refined, industrial-grade salt that appears on our tables and in processed foods.

It's worth remembering that Mother Nature has given us a taste for salt and every chef worth her - or his - 'salt' knows that what separates good food from great food is salt!

Each of these traditional foods is a book in its own right; indeed, each year, respected authorities are picking up their pens to set the record straight. In the chapters that follow, my contribution to this effort will be to outline why and how each of these important foods can optimise your energy, vitality and ultimately your health. And in so doing, I aim to inspire you to dig deeper and learn more. I'll share key recipes, tips and techniques which illustrate how easily and deliciously you can incorporate Granny's healthy, traditional foods into your life.

A note about eating seasonally

Eating and living seasonally is about much more than just taking random advantage of whatever produce happens to be available at the time.

Mother Nature has seen to it that our planet provides us with foods which will best nourish us for each and every season. Our place is to remember that we are part of Nature too and to reconnect with her wisdom by listening to our body and learning to follow our intuition to choose foods which yield their optimum nutritional potential when eaten in season.

When we adjust our diet and lifestyle to the seasons, not only do we benefit from the nutritional potential, but our health-promoting digestive microbes dramatically change too.

We've so closely co-evolved with our microbes - they're not just in our gut, we literally co-exist with them - that some would say that our human body is just a hot house for these tiny microbial masters, giving them a very comfortable home from which to orchestrate every aspect of our physical and mental health.

While they may be small, our gut microbes really are smart: they insist that we consume the foods which not only nourish us but allow them to thrive too. That really does mean eating with the seasons for optimum nutrition and not just because it sounds trendy.

Traditional societies and the ancient life-sciences like Ayurveda know the importance of eating seasonally. The emerging science of the human microbiome is catching up fast and showing us how these little critters make their displeasure obvious when we don't toe their line. Hippocrates held that all disease starts in the gut and it's so exciting when modern nutritional science - and our growing understanding of the fundamental role our gut microbiome plays in keeping us healthy - shows that he was right on the money.

A reminder about food provenance

Once upon a time, all our food, the food that our animals ate, the plants and the soil in which it grew and on which it was raised, was organic. In the chapters that follow, we'll see how far we've departed from the heritage that Mother Nature has provided and how it's affecting our health and our planet.

Please: try your very best to source your food as well as you are able, even if this means making sacrifices elsewhere.

Our health is our wealth.

As I mentioned earlier, pasture-raised and finished organic meats, dairy, eggs and wild-caught fish have a vastly superior nutritional profile, as do organic or cleanly raised and grown fruits, vegetables and herbs. This makes the shopping bill more expensive, but if you source your food wisely it will hurt less than you think. Make no mistake, your body will thank you and so will our planet.

A note about food as medicine

Food is our first and our best medicine and by changing our diet we can all - whether in sickness or in health - improve our health or achieve wellness.

Each of us is an individual with a unique constitution and health history, particularly if we're struggling with a specific, enduring or serious health issue. Anyone in this position will need a personalised nutritional-and-lifestyle approach, focused on their specific context. They'll also likely need support from an experienced healthcare practitioner to steer them along the path to wellness and optimum health.

Depending on the condition, if I were to need such a person, I'd probably want to find two: an experienced Functional Medicine doctor, working with a qualified Nutrition and Lifestyle Health Coach. I'd want them to work with me to address the root causes of my condition, understand the role of nutrition and lifestyle in health and disease, have practical experience of using food as medicine and be able to support me with practical steps to make sustainable food and lifestyle changes for better health.

As you read on, let's take with us the prophetic words of French physician - and arguably the father of the Paleo and low-carb diets - Antheléme Brillat-Savarin, who in 1826 wrote:

"Dis-moi ce que tu manges, je te dirai ce que tu es"

Tell me what you eat, and I will tell you what you are....

CHAPTER TWO

IT ALL BEGINS (and ENDS) IN THE SOIL!

"Ashes to ashes, dust to dust. Golden lads and girls all must,

as chimney sweepers, come to dust."

- English Burial Service
- William Shakespeare

You may find it puzzling that a book on the wisdom and science of traditional foods leads with a chapter on soil, but please, stay with me - all will become clear as we go!

When I made my decision to leave the corporate world and undertake professional chef's training, I finally settled on the Ballymaloe Cookery School, near Cork, in Ireland. Its near-coastal location looked beautiful, its international reputation spoke volumes and its organic ethos and focus on artisanal skill promised it to be a very special place indeed.

I couldn't wait. The prospect of learning classic French culinary techniques, honing my knife skills, making jus and rillettes, baking breads, working with organic produce and learning to master smears, stacks and other such cheffy endeavours was exciting. Boy was this course going to rock!

But on the first day of the first term in early January, I found myself not rocking the kitchen, but instead shivering in the middle of a cold, snowy field. As we huddled closely around the legendary Darina Allen, she bent to scrape away the snow and grab a fist-full of rich, black soil. The point she was indelibly making to a new intake of culinary students is one which any truly passionate chef will understand:

Good food and good cooking start in the SOIL, not in the kitchen!

I've written elsewhere how the experience of learning and working at Ballymaloe changed my life and in so doing, I hope the 'ripple effect' will help you to change your perception of what we can all too easily call 'dirt'. I implore you to remember that your good health starts in the soil.

Just as a good chef knows that the source of the produce determines the quality of the final dish, any committed farmer knows that the value of soil isn't only about what ends up in the kitchen. As Gerry Ross (Kupa'a Farm) says in his YouTube documentary *It All Starts in the Soil*:

"If you're a farmer, the soil is your bank account."

The soil is the foundation of a farm, so it makes sense to prioritise time, effort and investment in the soil if you want the best return. But as we'll see here (and rather painfully too) it isn't only farmers who need to be checking their bank accounts - it's every single one of us: our health is our wealth.

Before we start, I'd like to give you a heads up. If you've never got down and dirty in the soil or given it much thought, you may find this chapter far removed from your everyday life and kitchen. But I promise you… it isn't! Trust me when I say that every one of us needs to be aware of what's at stake when we don't look after our soil and believe me, as you read on, you'll find scales falling from your eyes.

The subject of soil is huge and there's a lot of ground to cover (pun most definitely intended!), so I've been selective in what I present here but it should give you a much clearer perspective on the 'state of the nation', as it were.

Topsoil - we've all heard of it

Topsoil: that dark, crumbly stuff that passionate farmers, growers and gardeners make such a fuss over and work so hard to improve.

Why the fuss? Because topsoil is the 5-20 cm layer that sustains ALL land life on this planet, whether plant, animal or human. The humble topsoil is home to this planet's highest concentration of organic matter, nutrients and micro-organisms and it's where most of the Earth's biological activity occurs. This amazing combination of minerals, rock particles, organic matter, air, water and living organisms (bacteria, fungi and archaea) ultimately provide us and our animals with our food and fuel. Healthy soil reduces the impact of drought and floods and can store more carbon than all the rain forests in the world.

But we're losing it - literally!

We don't need to be soil scientists to be persuaded that healthy soil, like clean air and clean water, is critically important to life as we know it. But consider this:

- we're losing the equivalent of 30 football pitches of soil every single **minute**.
- 25% of the planet's arable soils are *severely* degraded.[1]

You might well be wondering how we've managed to mess things up so badly? Well, I'm guessing you won't be too surprised to learn that modern-day industrial farming practices and exploitative corporate and business interests have soil on their hands.

In his book *Everything I Want to Do Is Illegal: War stories from the local food front*, regenerative farmer speaker and activist Joel Salatin writes:

> **"A farm includes the passion of the farmer's heart, the interest of the farm's customers, the biological activity in the soil, the pleasantness of the air about the farm - it's everything touching, emanating from, and supplying that piece of landscape.**
>
> **A farm is virtually a living organism.**
>
> **The tragedy of our time is that cultural philosophies and market realities are squeezing life's vitality out of most farms. And that is why the average farmer is now 60 years old. Serfdom just doesn't attract the best and brightest."**

Stay calm… this isn't a technical chapter about soil science and farming, neither of which I'm qualified to write about. Instead, I'd like to raise your awareness of how some of the key issues have impacted the quality and nutritional value of our food and our health. My intention is to encourage you - as enlightened individuals and informed decision makers - to demand and make better food choices that better support your health and the health of this precious planet that feeds us. So, let's begin at the beginning, by taking a look at microbes.

The fascinating world of microbes

Microbes are everywhere. These microscopic, single-cell micro-organisms (bacteria, fungi and archaea) are the oldest form of life on Earth, dating back over 3.5 billion years. At its most fundamental level, life on our planet is deeply co-operative - a symbiosis of beneficial relationships between different life forms - and microbes play a starring role in mediating those relationships and in the development and maintenance of all life on this planet, not least our own.[2]

Our human microbes - clever little critters

Our human microbiome (think of it as a hidden, dispersed organ) comprises the sum and total of micro-organisms that live on and inside our body. Different colonies of these microflora have co-evolved with our human cells and reside on the surface and in deep layers of:

- our skin and mammary glands
- our saliva and oral mucosa
- the conjunctiva in our eyes
- and crucially, our gastrointestinal tract and large intestine, where the majority of our microbes live.

We can actually think of ourselves as human super-organisms - in fact, we may be even more microbial than we are human! While there's no precise measurement of the ratio of our 10 *trillion* human cells to our microbial cells, science estimates a range from 1:1 (equal numbers) up to as much as 1:10 (10 times more). Either way, this gives us plenty to think about.[3]

Put bluntly, we couldn't survive without our microbes. Although science has only recently recognised the existence of the microbiome, these beneficial bacteria are crucial to our health, our well-being and our very survival. They help us to:

- digest our food
- train and regulate our immune system
- crowd out and protect us against pathogenic bacteria
- produce a range of essential nutrients like vitamin B12 & vitamin K.

They even determine our appetite and shape our behaviour.[4]

My own training in the GAPS (Gut and Psychology/Physiology) Protocol is based on healing and sealing the gut and restoring digestive health. Modern science is showing that autoimmune diseases and many chronic and degenerative diseases and mental illnesses are rooted in the dysfunction of the gut microbiome, leaving the way open for inflammation and subsequent disease.

The authors of a recent review[5] on the human microbiome and autoimmunity sought to demonstrate how dysbiosis of the human microbiome can drive autoimmune disease. They concluded that humans are superorganisms, harbouring an extensive microbiome, which has been shown to differ in patients with autoimmune diagnoses:

> **"The catastrophic failure of human metabolism observed in autoimmune disease results from a common underlying pathogenesis - the successive accumulation of pathogens into the microbiome over time, and the ability of such pathogens to dysregulate gene transcription, translation, and human metabolic processes.**
>
> **Autoimmune diseases are more likely passed in families because of the inheritance of a familial microbiome, rather than Mendelian inheritance of genetic abnormalities."**

Soil microbes - very clever little critters

Patrick Holden, farmer, founder and chief executive of the Sustainable Food Trust (and former Director of the Soil Association), suggests in his article *The Soil is the Stomach of the Plant* that even mainstream soil scientists are reaching a consensus that micro-organisms are crucial for soil and human health:

> **"The key concept that has changed my thinking on farming is to understand that the soil surrounding a plant's root zone is effectively its digestive system, or 'stomach'.**
>
> **The layer of healthy topsoil, thriving with micro-organisms, which covers much of the land's surface, is in effect a vast digestive system - the collective stomach of all plants, breaking down soil nutrients into bio-available forms that plants can absorb.**
>
> **Without the presence of micro-organisms, the mechanics of the digestive system can still function to a certain degree .... however, the long-term vitality and health of plants, animals and people is centrally dependent on**

the presence and diversity of micro-organisms, in the soil and [human] gut respectively."

It's clear then that the quality, nutritional status and health of the microbes in our soil determine the nutrients in our food and the very fabric and health of our body.

So, how has it all gone so horribly wrong?

Conventional farming systems

Counter-intuitively, 'conventional' farming systems don't employ time-honoured, traditional farming methods: they're typically resource- and energy-intensive and rely on industrial farming inputs such as synthetic chemical fertilisers, pesticides, herbicides, genetically-modified organisms (GMOs), monocultures and intensive tillage (preparation of soil by digging, stirring, and overturning). Conventional methods became widespread during the late 19th century on the promise of increased yields on less acreage and with lower labour cost, all of which meant increased profitability.[6]

Has the promise delivered?

Monocultures, intensive & factory farming

Put simply, Mother Nature hates monoculture.

Think of vast fields of wheat, barley, rape seed or soya crops, or plantations of a single species of fruit tree, or furrowed fields planted with a single vegetable crop. This is monoculture.

Think of thousands of livestock and poultry - cattle, sheep, pigs, chickens, turkeys - raised on large-scale, intensive farms, often in close confinement and fed an unnatural diet of growth-promoting grains and soya-based proteins. This is monoculture.

Monoculture - also known as monocropping - is a modern commercial agriculture and farming practice, the aim of which is to increase yield (and profits) by cultivating a single species or type of plant or raising a single breed of animal. The theory is that the farmer provides only for the needs of a single species, with its own individual characteristics, in order to grow a successful crop.

The promise is that the economy of scale allowed by cultivating a single crop (for example, the use of a single automated harvesting method) will boost profits for the farmer.

Monoculture has meant that of the huge number of species of plants and animals available for human consumption, we now use only a few. According to the UN's Food and Agriculture Organisation, 75% of our total food supply comes from a mere 12 plant species and over 90% of livestock production comes from only 15 mammal and bird species.

Monocultures have significant negative impacts on the ecological systems of the Earth and are an environmental disaster. Modern crops and livestock depend on hundreds of thousands of other species, including insects and birds that pollinate crops and feed on pests, and numerous microbial species that live on and in plants and animals which are especially critical to their survival. Mother Nature created and loves diversity, but the lack of diversity in the monoculture system eliminates evolutionary controls, leaving:

- an insufficient range of insect species in a specific location to ensure that a single population does not get too large
- no varieties of plant-based topsoil nutrients like legumes and clover
- fewer species of microbes and bacteria
- less soil integrity with fewer plants of different root depths.

Pathogens spread more readily, with less resistance and with a more severe impact, when the host plants (or animals) are more genetically uniform and crowded. Outbreaks of disease, invasions of insects and climatic anomalies cause crop and animal failures. This is a big problem.[7]

Chemicals are the problem, not the solution!

Enter the chemicals - conventional agriculture's superhero; a large supporting cast of synthetic herbicides, insecticides, bactericides, fertilisers and antibiotics, all ready to save the day. But actually, they are creating an even bigger problem.

These chemicals indiscriminately kill or damage wildlife, beneficial insects and native plants, while also depleting the diversity of neighbouring ecosystems. Much of this synthetic matter remains in the soil, unprocessed by micro-organisms, where it leaches into ground water, contaminating locations far from where it was originally applied.

However, nature is adaptable. Organisms under threat evolve to resist these artificial insecticides and herbicides, so new inorganic methods must be developed continually to combat each new threat. More and more chemicals are being applied to monoculture crops in a hopeless cycle of damage and control.

Soil degradation is inevitable and as ground cover crops are eliminated, the soil loses its natural protection from erosion by wind and rain, ultimately leaving huge areas of land unproductive for agriculture.

In some countries, this means that forests and traditional grasslands are then cleared to provide new land for intensive agriculture (and increasingly, for GM soya cultivation), starting the whole dismal, damaging cycle all over again. In this context, consider for a moment the consequences of the exponential rise in demand for a plant-based or vegan diet on the environment.

Water misuse and pollution are also a result of monocultures. Lack of topsoil and ground cover plants undermines moisture retention in the soil and increases rain run-off. Modern monoculture relies on huge amounts of water to irrigate the crops, so water must be pumped from lakes, rivers and reservoirs, also affecting those aquatic ecosystems. One of the most common water pollutants is from the run-off from synthetic chemical fertilisers, pesticides and antibiotic residues used by monoculture operations.

Toxic animal waste is also produced in vast quantities by intensive animal farms and huge confined animal feeding operations (CAFOs). Storing and disposing of this waste (and its accompanying residues of antibiotics, pharmaceutical drugs and pathogenic bacteria) often results in pollution of water supplies, not only through leakage and overflows, but also through spraying the waste onto farm fields as fertiliser. Once a saturation point has been reached, the contaminated waste runs off into nearby water systems.

Huge inputs of fossil-fuel energy are needed to harvest, process, sort, pack and transport the products of large-scale, intensive and factory operations. Some opinions estimate that it takes TEN calories of fossil-fuel energy to produce just ONE calorie of food energy. And that's just the end-point: consider the environmental damage and costs along the entire chain of fossil-fuel energy production.

Already, we're seeing a very unhappy picture of what has come to be called, ironically, 'conventional' agriculture.

To fully understand how agricultural and industrial chemicals impact the environment, our food and our health, we need to start rooting around in and scratching below the surface of the soil that's been supporting our food production for millennia.

I could write a whole separate book on this vast subject; however here are the main villains in this story of global proportions:

Commercial fertilisers - our soils must contain three main macronutrients to support healthy plant growth: *nitrogen* for leaf growth; *phosphorus* for the development of roots, flowers, seeds and fruit; and *potassium* for strong stem growth, movement of water in plants and the promotion of flowering and fruiting. All are important, but nitrogen is key: agricultural crops like corn, wheat, barley, potatoes or rice deplete nitrogen from the soil and unless it's replenished, the soil becomes infertile.

Until the early 1900s, farmers used traditional practices for enriching soil nitrogen, but with the advent of commercially-produced synthetic fertilisers, which held (empty) promises to feed the growing world, these have come to dominate and are indispensable to industrial food production.

On any level, this not good news, for while Mother Nature has seen to it that her soils are receptive to *natural* fertilisers, she's not at all happy with our meddling. We are clearly seeing the global impact of synthetic nitrogen, phosphate and potassium fertilisers - environmental pollution, radioactive waste, food nutrient depletion and neurotoxic drinking water, among many others.

Pesticides, fungicides and herbicides significantly impact our environment, food and health

Key amongst these are organophosphates and glyphosate.

Organophosphates were initially developed as chemical weapons in Germany in the 1940s. They have since become a primary 'weapon' against agricultural pests, killing insects by disrupting their brain and nervous system. And, as we now know, the same is true in human adults and children.[8, 9, 10]

The weed killer glyphosate - commonly marketed as *Roundup* - is the world's premier weed killer and a broad-spectrum herbicide that is routinely sprayed on most cereal crops before harvest, including the wheat, corn, barley and soya that are destined for animal feeds.

Glyphosate is also the basis for supporting genetically-modified crops, which absorb high levels of the herbicide without themselves being killed. Because glyphosate survives digestion, if animals eat it so do we! Indirectly, it gets passed on to us in the food chain and new, independent science speaks daily of the pervasive and destructive impact of glyphosate on our health and on almost every aspect of life on this planet.

It destroys our gut microbiome and disrupts the integrity of our digestive tract. It is a neurotoxin and is widely implicated as a powerful endocrine (hormone) disrupter which can cause cancerous tumours, birth defects, and other developmental disorders, such as autism. The WHO International Agency for Research on Cancer has concluded that glyphosate is a *"probable carcinogen.*"[11] While their decision provoked a storm of controversy, landmark litigation in the USA has validated and upheld the concerns of independent science.[12]

Little is known of the long-term health consequences of glyphosate ingestion, as safety tests have never been carried out, but the science is coming. Recent research in 2017 by King's College, London has found that glyphosate actually causes non-alcoholic fatty liver disease (NAFLD), even in very low doses. NAFLD is now the most common cause of liver disease in the West.[13]

Worryingly, the Pesticide Action Network's (PAN UK) 2017 report *Food for Thought* showed unacceptable levels of 123 different pesticides to be present in the food provided through the Department of Health's School Fruit and Vegetable Scheme (SFVS), some of which are linked to serious health problems such as cancer and disruption of the hormone system. Multiple residues were found on the produce. This is a serious concern, as the scientific community has little understanding about the complex interaction of different chemicals in this cocktail effect. PAN UK assert that, for just an extra 1p per day, all the core produce given out by the SFVS could be switched to organic.[14]

Genetically-modified organisms (GMOs) have huge consequences for our environment, food and health. Humans have been farming for around 12,000 years, but plants produced by GMO technology are brand new to our environment and to our diet: they've only been in our food system for about 20 years. The subject of GMOs is hugely controversial, and the debate is set to continue with critics arguing that GMOs are turning *"our food system into a large, uncontrolled experiment, with some disturbing consequences."* [15]

In genetic engineering, bio-technologists manipulate an organism's DNA, artificially adding, removing or changing it in the laboratory and scientists are only beginning to understand exactly how different genes interact with each other, with unintended side-effects now emerging.

The biggest area of contention is that the biotech companies which develop and release GMOs into our environment, animal and human food chains do so with woefully inadequate - or, in many cases, not any - safety testing. There is a lack of understanding of how they might alter ecosystems, farming practice and the food we eat, and it is poorly understood how consuming GMOs is affecting our very physiology and our health.

Fortunately, most of us in the UK don't directly eat food containing GM ingredients (let's pray that this continues post-Brexit, as our food safety policies have been largely EU-led), but the animal products that we eat certainly do contain GM ingredients. Because GM-fed animal products don't have to be labelled as such, unless we buy organic, we're unwittingly eating eggs, poultry, milk and dairy products, red meat and farmed fish from animals that have been fed GM soya and/or maize, and which has been sprayed repeatedly with glyphosate.

I strongly encourage you to take the deeper dive into these issues in Appendix 2 - Chemicals, Our Food, Our Health and Our Environment. Hold your nose and jump in to explore these murky waters. What you'll find there will surely shock you into demanding and making better choices for your health and for our planet.

Enough glum! Good news is coming

It would be easy to conclude that we're in a thoroughly desperate situation with no way out. But the tide *is* turning and it will turn faster if YOU are part of that tide. The internet and social media platforms are powerful vehicles for the democratisation of information: with a couple of clicks we can search for, consume and share information across the planet.

This means that we are all becoming more aware, more informed and can be more confident participating in this debate. We can witness how our decisions - and more importantly, our *actions* - are changing the way our environment is protected, how our food is grown and produced and how our health is restored.

But we must act. As consumers, every conscious buying decision is an act in favour of regenerative agriculture and sustainable food production, a step away from disease and towards better health. As mindful guardians of the integrity of our planet and its interconnected web of life, each buying decision is an investment in a better, healthier future for our children and theirs.

Organic is our birth-right

We can put to rest the view that organic food is an expensive, elitist, middle-class indulgence. Back in the day, all our food was organic and enjoyed by our forefathers, whatever their income and status. For me, organic food truly is a birth-right and one which everyone should be demanding and those of us who are better informed and equipped *must* speak up for those less able.

Organic is nature itself

Organic farmers (certified or not) don't rely on synthetic or petroleum-based pesticides and fertilisers, so farming organically significantly increases soil health, reduces soil and water contamination and consequential damage to wildlife.

To reduce the need for using chemicals to manage diseases, organic farming practices include the selection of diverse crop varieties with natural resistance to particular pests and diseases. Rotating crops also helps break cycles of pests and disease and builds fertility into the soil, making a major impact on the quality of our food and on environmental sustainability.

A farmer, grower or producer holding a formal Soil Association organic certificate can explicitly claim cleaner, healthier soil and/or feeds. For the consumer, this assures cleaner, safer, more flavoursome and nutritionally-superior meat, dairy, fruit and vegetables.

Animals raised organically are happier and healthier, and this is reflected in their nutritional quality. Because intensive farming practice raises agricultural animals in close quarters and in high populations, antibiotics are used frequently as a matter of necessity to keep them healthy. The use of antibiotics on organic farms is carefully monitored - almost two thirds of all antibiotics used in the EU are given to farm animals and these are passed to us through the food chain and ultimately end up in our environment.

Around 60% of each antibiotic dose is not metabolised by the animal and is excreted in its manure, which is then spread as fertiliser on farm fields. As a result, antibiotics are increasingly found in fields worldwide, leaving scientists and public health officials with a serious 'run-off' issue: the toxic antibiotic residues from agricultural land flow into streams and rivers, impact soil microbiota and are taken up by crops.

In the UK, the Soil Association regulations require that, whenever weather and ground conditions permit, organically-raised animals must be truly free-range and have access to pasture. Their diet must be as natural as possible, free from GMO feeds, and they must be free to graze and forage naturally on organic pasture - grasses and other crops - where only natural fertilisers are used and chemical pesticides are severely restricted. The extra space they enjoy helps to reduce stress and disease, so the need for antibiotics is also greatly reduced.[16]

As we'll see in later chapters, organic meat, dairy products and eggs - indeed all organically farmed foods - are not only healthier for the animals and the planet, but they're nutritionally superior to those 'conventionally' produced.[17,18]

That said, it's worth remembering that many small producers do employ traditional rearing, pasturing and growing methods and farm to organic (and even tougher) biodynamic standards,[19] but don't seek formal organic certification as it's often prohibitively onerous and costly.

Buying from smaller, local producers brings myriad benefits above and beyond a simple cash transaction. The nutrient content of local produce will be higher than produce shipped many hundreds of miles, over which time levels of vitamin C and B can decrease significantly.

You'll get more choice as local growers are more likely to offer heirloom and other varieties not found in larger grocery stores, which also helps to maintain the genetic diversity of the plants.

Buying local produce supports local farmers and local jobs, helping to strengthen your local economy and your community. Also, your purchase helps to reduce the greenhouse gas emissions that come hand-in-hand with large-scale food production, packaging, storage and transport.

It's true that organic is more expensive, but producers and retailers will always respond to market pressures and market forces dictate that the greater the demand, the greater the supply and so the lower the cost. These days everyone has access to the internet: go online to find local, small producers selling directly to the public, or buy direct from producers online. You'll find that with a small amount of determination and ingenuity, it is possible to buy organic *and* save the pennies.

And we'd all do well to heed this wisdom: *Pay the farmer now or pay the doctor later.*

Organic and pasture-raised

Intuitively we know that organic is a safer, healthier and more nutritious choice and the evidence is growing daily. However, it's very important to understand that organically-raised animals often receive a diet high in organic grains.

For optimum health, ruminants like cows and sheep need diverse pasture including grass, clovers, and legumes but not grains. Ruminant animals (and indeed humans) find grains difficult to digest, causing inflammation that leads to sub-optimal health. This impacts the meat and dairy products from these animals and it also impacts our health. Choosing organic, pasture-raised animal products of every kind - meats, dairy, eggs - is by far the healthiest and most nutritious option.[20]

We *can* farm without pesticides

A recent, definitive French study[21] shows that almost all conventional farms could significantly cut their use of chemicals while producing just as much food. In comparing pesticide use, productivity and profitability of almost 1,000 conventional farms of all types across France with similar farms using either high or low levels of pesticides, scientists found that 94% of farms would not experience decreased levels of production if they cut pesticides, and 40% of these farms would actually produce more.

The study found that lower levels of insecticide use would result in increased production in 86% of the farms and that no farms would experience a decrease in production. The research also indicated that 78% of farms would be equally or more profitable when using less pesticide of all types.

Indeed, by employing agro-ecological principles of diversifying crops, crop rotation and intercropping - like planting marigolds at the end of strawberry beds and perennial flowers such as lavender in between them - studies are showing that farmers are able to manage pests, break up pest and disease cycles and limit damage to harvests. Other benefits come from improvements in soil health, relief from the pressure of soil-borne diseases, better management of nutrient balance and improvements in water retention.[22]

For example, organic strawberry grower Javier Zamora, who farms in northern California, is showing that farmers can reduce pesticide and fungicide use by designing farm ecosystems with built-in pest control systems, reducing the load of toxins that affect soils, water supplies and local communities. While diversifying his crops hasn't eliminated pests, it's reduced the detrimental impact of pests on his harvests and eased pressure of soil-borne diseases.[23]

"I make sure before and after strawberries there's always something different," said Zamora, whose JSM Organic Farms has expanded from 1.5 acres to over 100 acres in just five years. *"I normally plant broccoli right after—no potatoes, no tomatoes, no eggplant in the three years between strawberries. Those things host the same diseases."*

Strawberries are amongst the most pesticide-sprayed crops on the planet, so given how much children love to pick and eat them, this can only be good news!

Beyond organic

There is a growing body of opinion that, whether conventional or organic, all large-scale agricultural operations are unsustainable. What really matters is whether the farming systems that produce our food are building, improving and nurturing soils, or exploiting them for short-term gain. Many experts and organisations are now calling for small-scale, regenerative agriculture and sustainable food production.

Small-scale rules the world

Commercial agriculture has come to feed the developed world and 'experts' insist that conventional, large-scale agriculture is needed to feed the whole world - without it, we're doomed to large-scale famine and starvation. However, the global reality is that most of the world's farmers, producing over 75% of the world's food, are to be found working on family farms, almost three-quarters of which are only around 2.5 acres in size!

In 2016, the Environmental Working Group (EWG) in the USA found that almost 90% of US agricultural exports went to developed countries where levels of hunger are low. Hardly the 'global-agro-industry-is-needed-to-save-the-world' myth that we've been sold, is it?

Small-scale *can* feed the world

Perhaps the loudest cry from supporters of large-scale, conventional agriculture is that organic farming produces lower yields and that this may well lead to global starvation.

Evidence from an extensive meta-analysis[24] of 115 studies (conducted in 2015) confirmed the findings of previous studies - that organic production averaged around 20% less than conventionally-grown crops.

However, in the same study, when crop yields on conventional farms were compared with those on organic farms where regenerative methods - like planting cover crops and crop rotation - were employed to build soil health, the gap shrank to below 10%.

Now let's factor food waste into the equation: evidence shows that 25% of all food produced worldwide is never actually eaten. UK studies, published in 2013 and 2016, showed that households, hospitality services, food manufacturers, retailers and wholesalers threw away 10 *million* tons (worth £17 billion a year), 60% of which could have been put to use.[25]

Each year the United States alone throws out over 66 million tons of food, more than enough to feed the near-50 million Americans who regularly face hunger. So even taken at face value, the oft-cited yield gap between conventional and organic farming is smaller than the amount of food we routinely throw away.[26]

Small-scale, but perfectly formed

According to a 1992 agricultural census report[27], small, diversified farms are able to produce more than twice as much food per acre compared with larger farms:

> **"While large farms excel at producing a lot of a particular crop - like corn or wheat - small diversified farms produce more food and more kinds of food per hectare overall."**

And it's becoming clear that the economies of scale enjoyed by high-volume industrial processes don't necessarily apply to agriculture. As far back as 1989, research studies[28] were concluding that:

> **"Well-managed alternative farming systems nearly always use less synthetic chemical pesticides, fertilisers, and antibiotics per unit of production than conventional farms… And while mechanization can provide cost and labour efficiencies on large farms, bigger farms do not necessarily produce more food."**

We've come a long, long way in this chapter… from dust, to microbes, to soil, to chemistry, farming systems and ecology. We've learned how human interference with nature is a risky and often unpredictable business and how the way forward lies in going back and working with Mother Nature and farming regeneratively and sustainably.

The future of farming - building healthy soils and gaining healthy profits?

For decades, Allan Savory, founder of the Savory Institute, has worked tirelessly to stop two-thirds of the world's grasslands turning into desert, a process known as 'desertification'. Through regenerative grazing, his commitment to an approach called 'holistic land management' is bringing about the restoration of arid land all over the world. Here, domestic livestock are managed in a way the matches nature's rhythms and cycles and mimics the behaviour of now long-gone herds of livestock bunched and moved across the globe.[29]

Grasslands are hugely important, since they sequester more carbon from the atmosphere than any other terrestrial ecosystem, including rain forests. Although conventional farming systems have come to see grazing animals as enemies to the grass plants, nothing could be further from the truth: nature evolved and uses grazing animals to provide biological decay for the world's grasslands. In fact, if grass plants are left to die undisturbed, their 'skeletons' will remain for years, acting like umbrellas to shade out seedlings and prevent future generations of seeds from germinating.

As we have seen, it's the job of soil microbes - and insects - to break down decaying biological growth back into the soil, but these critters need water to sustain them, so in areas of drought or low humidity they go dormant. Nature is left without a mechanism to break down the dried-out grasses before the next growing season.

Enter our ruminant grazer superhero. Unlike human animals, grazing animals - whether they be domestic cows, sheep, or wild grazers like impalas and water buffalo - have gut microbes which can break down and digest tough, cellulose-rich grasses.

When a cow, sheep or impala takes a bite of grass, it passes to their rumen - the initial chamber of their stomach - to ferment. Here, the animal's gut microbes digest most of their meal for them and at the same time these happy critters multiply wildly.

Some hitch a ride on the broken-down grass and pass through the animal's digestive system to serve as an important secondary source of nutrients, making their food more bio-available. And, as we'll see in the Cultured and Fermented Foods chapter, this is also a very good thing for humans.

> **"The grazer, with its ability to roam and move about, becomes a portable pack of microbes sweeping the land. The microbes in the soil are dormant because of lack of water, but the microbes in the ruminant's gut are flourishing because she can get to streams, springs, lakes and rivers to provide them the moist environment that they need.**
>
> **And with the help of millions upon millions of grazers bunched and moving, nature is able to provide the role of biological decay and remove the dry grass before the next season of growth comes."** [30]

So, now are you're getting the picture?

The future of food - we still need animals

Nearly half (40%) of the Earth's land consists of grassland ecosystems, home to - and work for - over a billion people. We've seen the crucial role played by grazing animals in protecting the fertility and regenerating these grasslands.[31]

We should also remind ourselves that many of these areas aren't suitable for agriculture, so growing grain crops, vegetables and orchards is very often not a sustainable option.

In a recent interview[32] Joel Salatin, speaker and founder of Polyface Farms in the USA, summarised several key issues through an ecological lens. It's the *"historical algorithms"*, says Salatin, that provide templates which have stood the test of time and are ones that we should follow.

Nowhere on the planet is there an 'animal-less' ecology, because animals spread fertility. Photosynthesis grows the plants, plants mature and decompose, leaving their minerals and biomass to move gravitationally downhill and create fertile valleys, but also leaving depleted hillside slopes and ridges.

Animals (the only things in nature that can defy gravity) move all this valley fertility back up onto the hillsides and ridge tops. One reason that animals want to move up to hilltops is predation; the predator-prey relationship ensures what Salatin calls the *"democratisation of fertility."*

In other words, animals are the vehicles by which nature spreads around fertility, healing the landscape by transmuting feed stuffs into a concentrated form, biologically and enzymatically active, which leaves the land richer. The build-up of that fertility is what the grain and corn cropping industries are still mining today, at least where they haven't worn them out.

All the deep soils on the planet did not develop under forests, shrubs or bushes, but from prairies and grasslands where waves of herbivores and predators moved across the terrain in a *"choreography of disturbance and rest."* But most of the land on the planet's surface is not conducive to growing arable crops, which require very specific conditions and heavily deplete the soil's resources.

Grain cropping annuals (like cereal crops) have always been land *deteriorators*, while the perennials (the grasses and clovers) and the animals which feed upon them, have been land *builders*. Diversified farming systems, where both plants and animals mirror ecology, have been the mainstay of farming throughout history.

Back in the day, when farmers depended on animal power for their farms' energy resource, at least one third of the land on the farm was set aside for areas where animals could feed.

Historically, animals provided nutrition without the need for storing food. The Native American, for example, would eat huge amounts of bison meat per day - you might call this 'real time' nutrition.

These days, it's easy for people to forget that our food security is far less simple than it was for our ancestors and is wholly dependent on technologies. With the transition from nomadic hunting and gathering to predominantly sedentary agricultural practices came problems with managing and eradicating the pests, mice or moulds that affect grain growth, harvest and storage.

Ultimately, this has driven the need for dehydration processes and for commercial refrigeration and temperature-controlled storage.

Everything in nature is either eating or being eaten: from the old and weak wildebeest who perish in the annual migration across rivers of the Serengeti - leaving feasts for predators, crocodiles and vultures - to the compost pile teaming with microbes, worms and bacteria.

"I think we need to flip the script on how we produce it, how we manage the animals, and rethink the infrastructure for how it is processed and distributed."

- Chris Kerston
www.savory.global [33]

Going forward, it's clear we need to eat less but *better* meat and make sure that all meat production is regenerative: production that heals, restores and adds value to the earth and provides us with excellent nutrition.

It's also very clear that we need to evaluate the wisdom of the increasingly agitated calls for a plant-based (or exclusively vegan) diet as a means of saving the environment. In fact, we need to "*flip the script*" on everything we put into our mouths and re-learn the food wisdom that will take us back to truly sustainable food production and better health.

Patrick Holden, Founding Director of the Sustainable Food Trust, sums it up perfectly:

"My message is simple: a healthy diet should work backwards from the most sustainable way to farm, and that ideally means eating the foods produced by mixed farms using crop rotations which include a fertility building phase,

usually of grass and clover grazed by cows and sheep, but also pastured pigs and poultry.

Industrial farming has been an extractive industry. We have dined out on the natural capital of the soil that previous generations have laid down for us. We need to fix that because the environment in which a plant or animal is produced goes a long way to determine its nutrient value when consumed by humans."

What can we do NOW?

- ✓ Take responsibility and educate ourselves, our family and our friends
- ✓ Reconnect with nature and with the sources of our food
- ✓ Demand clean, healthy food from farmers, producers and retailers
- ✓ Stay informed, ask questions, lobby food producers, supermarkets and policy makers
- ✓ Make responsible buying decisions
- ✓ Buy local-grown and organic whenever possible
- ✓ Stay connected with nature and engaged with each other.

To conclude this chapter, I'll leave you with these words of wisdom on sustainability from Satish Kumar, an internationally-respected peace and environment activist:

"The challenge for all mankind in the twenty-first century is to find humility and reconnect with nature. We need to understand that nature is not just 'out there'; we are nature too. The word 'nature' means birth; 'natal' 'nativity' 'native' and 'nature' all come from the same root.

Whatever is born and will die, is nature. Since we, humans, are also born and will die, we are nature too. Thus, nature and humans are one. Therefore, we need to understand that what we do to nature, we do to ourselves. If we harm nature, we harm ourselves."

- Satish Kumar: *Soil, Soul & Society* [34]

We would do well to heed them.

SOIL Recipes

When thinking about a recipe section for soil, I'm afraid my creativity couldn't get past the idea of Mud Pies! But, before we dismiss the idea completely, did you know that soil could be considered a traditional food?!

Geophagia - the practice of eating dirt, especially claylike soils - is classified as an eating disorder, in which people consume non-foods such as cigarette ash and paint chips. However, it seems that animals and people have been doing this for millennia and the practise may well be adaptive!

Some scientists believe that animals and people eat soil because it contains minerals such as calcium, sodium and iron, which support energy production and other vital biological processes. However, reviews have shown that the practice adds only small amounts of minerals to the diet and can in fact act as an anti-nutrient, interfering with the absorption of digested food from the gut into the bloodstream.

Another (more likely) explanation is that eating soil, particularly clay soils, is detoxicant. Clay molecules have a negative charge and so bind easily to the positively charged toxins in the stomach and gut (lipopolysaccharides or endotoxins), preventing them from entering the bloodstream and taking them out of the body in faeces.

Some indigenous peoples prepare meals of potatoes and acorns with clay - these foods are bitter because they contain small amounts of toxins, so the clay acts as a detoxicant. That said, in the interests of encouraging you to read the rest of this book, I'll spare you the dubious pleasure of experiencing 'dirty' recipes - save one *very* special recipe, which I'm really pleased to be able to share here.

DONNA'S MISSISSIPPI MUD BROWNIES

Donna Crous is a hugely talented food photographer, primal health coach and a multi-award winning fellow UK Health Blogger. Donna's recipes and her photography are amazing and are all designed with your good health in mind. They're wholesome, natural and many of them can be enjoyed by those who struggle with food intolerances and allergies.

So, if only one recipe was to represent the Soil chapter, I reached out to Donna…

"These brownies have fudgy, but light consistency - I've made them so many times that I've actually lost count. In the past, I've mixed in orange zest (simply add orange zest to the batter and squeeze the juice over the top once finished baking).

You can add nuts, drizzle with melted chocolate or anything else that can make these guys a firm family favourite!"

- Donna Crous
eighty20nutrition.com

What you'll need:

Ground almonds: 500g (2 cups)
Medjool dates: 7-10 (pitted, chopped)
Ground flax seed: 125g (½ cup)
Organic cacao: 125g (½ cup)
Nut, coconut or full cream milk: 250mls
Almond butter: 1 tbsp
Eggs: 3
Bicarbonate of soda/baking soda: 1tsp
Sea salt: (Maldon, ½ tsp)
Raw apple cider vinegar: 1 tsp
70% dark chocolate chips or good quality dark chocolate chopped: ½ cup

What to do:

1. Preheat the oven to 150°C (Fan) or Gas Mark 3.

2. In a food processor, pulse the dates, almond flour, flax meal, and cocoa together until the dates are chopped.

3. Add the rest of the ingredients, excluding the chocolate chips, and give the mixture a good blitzing, then stir in the chocolate chips.

4. Transfer the batter to a prepared brownie tin or 8x10 inch silicon baking tray and bake for 25min.
5. Remove from the oven and leave to cool
6. Cut into squares and try not to eat all at once!

CHAPTER THREE

EGGS

"When I hold an egg in my hand, I feel that it represents the image of the universe, and it awakens and increases my respect for life."

- Michel Roux

Eggs are one of the oldest foods of all and have always been prized in the mythologies, religions and cultural practices of the world. Hailed as one of Mother Nature's perfect foods, they're regarded as symbols of rebirth, renewal, new beginnings and fertility.

For me as a nutritional chef, eggs are the quintessential, traditional, nutrient-dense food and their culinary versatility is legendary.

I completely agree with acclaimed chef - and total master of egg cuisine - Michel Roux when he concludes:

"The egg is the simplest and most complete food, highly nutritious and versatile enough for the quickest of meals, or the smartest of dinner parties."

One of the most widely celebrated 'eggsociations' in this part of the world is with Easter. Before intensive farming took hold, hens stopped laying eggs during the cold, dark winter months to conserve their energy and maximise the survival potential for their chicks. They'd then resume prolific laying in spring, coinciding with Easter, hence the association. Today, the light and heat in a commercial hen's environment is manipulated so she continues laying all-year round, which is unnatural and has damaging consequences.

Nowadays we're consumers of all kinds of eggs; from ducks, bantams, quails, pigeons, gulls, guinea fowl, pheasants and even from emus. Although I must say, I've never tried an emu egg!

I'm going to focus on the humble hen's egg, since this is by far the most common type of egg used in our homes and in restaurant kitchens. The UK egg industry's figures for 2017 tell us that we eat over 34 million eggs every day.

Is it true that 'eggs are eggs'?

We often use the saying *"As sure as eggs are eggs"* when we're certain or confident about something, but these days it's difficult to be certain about an egg. Let's 'eggsplore' why. Sorry - couldn't resist!

Did your egg enjoy a 'natural' life? Although rare nowadays, a natural life for a laying hen (and indeed a chicken raised 'for the table') is one of true free-roaming. Mother Nature intended hens to scratch around eating bugs, worms and other sources of protein and, ideally, following in the footsteps of their bigger ruminant friends as they graze, moving from one healthy, unsprayed pasture to the next, flipping up the dried 'pats' to feast on the bugs beneath. Let's be clear: chickens are neither vegetarian nor vegan.

Eggs might roll, but not many rock

With the pervasive growth and roll-out of monocultures in both animal and arable farming, we consumers have seen our eggs predominantly limited to those produced from hens kept in cages or raised in barns. Unlike the domestic backyard hens of yesteryear, kept in relatively small flocks with access to a varied diet of grass, pasture, worms, and all manner of bugs and kitchen scraps, these modern laying hens spend their lives in confinement in vast, intensive houses, fed a diet of commodity grains, soya and other questionable ingredients.

Modern laying hens have been bred to lay, relatively prolifically, all year round and are expected to meet financially-driven egg production targets. This means that their protein requirement is much greater than that of their ancestors and to meet this requirement from non-grain protein sources, huge quantities of feed would need to be ingested daily. This would be extremely difficult and often not viable, without substantial supplementation (wholly or in part) with a high protein, grain-based diet.

Unfortunately, the same beginnings are true for the increasing number of eggs marketed as 'free-range' but still produced by hens reared in large, commercial operations. To be legally compliant and their eggs labelled 'free-range', producers must merely give their chickens access to the outside - usually via narrow, low-level flaps around the perimeter of their huge barns or sheds.

However, chickens aren't the bravest (or smartest) of birds and they know their place in the 'pecking order'. Unless they've been reared outside before they start laying, their internal environment quickly conditions them to avoid venturing outside. Few are brave enough to fight their way to the perimeter of the sheds, let alone enjoy the little outdoor space that has been made available to them.

In his book *Folks, This Ain't Normal: A Farmer's Advice for Happier Hens, Healthier People, and a Better World*, Joel Salatin writes:

> **"In half a century, we've never bought a pound of chemical fertiliser and don't apply pesticides, herbicides, insecticides, or any other-cide to our plants and animals. Our animals don't do drugs. Instead we move them almost daily in a tightly choreographed ballet from pasture spot to pasture spot. They aren't confined in concentrated feeding operations. The herbivores receive no grain and the omnivores receive local, no-transgenic modified organism supplemental grains (GMO-free)."**

Man vs Mother Nature comes at a cost...

Monoculture. Agrochemicals. Industrial food production. GMOs. Glyphosate. It's all a far cry from the way Mother Nature shaped traditional farming methods and the human food wisdom of millennia. The changes in agriculture and food production have come at a cost that's only just becoming clear, and not only to our humble hen's welfare and her eggs: it's costing us and our environment. As we've seen, unless we buy organic, we're unwittingly eating eggs from animals (both within and from outside the UK) fed with antibiotics, GM soya and/or maize and seasoned with glyphosate.

So, what's actually in your egg?

All eggs carry the nutrients to enable life, so it's no surprise that the eggs we consume are an almost perfect food to sustain our life too. Just check out the amazing nutrition in the humble hen's egg:[1]

Nutrient	Egg White	Egg Yolk
Protein	60%	40%
Magnesium, Potassium, Sodium	10-25%	
Vitamin B3	90%	10%
Vitamin B2	62%	38%
Total Fat	10%	90%
Omega-3 Fats	0%	100%
Vitamin A, D, E, K	0%	100%
Carotenoids	0%	100%
Vitamins B5, B6, B12, Folate, Choline	10% or less	90% or more
Calcium, Phosphorus, Zinc, Copper, Iron	10% or less	90% or more
Manganese	30%	70%
Vitamin B1	25%	75%
Biotin	20%	80%
Selenium	41%	59%

Source: whfoods.com

Although our body needs the full range of nutrients found in a whole egg - as each contributes to our optimum health (so please, just forget those 'egg white' omelettes!) - there are some star players:

Vitamin A - an important anti-oxidant that protects our cells from free-radical damage (responsible for ageing) and it plays a key role throughout our body. It's critical for good vision; supports healthy skin, hair and nails; plays an important role in healthy tooth and bone growth; is essential for reproduction; plays a role in cell division and cell growth; and crucially, it supports our immune system.

Just to be clear: true (pre-formed) vitamin A can only be obtained from animal sources such as organ meats, animal fats, milk, yoghurt, cheese and, of course, egg yolks, the very foods our grandparents (and theirs) grew up eating.

Sadly, it's a dangerous misconception that beta-carotene (vitamin A's precursor and found in vegetable sources) is the same thing: it isn't. Our body must first convert beta-carotene to vitamin A before we can benefit. As Nora Gedgaudas[2] explains in her article *Vitamin A Under Attack Down Under*:

"Critical fat-soluble nutrients, particularly true vitamin A (found only in animal sources) and D, were especially high in primitive and traditional diets - often ten times higher than in modern diets (Dr Weston A. Price).

Beta-carotene, a fat-soluble nutrient, is not, contrary to popular press, the equivalent of vitamin A, nor is its conversion to vitamin A, a simple matter.

Children under the age of five and individuals with liver or thyroid impairment cannot make this conversion at all."

By the way, did you know that thyroid dysfunction is epidemic in the West and is hugely under-diagnosed? [3]

Vitamin D - although now known as the 'sunshine' vitamin, its active form is a steroid-like hormone which impacts every cell in the body. Most important for us are vitamins D3 and D2. Vitamin D is available in a nutrient-dense diet, but relatively few foods contain it, so while diet is important, it's not our best source of vitamin D.

The most important natural source of vitamin D comes from the interaction of the sun's UVB radiation with the precious cholesterol stored in our skin. However, unlike our ancestors, our indoor jobs and lifestyles, sun-phobia and over-use of heavy sunscreens means that very few of us get enough of this important, immune system-critical vitamin.

The result is epidemic vitamin D deficiencies and the public are advised that every man, woman and now every child needs to supplement their diet; however, the standard advice is to supplement with vitamin D2, which is a less-than-optimally metabolised in comparison to Vitamin D3.

Good science shows us that supplementing with vitamin D must be managed very carefully. If it's not balanced with vitamin A and vitamin K2, it can result in calcium dysregulation - where calcium is wrongly deposited in organs and soft tissue, like the kidneys - causing calcium kidney stones and calcification in soft arteries leading to arterial and heart disease.[4]

How much better then, to follow Granny's traditional wisdom and eat your whole eggs frequently, and make sure to get regular, sufficient and intelligent sun exposure?

Selenium - is required to enable our body (primarily in our liver and gut) to convert thyroid hormone from the inactive (known as T4) to the active form (T3) ready for use in every cell.

As I've mentioned, thyroid dysregulation and disorders are epidemic and egg yolks, due to their selenium content, are nature's thyroid support 'supplement' - around 40% of the selenium is found in the white and 60% in the yolk.

Cholesterol - back in the day, our forefathers were advised to *"Go to work on an egg"*, but this wisdom fell from grace as poor science demonised eggs for being high in cholesterol, and we were warned to limit them to just one or two per week.

Thankfully, modern science has confirmed the traditional food wisdom and it's now widely accepted that we were wrongly advised to limit eggs. However, those with a genetic disorder such as hypercholesterolemia might still need to limit consumption.

As we'll see in the Fats chapter, good science is showing us that cholesterol is a vital structural molecule and an essential part of every single cell membrane: quite simply, without it we'd die. In fact, study after study is showing us that higher cholesterol is protective, especially as we age, and especially for women.[5]

We've seen the importance of the interaction of sunlight with the cholesterol in our skin in the process of making the steroid-like hormone, vitamin D. Cholesterol is also used to make hormones like testosterone, oestrogen and cortisol and so plays an important part in our hormonal health and fertility.

Aa a powerful healing agent, our levels of cholesterol rise during periods of stress, or when inflammation is present. Several studies have now linked low cholesterol with depression, suicide and acts of violence.[6]

While it is true that eggs are high in cholesterol, cholesterol in the diet doesn't necessarily raise cholesterol in the blood. Our own liver produces large amounts of cholesterol every single day. When we eat more eggs, the liver just produces less - smart liver!

Eggs have also been shown to have beneficial effects on HDL (high density lipoprotein, so-called 'good' cholesterol) and turn small LDL (low density lipoprotein, 'bad' cholesterol) into larger LDL particles.

Choline - egg yolks are the most concentrated sources of choline, critical for a process called methylation. Building your DNA, exchanging signals in your brain and detoxifying your liver are just some of the important processes that are dependent on methylation.

Choline has a unique, soap-like structure which helps to keep our cell membranes fluid, yet mostly impermeable. It's the backbone of acetylcholine, a key brain-signalling molecule (or neurotransmitter). The part of your nervous system that runs your heart and keeps your intestines moving along runs largely on acetylcholine, and your muscles require a signal from acetylcholine to tell them to contract.[7]

Why are pastured eggs so special?

Although most of us are by now familiar with the expression *"You are what you eat"*, we need to be conscious that we're also what we eat eats. A natural life for a laying hen is one of true free-ranging in small flocks on healthy, unsprayed pastures, eating bugs, worms and other sources of protein. It won't surprise you that eggs from pastured hens are more nutritious[8] and much more delicious than the conventional eggs you'll typically find at the supermarket.

A study by researchers in Penn State's College of Agricultural Sciences in 2010 has shown that eggs produced by chickens allowed to forage in pastures are higher in some beneficial nutrients than eggs from hens that are not free-range or pasture-fed.

The researchers examined how moving pastured hens to forage legumes or mixed grasses influenced hen egg omega-3 fatty acids and concentrations of vitamins A and E. They also compared the eggs of the pastured hens to those of hens fed a commercial diet and found the differences to be striking! [9]

Depending on the composition of the pasture - grasses, legumes, seeds, worms, grubs and adult insects - pastured eggs are:

- higher in vitamin A
- higher in vitamin E (25% - 200%)
- higher in vitamin D (25%)
- lower in cholesterol
- lower in saturated fat
- have a healthy ratio of omega-6 to omega-3 fatty acids.

It's important to keep our consumption of the fatty acids omega-6 and omega-3 in the right balance. While we need both to work in opposition, too much pro-inflammatory omega-6 will promote inflammation.

Nutritional anthropologists have found that humans evolved to eat an optimal balance of equal amounts of omega-6 and omega-3, however a ratio of four times as much omega-6 to omega-3 is still acceptable[10] and one that should be reflected in what we eat.[11]

Worryingly, an average supermarket egg from hens raised in confined barns or sheds and typically given high protein soya feed (which unless it's organic, is likely to be genetically modified and glyphosate-treated) can have an extremely high ratio of a whopping 20 times the amount of omega-6 to omega-3!

By contrast, eggs from hens raised on diverse organic pastures can have a very healthy and anti-inflammatory inverse ratio of omega-6 to omega-3 - i.e. five times as much omega-3 as omega-6; great news for lowering our triglyceride levels and risk factor for cardiovascular disease.[12]

An organic egg producer I spoke to recently tested his eggs against others for omega-6 and -3. The battery-cage eggs that were marketed as large were found to contain huge amounts of linoleic acid (an inflammatory omega-6 fatty acid), which the egg industry uses to push hens to create the larger eggs.

In a 2018 paper in the British Medical Journal's *Open Heart*, Dr James DiNicolantonio argues for compelling evidence that omega-6 linoleic acid promotes coronary artery disease (CAD).[13]

So, depending on their provenance, large eggs may not be best!

As we shall see in later chapters, our high consumption of inflammatory omega-6 fatty acids (typically 16 times omega-6 to omega-3) contributes to many of today's health issues. When we consider the amount of grain-fed meat we eat, how much grain we directly consume and the damaged omega-6 vegetable oils we ingest from cooking oils and those hidden in processed foods, it's not difficult to see how modern food is creating chronic systemic inflammation in our bodies.

The egg producer above told me that before the BSE scare (bovine spongiform encephalopathy or 'mad cow' disease) when hens were fed meat and bone meal, rather than the almost exclusively vegetarian grain-based diet they're given today, farmers had far fewer issues managing their hens' health. The same producer uses hens to follow-on behind the cows when he moves the cattle to a new pasture: the hens not only get the nutritional benefits from the grass, but they can enjoy a protein-rich feast from the bugs which hide under the cow pats. He also tells the story of eggs from hens who lived on a dairy farm: the hens came up to the farmer daily for their milk, after he finished milking his cows and their yolks looked lovely and the eggs were excellent quality.

Dr Natasha Campbell-McBride (my GAPS teacher and mentor, who is also a small-holding farmer) recommends giving hens a regular treat of raw ground meat.

I must say, our backyard flock of six laying hens devour raw milk, kefir, home-made yoghurt and ground meat!

Nowadays, most hens have derived some of their protein requirement from wheat, but high-protein, GM soya feed certainly should not be on the menu for our laying hens, or indeed for any animal.

'Unscrambling' your eggs

How free-range is your 'free-range' egg? Egg labelling is notoriously confusing and wide open to cynical marketing manipulation - the British Hen Welfare Trust provides a description of the various egg production environments.

At the time of writing, there is no definitive or agreed consensus, so you'll have to do a little detective work for yourself and ask a few questions - a genuine producer will be happy to explain his or her methods.

Below is summary guide I've put together to help inform your questions:

3* Organic Pastured Eggs**	These are the 'real deal' from hens genuinely free to roam on diverse, organic pasture (no synthetic pesticides or herbicides); bulk of feed is from grass or forage; no soya/GM feeds; no antibiotics/hormones.
2Organic Grain-fed Eggs, labelled free-range**	These eggs may be from hens which genuinely free-range (as above), but they can also be from hens raised in confinement (in multi-tier hen-houses, or in sheds) with some access to outdoors, fed on organic grains, including organic soya (no synthetic pesticides/herbicides); no antibiotics/hormones/GMOs.
1* Non-Organic Eggs, labelled free-range	These may be from hens which genuinely free-range, but they can also be from hens raised in confinement (in multi-tier hen-houses, or in sheds) with some access to outdoors, fed on non-organic grains (including GM soya), sprayed with synthetic pesticides/herbicides); usually subjected to antibiotics.
0* Non-Organic Eggs	The typical supermarket egg, from hens raised in confinement (caged, colony, or in barns) with no access to outdoors, fed on non-organic grains (including GM soya), sprayed with synthetic pesticides/herbicides); usually subjected to antibiotics/hormones.

Where can you find a good egg?

For me, it's in my own backyard. By keeping laying hens and choosing feed that is soya-free and organic, you'll have great quality eggs. Four hens will provide a family with nutritious and spanking fresh deliciousness every day.

If that's not an option, make friends with (and treat nicely!) a neighbour or local small-holder who keeps hens. Source eggs from trusted and committed suppliers such as: Riverford Organic Farmers, or Abel & Cole; a regional/local farming co-operative; Farm Drop; and other sources like The Open Food Network. Always check welfare standards and practices.

You can also check out the British Hen Welfare Trust's participating pastured egg producers or search online for up-to-date information on comparable welfare standards and practices.

A little egg wisdom:

A fresh egg has a plump white; an older egg has a runny white; older eggs sit more upright or float when placed in water. A freshly laid egg is difficult (if not impossible) to peel when hard boiled - so if you want hard-boiled eggs, then steam them for 15-20 mins and they'll peel easily.

However, eggs from older hens will have more watery whites, so if you want to poach your eggs, then use them as fresh as possible, or the whites will be stringy. Pullet eggs - the hen's first eggs - are extremely nutritious. While they may look small, they actually pack a punch as the yolk/white ratio is closer to 50:50 compared with eggs from mature hens.

Various studies have shown no difference in bacterial contamination between eggs that have been stored at room temperature versus those stored in a fridge.

If the egg's shell is cracked, always discard the egg, unless you've cracked it yourself, in which case transfer it to a clean, lidded container and use it within 24 hours. Eggs have porous shells, so the best advice is to store them away from foods with high odours like cheese, garlic or onions.

I store mine in the fridge, on a shelf, in their cartons. We love poached eggs and I find this keeps the eggs fresh for ages and the whites stay nice and plump. Happy days!

A note about raw eggs

Marilyn Monroe was reputed to subsist on a diet of raw eggs, raw milk, raw carrots and liver. She was a wise woman, as raw eggs offer several nutritional benefits over cooked.

For example, they contain around 33% more vitamin D and omega-3 and are the major source of choline, a single raw egg offering 35% of adequate intake for a female.

However, consuming raw eggs is controversial, not least due to the (albeit small) risk of bacterial contamination. So, let's reiterate an earlier discussion: the nourishment we get from plant foods depends entirely on the quality of the soil in which they grow and the same is true for animal foods, including eggs.

The nourishment we get from an egg depends on the lifestyle and health of the hen who produced it. Newly-gathered eggs from healthy hens, free to roam in the fresh air, enjoying high-quality diverse pastures (or even your own back garden) will be more nutritious and often safer than any supermarket egg, or those from large, poorly managed, commercial operations. Know your supplier is the rule here.

It's also worth pointing out that raw egg whites are less digestible that cooked whites[14] so like Marilyn, you might want to stick to the raw yolks and save and freeze the whites for those meringues - in moderation!

Everyone must make his or her own judgment call about eating raw eggs, particularly younger people, older people and pregnant women. According to the George Mateljan Foundation, an online resource for the *'World's Healthiest Foods'* it's worth noting that, on an individual basis, a person who eats one egg per day would expect to consume a contaminated egg only once every 54 years.[15]

So, if you do plan to include raw eggs in your diet, get them from a local source that not only produces certified organic eggs, but also provides a genuinely natural outdoor lifestyle for the hens, including a pasture-based diet from a natural landscape with ecologically balanced vegetation. Or, do as I do, and get a few hens of your own!

Art of the egg...

> **"If you want to learn how to cook, start with eggs. That's my advice."**

- Delia Smith

Delia began publishing her now classic *How to Cook* series some 20 years ago, by dedicating three chapters to the art and science of how to cook an egg any way you choose. For my money, Delia's advice can't be beaten, and I highly recommend adding the series to your culinary bookshelf. She also has some excellent video tutorials on her website.

The subject of what to do with an egg would provide content for several books, but here are a few of my simple ideas:

Whole eggs - use them solo, in recipes, soups and broths.

Egg yolks - use yolks to enrich soups, broths, sauces, luxurious desserts. Use super-fresh eggs yolks in milkshakes, smoothies, fresh fruit juices, quick mayonnaise made with yoghurt.

Egg whites - meringues (older egg whites are easier to whisk), sweet/savoury mousses, tempura batter, coconut macaroons, bread glazes.

Egg shells - ground egg shells, sourced from the best eggs, are a traditional source of calcium, especially for anyone with a true milk intolerance or allergy - just grind them to a powder and add to soups, casseroles or sauces.

Eggs-for-breakfast - boiled, poached (use very fresh eggs or the whites will spread), scrambled, fried, baked, omelettes, frittatas, muffins.

Eggs-for-lunch - make them 'portable' - frittatas, muffins, egg mayo/salads, quiches.

Eggs-for-supper - again, omelettes, frittata, quiches (add mixed green leaf salad, buttered or roasted veggies).

Eggs-for-sweets & treats - meringues, custards, soufflés, tarts, cakes, bakes, breads, the list goes on and on!

EGG Recipes

AVOCADO & SPINACH BREAKFAST SMOOTHIE

(Serves 2, gluten/grain free)

It's delicious, nutritious and rich in proteins, fats and probiotics. Adding fresh, organic, truly free-range egg yolks not only gives flavour and smooth texture but will provide an extra powerful hit to keep you going into the afternoon.

Spinach is a high nutritional hitter and while we think that raw green smoothies are super-healthy, raw and cruciferous vegetables cause us problems with thyroid production and irritate our intestinal tract. Spinach is one such vegetable.

I recommend always cooking spinach, as raw spinach contains goitrogens which block the production of thyroid hormone and impede metabolism. It also contains oxylic acid, a very irritating substance to the mouth and intestinal tract and it blocks iron and calcium absorption, contributing to the formation of kidney stones.

What you'll need:

Avocado: 1 (peeled, stoned, roughly chopped)
Banana: 1 small (peeled, roughly chopped)
Fresh ginger: 1 heaped tsp (finely grated)
Collagen hydrolysate: 1 tbsp (*non-setting* gelatin powder – see the Bone Broth chapter)
Spinach: 100g (cooked, well-drained and roughly chopped)
Organic Greek natural yoghurt: 2-3 generous tbsp (Yeo Valley is good)
Kefir (optional): 250ml
Organic, free range egg yolks: 1-2 (optional, must be very fresh)
Coconut milk/ Organic full-fat milk: 400ml (approx.) raw/Pasture Promise/unhomogenised
Organic virgin coconut oil: 1 heaped tbsp (melted & cooled slightly)

What to do:

Blitz together in a food processor/blender until smooth.

CHORIZO & RED PEPPER FRITTATA

(Serves 2, gluten/grain free)

This delicious stove-top frittata is a meal in a pan, with a great balance of proteins, carbs and fats. Served solo, it will sort you out for breakfast. Great for the lunch box, just add a serving of slaw. And it makes an easy supper - just add your choice of a simple tomato, or green leaf salad, or buttered vegetables.

What you'll need:

Extra Virgin Olive Oil: 2 tbsp
Sweet potato: 1 medium (peeled, coarsely grated)
Chorizo: 8 slices (wheat-free, uncooked is best, small dice)
Red peppers: 6 tbsp (finely chopped)
Eggs: 5 large (organic, pastured or truly free-range, beaten)
Spring onions: 4 (finely chopped)
Flat-leaf parsley: 2 tbsp (finely chopped)
Mature Cheddar or Manchego: 100g (finely grated)
Sea salt: to taste (Maldon)
Ground black pepper: to taste
Oregano (dried): ½ tsp (or 1 tsp freshly chopped)

What to do:

1. In a 20cm (8in) frying pan, heat the olive oil. Add the sweet potato and cook until just tender.

2. Add the red pepper and cook gently for 5 mins until softened.

3. Add the chorizo and cook until slightly crisp.

4. Beat together the eggs, spring onions, oregano, half the parsley, salt and pepper.

5. Turn down the heat and add the egg mixture to the frying pan.

6. When the mixture has set on the bottom, add the grated cheese and stir gently to incorporate.

7. Cover the pan and cook very gently for about 7 - 10 mins, until the frittata has set all the way through. Reduce the heat to make sure the bottom doesn't burn.

8. When the top is set, sprinkle with the remaining parsley and serve.

Note: If you want to finish the frittata under the grill: reserve a tablespoon of grated cheese, and when the bottom and sides of the frittata are set, sprinkle with the cheese and place the frying-pan under a medium-hot grill until set and slightly risen.

A PROPER, Real Custard

No discussion on the value and use of an egg could possibly omit a classic custard. A thing of unctuous beauty, made-from-scratch proper custard has stood the test of time and is good enough to eat on its own. It puts the gloopy supermarket offerings to shame.

What you'll need:

Organic full-fat milk: 575ml (raw/Pasture Promise/unhomogenised)
Vanilla pod: 1 (split in half, seeds scraped out)
Egg yolks: 6 (organic, free-range, freeze the whites for meringues)
Caster sugar: 2 tbsp
Arrowroot: 1 tbsp

What to do:

1. Pour the milk into a heavy-bottomed pan, with the vanilla pod and seeds, set on a gentle heat.

2. Stir, then slowly bring to a very gentle simmer: don't allow it to boil or you'll scramble the eggs.

3. While the milk is heating, beat the yolks, sugar and arrowroot together in a large heatproof bowl.

4. Remove the vanilla pod from the hot milk and then pour the milk on to the yolk and sugar mixture, stirring vigorously as you go.

5. Pour the custard back into a clean, dry pan and turn the heat right down. Stirring continuously, heat until it coats the back of your wooden spoon, scraping the bottom as you go. Be patient, if the heat is too high the eggs *will* scramble. The longer you cook the custard, the thicker it will get.

6. Pour the custard into a jug and serve straight away or press cling film on to the surface if you want to avoid a skin forming over the top.

CHAPTER FOUR

MEAT IS A TREAT! (and OFFAL ISN'T AWFUL)

"You, as a food buyer, have the distinct privilege of proactively participating in shaping the world your children will inherit."

\- Joel Salatin

The subject of eating meat, what kind of meat to eat and even whether we should be eating it at all, is becoming more and more controversial. Although humans have been meat eaters throughout our evolution, today many believe that eating meat causes us - and the planet - all kinds of harm. From the pro-meat Ancestral/Paleo enthusiasts, to the no-meat vegetarians, to the plant-only vegans, opinions are deeply divided.

Eating meat, particularly red meat, has taken the blame for everything from heart disease to diabetes and cancer, and also its environmental sustainability is persistently questioned. Let me be clear from the start: I believe that eating intelligently- and ethically-sourced meat is a *very* important element in a healthy, traditional, nutrient-dense diet.

As we saw in the Soil chapter, with holistic, planned grazing and regenerative farming practices, raising animals and consuming their meat is, according to the Savory Institute, the key to *"a life of enduring returns for the land and all who depend on it."*

With an informed and considered approach, it is perfectly possible to enjoy good health on a plant-based and meat-free diet. But it's much harder (some would say impossible) on a strictly vegan diet and I (like many others) would argue that globally, an exclusively plant-based diet is environmentally unsustainable.

Eating meat today certainly isn't as simple as it used to be, and in this chapter we'll see why.

But first, let's rewind...

Go back some 10,000 years and imagine the Earth's vast prairies and fields populated by wild cattle and other animals roaming free, chewing leisurely on Mother Nature's bounty of healthy grasses, edible plants, insects and whatever else was natural to that environment.

Now, fast-forward to today. In our mind's eye, we see sheep and cattle dotted about the countryside, grazing freely on lush green grass, living the life of Riley, before giving us our comforting midweek casserole, succulent Saturday night steak or delicious Sunday roast.

And in the next field, following in their footsteps, see those flocks of chickens? Their heads down, scraping and pecking for bugs and other morsels, slowly growing plumper and plumper each day until they're ready for market.

Just check out those fat porkers, happily rooting around, snouts digging into the ground all around, snorting, grunting and playing games, before gifting us the best bacon, sausages and crackling ever.

Let's just understand the basics: cows and sheep eat grass, right? Isn't that what they were designed to eat? Pigs root and chickens peck and scratch, right?

Indeed, in her infinite wisdom, Mother Nature carefully crafted a very neat food production line for our benefit and for the planet she has gifted to us. Take cows as an example: their complex, ruminant, four-compartment stomachs and digestive tract can turn tough, indigestible cellulose plant matter - the grasses they eat - into the almost perfect formula of nutrient-dense proteins and fats - the meat we eat - that our digestive systems are well-equipped to handle over thousands of years' evolution. Yes: cows and sheep eat grass, so we don't have to.

But, do they actually eat grass? Sadly, most don't, and if your memory's a little short - and whose isn't these days? - let's have a quick refresher on animal feed.

Cows should eat grass and sometimes they do, but most of the meat we buy from supermarkets - and often from the average butcher on the High Street - is from animals reared in confined conditions on ever-growing intensive farms and fed on grains. In common with our laying hens in the Eggs chapter, the animals we eat today are increasingly raised this way.

And folks, this isn't natural and it's certainly not healthy.

What's in the feed?

We saw in the Soil chapter how glyphosate - the broad-spectrum herbicide - is routinely sprayed on most cereal crops before harvest, and that includes crops like soya and corn that are destined for animal feeds. We saw that animal feeds, unless organic, will have been genetically modified, particularly from the soya component which satisfies the protein requirement in animal feeds; about 80% of the world's soya is now GM and the majority of animal products produced and sold in the UK are fed on at least some GM feed.

Of course, organic soya can be sourced, but organic or not, soya is a plant-based oestrogen - phytoestrogen. Phytoestrogens occur naturally in many foods, including eggs and cheese, but the levels in soya are significantly higher than any other food.

Animals consuming a soya-based diet have much higher levels of phytoestrogens in their tissues and eggs than those which are pasture-raised. Therefore, when we humans consume these animal products, we consume higher levels of phytoestrogens too.

As a phytoestrogen, soya acts in the body to interfere with the its endocrine system and produces adverse developmental, reproductive, neurological and immune effects in both humans and wildlife.

Soya consumption has been linked to: suppression of thyroid function, affecting the metabolic efficiency of every cell in the body; breast cancer in women; and infertility in men. Damage is believed to be most severe during prenatal or early pregnancy exposure.[1]

"A litany of health benefits including a lowered risk of osteoporosis, heart disease, breast cancer, and menopausal symptoms, are frequently attributed to phytoestrogens but many are also considered endocrine disruptors, indicating that they have the potential to cause adverse health effects as well.

Of even greater concern is that emerging evidence suggests that exposure to these compounds may, in fact, pose a risk to some groups, particularly infants and the unborn.

Consumers should be aware that soy contains endocrine disrupting compounds and make dietary choices accordingly."

- Heather Patisaul
Pros and Cons of Phytoestrogens

What's the beef with feeding grain?

If cattle and sheep are ruminants, designed to eat grass, why feed them grains at all? The answer is simple: grain is cheap, and animals fed on grain fatten quickly, so their time-to-market is shorter. While grain-fed systems make healthy profits for agri-business, they're not healthy for the animal or its consumer.

Inflammation

A ruminant's gut is normally pH-neutral and so best-suited to a diet of grasses. However, the highly acid (and inflammatory) nature of a grain-based diet makes, for example, a cow's gut unnaturally acidic. Inflammation causes bovine heartburn and allows a whole range of harmful parasitic bacteria (such as E-coli) to proliferate.

In humans, the health, integrity and efficiency of our digestive tract is paramount to every aspect of our health, not least to our immune system, 80% of which is actually located in the digestive tract. When these two systems fail, we fall prone to disease. Animals are no different: when cattle and other ruminants are fed grains (whether GM or not) and kept indoors in crowded conditions, they fall prey to inflammation and infections and need to be treated with regular doses of antibiotics to keep them going long enough to get them to market. Indeed in 2015, NHS Choices[2] said this:

> **"A considerable amount of antibiotics are used in healthy animals to prevent infection or speed up their growth. This is particularly the case in intensive farming, where animals are kept in confined conditions."**

And more inflammation

A high-grain diet will also radically change an animal's omega-6 to omega-3 ratio, which as we've seen, should optimally be a in ratio of 1:1. Research shows that if ingested omega-6 exceeds omega-3 in a ratio greater than 4:1, then people have more health problems. Grain-fed animals can have ratios in excess of 20:1, while traditionally reared grass-fed animals are 3:1. Quite a difference.

Give them grass!

While most cattle spend the majority of their early lives on pastures eating grass before moving to intensive grain finishing to fatten them ready for market, grass-finished beef cattle remain on a pasture-and-forage diet. The meat from grass-fed and finished cattle can contain more than four times the vitamin E found in grain-fed animals and is much higher in conjugated linoleic acid (CLA), associated with lower heart disease and cancer rates. When examining the health effects of meat, it's important to realise that not all meat is created equal.

Many studies on red meat, especially those conducted in the US, primarily examine meat from factory-farmed animals that have received grain-based feeds, so it's important to remember that much, if not all, research on how eating meat impacts our health (especially the much-demonised red meat) has been done on intensively or factory-farmed, grain-fed animals.

It's a sad fact that our insatiable appetite for cheap food, fuelled by supermarket competition for market share, has forced dramatic changes in how farmers produce our meat. In the unrelenting market pressure to keep costs down, control prices and keep margins high, agri-businessmen - formerly known as farmers - have been pushed to develop ever more intensive and more lucrative methods of rearing and feeding livestock.[3,4]

And remember, even though 'free-range' and 'organic' animal products - whether chicken/eggs, beef/dairy, lamb or pork - may be more ethically raised and superior in taste to those intensively reared, most have still been fed an unnatural, grain-based diet, which directly impacts our health.

Why does it all matter?

A farmer, grower or producer bearing a formal Soil Association organic certificate indicates cleaner, healthier soil - and feeds - and thus cleaner, safer and more flavoursome meat and dairy products. Add to this 'pasture' or 'grass-finished' and you're now talking *real* meat.

That said, it's always worth repeating the point I made earlier: there are many local or smaller artisan farmers, growers and producers who employ traditional rearing and pasturing methods and farm to organic - and even tougher biodynamic - standards, but who aren't formally certified, often because certification is onerous, costly and frequently anomalous.

War and Peace

I could easily compete with *War and Peace* on the subject of meat, so here I'll simply focus on the key issues around our carnivorous predilection that have been the brunt of demonisation by the media and by the scientific community. Almost daily, we read alarmist headlines in the media, warning us of the grave dangers of eating meat and particularly red meat. So...

First, let's define 'meat'

Red meat - meats that are 'red' when raw - from cattle, buffalo, sheep and lambs, goats, pigs etc.

White meat - meats that are 'white' when cooked - from poultry such as chicken and turkey.

Conventionally-raised meat - the animals are often intensively farmed and/or kept in confinement and fed on grain, soy and GM-based diets, treated with drugs that encourage maximum growth and antibiotics to maintain health.

Grain-fed organic meat - this meat comes from animals that have been given organic feed without chemicals, drugs or hormones.

Grass-fed organic meat - this meat comes from any animal that has been naturally fed on grass or pasture and raised organically, without chemicals, drugs or hormones.

Processed meat - these products are most often from conventionally and/or intensively raised animals and go through various industrialised processing methods. Processed meats include bacon, sausages, salami and other products made with meats that have undergone high processing and manipulation and adulteration with additives, preservatives and various other undisclosed processing aids.

However, we need to make a big distinction between these kinds of products and the artisanal sausages, cured and naturally fermented meats made by time-honoured methods, from traditionally-raised animals.

Red meat: are the warnings correct?

Well, yes and no. Firstly, there's no doubt about it: We are all eating more meat than is good for our health, as well as consuming too much cheap, low-quality processed meat instead of higher quality options. The effects of red meat on health outcomes has been studied intensively and reviews of the literature for observational studies *have* found associations between eating red meat and an increased risk of cardiovascular disease, diabetes, cancer and death.[5]

But before you run for the hills, let's just take a step back and remember that not all meat is created equal and this is particularly important in a research context: unless we make a clear distinction between different kinds of meat, we're comparing apples with cabbages. We need to firmly bear in mind that the research data (much of it derived from flawed US observational studies which have been hugely influential in shaping current nutritional dogma) has come almost exclusively from studies which examine meat from intensively reared, factory-farmed, grain-fed animals and often have not distinguished between unprocessed and highly processed meats.

> **"Highly processed and adulterated "factory-farmed" meats like salami and hot dogs are lumped together with grass-fed, organic meat as if they're the same thing. It's likely that very little of the meat people ate .... was from pasture-fed animals. Factory fed animals are fed corn (high in polyunsaturated, omega-6 fat), antibiotics, and hormones, all of which negatively impact human health."** [6]

We also need to ask another important question: how reliable is the quality of the research? You may need a glass of something to fortify yourself, but I recommend you try Appendix 3 - A Deeper Dive into Good vs Bad Science to get a feel for why so much of what we read and hear is contradictory or just plain wrong.

The problems with research studies highlighted in Appendix 3 go a long way to explaining why going back to examine what kept our ancestors healthy is a valid approach to informing optimum nutrition today.

A closer look at red meat and nutrition

All red meat is rich in vitamins, minerals, antioxidants and other nutrients that can have profound effects on our health. Traditionally-raised, organic red meat is one of the most nutritionally complete foods for human health.

- **Vitamin B12** - animal-derived foods are the *only* dietary sources of vitamin B12, an essential nutrient that is important for blood formation and the function of the brain and nervous system.

- **Zinc** - Beef is rich in zinc, a mineral important for body growth and maintenance.
- **Selenium** - meat is generally a rich source of selenium, an essential trace element that is a powerful antioxidant that fights oxidative stress and helps to defend the body from chronic diseases, such as heart disease and cancer.
- **Iron** - found in high amounts in red meat, mostly in the heme form. Heme iron is absorbed more efficiently (typically at a rate of 7-35%) compared with the non-heme iron found in plant foods (typically absorbed at a rate of 2-20%).
- **Niacin** - vitamin B3. Niacin has various important functions in the body. Low niacin intake has been associated with increased risk of heart disease.
- **Vitamin B6** - a family of B-vitamins, important for blood formation.
- **Phosphorus** - widely found in foods, phosphorus intake is generally high in the Western diet. It is essential for body growth and maintenance.
- **Creatine** - abundant in meat and an important energy source for muscle growth and maintenance.
- **Taurine** - found in fish and meat, taurine is an antioxidant important for heart and muscle function.
- **Glutathione** – the 'master' antioxidant found in most whole foods, glutathione is particularly abundant in meat. It is found in higher amounts in grass-fed beef than in grain-fed.
- **Conjugated linoleic acid (CLA)** - a natural ruminant trans-fat that has health benefits when consumed as part of a healthy diet.
- **Cholesterol** - a sterol found in animal fats, and also produced by the human body where it has many functions. Dietary cholesterol has little effect on blood cholesterol and is therefore not considered a health concern.

Overall, grass-fed beef is more nutritious than grain-fed, containing plenty of heart-healthy, inflammation reducing omega-3s, the fatty acid CLA, along with more vitamins A and E. In addition, organic meat is even better - recent studies have found that omega-3 fatty acids are 47% higher in organic meat, protecting against cardiovascular disease and cognitive decline.[7]

Red meat or white meat - which is better?

I have to dispel the popular myth that eating white meat - particularly lean white meat - is better for our health than eating red meat. Nutritionally, it is not.

The benefit of eating red meat rather than white, lies in red meat's fatty acid profile. In ruminants - cattle, goats, sheep - the fat comprises approximately equal parts of saturated and monounsaturated fat, with only a very small amount of polyunsaturated fat. This is a very good thing as we'll see in the Fats chapter. For those on a budget, red meat (especially the cheaper, slow-cook cuts) is a better choice over pork or poultry because it delivers the healthier, mostly saturated and mono-unsaturated fats.

In traditional diets, all parts of the animal were used, not just the lean muscle meats: eating 'nose-to-tail' wasn't just some foodie trend! Collagen makes up about 50% of the protein mass of an animal and is free from the pro-inflammatory amino acid tryptophan, which our body then converts to serotonin, a neurotransmitter known for its contribution to feelings of well-being, stabilising mood, reducing depression and regulating anxiety. Although it's seen as a 'brain chemical', most serotonin is actually found in the gut, helping us with our sleep, with eating and digesting our food and with maintaining bone health.

Our ancestors favoured the tougher, fattier (and cheaper) cuts of meat with plenty of gelatinous connective tissue, and bone broths rich in collagen and gelatin (the 'cooked' form of collagen). However, over recent years these old-fashioned cuts have been shunned in favour of quicker-cooking lean meats, particularly chicken breasts and lean, tender (and expensive) cuts like fillet and tenderloin.

When our ancestors consumed the old-fashioned cuts (together with oxtails and chicken feet) they were consuming about half as much tryptophan in proportion to other amino acids. Today, our high consumption of lean meats means we are consuming much more tryptophan and therefore producing high levels of serotonin. Research has shown that excess serotonin can lead to a broad range of harmful effects: for example, inflammation, hypertension, bronchoconstriction, fibrosis, impaired learning and neurological damage.[8]

But what about red meat and cancer?

Scientists have speculated whether eating red meat causes cancer since the mid-1970s. However, as Dr Carrie Ruxton, a dietician at the UK Meat Advisory Panel points out:

"There are no agreed mechanisms which point to how red meat could cause disease or death... even the evidence on bowel cancer, which is the area with the most data... has not provided a consensus on mechanisms."

While some individual and observational studies have found that red meat consumption is associated with an increased risk of colorectal cancer, a 2010 meta-analysis looked at 35 studies which claimed to have found an association between red meat and cancer and uncovered numerous problems with these studies: often the associations were weak and not distinguishable from chance and in some studies, there was a *decrease* in cancer rates among people who ate the most red meat. [9]

I think it's well worth reiterating: a major problem with interpreting the data from the majority of studies like these is that they fail to compare or distinguish the effects on health of eating grass-fed vs factory-farmed meat or wholly unprocessed meats vs highly processed meats and their products.

Another major problem is that earlier studies did not consider the role of the gut microbiome. More recent research suggests that the composition of our gut microbes may directly interact with dietary factors in the risk of developing cancer.

Someone with a dysbiotic microbiome (one compromised by the proliferation of certain strains of gut microbes) may be at increased risk for cancer if he or she consumes high amounts of either fresh or processed red meat, whereas a patient with a normal, healthy microbiome may not. [10]

What about red meat and cardiovascular disease?

A recent (2018) and well-designed study by Czech researchers[11] reviewed average food intake of a wide range of items between 1993 and 2011, in 158 countries. The team looked for associations with cardiovascular disease (CVD):

"How many times have we looked at the attacks on real food (red meat, eggs, dairy products etc) emanating from the Harvard School of public health and lamented the fact that they never seem to investigate processed

food or even all food? This Czech study has done what we have been longing for a research team to do for some time."

The study found several foods/food groups had strong inverse relationships (the higher the consumption, the lower the incidence) with CVD deaths in European men and women. The researchers found that fats and proteins from all sources (including animal), as well as fruits, coffee, oranges and cheese were all strongly associated with lower deaths from cardiovascular disease. [12]

In her review of the study, obesity researcher Dr Zoë Harcombe suggested:

"Some of the relationships were almost as high as will ever be seen in statistical analysis."

A word of caution: red meat and iron overload

Red meat contains primarily heme iron, a form that is absorbed and utilised much more efficiently than the non-heme iron found in plant foods, and even small amounts of meat can aid in the absorption of non-heme iron.

For most of us, especially those with iron-deficiency anaemia, the iron from red meat is beneficial and this is particularly important for women who are pregnant (or wish to become pregnant) as iron is crucial for the growth and development of the foetal brain.

However, for people with iron overload conditions like hereditary hemochromatosis, it's probably best to limit food high in iron (such as red meat) or take steps to limit the absorption of heme iron.

If you suffer from iron overload, limit or avoid drinking orange juice near (or with) a red meat meal, as the juice acts to enhance iron absorption. On the other hand, drinking coffee with red meat inhibits iron absorption, so if you have iron overload, or if you're enjoying a lean muscle cut, then adding a spoonful of gelatin powder to your coffee will both help protect against iron and help digestion.

How about processed meat?

Cured and processed meats are frequently demonised and indeed, the mass-produced, ultra-processed, flavour-enhanced sausages, cold cuts and bacon should, by now, have left you with second thoughts.

However, preserving food by curing, smoking, pickling and salting and making use of every scrap of the precious animal were all traditional 'processing' practices in every civilization throughout the millennia. Knowing a food's provenance helps you to make a better buying decision. Next time you hear, or read a damning report on processed meat, please stop and think of apples and cabbages!

Ask yourself: how was it reared? What was it fed and by whom? How and where was it processed? If your sausages and bacon come from next door's farm, or your salami from a local producer (or even better, if you've actually made them yourself from trusted sources) then just enjoy.

While controversy continues to rage around the issue of consumption of nitrites and nitrates in processed meats, a review by Tang et al (2011)[13] examined the published literature on the health benefits vs risks of consuming nitrite and nitrate and found both cardiovascular and cellular benefits:

> **"The major source of exposure of nitrite and nitrate comes from the consumption of nitrate-enriched vegetables. The preponderance of epidemiological studies shows a very weak association with consumption of meats and certain cancers, which contain very little nitrite and nitrate.**
>
> **Nitrite and nitrate in certain foods and diets can be metabolized to nitric oxide and promote cardiovascular benefits and cytoprotection."**

The researchers concluded that "*the collective body of evidence suggests that foods enriched in nitrite and nitrate provide significant health benefits with very little risk.*"

What can we learn from the science?

Well, it seems that the evidence has left at least one globally-recognised leader in the fields of ancestral health, Paleo nutrition and functional and integrative medicine, with this general conclusion:

> **"At this point, given what the research indicates, I do not feel that modest consumption of cured or processed meat is likely to pose a significant health risk, provided you are doing other things right (i.e., nurturing your gut microbiome, eating nutrient-dense, real foods, exercising, etc.). I think there is even less evidence suggesting that we should limit consumption of fresh red meat, especially when it is cooked using gentle methods (rather than charring it) and when you eat from nose-to-tail."**

- Chris Kresser

And I completely agree!

Hey - what about the chooks and porkers?!

Broadly, all of the main points above apply to all meats. However, as I've outlined above and will do again in the Bone Broth chapter, frequent and/or excessive white or lean meat consumption doesn't lead to optimal nutrition. Well-sourced, grass-fed and finished red meat, slow-cooked on the bone, is by far our best choice

That said, we just can't ignore our love affair with poultry, side-line that unctuously melting pork belly, or deny ourselves the delight of a piece of salty, crunchy crackling!

Provenance is king not only in terms of ethics, quality and flavour, but crucially in terms of our health. On every level, sourcing and cooking a traditionally pasture-raised, organic chicken, or enjoying a crispy-crackling, succulent pork joint from a truly outdoor-reared pig is a million miles away from the experience of consuming their intensively-reared poor relations.

Did you know that over 50 billion chickens are reared annually to provide us with meat and eggs? That's around seven times the number of people on earth and that most of this poultry will be intensively produced.

Many volume producers are increasingly using misleading labelling which implies that their product - particularly chicken - comes from small-scale farmers or higher-welfare sources:

> **"Beware of false brands. This is where a name is created to suggest something about the origin of the chicken, without actually having any real basis in fact. For example, chicken in a discount supermarket labelled "Sunny Forest Farms Chicken" is unlikely to be from a small farm in a forest, with chickens given access to sunshine. It is simply clever marketing of standard, intensively-produced chicken."**

- Daniel Nowland
The Truth About the Chicken Industry

Sourcing healthy meat is so important but knowing where to source it is confusing and labels don't help much either.

What's in a label?

Pasture-raised, free-range, organic, barn-raised, Freedom Foods, farm assured, locally produced, outdoor-reared… what does it all mean? Food labels should be simple, clear and informative, and various organisations are campaigning for this. It will help to look out for…

Organic	Standards are defined by law, and farmers and processors must be certified. Organic systems provide high levels of animal welfare, so animals can go outside for part - or all - of their lives, don't use chemical fertilisers or pesticides and the routine use of antibiotics is not permitted. However, unless raised on grass or pasture, these animals receive varying proportions of organic grains.
Free-range	Chickens and pigs can go outside for at least part of their lives, allowing them to be more active and exhibit more of their natural behaviours compared with intensively-reared animals. Free-range chicken typically contains less fat than intensively-reared chicken, as well as being tastier. But as we saw for laying hens in the Eggs chapter, the extent to which any chickens are truly 'free-range' varies hugely; many are likely never to see the outdoors.
Pasture/grass-fed	Signifies the traditional practice of grazing cattle, sheep, hens and table chickens on pasture as opposed to the conventional intensive practice of fattening them on grains. Pasture-raised animals are often - but not always - reared to organic standards or certification and some will be grass-finished.
Outdoor bred/reared	Refers to pigs born in systems with outdoor space, then brought indoors for fattening after weaning (outdoor bred) or spend around half their life outdoors (outdoor reared).

RSPCA Assured	The RSPCA's labelling and assurance scheme dedicated to improving welfare standards. About 30% of pigs in the UK are reared under this strict labelling scheme which covers both indoor and outdoor rearing systems and ensures that greater space and bedding material are provided.
Freedom Foods	This is the RSPCA's higher animal welfare standards and labelling scheme that includes beef, chicken, pork and turkey. Freedom Foods allows free-range, organic, indoor and outdoor farms to join its scheme as long as the RSPCA's welfare standards can be met.
Happerley Provenance	This is a unique certification in the making. Using block chain technology to create a transparent and traceable food chain from production to plate, a Happerley 'passport' will enable the consumer to see the ingredient supply chain from restaurant, retailer, butcher, baker right down to the farmers and growers - without "smokescreens, disingenuous labelling, fake farm brands and cynical use of the word local."
Farm assured/Red Tractor	This label says nothing about how the animal was reared but provides traceability back to the farm. Inspection standards include food safety and hygiene and basic - rather than higher - animal welfare standards.
Locally-sourced, farm fresh, natural	These labels tell us nothing about how the animal was fed and reared, nor do they guarantee the animals have been reared in higher welfare systems. So unless we know otherwise, we should assume nothing.
No label	Tells me to assume the worst!

I recently came across a useful chart informing customers how chickens are raised - I'm sharing it overleaf, since it helps us to ask the right questions of our farmer, producer or butcher.

For me, the peace of mind for my health and my conscience that comes with finding a trusted source for organic, traditionally-raised, truly free-range meat is more than worth the effort.

And, with Brexit approaching, consider this:

"We stand at a cross roads. Will our leaders create new trade deals that sweep aside sustainability standards, climate change commitments, fair dealing, consumer protection, humane production and investment in international development, bowing to intense pressures to deregulate? Or will the UK choose a better path, towards a healthy, fair, humane and sustainable food and farming system?"

- Sustain Alliance for Better Food and Farming

Eating nose-to-tail - like Granny did

Traditional cultures valued every part of the animal and particularly prized offal and organ meats. Our grandparents' traditional diets included these 'forgotten' foods too, providing them with a richly balanced intake of a wide variety of nutrients and important amino acids found in connective tissue around bone, which ease digestion, heal your gut lining and act as anti-ageing supplements befriending your eyes, skin, hair and joints.

Sold by us				**Would never be sold by us**
	Organic (under normal circumstances)	**Organic (under temporary 'high risk' restrictions)**	**Free-range (reared for Swillington by Loose Birds)**	**Factory-farmed birds (source: *The Guardian*)**
Birds	Reared from day-old chicks, slow grown for 3 months	Reared from day-old chicks, slow grown for approx. 3 months	Reared from day-old chicks, slow grown for approx.3 months	Bred to grow unnaturally fast. Deaths from heart attacks that cannot supply enough oxygen to oversized breast muscles. 33-38 days old at slaughter
Feed	Organic certified feed; no routine antibiotics	Organic certified feed; no routine antibiotics	Custom-milled, non-organic feed; no routine antibiotics	Water and feed are medicated with drugs to control parasites or with mass doses of antibiotics
Housing	Small, high-welfare groups in wooden sheds (approx. 200)	Small, high-welfare groups in wooden sheds (approx. 100)	Small, high-welfare groups in large, open arks (approx. 400)	Artificially-lit shed of around 20-30k birds
Access to outdoors	Free to roam during the day	Temporarily housed	Free to roam 24 hours	No access to outdoors or natural light
Slaughter	Pre-stunned and slaughter in high-welfare on farm abattoir (Swillington)	Pre-stunned and slaughter in high-welfare on farm abattoir (Swillington)	Pre-stunned and slaughter in high-welfare on farm abattoir (Harome)	High throughput abattoir, can include use of shackles, gassing and no requirement to pre-stun
Butchered	Butchered and packed on the farm at Swillington	Butchered and packed on the farm at Swillington	Butchered and packed on the farm at Swillington	Part of a worldwide chain

Source: *Swillington's Organic Farm*

Why offal isn't awful

Poor old offal: always an afterthought, but prized by our ancestors, who ate the offal and left the lean muscle meats for their animals to eat!

Offal comprises the parts of the animal that we foolishly throw away: the organ meats from functional internal organs - liver, kidneys, heart, brain - or those derived from tongue, oxtail and intestines. We need to get over our aversion to offal, because for our health's sake, it needs to be back on our tables.

Why? Quite simply, because offal and organ meats are amongst the most nutrient-dense super-foods on the planet. These powerhouses are: rich in anti-inflammatory vitamin A anti-oxidants; rich in heart and brain protective B vitamins and in CoQ10; a powerful tool in preventing anaemia; and an important aid to fertility and healthy pregnancy.

Liver from grass-fed animals is one of the most nutrient-dense foods available to us and practically every cuisine has a number of liver specialities. Liver is immensely rich in true vitamin A, and Dr Weston A. Price found that the diets of the traditional peoples he studied contained at least 10 times more vitamin A from animal sources than did the Standard American Diet of his day. No doubt he would find an even greater difference now.

Another word about vitamin A

It's worth repeating here that the carotenes found in plant-based foods need to be converted to vitamin A in our upper intestine; however, young children, older people and those with digestive issues are not able to make this conversion.[14]

Banish your offal fears

Although most offal meats do have a fairly strong taste - but one which can readily be re-acquired - a little goes a long way. As we'll see in the recipes below, there are lots of ways to incorporate a little offal into a deliciously rich stew, casserole, ragù, burger, meatloaf, or pâté… and - don't run for the hills - we can even benefit from eating it raw, as tiny frozen 'liver pills'!

On cooking your meat - a word of caution

A number of studies implicating red meat in cancer formation suggest that it may not be the meat itself that is contributing to the increased health risk, rather the harmful compounds that form when the meat is incorrectly cooked… or burned on the barbecue!

When meat is cooked at a high temperature, it can form a variety of compounds, which have been found to cause cancer in animals; but once again, these studies have been criticised and as yet, there is no definitive answer. However, these bitter-tasting burnt offerings make no sense at all to our palate, so avoiding burning your meat is probably the most sensible thing to do. I favour lower heat cooking methods - low and slow for the best flavour - and use a clay pot which I find browns the meat without burning it.

If you do want to grill, fry or barbecue meats, marinating them for at least an hour in an acidic marinade can significantly reduce the formation of harmful compounds, as can keeping a water spritzer to hand to douse down a flaming barbecue as you cook.

Granny knew best

Although red meat has become one of the most controversial foods in the history of nutrition, if sourced well, it's one of the most nutritious and delicious foods available to us. Back in the day meat was - relatively - far more expensive than it is now; as Granny used to say: "*Meat is a treat*!"

What would Granny say now?

- Eat less meat but make it better quality. Yes, it will cost a bit more, but you'll pack in much more nutrition - and flavour - so you won't need to eat as much.

- Wherever possible, don't buy your meat from retailers who source their meat from conventional or factory farms. Source traditionally raised, grass-fed and finished, organic meat - and its products - from local farms, or farms which work with Nature, not against her.

  Even if a farm hasn't got formal organic certification, many traditional farmers take great pride in time-honoured farming methods and are rightly proud of their soil and long heritage of producing clean, healthy meat.

- Search online for a source near you - you'll find one - and buy in bulk, or club together with family and friends to bring down costs. Make your freezer your best friend and tend it well.

- While you may love your rump or fillet steaks and Sunday's roast topside or sirloin, these are the lean muscle meats that lack those important anti-inflammatory amino acids. When you do eat leaner cuts, consider supplementing with anti-inflammatory, grass-fed bone broth or a good quality gelatin powder (see the Bone Broth chapter).

Better still choose the cheaper - and yes, fattier! - on-the-bone cuts with plenty of the connective tissue which yields the full range of amino-acids. Slow cook them for the best nutrition and flavour.

Slow cooking is new fast food: you'll pile a bunch of ingredients into a pot, switch it on and you'll come back to a delicious meal and a home that smells of… a home!

- Remember: as far as the food industry is concerned, it's *your* buying decisions that ultimately determine their market, the health of their product and the welfare of our animals and soil.

  And, consequently, your buying decision also determines your health.

- Finally: always remember that good quality, healthy meat from healthy animals, reared and fed traditionally is a treat.

MEAT and OFFAL Recipes

BURGERS - EVERY WHICH WAY!

Once you've made your own, you'll never want to waste your money on the additive-enhanced, overcooked and increasingly expensive specimens on offer at fast-food joints and most restaurants. Making burgers at home is fun (kids love making up their own) and it's speedy: because the meat has been finely minced, the fibres are broken down well and cook quickly.

On making burgers

You can prepare and refrigerate burgers well in advance, as long as the meat hasn't previously been frozen. Open freeze the raw burgers - line an oven tray with greaseproof or parchment paper, lay the burgers on the paper in a single layer and place them in the freezer. When frozen, remove and wrap them with a single layer of parchment in between each and then label and date them.

You can also open freeze cooked burgers - cook them gently, without over-browning, and make sure they're completely cold before freezing. Defrost thoroughly, re-heat in a hot oven and finish under a hot grill.

If you're not cooking your burgers straightaway, make sure the onions, red peppers (and any other added vegetables) are *completely* cold before adding them to the burger mix.

Adding milk-soaked bread is optional, but it gives a moist, lighter texture to the burgers and adding an egg yolk helps everything bind together nicely.

Classic herbs for burgers:

Lamb: mint, thyme, lemon thyme, oregano, basil, coriander, flat leaf parsley
Pork: sage, marjoram/oregano, flat leaf parsley
Beef: thyme, oregano, coriander, tarragon, horseradish root, flat leaf parsley.

Classic spices:

Lamb: garlic, chilli, paprika, cinnamon, ground cumin, ground coriander, turmeric
Pork: garlic, chilli, ground fennel, paprika, smoked paprika, ground star anise
Beef: garlic, chilli, cinnamon, ground cloves (a pinch), paprika, ground cumin, ground coriander.

On serving burgers

Forget the tired old burger buns (too pappy) or the trendy brioche buns (far too sweet). Lightly toast thick slices of sourdough bread, spread over home-made mayonnaise or aioli, a slaw or some spicy salad leaves and top with your burger. Dress with a thick slice of tomato and some caramelised red onion chutney, or spoon on some kimchi.

Or spice it up with a dollop of tasty relish and serve with a fresh, zingy salsa on the side. Or, top the burger with some well-seasoned mushrooms sautéed in a little butter, garlic and a good squeeze of lemon juice and add a good nugget of blue cheese to melt over it all. Or serve the burger in a home-made wrap or flat-bread. Or, wrap all this deliciousness up in a large, crispy (organic) salad leaf and enjoy.

HERBED BEEF, FETA & RED PEPPER BURGERS

(Serves 4)

What you'll need:

Onion: 1 medium-large (very finely diced)
Red pepper: 1 large (finely diced)
Good quality beef mince: 750g
Herbs of choice: 2-3 tbsp (finely chopped)
Good quality bread: 2 slices (preferably sourdough, crusts removed, soaked in a little milk*)
Sea salt: 1½ tsp (Maldon)
Ground black pepper: ¾ tsp
Organic, free-range egg yolk: 1
Feta: 75g (cut into very small dice)
Olive oil: 2-3 tbsp for frying

**Omit for gluten/grain free*

What to do:

1. Over a medium heat, sweat the onion, red pepper and a little salt and pepper in a tbsp of oil, until the vegetables are softened, but not browned. Set aside and let cool down.

2. Squeeze out the milk from the bread and in large bowl and with your (very clean) hands, mix and 'squish' together the ingredients - except the feta - making sure all the ingredients are really well combined.

3. With wet hands, form the mixture into 8 fairly flat patties and push the diced feta into half the patty. Fold the other half of the patty over the cheese and press together lightly so that the burger is sealed. Try not to let the feta come through the mixture to avoid it leaking and burning during cooking.

4. Over a medium heat, fry the burgers in a thin film of oil, until just browned on one side. Turn and brown the other side, adjusting the heat and turning until the burgers are nicely browned on each side and cooked through to the middle.

Serve with: Tomato, Coriander and Sweet Corn Salsa and a Green Leaf and Cucumber Salad dressed with lemon juice.

PORK & CHORIZO BURGERS

(Serves 4)

The addition of chorizo sausage and the compliment of herbs and spices takes these burgers to another level. We often enjoy these for a weekend brunch, with buttered, wilted spinach and poached eggs.

What you'll need:

Good quality pork shoulder: 500g (finely minced)
Chorizo cooking sausage: 250g (skinned, well broken up)
Fennel: 2 tsp (finely ground)
Paprika: 2 tsp (ground)
Smoked paprika: 1 tsp (ground)
Spring onions: 6 (halved and quartered lengthways and very finely sliced)

Garlic: 1 fat clove
Red or green chilli: 1-2 small (seeds optional, very finely chopped)
Flat leaf parsley: 1 tbsp (heaped, finely chopped)
Egg yolk: 1
Sea salt: Maldon (to taste)
Ground black pepper: to taste
Olive oil: 1 tbsp

What to do:

1. Put the meats in a mixing bowl and, using your hands, combine well with the remaining ingredients.

2. To check for seasoning, pat down a 10p size nugget of the mixture and fry it over a medium heat until golden and cooked through. Taste and adjust seasonings until you're happy with the flavours.

3. With wet hands, divide the mixture into 8 balls and pat down to form thick patties.

4. In a frying pan, fry the burgers in a thin film of fairly hot oil for 2 mins until sealed and beginning to brown on one side, then turn down the heat and continue to cook the burgers until nicely browned. Turn and brown the other side, adjusting the heat and turning the burgers until they're nicely browned on each side and cooked through to the middle.

Serve with: Spicy Tomato, Red Onion and Chickpea Salsa and a simple Green Leaf and Cucumber Salad dressed with lemon juice.

LAMB KOFTAS

(Makes 8)

These koftas (made with lamb or hogget) are fun, they're really easy to make and far, *far* nicer and healthier than anything you can buy.

What you'll need:

Minced lamb or hogget: 750g
Coriander: 2½ tsp (ground)
Oregano: 2 heaped tsp (dried) or 1½ tbsp (fresh, finely chopped)
Red chilli: 1-2 or to taste (deseeded and finely chopped)
Red chilli pepper: ½ tsp
Paprika: 1 tsp (ground)
Fresh ginger: 1 tsp (heaped, finely grated)
Garlic: 2 cloves (peeled and crushed)
Soft, dark brown sugar: 1 tsp
Fish sauce: 1 tsp (optional)
Fresh mint: handful of leaves (finely shredded)
Egg yolk: 1 small
Sea Salt: (Maldon, to taste)
Ground black pepper: to taste
Wooden skewers: 8
Olive oil: 1-2 tbsp for frying

What to do:

1. Soak the skewers in warm water for 30mins.

2. Place all the ingredients in a bowl and, using your hands, combine them thoroughly.

3. To check for seasoning, pat down a 10p size nugget of the mixture and fry it over a medium heat until golden and cooked through. Taste and adjust seasonings if necessary.

4. With wet hands, divide the mixture in 8 tight balls, then form each ball into a thick tube and thread the tube onto the skewers.

5. Oil the koftas liberally and, over a medium heat, fry them until just browned on one side. Turn and brown on all sides, adjusting the heat and turning until they are nicely browned and cooked through to the middle.

Serve with: Tzatziki and accompany with a Tomato and Onion and/or Crisp Green Salad.

MAGIC MINCE

I call it 'magic' mince since it's not only versatile but, because it generally comes from the less fashionable parts of the animal, it will be highly nutritious, and full of flavour and much cheaper than less versatile prime cuts.

An equal mix of these cuts will give you great mince:

Lamb: shoulder + neck
Pork: belly, shoulder + leg
Beef: shoulder, skirt, blade, rump + sirloin

You can also mix beef with pork mince, or lamb with beef mince. A traditional Italian ragù and meatballs are both made from a 50/50 mix of beef and pork.

On cooking mince

One of the greatest sins when cooking mince is to brown it over a less than high heat, while stirring it, bashing it and smashing it to bits. The result will be an unappetising homogenous, stewed slurry.

So, I encourage you to depart from the usual advice to bring meat up to room temperature before cooking it and make sure your mince is *well* chilled before starting to brown it. Add the mince in teaspoon-sized nuggets to a well-oiled pan (use coconut or olive oil, lard or beef dripping) in small batches, over a fairly high heat. Don't prod, poke, or otherwise interfere with it, until one area is nicely browned and only then, carefully turn it over, with a wide spatula, so it browns evenly.

If you're adding any liquids, stocks or sauces to your mince during cooking, stir them in gently. All this will mean that your finished dish will have much more flavour from the caramelisation in the sugars and you'll create a pleasing texture and bite.

On choosing seasonings, herbs and spices

Use good a quality, healthy sea salt such as Maldon (grind the flakes) and freshly ground black pepper. Don't be afraid to season well - it makes a huge difference to final flavours if meat is under-seasoned and remember that it's difficult to over-salt your food if you cook it from scratch at home.

The herbs and spices you choose are to your personal taste: think about which herbs and/or spices will best compliment the meat that you're using, but don't over complicate: keep it simple, and use plenty. To test for seasoning, fry-off small nuggets until you're satisfied: taste, taste, taste – and be patient! NB: the nugget tip is for burgers.

BEEF & BLACK BEAN CHILLI

(Serves 4)

We love this dish at home - it's full of flavour from the chocolate, herbs and spices, with a nice kick from the chilli. If you don't like it too hot, go easy on the chilli in the recipe and serve very thinly fresh chillies on the side. I like to finish each bowl with a dollop of thick, well-seasoned yoghurt and strew strips of oven-roasted red peppers over the top.

Using the following recipe as a framework, you can experiment with adding in pork or lamb mince and play about with the spices - it will all be delicious.

What you'll need:

For the beef:
Olive oil: ½ tbsp
Minced beef: 750g (well chilled)
Sea salt: 1 tsp (Maldon)
Ground black pepper: ½ tsp

For the flavour foundation:
Olive oil: 1 tbsp
Onion: 175g (finely diced)
Carrots: 100g (finely diced)
Celery: 100g (finely sliced)
Sea salt: ½ tsp (Maldon)
Ground black pepper: ½ tsp
Garlic: 2 fat cloves (very finely sliced)

For the sauce:
Chopped tomatoes: 1 x 400g tin
Black Beans: 1 x 380g brick
Brown sugar: 1 tsp (level)
Ginger: 1 tsp (heaped, finely grated)

Paprika: 1 tsp (heaped)
Cinnamon: ½ tsp
Chilli powder*: 1 tsp (level, or to taste)
Oregano: 1½ tsp
Sea salt: 1 tsp (Maldon)
Fish sauce/apple cider vinegar: 2 tsp (optional)
Cocoa Powder: 1 tsp (level)

**Or, use 1-2 fresh bird's eye chillies. Finely slice and adjust the heat to taste by removing seeds.*

What to do:

Beef:

1. Heat the oil in a large broad oven-proof casserole (or frying pan). Pick off walnut sized nuggets from the chilled beef mince and brown them, a few at a time, over a high heat. Don't over-fill the pan or move them too much or they will stew and break up. Transfer the meat to a plate.

2. Set the oven at 180°C (Fan) or Gas Mark 6.

Flavour foundation:

3. In the same pan, on a gentle heat cook the onions, celery and carrots, with half the salt and pepper, covering the pan and sautéing gently until well softened and just beginning to brown.

Sauce:

4. Return the meat to the pan, add the sauce ingredients and the black beans. Stir well (but carefully) and gently bring up to a simmer. Taste and adjust for seasonings - add a little more salt and sugar if needed, as this brings out the heat of the chilli.

5. Cover and place the chilli in the oven for 1 hour, stirring occasionally. Taste and adjust for seasonings and add a little water if too dry.

6. Reduce heat to 160°C (Fan) or Gas Mark 4 and cook for a further 45 mins, or until meat is very tender.

Let the chilli stand for at least 15mins, or longer - the longer the better - before serving. Serve with plain white rice.

MOROCCAN SHEPHERD'S PIE WITH SPICED PARSNIP CRUST

(Serves 4)

These days, lamb has fallen out of favour, but it's a truly delicious meat and lends itself well to herbs and spices.

To be clear, a sheep in its first year is called a lamb, and its meat is also called lamb. The meat of a sheep older than one year is called hogget. The meat of an adult sheep is called mutton. As the sheep matures, so does its meat, with mutton having a richer, deeper flavour than hogget or lamb and requiring longer, slower cooking.

While it's not traditionally English, this Shepherd's pie is deliciously different with aromatic Middle Eastern spices and a spiced parsnip crust. I have a couple of friends who run gastro-pubs and I'm chuffed to say that they have my dish on their menus. People love it - I hope you do too.

What you'll need:

For the lamb:
Olive oil: 1 tbsp
Lamb/hogget mince: 750g (well chilled)

For the flavour foundation:
Onions: 1 large (finely chopped)
Celery: 2 medium sticks (finely chopped)
Carrots: 2 medium (diced small)
Sea salt: 1½ tsp (Maldon)
Ground black pepper: ¾ tsp
Plain flour: 1½ tbsp (can be gluten-free)
Garlic: 3 cloves (very finely sliced)
Ground cumin: 1½ tsp
Ground cinnamon: 1½ tsp
Mixed spice: 1½ tsp
Chicken stock or water: 650mls
Orange: grated zest + juice
Tomato purée: 2 tbsp

For the Spiced Parsnip crust:
Floury potatoes: 500g (cut into chunks)
Parsnips: 500g (chopped)
Butter: 40g (unsalted)

Ground cinnamon: ½ tsp
Chilli flakes: ½ tsp (optional)
Natural yoghurt: 50ml (thick)
Paprika: ½ tsp
Sea salt: to taste
Ground black pepper: to taste

What to do:

Lamb:

1. Heat the oil in a large broad oven-proof casserole (or frying pan). Pick off walnut sized nuggets from the chilled lamb mince and brown them, a few at a time, over a high heat. Don't over-fill the pan or move them too much, or they will stew and break up. Transfer the lamb to a plate.

Flavour foundation:

2. In the same pan and on a gentle heat add the onions, celery and carrots, with half the salt and pepper. There will be plenty of fat left in the pan, so cover and sauté very slowly until well softened and just beginning to brown. Put the lamb back in and add the flour, stirring gently.

3. Pre-heat the oven to 180° (Fan) or Gas Mark 6.

4. Add the garlic and spices to the meat mixture and cook for another 2/3mins and then add the chicken stock/water, orange juice and zest and tomato purée. Stirring very gently, bring everything up to the boil.

5. Check the seasoning, cover and transfer to the oven for 20 mins and then reduce the heat to 150°C (Fan) or Gas Mark 3 and cook for another 60-90 mins until the lamb is nice and tender.

PARSNIP CRUST:

6. Meanwhile, boil the potatoes in well-salted water and steam the parsnips separately until just tender. Don't over-cook the parsnips or they'll be too watery. Drain well and place a tea-towel over the pan and cover with a lid. Let sit for a few mins to absorb the steamy moisture.

7. Heat the butter in a large saucepan with the spices and add the potatoes and parsnips and mash, adding the yoghurt, cinnamon, chilli flakes (if using). Season with salt and pepper to taste.

8. Spoon the lamb into a pie dish, spread the mash on top roughing it up with a fork. Sprinkle with coarsely ground black pepper and paprika and return to the oven at 180°C (Fan) or Gas Mark 6 until golden. You may like to finish browning under a hot grill.

Serve with a fresh green salad.

OLD-FASHIONED, SLOW-COOKED BEEF BRISKET

For me, lean cuts of beef offer little in the way of flavour and are expensive. On the other hand, a meltingly flavoursome, slow-cooked beef brisket and buttery mash is just what a body needs at the end of a long day - and it won't break the bank.

Slow cooking is *so* obviously the new fast food, saving you time and energy and it's like having your own private chef. Just put everything in a slow cooker, or a covered oven-proof pot (I use my clay pot) in the morning and come back home to a kitchen full of love.

Brisket is an old fashioned and undervalued cut, but please don't be frightened of it. The secret is to give it time - *the lower and slower the better* - and to keep it moist and well covered. Brisket is full of beefy goodness, which melts into the surrounding broth; and it's even better if you can get the brisket on the bone - the minerals and other nutrients from the cut will leach into the already nutrient-dense bone broth braising liquid. That's Heaven, I'd say.

What you'll need:

Coconut oil: 2-3 tbsp (or olive oil)
Beef brisket: 1½ kg (grass-fed, on the bone if available) at room temperature
White onions: 600g (thickly sliced)
Carrots: 2 large (thickly sliced)
Celery: 2 sticks (thickly sliced)
Garlic: 2 cloves (thinly sliced)
Paprika: 1 tbsp
Chopped tomatoes: 1 x 400g tin
Collagen hydrolysate: 2 tbsp (see the Bone Broth chapter)
Molasses: 1 tbsp (or organic sugar, maple/date syrup)
Bone broth: 750ml (or enough to almost cover the meat)
Sea salt: 1 tbsp (Maldon, to taste)
Ground black pepper: 1 tsp (to taste)

Arrowroot powder (optional, for thickening)
English mustard: 1 tbsp (optional, for finishing)
Molasses: 1 tbsp (optional, for finishing)

What to do:

1. Heat a deep sauté pan over medium heat with the coconut/olive oil. Add the onions and cook on medium-low to medium heat, stirring frequently, for about 10 minutes or until the onions have caramelised lightly. Set aside.

2. Repeat Step 1 with the carrots and celery. Return the onions to the pan, add the spices and liquid ingredients to the vegetables and bring up to a simmer. Pour the mixture into the inset of a slow cooker.

3. Meanwhile, pat the meat dry and season it generously with salt and pepper.

4. Heat the sauté pan over medium-high heat and add a tbsp of coconut oil and turn on your vent or extractor fan, if you have one. Sear the brisket on all sides until the crust golden brown.

5. Nestle the brisket into the vegetables, fatty side up. Pile the vegetables over the meat.

Oven Instructions:

1. Cook in a covered casserole dish*. Start at 190°C (Fan) or Gas Mark 6-7 for 20 mins and then reduce heat for to 125-130°C (Fan) or Gas Mark 1-2 for 5 hours, or until very tender.

2. If you like a well-browned (but not burned!) top, place the brisket on a baking sheet and mix English mustard, salt and a little molasses and spread it over the top of the brisket. Place under a medium - hot fan assisted grill until browned to your liking.

** I like to use a terracotta brick or a Dutch oven (a covered cast iron pot). Note that these are both very efficient conductors of heat, so you may need to lower the temperature slightly to take account this).*

Slow cooker instructions:

1. Cover and cook in the slow cooker on LOW for 6 to 8 hours or until the brisket is very tender. Let rest for at least 20 minutes in the slow cooker set on WARM before serving. If your slow cooker doesn't have a WARM setting, transfer to a warmed, enclosed baking dish while resting.

Always allow the meat to rest for 20 mins, well covered, in a warm place before using.

The brisket can now be sliced or shredded immediately and served with the vegetables and juices. Or let the meat cool, then refrigerate overnight.

If you like thick gravy, carefully strain off the juices into a saucepan. Mix arrowroot to a smooth paste with a little water. Heat the juices, add the paste and whisk well until the sauce has thickened.

To reheat:
Heat the oven to 120°C (Fan) or Gas Mark 1-2. Transfer the brisket and all its juices to a baking dish and cover tightly with a lid. If whole, re-heat for 1 hour, or until piping hot all the way through. The exact time will depend greatly on the size and shape of the brisket; cut it into smaller servings or slices for faster reheating.

CLAY POT HERBED ROAST CHICKEN

Surely there can be no aroma in the kitchen, or better sight on the dining table than a well sourced, well-reared, perfectly roasted chicken?

When it comes to choosing cookware, one of the best ideas is a very old one: a clay pot. Unglazed clay pots and casseroles are non-toxic and take a long time to absorb heat; they then spread that heat evenly and slowly, cooking the food within to perfection.

This allows for the flavours of a dish to build slowly, for spices to penetrate more deeply, and for meats, even the tough cuts, to break down into succulent pieces and also helps the food retain more nutrients… and chicken, cooked this way, is utterly sublime.

What you'll need:

Chicken: 1.75kg
Onion: 1 medium (roughly chopped)
Carrot: 1 large (peeled, roughly chopped)

Garlic: 2/3 fat cloves (peeled, smashed)
Lemon: ½ medium (cut into thin wedges)
Thyme: 7/8 sprigs
Black peppercorns: 10
Whole cloves: 4
Olive oil: 1 tbsp
Paprika: 2 tsp
Unsalted butter: 1 tbsp, at room temp
Sea salt: Maldon, to taste
Ground black pepper: to taste

What to do:

1. Salt the chicken generously inside and out. Cover, and allow to come to room temperature for about an hour.

2. Heat the oven to 180˚C (Fan) or Gas Mark 6.

3. Lightly rinse the salt from the chicken and dry well with kitchen paper. In the bottom of the clay pot, make a trivet with half the chopped onion, carrots, peppercorns, cloves and one clove of garlic.

4. Oil the chicken well and push the remaining onion, carrot, garlic, thyme, peppercorns, cloves, butter and lemon wedges inside the cavity.

5. Set the chicken breast-up on the vegetables and rub in a good grinding of black pepper and the paprika.

6. Place the chicken the oven, uncovered, for about 20 mins at 180˚C (Fan) or Gas Mark 6, then turn it over (breast-down), cover and reduce the temperature to 140˚C (Fan) or Gas 2-3.

7. Cook for a further 30 mins per 500g, until the inner thigh reaches 75˚C (or the juices run clear when pierced with a skewer).

8. When just cooked, remove the chicken from oven and strain off the juices into a separate pan. If necessary, return the chicken, breast side-up to a hot oven at 200˚C (Fan) or Gas Mark 7) for about 5-6 mins to brown up the skin.

9. Rest the chicken breast-down (lightly covered) for 15 mins, before carving or portioning.

10. Meanwhile, bring the chicken juices to a rapid boil to reduce by half. Add back the vegetables from roasting (or push them through a sieve).

Serve the chicken:

Very simply, with the reduced jus, roast vegetables and a mixed green leaf salad
More lavishly, with potato, celeriac and garlic mash, steamed green vegetables and thyme gravy.

A SIMPLE LAMB, NIGELLA SEED & SWEET POTATO CURRY

This recipe uses neck of lamb. Granny knew it as 'scrag-end' (it's *so* not!) and its thrifty value ensured it made a regular appearance on her table.

Lamb neck is an underrated, inexpensive and very flavoursome cut that needs long, slow cooking. On the bone, it often looks as though there isn't much meat, but it yields a surprisingly generous amount once cooked to tender perfection. Off the bone, it's known as neck fillet and is slightly more expensive. In my opinion, it's well worth the effort of buying and cooking it on the bone for the rich nutrients and flavour it yields.

You can use hogget or mutton for this recipe: the latter will need quite a bit more time to yield its rich deliciousness, so you may want to add the sweet potato (at stage 4) a little later on.

This rich curry is at its best served with plain steamed rice.

What you'll need:

Ginger: 1 thumb-sized piece (½ cut into matchsticks, ½ roughly chopped)
Onions: 2 (roughly chopped)
Garlic: 4 cloves (peeled and smashed)
Chicken or beef stock: 700ml (or water)
Coconut oil: 2 tbsp
Cinnamon stick: 1 (medium)
Ground coriander: 1 tbsp
Ground cumin: 1 tsp
Ground turmeric: 1 tsp
Nigella seeds: ½ tsp
Neck of hogget/mutton on the bone: 1.25kg, or 750g off the bone
Chopped tomatoes: 1 x 400g tin

Red or green chilli: 1 (deseeded and sliced)
Sweet potato: 1 medium (peeled and diced large)
Coriander: small bunch (stalks finely chopped, leaves roughly chopped)

What to do:

1. Put the roughly chopped ginger, onions and garlic in a food processor with 300ml of the chicken or beef stock and blitz to a smooth purée. Keep scraping down the sides and keep blitzing until you achieve as smooth a paste as possible.

2. Put the mixture into a deep sauté pan, cover with a lid and simmer gently for 15 mins. Remove the lid and cook until all the liquid has evaporated.

3. Add the coconut oil to the pan with the rest of the ginger, turn up the heat and fry, stirring, for 3-5 mins until it starts to colour, then stir in the remaining spices (except for the chilli), add the lamb and stir-fry until the lamb changes colour. Take care not to burn the spices or they'll be bitter – a splash of water will bring down the temperature.

4. Add the diced sweet potatoes, chopped tomatoes, remaining stock and the chilli. Season well and taste. Adjust the seasonings/spices if necessary, cover and leave to simmer slowly for at least 1 hour or longer, until the lamb is just soft. If the lamb is on the bone it will need longer, as will mutton.

5. Stir in the coriander stalks and cook for a final 30 mins until the lamb is really tender. If the mixture looks dry, add a little water to loosen it as it cooks.

6. Stir in the coriander leaves just before serving.

Serve with: Steamed rice, fresh mango chutney and a cucumber raita.

PORK BREAKFAST PATTIES

(Serves 3-4)

What you see is what you get with these breakfast patties. I love good quality sausages, but I also love that these breakfast patties are quick, easy and inexpensive. They can be made up in advance and frozen, or batch-cooked and then frozen; just remember to be quite generous with the salt and pepper since, in my experience, freezing tends to dull seasonings.

What you'll need:

Minced pork: 500g
Sea salt: 1tsp (Maldon)
Ground black pepper: ¼ tsp
Garlic: 1 clove (smashed, finely minced)
Shallots: 1 small (very finely diced)
Herbs/spices of choice: fresh sage, thyme, ground fennel, (smoked) paprika,
Egg yolk: 1 medium
Olive or coconut oil for frying

What to do:

1. In a large bowl, combine all the ingredients using your hands to knead everything together into a homogenous mass.

2. Test for seasonings by frying a small flat nugget in a little hot oil. Don't skimp on the salt - make sure you can taste the seasoning and if you're planning to freeze, then consider adding a little more.

3. Shape the patties into 6-8 small, tight balls and then gently flatten them down into even rounds (1-1½ cm thick) with your hands.

4. Cook the patties for 2 minutes on each side, or until cooked through.

To freeze: Place the patties (raw or cooked) in a single layer on a baking sheet and open freeze. Transfer frozen patties to a resealable bag. De-frost thoroughly and re-heat until piping hot.

CHICKEN LIVER PATÉ

Served on slices of freshly baked, or lightly toasted sourdough bread, this pate is sublime.

Liver is the BEST source of vitamin A (critical for vision, protein formation, cell growth, skin health). It's worth repeating that plant sources are not true vitamin A but contain carotenoids (like beta-carotene) which need to be converted to vitamin A before they can be utilized by the body. This conversion is, at best, inefficient and at worst the young, the elderly and those struggling with health issues cannot make this conversion.

So, eat liver! And this chicken liver paté is a great way to introduce it into your diet. Be aware that shop-bought patés often contain gluten (and other questionable ingredients) and the flavour often disappoints. This recipe is based on a Delia classic, it's really simple and it freezes well.

What you'll need:

Organic chicken livers: 225g very fresh (rinsed, trimmed, cut into even-sized pieces)
Brandy: 2 tbsp (optional)
Butter: 225g (organic, unsalted, plus extra if needed to seal ramekins)
Mustard powder: 2 tsp (level)
Garlic: 2 cloves (well crushed)
Sea salt: generously to taste, don't under-season
Ground black pepper: generously to taste, don't under-season

What to do:

1. Melt 25g of the butter in a heavy-based frying pan and gently fry the chicken livers over a medium heat for 3-5 mins, keeping them on the move and turning frequently. They need to only just cook evenly (over-cooked livers can be grainy and bitter - so err on the side of caution).

2. Remove the livers from the pan with a draining spoon and transfer to a blender or a food processor.

3. In the same pan, gently melt 150g of the remaining butter and then add to the chicken livers.

4. Pour the bandy (if using) onto any juices left in the pan and 'de-glaze' by swirling the contents around over a medium heat, then add to the chicken livers.

5. Add in the mustard and garlic and season generously with salt and pepper, then blend to a smooth purée. Check for seasoning and adjust if necessary - don't under-season. At this stage, the pâté will look very sloppy but will firm up as the butter sets in the fridge.

6. Divide the mixture between ramekins (or pots) smoothing the surface as much as possible.

7. Gently melt 50g of butter and pour a little melted butter over each of the pots to seal it (you may need a little more butter at this stage).

8. Leave the pots to get quite cold, cover with cling-film and refrigerate. They will keep well (if sealed) for 3 days and they freeze really well.

Serve with: Sourdough bread or rye crackers, sliced tomatoes, red kimchi and cornichons.

PORK, SPINACH & HERB TERRINE

(Serves 10 slices)

I first made this chunky terrine as a student at Ballymaloe Cookery School; I'd never made a terrine before and was really nervous. It came out really well and before I knew it, it'd been whisked away to Ballymaloe House for inclusion in the Sunday night Guests' Buffet!

This is real party piece and looks fabulous cut into thick slices, served on a wooden board, lined with green leaves and garnished with cornichons. Slices of crusty sourdough bread (or lightly griddled sourdough toast), red onion marmalade, fermented vegetables and red pepper salsa make a great accompaniment too.

The trick with a terrine is to season it really well, even to the point of slightly over-seasoning, otherwise it can taste bland when cold.

If you've never made a terrine, please have a go. It really is a very simple process, a bit like making a meat loaf, which is a bit like making a big burger. You can double the quantities to make two terrines, which you can then slice, wrap and freeze.

What you'll need:

Spinach: 380g (after large stalks removed)
Unsalted butter: 8g
White onion: 4oz (finely chopped, sweated down, cooled)
Streaky pork: 450g (fatty is better)
Pigs liver: 125g
Smoked lean bacon: 130g (after rind removed)
Unsmoked streaky bacon: 130g (after rind removed)
Garlic: I large clove (crushed)
Free-range egg: 1 (beaten)
Maldon salt: to taste (be generous)
Freshly ground black pepper: to taste (be generous)
Freshly ground nutmeg: to taste (be generous)
Freshly chopped herbs: 2-3 heaped tbsp (of choice: try a mix of parsley/chives/ marjoram/basil)

A terrine (19x13.5cms) or a loaf tin (20x10cms)
Olive oil for greasing and baking parchment for lining the tin

What to do:

1. If you don't have a robust food processer with a sharp blade, or a mincing attachment, ask the butcher to mince the meats for you - they need to be minced quite coarsely as this is a chunky terrine.

2. Remove any tough stalks from the spinach, wash and drain well. Put the leaves into a large thick-based pan over a low heat and cover. Stir after a few minutes and carry on cooking the spinach until it's well wilted; it will yield a lot of liquid, which you'll need to drain off.

3. When it's cooled enough to handle, squeeze and press the spinach in your hands until almost dry. Chop well and leave to cool.

4. Over a low heat, melt the butter in a small pan and add the chopped onions. Cover the pan and allow them to sweat down until soft, but don't let them brown. Leave to cool.

5. In a large bowl, mix all the ingredient together with your hands, seasoning it generously with salt, pepper and nutmeg. To test for seasoning, fry off a small part of the mixture - it should taste highly seasoned; if not add more seasoning.

6. Preheat the oven to 170˚C (Fan) or Gas Mark 5.

7. Lightly grease your tin with olive oil and line the tin with two strips of baking parchment, cut to fit the width and length with a little over-hang over the sides, pressing down the parchment firmly. Put the terrine mixture into the tin, patting it down gently with your hand. Cover with the lid or with a double layer of baking parchment topped with foil (don't allow the foil to come into contact with the meat).

8. Bake for 45 minutes, then remove the lid or cover and press lightly with your finger - the terrine will be surrounded by liquid and should yield to your touch. Continue to cook for another 15-20 mins, until the top is slightly browned.

9. Remove from the oven and allow to stand for several hours in a cool place, until the terrine reabsorbs most of the liquid. Remove from the tin and refrigerate until needed.

Serve with: Sourdough bread or rye crackers, sliced tomatoes, red kimchi and cornichons and assorted green leaves.

CHAPTER FIVE

THE RISE AND FALL OF MILK

"One day, my daughter Tybee came to me, and she said,

'I have so much love for you in my body, Daddy, I can't stop giving you hugs and kisses.

And when I have no more love left, I just drink milk, because that's where love comes from."

- Bruce Feiler

Milk - 'Mother' of civilisation

The emergence of civilisation is a cyclical process which, as we saw in the Soil chapter, ultimately rests on the health of our soil. Many cultures regard the Earth as our ultimate 'Mother' ensuring that the microbes in healthy soils produce the nutrients for the grasses that feed the animals, which in turn feed us.

According to the late Ron Schmid in *The Untold Story of Milk*, of those animals, "*the bovine tribes have been our best animal friends for a long, long, time.*"

Milk - the healer

Milk has a rich history as a builder of health and a healer. Once upon a time, milk was a valued medicine, prized and used by doctors everywhere to restore health. Until recent times, milk was given free to school children and valued by bodybuilders!

Hippocrates recommended milk and its products as "*wonderful food and the best medicine.*" Milk shaped the cultures that founded Western civilisation: no civilisation has ever arisen without the domestication of animals and the use of their milk.

Milk is the only organic substance purposely designed and prepared by Mother Nature as food and early humans made good use of this gift.

Some 20,000 years ago, all humans were hunter-gatherers and the most advanced followed the herds of antelope, reindeer, sheep, camels, goats, water buffalo and cattle and milked them when they could.

We know this because the earliest human artefacts include vessels containing residues of milk which pre-date the agricultural revolution by many thousands of years. About 12,000 years ago, the domestication of animals and the cultivation of plants marked man's transition from hunter-gather to agrarian farmer.

> **"Where people have travelled, the ox and the milk cow have followed. Rome was built on ground blessed by libations of milk. In America, the arrival of a shipload of cows saved the Jamestown colony from starvation. Cows went west with the settler, hitched behind wagons pulled by their brothers the oxen, feeding families and calves alike."**

- Ron Schmid
The Untold Story of Milk

In the course of his global travels, seeking out healthy populations in the early part of the 20th century, Dr Weston A. Price visited the villagers of Lötschental Valley, far above sea level in the mountains of Switzerland. Their location meant that the villagers had a very short growing period for any produce, so their diet relied heavily on various forms of dairy (milk, cheese, cream and butter) and their stored crop of rye.

Their milk came raw - straight from their cows and goats - without any processing and Dr Price found it to be no coincidence that the villagers enjoyed substantially better health than their neighbours, who were exposed to a more Western diet of processed foods.[1]

Milk - the 'demonic' drink

As we saw in Chapter One, present-day milk is now far from prized and dairy intolerance is rife, with people are increasingly blaming their poor health (for instance, eczema, asthma, allergies) on milk. Dairy-free recipes abound everywhere and all sorts of fiddled-with versions of 'milk' and milk substitutes - from soya, almonds, coconuts and oats - take pride of place on the supermarket shelf, while we've shunned the real deal for decades.

Of course, many animals produce milk - cows, sheep, goats, buffalo and even camels - and all have health benefits. Indeed some, such as goat's milk, suit those who have true intolerances. But here, I'm going to focus on the story of cow's milk.

What went so wrong? What is the back-story of milk? How did it fall from grace? And how did we come to be suffering from so many milk-related illnesses?

Let's begin with a history lesson...

American urbanisation

Once upon a time, all milk was raw - it was consumed literally 'straight-from-the-cow' with no additional processing. In the early 1800s, the explosive growth of cities in America led to unyielding demands for milk from the thousands of families who flocked to the cities to make their living.

As the cities grew larger and more crowded - particularly New York - the surrounding traditional grazing lands were lost; city families and communities could no longer keep their own cattle. Their milk supply depended on increasingly expensive imports from wider rural areas and dairy farmers struggled to meet demand.

Distillery dairies

At the same time, America lost its whiskey supply from the British West Indies, so grain distilleries began springing up in the cities to meet the demand. Whiskey production leaves abundant amounts of distillery 'slop' (an acid refuse of grain and water) and this was soon fed to city cattle by indiscriminate profiteers. Before long, distillery owners began to deliberately house dairies adjacent to the distilleries to cut costs and to feed cattle with the hot slop as it poured off the stills. 'Slop milk' became a profitable - but lethal - industry.

With this toxic diet, the cattle soon became diseased and emaciated, their milk so defective that it couldn't be used for butter or cheese. The cattle were kept and milked in appalling, unsanitary conditions allowing a host of pathogenic organisms to flourish and sicken people. What goes around comes around, and it's worth noting that with the growth of modern confined animal feeding operations (CAFOs), the clock has gone full-circle and hence the reliance on antibiotics to control infections.

Unbelievably, the 'slop' milk was fed to New York's children and by the mid-1800s, infant mortality accounted for half of all deaths in the city, mainly caused by diarrhoea, tuberculosis and other infectious diseases.

Tragically raw milk, once prized by countless generations across the globe, became the scapegoat that concealed the horrendous practices of greedy distillers.

Battle of the Giants - the stethoscope vs the briefcase. Guess who wins?

Despite the best efforts of milk reformers of the day (mainly doctors) to restore clean, healthy, raw milk to the population of cities to support the health of the children, the production of this filthy milk and its unhygienic distribution across America's first city continued for over a hundred years.

During this time, doctors (mainly paediatricians) continued their demand that milk production be certified in order to ensure a supply of safe, healthy raw milk for the treatment of disease.

However, businessmen had a different agenda. With no regard for milk's physical, bio-chemical or healing properties, they were keen to adopt a brand-new discovery that would ensure lucrative profits by producing milk that was bacteriologically sterile.

Louis Pasteur's new process of pasteurisation (heat treatment) was eagerly adopted by the growing number of milk processing operations across America, Europe and the UK (cutting traditional dairy farmers out of the equation), with contamination and food safety concerns being given as the justification for pasteurising raw milk.

Thankfully, distillery dairies have had their day, although sadly, deals are still being struck to feed cattle 'confectionery' waste from the food industry. But what does this all mean for the milk we drink today?

Milk is still milk - isn't it?

In fact, it's not - and that's a big problem. The vast majority of our milk now comes to us pasteurised and also homogenised. Let's take a closer look at why this is a problem.

Raw unpasteurised milk

As we saw above, raw milk is unprocessed - it comes straight from the cow - so retains its full, nutrient-dense complement of vitamins, minerals, beneficial bacteria and live enzymes. Such is the lobbying power of the milk processing industry in the USA that in some states, selling or consuming raw milk is actually illegal. In Scotland, the sale of raw milk is also illegal, while in the rest of the UK (at the time of writing) it can be sold directly to the public at the farm gate, or via the internet for home delivery, but only by closely monitored certified raw milk farms.

Pasteurised milk

Almost all of our milk is now pasteurised, or 'pre-cooked'. The process of pasteurisation does actually cook the milk (often at 72°C for 25 seconds, but methods vary) to destroy all the bacteria in the raw milk. Unfortunately, pasteurisation can allow shoddy producers to cover up poor dairy practices, practices that would not be tolerated among raw milk producers.

And since pasteurisation renders the milk product sterile, it also extends its shelf-life, making it more profitable for milk processors and retailers, but sadly not for dairy farmers.

However, pasteurisation has consequences for milk nutrition: it weakens or destroys important vitamins - vitamin C, vitamin A and around a third of the precious B vitamins. It also destroys the enzyme phosphatase, which we need to absorb calcium.

Pasteurisation also alters or destroys many amino acids, substantially reducing the digestibility of the protein (casein) in milk. Our body struggles to deal with these de-natured and incompletely-digested proteins and responds by triggering our immune system in an effort to defend us from what it perceives to be foreign invaders. Chronic exposure to these kinds of triggers ultimately increases our risk for developing full-blown immune modulated conditions, like food intolerances, allergies, asthma and eczema.[2]

As well as destroying any pathogenic bacteria, pasteurisation destroys the abundant beneficial probiotic bacteria in raw milk; these bacteria not only support our gut and the health of our immune system but prevent the milk from decomposing.[3] The net result of destroying the protective, beneficial bacteria is that while raw milk sours, pasteurised milk goes rancid.

Pasteurisation also destroys the heat-sensitive enzyme lactase, which we need to digest the milk sugar lactose. Is lactose intolerance springing to mind?

Homogenised milk

Most of our milk is also homogenised. This prevents the cream from rising to the top, so extends shelf-life and allows milk to be shipped over greater distances. Homogenisation allows dairy processors to mix milk from different herds without issue and makes it easier for them to filter out the fat and create two percent (full fat), one percent (semi-skimmed) and zero percent (skimmed) milks.

The main components of milk are protein (casein) particles and fat (lipid) globules. Homogenisation reduces the globule size by reheating milk and passing it under high, intense pressure through a tiny orifice. This process breaks down the fat molecules into much finer particles, so that they are dispersed evenly within the milk: there's no traditional cream line in homogenised milk.

The *Dairy Processing Handbook* explains the highly industrial process of homogenisation like this:

"Homogenisation has become a standard industrial process, universally practiced as a means of stabilising the fat emulsion against gravity separation. Homogenisation primarily causes disruption of fat globules into much smaller ones. Consequently, it diminishes creaming and may also diminish the tendency of globules to clump or coalesce.

Essentially, all homogenised milk is produced by mechanical means. Milk is forced through a small passage at high velocity. The disintegration of the original fat globules is achieved by a combination of contributing factors such as turbulence and cavitation. The homogenisation reduces fat globule size from an average of 3.5 μm in diameter to below 1 μm.

The newly created fat globules are no longer completely covered with the original membrane material. Instead, they are surfaced with a mixture of proteins adsorbed from the plasma phase."

Is homogenised milk healthy?

If homogenisation sounds a bit one-sided, favouring the milk processors - it is. While there are no health benefits to homogenising milk, there are several distinct health concerns.

Not only is the milk effectively re-pasteurised (by heating it again to a high heat), but the process changes both the physical and chemical properties of the milk. When fats are subjected to high heat, not only do they oxidise and become rancid, it's also argued that the violent destruction of the molecular structure of the fat (and the creation of smaller molecules) allows undigested milk proteins to pass through our gut lining into the blood stream. Absorbing undigested proteins provokes systemic inflammation and lays the foundations for chronic disease. Protein, fat and sugar particles in denatured milk easily pass through the intestinal lining and cause inflammation, immune responses and allergic reactions.[4]

Some have argued that oxidised fats contribute to heart disease, hypertension and hyperlipidaemia.

However, thankfully there has been a resurgence in the market for non-homogenised milk (organic and non-organic) and its availability in UK supermarkets is steadily growing.

De-mystifying milk choices

Nowadays our milk comes in such a wide variety of forms (no fat, low fat, mid fat, full fat) and is available in supermarkets, food stores and petrol stations everywhere. Our ancestors would be flummoxed by the variety we have available today, and, in my experience, so are many consumers.

Enjoy full-fat dairy

Let's put to bed the myth that full-fat dairy clogs arteries and results in cardiovascular disease. The Fats chapter blows the saturated-fat-will-kill-us-hypothesis out of the scientific waters. But let's consider an important study on the consumption of dietary dairy fat at this point.

This study[5], led by the University of Reading and published in April 2017 performed a meta-analysis on 29 studies and involved a total of 938,465 people, covering a wide spectrum of economic levels, lifestyles, genders, and ages from around the world, over the past 35 years to 2016.

The British and Dutch research team concluded that consuming dietary dairy fat has no negative effects on all-cause mortality (deaths), nor on mortality from cardiovascular disease (CVD) and coronary heart disease (CHD). This includes dairy fats of all types.

"No associations were found for total (high-fat/low-fat) dairy, and milk with the health outcomes of mortality, CHD or CVD. Inverse associations were found between total fermented dairy (included sour milk products, cheese or yoghurt."

We should note that 'inverse associations' mean that consumers of fermented dairy (a prized traditional food) lived longer and were healthier. Even though the dairy products involved with the 29 studies were mostly from 'nutritionally handicapped' pasteurised and/or homogenised milks, the study clearly shows us that it is not harmful to consume whole-fat dairy products, including cheeses, yoghurt, and butter.

So, despite all the evidence to the contrary, when we keep hearing in the media that full-fat milk and dairy products are harmful, we should remember the interests that are vested in maintaining the status quo. And we should also remember this:

"It's easier to fool people than tell them they've been fooled."

- Mark Twain

You can, with impunity, freely enjoy traditional full-fat milk and if you're concerned about weight you don't need to reach for semi and skimmed milk, since, as we shall see in the Fats chapter, the science is clearly telling us that fat does **not** make us fat.

Once upon a time, our milk choice was very simple and very healthy: organic, unpasteurised and full-fat and our supplier was our local dairy farmer. Now, the milk production, processing and marketing industries have created so many variables that we struggle to sort the wheat from the chaff when trying to make the best choice.

Even describing the variety of milk permutations is confusing, however, it might be helpful to keep in mind the (very) simplified table overleaf when next choosing your milk. It's not definitive, but it will help you to ask questions of your milk supplier:

THE VERY BEST:	GOOD:	NOT THE BEST:
CERTIFIED UPASTEURISED (RAW)	**PASTEURISED NON-HOMOGENISED**	**PASTEURISED & HOMOGENISED**
Straight from the cow	Intense heat-treatment	Secondary heat-treatment
Retains all vitamins, minerals, live enzymes & probiotics	Loses significant vitamins, & minerals, all live enzymes & probiotics	Fat molecules broken down & dispersed
Visible cream line	Visible cream line	No visible cream line
ORGANIC, 100% GRASS-FED, FULL FAT	**ORGANIC, 100% CERTIFIED GRASS-FED, FULL FAT / SEMI-SKIMMED**	**NON-ORGANIC MIXED FEED FULL FAT / SEMI-SKIMMED / SKIMMED**
Raised on organic pasture & forage crops	Raised on organic pasture & forage crops	Raised on non-organic pasture, grains and feed supplements
NO: Antibiotics, hormones, synthetic pesticides, herbicides, GMOs	**NO**: Antibiotics, hormones, synthetic pesticides, herbicides, GMOs	**EXPOSED TO**: antibiotics, hormones, synthetic pesticides, herbicides, GMOs

But is milk still milk and does it even matter?

Be under no illusion: most of the milk we drink isn't what it used to be. There's no denying that modern milk is a highly industrially-processed food 'product', of unknown provenance, which bears little resemblance to the traditional jug of natural, liquid food (and good medicine) on our ancestors' tables.

In fact, many would go so far as to class modern milk as a chemically-fortified white liquid, a 'fake' food. I think this matters and I'm not alone…

Kaayla Daniel PhD, author of *The Whole Soy Story*, thinks it matters:

"Today, so many health problems are associated with the cheap, commercial, pasteurised, ultra-pasteurised, homogenised, low fat and no-fat 'milk products' found in supermarkets, that milk itself has an image problem. The solution is 'real milk" - meaning raw, whole milk from clean, pastured, non-Drugged and happy cows or goats."

Thomas Cowan MD, author of *The Fourfold Path to Healing*, thinks it matters:

"The story of real milk - not the pasteurised, chemicalised, homogenised stuff for sale in supermarkets - is the story of real agriculture, real food and real health."

So does Mark McAfee, Founder, Organic Pastures Dairy Company & Founder of the Raw Milk Institute (USA):

"We are 'bacteria-sapiens' - our bodies need a biodiversity of good bacteria, raw fats and essential enzymes to stay healthy. Raw milk is a 'one-stop-shop' for these essential elements."

And so do organic dairy farmers Hook & Sons, who have been farming in Hailsham, East Sussex (UK) since 1959:

"You could almost say that they only have two things in common: they are both fairly white in colour, and both called milk! The more you understand raw milk, the more you realise what an amazing food it is."

Can milk still be a healthy choice?

Milk is a healthy, whole food. Let's get this straight - milk is one of the only substances that is actually meant to be a food from the get-go. Clearly, cows' milk is a primary food for calves, but we humans have been benefitting from drinking milk for some 8,000 years. Milk is immensely nutrient-dense and although animal milk wasn't directly intended for our consumption, it doesn't mean that it's any less nutritious or important for us. And, even though we aren't ruminant animals, we can digest milk.

Consider this: no one doubts the value of the nutrition available from many of the green vegetables that humans eat. Similarly, the grass, clovers and leaves that cattle and other ruminants consume are also rich in nutrients, but humans can't eat grass.

We lack the physical apparatus to digest the dense cellulose in grasses and leaves, or to deal with all the defensive compounds (phytotoxins) in the leaves. Luckily, left to their natural devices, ruminant animals that are traditionally raised on pasture can do both - they spend all day chewing the cud and their huge stomachs (all four of them) contain bacteria which work hard to ferment the green stuff, so their host animal can digest it. And ultimately, that host is us.

Over the course of human evolution and in the process of domesticating ruminant animals, our ancestors found that they could trust the mighty cow to detoxify and concentrate all the wonderful greens they consume into milk that is digestible by (and richly beneficial to) human animals.

Let's look at some reasons we benefit from eating quality dairy

As we saw in the Soil and Meat chapters, it's important to distinguish between products derived from livestock that have been raised on traditional pastures and those raised in confinement, on an unnatural and damaging grain diet. Dairy animals fed on grains deliver none of the real health benefits of pasture-fed meat and dairy foods.[6]

Dairy is a true nutritional powerhouse. No other food gives us protein, carbohydrates and fat in one single food which requires no cooking. Ron Schmid wrote in *The Untold Story of Milk* about a man who lived, in good health, on milk alone for more than 40 years!

Milk contains high-quality protein and all eight essential amino acids in perfect balance, so is non-inflammatory. This supports the whole body and particularly our liver, which needs a consistent supply of sufficient protein to do its job properly and detoxify other substances to which we're exposed. Although we've elevated the status of green detox juices to dizzy heights, they're actually very difficult for us to digest and to absorb the nutrients. Good quality milk is a much better option for detoxing.

Milk contains low levels of unhealthy polyunsaturated fats (PUFAs) and higher levels of saturated fats. As we will see in the Fats chapter, research is now consistently showing us that it's the saturated fats which are beneficial to health, while the real demons, promoting systemic inflammation and widespread cellular damage, are the once-applauded PUFAs.

Dairy is a source of calcium. Despite much nonsense to the contrary, milk is a good (although not the best) source of calcium. But here's the thing: the calcium, protein, sugar and fat in milk mean it's all digested efficiently, so milk supports not only bone and tooth health and energy production, but also the growth of gut friendly bacteria and it reduces the absorption of harmful substances from the colon (lipopolysaccharides or endotoxins) which can leak into the body and trigger an inflammatory response.[7]

Did you know that calcium is important in managing our stress levels? Most of the calcium in our body is stored in our bones but some, at very tightly controlled levels, also circulates in our blood. Under stress, we release high levels of a hormone known as PTH - parathyroid hormone. PTH signals our body to remove calcium from our bones and put it into our blood circulation.

But because blood levels of calcium are so tightly regulated, our body will look to dump any excess (as calcification) wherever it can: in our joints (ouch!); in soft tissue such as in kidneys (forming stones); or in arteries (promoting atherosclerosis and cardiovascular disease). Consuming adequate dairy can have a significant anti-stress effect on our body by suppressing the release of PTH and keeping body calcium in our bones, where it's meant to be.

Milk helps prevent tooth decay by binding to bacteria in the mouth, as well as providing essential minerals for strong teeth.

"Milk has sugar for energy in the form of LACTOSE (80% of the carbohydrate in milk) which, studies have found, does much less damage than glucose to teeth. Milk also contains casein which is a phosphoprotein and considered to be a protective factor in teeth health to prevent caries.

It does this by its ability to concentrate calcium and phosphorus in the plaque with the effect of reducing some of the plaque bacteria.

Furthermore, when milk is from organic grass-fed cows, which is usually the case with certified raw milk, the calcium in the milk is of the highest quality. That means your body will be able to make the most use of it to produce strong teeth and bones." [8]

Milk promotes soft, healthy skin. Our skin is an organ of absorption, as well as elimination - around 80% of what we put onto our skin hits the bloodstream within seconds. The abundance of nutrients in the right quantities in milk promotes healthy skin.

Remember that Cleopatra was reputed to have bathed in asses' milk? Wise woman.

So there we have it: if we consume enough good-quality milk, we keep stress levels down, energy up and calcium where it belongs - in bones and teeth and not in our soft tissue.

Raw milk - why is it so special?

You may have noticed that I've mentioned 'good-quality' milk several times, but what do I mean by this? Well personally, I am a huge advocate of certified raw milk, but I understand that it has become very controversial, much-maligned and poorly-understood.

Let me say that I'm not on a mission to persuade you here. I believe it's important that we understand the health benefits of raw milk and the issues around pasteurised, homogenised milk so that we can each make informed choices, based on sound, substantiated information, not on scaremongering and media hype.

Many of us have been prejudiced against raw milk by unjustified (and even plain wrong) public health and food safety warnings, issued by bodies like the Food Standards Agency (FSA) in the UK and a media hell-bent on bad news.

However, the food hygiene standards applied to raw milk dairies by the FSA (and the safety record for raw milk itself) far exceed those of its pasteurised poor relation. The FSA's latest recorded figures (2014) show that more than 500,000 cases of food poisoning each year are caused by known pathogens.

The most common food-borne pathogen is campylobacter, which results in some 280,000 cases every year. Clostridium perfringens causes 80,000 cases, and norovirus is third with an estimated 74,000 cases. Salmonella is the cause of the most hospital admissions, some 2,500 annually.

Poultry meat is estimated to cause 244,000 cases (or 84%) of food poisoning cases each year. Vegetables (particularly bagged salad), fruit, nuts and seeds caused the second-highest number of cases of illness, followed by beef and lamb.

Notice the absence, any mention of (or figures for) raw milk? That's because, despite occasional media reports where food poisoning incidents have been 'linked' to drinking raw milk, rigorous safety testing of the dairy farms implicated have failed to find any bacterial contamination.

The FSA states that consumption of raw milk is *"generally acceptable where appropriate hygiene controls are applied."*

Raw milk is *real* milk

In my personal opinion (and an exponentially growing number of like-minded consumers), the commercial milk available in supermarkets, food stores and petrol stations is bland, highly-processed and less-than-healthy, a white liquid product bearing little resemblance to the delicious healthful, nutritious and healing food our grandparents enjoyed.

It's heartening to see the increasing numbers of certified raw milk dairy farmers (who work hard for a pittance and struggle to keep going) unshackling themselves from the milk processing industry to sell their unprocessed, wholesome, healthy, nutritious milk directly to a public whose health desperately needs it.

Few of us are aware that raw milk from grass-fed cows was used as a medicine to treat (and often cure) a variety of serious chronic diseases: from the time of Hippocrates until just after World War II, this 'white blood' nourished and healed countless millions.

Raw milk is a living food, rich in beneficial bacteria, food enzymes, natural vitamins and heat sensitive immunoglobins (anti-bodies). The minerals (like calcium) are more bio-available in unheated raw milk and it's also rich in beneficial, probiotic bacteria which are critical to our health and support our own beneficial gut microbes.

Our gut microbes are responsible for stimulating and training our immune system (the first line of which is housed in our gut) to function correctly and keep pathogenic bacteria at bay. Indeed, they can be effective in the prevention and treatment of E. coli, rotavirus and salmonella infections. By consuming foods rich in beneficial bacteria (like raw dairy products), we can help to optimise the levels of beneficial bacteria present in our gut.

Raw milk is rich in natural food enzymes: lactase and amylase (to digest sugars); lipase (to digest fats); and phosphatase (to absorb calcium) are among many of these natural enzymes. These enzymes help our body to better digest milk and better metabolise its vital nutrients. Without these vital enzymes, the milk's natural sugars, fats and proteins can cause reactions in those prone to food intolerances.

Raw milk is packed with natural vitamins: the butterfat present in raw milk is rich in fat-soluble vitamins, particularly pre-formed (true) vitamin A, vitamin K and vitamin E. Raw milk is also rich in water-soluble vitamins like vitamin C and B-complex vitamins.

Raw milk from pasture-raised cows contains approximately 50% more vitamin E and 7% more folate than pasteurised milk. The natural vitamin C in fresh raw milk remains intact. Like food enzymes, vitamins are delicate and are largely destroyed by heat; therefore, pasteurised milks are fortified with vitamins, and those fortifying vitamins are synthetic, laboratory-created versions of naturally-occurring vitamins so are not treated the same way as natural vitamins by the body.

As we saw in the Meat chapter, food products from grass-fed animals are rich in conjugated linoleic acid (CLA). Raw butterfat is no exception, and this fatty acid compound is classified as a natural trans-fat, so offers many positive health benefits.

Indeed, research indicates that CLA is known to fight cancer (particularly breast, intestinal and bone cancers), hypertension and obesity.[9]

Raw milk is typically sourced from grass-fed cows, which means we're consuming this important fatty acid, but it's something that's missing from commercial, intensively-raised pasteurised and skimmed milk at the grocery store, and this includes organic milk from intensively-reared animals.

Certified raw milk farmers are small, local farmers who produce cleaner milk, by traditional methods, from healthy animals. Mastitis is endemic in dairy cattle raised on intensive farms and is a huge problem for the dairy industry.

Unless the farm is organic, the herd must be fed antibiotics routinely. Half of *all* antibiotic use in the UK is on these intensive farms, where animals are kept in such appalling conditions, they would be unlikely to survive without them.

The overall use of antibiotics per animal on UK farms increased by 18% between 2000 and 2010 and the problem is even worse in the US, where roughly 80% of all antibiotics are used on farms. At the same time, we humans are fast losing response to antibiotics - think antibiotic resistant super-bugs.

"Sick milk, from sick cows, makes for sick people."

- Jenny McGruther
nourishedkitchen.com

Raw milk is produced on farms where fewer cattle are spread out over relatively larger areas of land. In the main, the cows spend their time outside (with access to shelter when needed) and aren't fed on highly inflammatory feedlot grains, but graze on fresh, usually organic, pasture.

As we saw in the Soil chapter, we're using huge amounts of nitrogen fertiliser in the UK every year, with a pollution 'cost' for society that is two to three times higher than its commercial benefit to farmers. Since pastured cows also eat clover (a legume that puts huge amounts of nitrogen into the soil naturally) they are a valuable environmental asset.

By choosing to drink raw milk, we're supporting small, local farmers who value their customers, their herd and their environment. And we're also supporting sustainable and regenerative agricultural operations, not the monoculture of the dairy mega-industries.

Raw milk is not homogenised - the fresh, raw cream rises to the top and can be skimmed for making butter or used in delicious milk and cream-based recipes. Non-homogenised milk just needs a shake-up (unless you don't want to share!) before drinking to evenly distribute the cream into the milk.

Raw cream and butterfat are in their 'whole' state. As we have seen, homogenisation is an intense process that leaves the delicate fats subject to oxidisation, leaving the door open for chronic disease. Fresh raw milk is much easier on your stomach and digestive tract - the enzymes lipase, lactase and amylase work to break down and help us digest the components in the milk.

Raw milk naturally sours and produces a healthful, richly probiotic food (resembling yoghurt) as the lactic-acid producing bacteria get to work. It's traditionally known as 'clabbered milk' and is still consumed by many cultures. By contrast, these bacteria are killed by heat treatment in pasteurisation, so yeasts will rot the milk which will eventually turn rancid.

Raw milk supports local economies and the environment: because raw milk is produced and sold locally, without the involvement of a dairy processor, the money we spend goes directly to the farmer and stays in the local economy, rather than divided between retail chains, the wholesaler/milk processors and, lastly, the farmer. It also saves food miles compared with the pasteurised milk in our fridge which has invariably travelled long distances after leaving the dairy farm.

Certified raw milk is a truly delicious food - smooth, creamy and crammed full of powerful nutrients and well-tolerated and digested by many people with dairy issues, including lactose intolerance.

Ah, lactose intolerance: are all of us able to digest milk?

Milk contains the milk sugar lactose and all young mammals produce the enzyme lactase to digest it efficiently. It is often argued that humans lose the ability to produce lactase after toddler-hood, when we transition from milk to solid foods, and that this is a sign that we should avoid milk as adults.

However, not all adults do lose the ability to produce lactase. For example, groups in northern Europe, the Middle East and some parts of Africa technically have the genetic markers for lactase persistence: an ability to produce lactase and thus digest and tolerate lactose.

An evolutionary advantage has meant that lactase persistence has spread widely in populations who consume dairy. For instance, lactase persistence is estimated to be 89-96% in the British Isles and Scandinavia.[10]

Surprisingly, there are large numbers of people around the world who don't have the gene for lactase persistence, yet they don't appear to be lactose-intolerant - they can still drink milk. It's currently hypothesised that, in the absence of sufficient lactase, our gut bacteria are digesting the lactose for us. Clever little critters![11]

Certainly, many people who now seek out and drink raw milk find it to be digestible, so maybe the destruction of the lactase during pasteurisation is an important factor underlying a lot of digestive issues? Indeed, there is numerous anecdotal evidence suggesting people who, once they started drinking raw milk, could then go on to tolerate pasteurised milk.[12]

Conclusion

Well, as you can see, the rise and fall of milk is a sorry and largely untold story. I hope I have gone some way to putting the record straight and to encouraging your interest in trying one of Mother Nature's nutritionally perfect gifts?

I make no apology for re-stating that raw milk is real milk, and is vastly superior to pasteurised, homogenised milk.[13]

What if you are (or think you may be) lactose-intolerant?

Of course, many of us do have difficulty tolerating milk: for instance, bloating or excessive wind … and nobody likes excessive wind!

Some tips on what to do if you want to be able to drink milk, but think you can't:

Give milk a chance. Start drinking milk regularly. It takes about two weeks for the body to get used to a new food and up-regulate the enzymes necessary to digest it.

If you've never given drinking milk a chance by introducing it very slowly and persisting over at least two or three weeks, you may not have allowed your digestive system and gut bacteria adequate time to adapt.

Start slowly. Try a teaspoon a day (really!) and work up to the amount you want to consume. Consider your selection of the type of milk before starting out to give yourself the best chance of adapting (see below).

Buy organic. If the milk is not organic, then it may be the pesticides (remember glyphosate?) and/or other toxic contaminants in the feed (or used in husbandry of the cattle) that are to blame. The chemical contamination of commercial, industrially-produced pasteurised milk should be of concern to us all, not just those with an intolerance.

Give up wheat. This sounds odd, but many of us have bowel damage from consuming improperly prepared wheat and/or gluten intolerance. Because milk is digested at the site of the damage, you can see how this may exacerbate the whole issue.[14]

Try giving up wheat and similar grains for at least a month (it may take longer), focus on healing your gut (see the Bone Broth chapter) and then try introducing milk slowly.

Beware casein. It may not be the lactose (the milk sugar), but something else in the milk that isn't being digested. Some people find casein, the main protein in milk, hard to digest, particularly those with gluten sensitivity or intolerance.

Beware the additive carrageenan. A thickening agent and a powerful allergen commonly added to milk products.[15]

Buy milk from pasture-fed cows. Remember, an unnatural, grain-based diet causes digestive distress and systemic inflammation in cattle and in humans, particularly for those with an already compromised gut lining - think leaky gut. If the cow is suffering, ultimately so might you be.[16]

Try different brands of pasteurised, non-homogenised milk (you'll see the cream on top) from smaller or closed herds. Bear in mind that what the cows eat will ultimately affect their milk & consuming allergenic weeds or mouldy grains (instead of grass) can be highly allergenic to us too.

Find a source of certified raw milk locally or search on-line.[17] Many people who can't tolerate heat-treated, commercial milk have no problems with drinking raw milk, since it still has its lactase enzymes intact; this aids digestion and it's theorised it can trigger your body's own production of the necessary enzymes.

It also gives your body a dose of the bacteria that your own gut flora will need to help digest milk, if you truly do have low lactase production.[18]

Try home-pasteurising raw milk. Certified raw milk is extremely safe, but if you're concerned about drinking it, pasteurising it yourself is easy and much less damaging, so it's a healthier option.[19]

Try different forms of dairy. For example, fermented dairy like yoghurt, kefir and cheese are all lower in lactose (see the Cultured and Fermented Foods chapter). Try these and observe your reaction.

Then try lower protein dairy (like cream) and again, observe your reaction - this can give you a clue as to which part of dairy (lactose or protein) is causing problems for you and remember that food intolerances can be secondary to another problematic food.

On a final note, it's important to be clear on allergy vs intolerance

With an allergy, the body makes an antibody to fight off a specific food; when the food is next consumed, it triggers the release of histamine and other substances, with immediate and potentially life-threatening effects. But true allergies are very rare - if you have an allergy, you'll almost certainly already know about it.

Children with a cow's milk allergy often outgrow it by the age of five, so true milk allergy in older children and adults is very uncommon.

An intolerance is more common, and its onset is usually much slower, accompanied by symptoms such as fatigue, bloating, digestive issues, joint pains, rashes and eczema. Food intolerances[20] are often linked to (and can underlie) a wide range of chronic health conditions.

Please: STOP fearing milk!

If you want to drink milk, try following the above guidance and don't rush it. You may experience a little digestive upset at first, but assuming no serious negative effects, your gut bacteria will gradually adjust and away you'll go.

And give us *real* cheese, please

By the early 18th century, a variety of traditional British regional cheeses (Cheddar, Cheshire, Lancashire, Double Gloucester, Red Leicester, Stilton, Wensleydale, Caerphilly and Sage Derby), made by time-honoured slow methods were well established.

However, by the mid-1940s, industrialisation had put an end to traditional cheese-making and today's mass-produced products bear little resemblance to the full-flavoured, nutritious local cheeses enjoyed by our grandparents and theirs.

Today, nearly all cheese production is heavily industrialised, pasteurised and standardised, and is processed with industrially-manipulated starters to curdle the milk and modified with enzymes to produce a concentrated cheese flavour.

Happily, however, with each passing year more and more traditional, artisan handmade cheeses are once again being produced in the UK, where each batch uniquely differs from the last, depending on the seasons, the animal's feed, the 'terroir' or environmental conditions. And increasingly, it is being made with raw, rather than pasteurised milk. For my money, it's got to be raw to be real.

But, be it milk or cheese, good quality, grass-fed organic full-fat milk is at the heart of the matter and approached mindfully, both can be your friend, not your foe.

MILK Recipes

Milk is a food, not a beverage - always sip milk-based drinks *slowly,* taking time to enjoy their deliciousness and know that your body is saying thank you!

Whole, full-fat milk-based drinks make a great breakfast stand-by, a portable no-fuss lunch or a mid-afternoon snack and a comforting bed-time drink. I'd encourage you to experiment with the ingredients and always include as many of the good guys (like raw egg yolks, kefir, gelatin powder, raw honey) as you can. There's no wrong or right way to enjoy the benefits, just *your* way.

For probiotic super-nutrition, I use certified, unpasteurised raw milk. If you're using pasteurised milk, *please* make it full-fat, organic, pasture-fed and non-homogenised.

REAL STRAWBERRY MILKSHAKE

(Serves 2)

Simple milkshakes are a great way to get kids (and yourself!) off those appallingly sweet, chemically enhanced, highly-processed fake milk drinks and on the road to real milk. Once you start making your own fruit milks and smoothies you won't want to look back.

Organic strawberries (other berries, or indeed any soft fruit) ramp up the nutritional value and add flavour. You can use fresh or frozen strawberries and the quantities needn't be precise.

For a super-nutritional hit, replace a ¼ cup of the milk with powerfully probiotic kefir and whisk in a couple of teaspoons of gelatin powder - the *non-setting* collagen hydrolysate.

What you'll need:

Organic strawberries: 1 mug-full, hulled & roughly chopped
Unrefined sugar: (or raw honey): to taste
Water: ½ cup
Full-fat milk: 1 ½ cups (raw, or organic, non-homogenised)
Optional, but excellent: ¼ cup of kefir and/or 2 tsp of collagen hydrolysate

What to do:

1. In a medium saucepan, heat the strawberries, water and sweeten the mixture to taste.

2. Bring the mixture up to boiling point and let it bubble for about 10 minutes until it reduces and thickens slightly. It's likely to 'spit', so take care not to burn.

3. Let the mixture cool slightly, and then push everything through a mesh strainer into a small bowl. Set the strawberry syrup aside to cool*

To serve, whisk two or three tablespoons (or your desired amount) of strawberry syrup into glasses of chilled milk, or milk/kefir, and whisk in the collagen powder.

Enjoy, slowly and later, make another one!

**The syrup will keep well for several days in the refrigerator.*

ORANGE & GINGER SPICED RICE PUDDING

(Serves 4)

On a wintry day, what better food fantasy can there be than the thought of sliding a spoonful of rich, velvety deliciousness slowly into an expectant mouth? That's a rice pudding for you!

Oranges - the sunniest of fruits - are at their juicy best during the bleak winter months, just waiting to spill out their fresh, sweet nectar for our delight. Accompanied by warming spices like cinnamon, ginger and nutmeg, this orange rice pudding is a marriage made in heaven. Food heaven. Try it.

For a summer treat, make the recipe slightly looser (it'll firm up as it stands); it's delicious served cold in dessert or whisky glasses, drizzled with double cream and twists of candied orange peel. And rice pudding certainly isn't just for dessert - there's no shame and every benefit from having it for breakfast.

What you'll need:

Unsalted butter: 37½ g, plus 1 tbsp
Ginger root: 2 tsp, finely grated
Cinnamon: 1½ tsp, ground

Nutmeg: 1½ tsp, finely grated
Short grain (pudding rice): 80g
Full-fat milk: 375ml
Double cream: 375mls
Unrefined sugar: 37½ g, plus 1 tablespoon (or use honey to taste)
Oranges: 2 large (zested, peeled horizontally to remove pith and cut into thick rounds)

You'll also need a heavy based saucepan, or other flame-proof and ovenproof dish.

What to do:

1. Firstly, soak the rice in cold water for at least an hour (this will soften the grain, make it easier to digest and will substantially reduce the cooking time). Drain the rice well.

2. Stir the sugar, milk and cream together well.

3. Melt the butter in your pan of choice and add the rice. Stir well to coat all the grains - the rice should not sizzle at all. Add the ginger, cinnamon, one teaspoon of the nutmeg, the orange zest and pour in about half of the milk and cream mixture, stirring well.

4. Increase the heat to medium and bring the liquid up to very slow simmer, then add the sugar, stirring well until dissolved.

5. Set the oven to 180°C (Fan) or Gas Mark 6.

6. Cook the rice on the stove top for about 15mins, on a very slow simmer, until it has softened, but is still quite al dente. You'll need to stir frequently, topping up the liquid to maintain a soft, creamy consistency.

7. Give the rice a final stir, adding more liquid if necessary (if you're planning to serve cold keep it on the looser side) and transfer it to an ovenproof dish.

8. Sprinkle over the remaining nutmeg and place in the oven for around 20mins until the rice is quite sticky and the top has set and is browning nicely.

9. Let the pudding sit for 5 mins or so before serving and while it's resting, melt one tablespoon of butter in a hot frying pan and sprinkle in one tablespoon of sugar. Add in the orange rounds and let them caramelise lightly on one side.

10. Arrange the orange slices over on the top of the rice pudding. Serve the pudding hot or cold, on its own, or with a little cream, Greek yoghurt, or ice cream.

Enjoy your bowl of comforting, delicious winter sunshine!

VANILLA CREAM TERRINE WITH RASPBERRIES & BLACKCURRANT COULIS

A simple and simply healthy treat you'll want to make again and again. *Note*: this is one you'll want to start the night before, or first thing in the morning to give the terrine a chance to set well.

What you'll need:

For the terrine:
PURE vanilla extract: 2 tsp
Whipping cream: 425ml
Grass-fed gelatin powder: 11g*
Caster sugar: 75g (or reduce to taste)
Plain Greek yoghurt: 425ml (organic)

For the blackberry coulis:
Blackcurrants: 225g (de-stalked)
Caster sugar: 75g

For the garnish:
Raspberries: 175g
Fresh mint leaves

Kit:
1 silicone tray/box/container 10cms x 10cms x 10cms

* Make *sure* you use regular 'setting' gelatin power (**not** collagen hydrolysate) or the liquid won't set... I have been there!

What to do:

1. Bring the cream to room temperature and in a small bowl, mix 5-6 tablespoons of cream with the gelatin powder. Stir well and leave it to soak for a few minutes.

2. Meanwhile, place the rest of the cream in a saucepan with the sugar and heat gently, just until the sugar has dissolved (it's important not to overheat the cream, so draw the pan off the heat as soon as you can feel all the sugar has dissolved).

3. Then add the soaked gelatin to the hot cream, put the pan over a low heat and whisk everything together well for a few seconds. Again, don't over heat and don't worry if you have a few small lumps - they'll sieve out in the next stage. Remove the cream mixture from the heat.

4. In a mixing bowl, stir the yoghurt and vanilla together, then pour in the gelatin cream mixture through a fine sieve.

5. Mix everything together very thoroughly and pour the mixture into the container, allow to cool, then cover and chill in the fridge for at least 4-6 hours or preferably overnight until it's set.

To make the blackcurrant coulis:

1. De-stalk the blackcurrants and then sprinkle them with the sugar in a bowl. Leave to soak for 30 minutes, and then blitz them in a food processor or blender, until as smooth as you can get them.

2. Then sieve the pulp into the bowl to remove the pips. Taste to check that you have added enough sugar, then pour into a jug and chill until you're ready to serve the terrine.

To serve:

1. Slide a palette knife around the edges of the container just to loosen the terrine, then carefully dunk the bottom of the box into a bowl of warm water for a few seconds.

2. If serving the terrine at the table, place a flat plate over the top of the container and turn the whole thing over, giving it a firm shake as you set it down. The decorate the top with raspberries and mint leaves, in such a way that you can easily cut it into six portions at the table. You can drizzle a little coulis over the top and serve the remainder in a separate jug.

3. Or, turn the terrine out onto a board and cut it into six slices. Arrange each slice on a serving plate, spoon a little blackcurrant coulis over opposite corners of each one and decorate with the fresh raspberries and mint leaves.

Either way... ENJOY!

CHAPTER SIX

GIVE US BACK OUR DAILY BREAD

"How can a nation be called great if its bread tastes like Kleenex?"

- Julia Child

Not only does most of our daily bread taste like Kleenex but sadly, it actually resembles it too. But if that were the end of it, there would be no need for this chapter.

I think (and I'm in good company) that it's no exaggeration to say that our time-honoured, traditional bread has been stolen from us and as a result we've been getting sicker and sicker.

Who stole the wheat?

Wheat, that ancient grain and the raw material for the 'staff of life', has been intensively hybridised and grown in high-yield monocultures, to produce a high-protein, chemically contaminated, highly processed - and highly profitable - product for growers and the baking industry.

Sadly, it's done nothing for us.

The 1870s saw grain milling revolutionised by the invention of steel rollers. Compared to traditional stone-ground methods, which were slow and mashed all parts of the grain together, steel mills were fast, efficient and could separate the component parts of the grain to produce pure, fine white flour at low cost. People loved it.

Why is modern wheat a problem?

- It's hybridised

Almost all of the wheat we eat today is high-yielding dwarf wheat with shorter stems and much larger heads, which produces a much greater yield. However, back in the day, our forefathers grew and ate ancient varieties of lower protein, gut-friendly wheat like emmer, einkorn and kamut and they encountered few of the problems associated with the wheat we eat today.

'Modern' wheat was developed in the 1960s by cross-breeding and crude genetic manipulation and now it rules he world. While it's much cheaper and more profitable to produce than older varieties, hybridisation markedly changed the nutrient and the protein composition of the wheat plant itself.

Since the 1960s, we have seen the important mineral nutrients in wheat (like zinc, copper, iron and magnesium) decrease by up to 30%; older varieties also contained greater amounts of selenium - critical for our ability to produce thyroid hormone and selenium deficiency is common in hypothyroidism.[1]

- It's higher in protein

Back in the day (well in my day, at least!) as kids, we frequently made a sticky mess by mixing flour and water into a gluey paste. This stickiness is a key property of the gluten protein in flour; in fact, the word 'gluten' itself is derived from the Latin word *glutinis* meaning 'glue'. Traditionally, flour-based pastes have been put to use in paper-making, wallpaper paste, paper-mâché and play-dough; given this property, it's not hard to see that it can be very difficult to digest.

Although gluten is the term that we're most familiar with, it's not a single protein but a combination of much smaller gliadin proteins and longer glutenin molecules.

Over 50 years of wheat hybridisation has increased the expression of a particular amino acid sequence Glia(a)9, which is closely linked with the ability to trigger coeliac disease. Glia(a)9's dramatically increased presence in modern wheat mirrors the huge increase in coeliac disease, leading many researchers to speculate that modern wheat may be much worse for people with this disease (and maybe for all of us?) than older varieties of wheat. [2,3]

The long strands in the glutenin component of gluten lend structure and elasticity to dough, determining the baking characteristics so important to modern bakers. This is why wheat has been subjected to so much genetic manipulation to produce specific baking characteristics in regard to firmness, stretchability and crust formation.

"Geneticists therefore bred and cross bred wheat repeatedly to achieve desired baking characteristics, bred wheat with non-wheat grasses to introduce new genes, used chemicals and radiation to induce mutations that included new and unique changes in glutenin characteristics."

- Dr William Davis
Wheat Belly Cookbook

This genetically-manipulated, hybridised wheat (and the refined, nutritionally-deficient flours it produces) is designed to run smoothly, efficiently and at speed through the industrial grain rollers, mixers and ovens of the milling and baking industry. It arrives at production facilities contaminated by all manner of agri-chemical residues (unless it's organic) to be transformed into our daily bread.

- It's lower in nutrition

Absent from refined white flours, is the whole grain - those portions of the wheat that are richest in nutrients: proteins, fats, vitamins and minerals. These ultra-processed products yield so little nutrition that, in the UK at least, there is a requirement to add back in synthetic nutrients in a somewhat misguided attempt to enrich a nutritionally deficient food 'product'.

"And, beyond being cheap and wildly popular, this new type of flour shipped and stored better, allowing for a long distribution chain. In fact, it kept almost indefinitely.

Pest problems were eliminated because pests didn't want it. Of course, we now know that the reason it keeps so well is that it has been stripped of vital nutrients.

The bugs and rodents knew this way before we did."

- David Zivot
Grainstorm Heritage Baking - grainstorm.com

Dr William Davis describes our modern wheat thus:

> **"This thing being sold to us called wheat - it ain't wheat. It's this stocky little high-yield plant, a distant relative of the wheat our mothers used to bake muffins, genetically and biochemically light-years removed from the wheat of just 40 years ago."**

- It's full of processing aids and additives

In 1961, research bakers at Chorleywood in Hertfordshire, UK, developed a process where hard fats, extra yeast and a number of chemicals were added to flour and then mixed at high speed, producing a dough that was ready to bake in a fraction of the time it took to bake breads by traditional methods.

This method has become known as the Chorleywood Bread Process and since its inception, a dizzying variety of 'not on the label' processing aids and additives have thus been employed to facilitate the speedy transformation of this deficient wheat into the pappy product that has become known as 'bread':

> **"Extra yeast, extra gluten, fat to improve crumb softness, reducing agents to help create stretchier doughs, soya flour to add volume and softness, emulsifiers to produce bigger, softer loaves and retard staling, preservatives - to extend shelf-life, and any of a wide variety of enzymes, legally defined as "processing aids" which do not have to be declared on the label."**

- Barbara Griggs
The Guardian: *The rise and rise of sourdough bread*

- It's done and dusted at the speed of light

Now, our 'freshly-baked' loaf is good to go in a mere three hours: from first mix to spraying with anti-stale agents, wrapping in mould-inhibiting plastic packaging and then journeying hundreds of miles across the county, its crumb-less form finally comes to rest neatly and almost indefinitely on the store shelf, ready for us to enjoy.

And don't let that enticing in-store crusty loaf aroma fool you: packaged or not, whether it's baked in a production facility or in-store, nearly all the bread eaten in the UK today is produced by the Chorleywood method.

It's to our shame that this British bread of ours is now the most chemically treated in Europe.[4] As we shall see, if dough is not allowed to ferment for several hours, there is little chance for natural bacteria to breakdown the harmful elements (anti-nutrients) in the grain and to make important nutrients available to the human body.

Is it really any surprise that millions of us can't eat these loaves without experiencing a host of digestive issues? By contrast, are you the one of many who feel just dandy eating European breads?

Agrichemicals and GMOs rear their ugly heads - again!

We saw in the Soil chapter how the use of fertilisers, herbicides, insecticides and pesticides has seriously damaged soil health, polluted waters and human health via food chain contamination, particularly via wheat and cereal grains. Is there anything else to say here?

Just a couple of brief reminders:

Agrichemical residues

The Pesticide Action Network (PAN) UK's 2013 analysis of the UK government's own data on the pesticide residues concluded that, in both supermarket own-brand and leading brand-name loaves, 63% (nearly two in every three loaves sold in the UK) contained traces of at least one pesticide and that 25% contained residues of more than one pesticide. Contamination remained at these levels for at least a decade.

The most frequently detected pesticide was glyphosate (sold under the brand name *Roundup*) followed by chlormequat, a plant growth regulator used on cereal crops, plants and vegetables and malathion, an organophosphate insecticide. If you need reminding of the misery these chemicals cause, re-read the Soil chapter and delve into Appendix 2 - Chemicals, Our Food, Our Health and Our Environment.

And, let's not forget cereal bars, noodles and other starchy foods - they also contain these highly toxic chemical residues. PAN's report found that 90% of cereal bars, and 38% of the noodles had at least one pesticide residue.

Bearing in mind that many food products contain more than one chemical residue (and little is known of their multiplicative effects) and given the volume of evidence against endocrine and gut-disrupting and neurotoxic chemicals (glyphosate and organophosphates) it surely beggars belief that we continue to be subjected to these ingredients in our daily bread and in our children's favourite cereal bars and noodles.

Gluten? Or glyphosate?

The number of people diagnosed with gluten intolerance and coeliac disease has also risen in tandem with the increased use of glyphosate in agriculture, especially with the recent practice of drenching grains in the herbicide right before harvest, which started in the 1980s and became routine in the 1990s.

This has raised the issue of whether we are gluten or glyphosate intolerant. In their 2013 study, (largely ignored by the media) senior independent research scientists Anthony Samsel and Stephanie Seneff published a meta-analysis of nearly 300 studies in the journal *Interdisciplinary Toxicology*[5] linking the growing problem of coeliac disease and gluten intolerance worldwide - but particularly in North America and Europe - to glyphosate ingestion.

Samsel and Seneff argue that the symptoms of gluten intolerance and coeliac disease are shockingly similar to symptoms expressed in lab animals exposed to glyphosate and point to the evidence that glyphosate affects the digestive systems of fish, decreasing digestive enzymes and bacteria, disrupting mucosal folds, and destroying microvilli structure in the intestinal wall.

Studies have repeatedly linked glyphosate-containing chemicals to non-Hodgkin's lymphoma, a type of blood cancer. However, hope is on the horizon in regard to glyphosate: recent landmark litigation in the USA has validated and upheld the concerns of independent science when a jury found in favour of the plaintiff, who alleged that exposure to Roundup weed killer gave him cancer.[6]

Genetically modified wheat - do we want this?

Until recently there was no GM wheat grown for public consumption in the UK. Earlier trials of GM wheat - in 2015 - were carried out by government-funded Rothamsted Research[7] (via the Biotechnology and Biological Sciences Research Council).

Rothamsted, a major research player in the international bio-tech arena, offers what it calls a "cereal-transformation service" to generate transgenic wheat plants:

"The Cereal Transformation Group has a long history of wheat transformation research and has developed optimised protocols for both particle bombardment and Agrobacterium-mediated transformation, successfully transforming over 40 different wheat and wheat-related varieties.

Advice is available on all aspects of transformation from the design stages such as suggesting promoters to drive transgene expression or providing appropriate cloning constructs for either over-expression of genes or their down-regulation by RNAi, to assistance with crossing transgenic plants or taking transgenic lines to field trial.

A more recent addition to transformation technology is genome editing which offers the possibility to generate highly targeted mutations in the host genome. Some success has already been achieved in modifying specific target genes and the intention is to add this to the range of services offered."

Rothamsted was funded - to the tune of almost £3 million of public funds - to carry out a trial in which their genetically-modified wheat was designed to release a scent that would drive away aphids or pests, so allowing the crop to flourish. It failed spectacularly, with no significant difference between the GM and non-GM strains. In testament to this monumental waste of public money, the late Peter Melchett, former Policy Director at the Soil Association, dismissed the trial as redundant:

"The GM wheat trial at Rothamsted was a waste of time and money, whether it worked or not. Aphids are not a significant problem on wheat crops in the UK, which is confirmed by the fact that organic farmers, using no insecticides, do not have significant problems with aphids attacking their wheat crops, with no use of pesticides."

Despite this expensive failure, in early 2017 Rothamsted received the go-ahead for another open-air trial of GM wheat. Despite a detailed objection submitted by over 30 organisations - including GM Freeze, the Soil Association, Friends of the Earth, the Biodynamic Association, Mums Say No to GMO and The Real Bread Campaign - DEFRA (the Department for the Environment, Food and Rural Affairs) approved the application.

"We are disappointed but not surprised to hear that it is going ahead. We raised a number of technical concerns about the application itself and highlighted the potential for GM wheat to escape into the wild, as has happened repeatedly with GM wheat trials in the USA.

But beyond all the technical detail, we believe that Rothamsted researchers have totally missed the point - what is the purpose of growing more wheat in the first place?

World food production already far exceeds the needs of generations to come but people still go hungry. Nobody is starving because of some fundamental flaw with photosynthesis; they are starving because they are poor. Techno-fixes like GM wheat suck up public funding that could make a real difference if it was spent on systemic solutions like waste reduction and poverty eradication. Then we could all enjoy food that is produced responsibly, fairly and sustainably."

- Liz O'Neill, Director, GM Freeze
GM Wheat will be planted in Hertfordshire - gmfreeze.org

I can't improve on David Zivot's summary of the depths to which we have sunk with our 'modern' bread:

"First we invented mechanical technologies to turn wheat into barren white flour. Then, we invented chemical and genetic technologies to make it resistant to pests, drought and blight and easier to harvest, dramatically increasing yield per acre.

And, while we were tweaking genetics, we also figured out how to increase glutens for better "baking properties" (fluffier results).

Put another way: We have mutant seeds, grown in synthetic soil, bathed in chemicals. They're deconstructed, pulverised to fine dust, bleached and chemically treated to create a barren industrial filler that no other creature on the planet will eat. And we wonder why it might be making us sick?"

High-tech bread shenanigans vs simple, traditional sourdough bread

For millennia after the first agrarians planted their ancient grains like einkorn, emmer and spelt, cereal grains were simply crushed into a rough porridge, or baked as a heavy, flat bread. And then…

> **"Some baker, somewhere, around 6,000 years ago, noticed that the flour and water mix he'd left lying around forgotten was doing something odd. It was bubbling, fermenting; it was expanding; it looked off. It smelt a bit funny.**
>
> **He stuck it in the oven nonetheless - waste not, want not - and became the first human being to sniff that wonderful aroma: the smell of baking bread.**
>
> **The taste and texture were different too: his bread was chewier, it had a more interesting flavour. Perhaps he began experimenting himself; maybe he told other bakers…"**

- Barbara Griggs
The Guardian: *The rise and rise of sourdough bread*

I love this description although, historically, it probably isn't the whole story. Gradually, this fermentation technique spread around Europe and the Middle East and sourdough was born. It had just three basic ingredients: flour, water and salt (and a fourth ingredient - time - made it a healthy, digestible and satisfying food that our forefathers enjoyed).

Anyone who has ever experienced the wonder of an authentic, slowly-fermented organic sourdough loaf will agree that this is bread as it should be: easily digestible, sustaining, flavour-some and utterly delicious. And healthful. We make organic, long-fermented sourdough regularly at home and I always feel the need to say a big "thank you" for my daily bread.

Referring back to Dr Weston A. Price's work in the 1930s, his research recorded that the inhabitants (especially the children) in the Swiss village of Lötschental lived very healthily on their primary daily rations of raw milk, cheese and butter atop a chunk of *roggenbrot* - rye sourdough. This was in stark contrast to the health of their neighbouring Westernised-diet communities beset by tooth decay, dental deformities or tuberculosis. Imagine if these staples were the basis of our children's school meals today!

Not a panacea for everyone

Those with Type 1 or Type 2 diabetes should note that sourdough raises blood sugar far less than any other bread. In a 2008 study published in *Acta Diabetologica*, subjects with impaired glucose tolerance were fed either sourdough or ordinary bread. The sourdough bread produced a significantly lower glucose and insulin response. The bacteria which ferment the dough consume the sugars in the flour and produce carbon dioxide, which causes the dough to rise, so more of the sugar is processed by these little critters, leaving less of it to be processed by us.

Indeed, those with Type 1 diabetes might be well advised to investigate the possibility of a co-existing gluten condition. A team from the Center for Coeliac Research in Massachusetts - which included Dr Alessio Fasano, a paediatric gastroenterologist and major figure in the research into and treatment of coeliac disease - recently reviewed the role of gluten as an important player in the pathology and development of Type 1 diabetes and associated coeliac disease. They concluded:

> **"The high rate of comorbidity between these two autoimmune diseases and their rapidly increasing prevalence in the last few decades underscore the importance of screening in high risk patients and the need to further explore and detail the contributory role of environmental factors that may be involved."** [8]

We now know a lot more about conditions like coeliac, sub-clinical coeliac, silent coeliac and non-coeliac gluten sensitivity. There is growing evidence from studies with those who suffer from non-coeliac gluten sensitivity (gluten intolerance) and even for some with the coeliac disease (the most extreme form of reaction to gluten and an autoimmune disease) that authentic, long-fermented sourdough bread may be better tolerated, with studies showing that long-fermented dough produces no symptoms and, on biopsy, no changes in the intestinal lining.[9]

It's thought that the natural wild yeasts and lactobacilli bacteria present in the dough get to work in the fermentation process, to pre-digest the gluten (a protein found in all forms of wheat, rye and barley), fully break down the carbohydrates and deal with the anti-nutrients and toxins (phytates and lectins) present in all grains.

The incidence of coeliac disease itself has been growing exponentially over the last few decades. In a study which compared blood samples taken from 10,000 people 50 years ago with those taken in 2009, researchers found a 400% increase in the markers for full-blown coeliac disease.

Because full-blown coeliac is diagnosed by biopsy, we can't know precise numbers, but it's conservatively estimated that more than one in 100 of us has the disease but are either not diagnosed (sub-clinical) or are symptom-less (silent-coeliac), even though our gut is compromised or damaged.

Millions more of us may be gluten-sensitive. Non-coeliac gluten sensitivity (NCGS) is something that's increasingly recognised as a problem in many countries across the world. This is a new area for research and the exact role of the immune system is unclear.

There are no specific diagnostic tests or reliable statistics for gluten sensitivity, but in the US alone, one estimate puts it as high as 18 million people.

Indeed, some physicians argue that NCGS may be a much more serious problem than coeliac disease itself. Because individuals are not reacting to the same proteins that signal full-blown coeliac, they will remain undiagnosed, and may continue to eat gluten for the rest of their lives, putting themselves at serious risk for autoimmune and other diseases.[10]

Anyone struggling with leaky gut, aching joints, brain fog, fatigue, IBS, Crohn's disease, arthritis, skin conditions or any autoimmune disorder is well advised to reconsider their consumption of wheat and/or gluten grains.[11] However, this is no easy task since nearly all processed and convenience foods contain gluten - ubiquitous in the food industry as a food 'glue'.

Yet another incentive to cook-from-scratch?

Dr Fasano has set out a Gluten Contamination Elimination Diet[12], which basically eliminates all processed foods:

✓ **Allowed**: brown and white rice; all fresh fruits and vegetables; fresh meats; fish; eggs; dried beans; unseasoned nuts in the shell; butter; plain yogurt; plain milk, and aged cheeses; oils; vinegar (except flavoured or malt); honey; salt. Beverages allowed include 100% fruit juices, water and Gatorade.

X **Not allowed**: millet, sorghum, buckwheat or any other grains, seeds, or flours; frozen, canned, or dried fruits and vegetables; lunch meats; ham; bacon; seasoned or flavoured dairy products; processed cheeses; flavoured and malt vinegars.

! **A health warning**: avoid commercially produced gluten-free products.

Most commercial gluten-free versions of wheat-based foods are actually just highly processed junk food. Read the labels and you'll find combinations of rice starch, corn-starch, tapioca starch, potato starch and guar gum as a substitute for white flour. These are the same kind of highly refined industrial starches that spike blood sugar as much as - or even more than - white flour. And they contain a host of emulsifiers, pesticide residues and so on.... and on and on.

Grains - are they healthy anyway?

As a species, we've only been consuming cereal grains for a heartbeat of the time in our two million-year evolution as hunter-gatherers. Within the Paleo and Ancestral Diet community, there's a significant body of opinion that calls on evolutionary evidence to argue that an agrarian, grain-based diet may fundamentally underlie many of our modern chronic diseases, as well as inflammation, infection, anaemia, diseases of the bones and teeth and other degenerative conditions.[13]

In less than 150 years since the forced abandonment of their hunter-gatherer diet, the prevalence of diabetes among the First Nations indigenous people in Canada is epidemic, about 3-5 times the national average.[14]

However others, like the Weston A. Price Foundation traditional foods movement (see Chapter Two - Nourishing Traditionally) hold grains, properly prepared, to be one of the most important foods in human history, revered and widely eaten by traditional peoples across the planet, with a rightful place in a varied, nutrient-dense diet. So, who's right?

Both? Neither? It depends.

The problem with grains - anti-nutrients

Anti-nutrients are natural or synthetic compounds found in a variety of foods, especially grains (the seeds of cereal grasses) but also in beans, legumes and nuts. These anti-nutrients interfere with the absorption of vitamins, minerals and other nutrients and they can also disrupt digestive enzymes and so prevent proper nutrient absorption.

Anti-nutrients can also be found in plant roots, vegetables, leaves and fruits, although these are at much lower levels and usually have benefits, as opposed to mostly harmful effects. Two particular anti-nutrients can give us serious grief: phytates and lectins. During digestion, most of the phytates we consume are broken down in our stomach and small intestines.

However, because phytic acid 'binds' minerals (like magnesium, calcium, iron and zinc) in our gut before they are able to be absorbed, these key nutrients are less available to us. Ultimately, this can lead to nutrient deficiencies and also reduces the digestibility of the macro-nutrients - starches, proteins and fats.[15]

Let's look at phytates

Whole cereal grains (wheat, maize, rye, barley, oats, sorghum, millet, rice) are essentially seeds, as are nuts, beans/legumes and oilseeds (sesame, sunflower, linseed, rapeseed and soya bean).

All contain varying amounts of phytic acid. When phytic acid is bound to a mineral within the seed, it's known as phytate. These stored phytates provide energy for the sprouting seed to grow. Many other vegetables also contain phytic acid, but in lower amounts - the most concentrated sources tend to be whole grains (concentrated in the bran) and beans (in the protein). When whole grains are refined (as in white flours) little or no phytate is retained.

On the other hand, some experts propose that phytic acid in whole grains and beans, by binding minerals, acts like an anti-oxidant and prevents the formation of harmful free radicals and has protective properties against cardiovascular disease, cancer and diabetes.

Let's look at lectins

Lectins are plant proteins and are abundant in grains and raw legumes. They are found on the seed coat and in the part of the seed that becomes the leaves when the plant seed sprouts.

Mother Nature is smart and has provided many plants and fruits with lectins (around 53 fruits, vegetables, spices and other commonly eaten plants) as a natural, defensive armour against micro-organisms, pests, and insects. It's thought that lectins evolved as a way for a plant's seeds to remain intact as they pass through a predator's (animal or human) digestive system, for survival, dispersal and further reproduction.

Although they're very good news for plants, many experts argue that lectins can give us grief. Indeed, consuming grains and legumes raw can result in nausea, diarrhoea and vomiting - think red kidney beans. Some experts suggest that many instances of apparent bacterial food poisoning may in fact be lectin poisoning, and even when cooked, lectins often cause flatulence.

Normally our gut lining is able to repair very quickly, but some experts argue that lectins retard this process and can exacerbate leaky gut (intestinal permeability), a condition in which the lining of the small intestine becomes damaged, allowing undigested food particles, toxic waste products and bacteria to 'leak' through the intestines and flood the blood stream.

The theory is that because lectins are resistant to human digestion, they enter the blood stream (via a leaky gut) unchanged; our immune system recognises them as foreign proteins and produces antibodies to fight them. In this way, many of us - especially those with an already compromised or damaged gut lining - can become intolerant to lectins after an immune response has been consistently provoked.

Symptoms can include general inflammation, skin conditions, joint pain and other chronic disorders associated with leaky gut, such as IBS and Crohn's and many other autoimmune mediated conditions.

However, the case against lectins isn't open and shut. Other experts have pointed out that the evidence against lectins is flawed, in that large amounts of raw lectin were fed to the animals in the studies, much more than we would ever consume cooked in the context of a whole food diet. We know that cooking legumes well deactivates lectins dramatically and that other components in the food (like simple sugars) bind to lectins and diminish their effect. Peanuts (surprisingly) are one legume which for a number of reasons it may be wiser to minimise or avoid.[16]

Traditional methods for sprouting, soaking and fermenting grains		
Soaking and sprouting	**Soaking** is the process of putting any sproutable food - seeds, grains, nuts or legumes - in water for a period of time. **Sprouting** allows the soaked item to germinate and further enhances the density and bioavailability of the nutrients and digestibility and of the grains. After sprouting, the food can be dehydrated and ground into flour.	**Phytates:** Sprouting and malting grains decreases phytic acid. **Lectins:** Sprouting grains, seeds and beans decreases the lectin content by de-activation during the sprouting process, or by germination, where the lectins are eliminated via the sprouted seed coat. However, beware eating certain legumes raw - think red kidney beans for example.
Soaking and cooking	This is the classic method of preparing grains and beans; the whole seed or kernel is soaked, often in some acidified liquid like whey or lemon juice, for a period of time before cooking.	**Phytates:** Soaking and cooking grains can reduce phytic acid (and many other anti-nutrients). **Lectins:** Long soaking in several changes of water and adding baking soda (sodium bicarbonate) helps neutralise lectins.

Fermenting	Cultures with a history of grain eating traditionally have used some form of fermentation to treat grains, as in the sourdough process.	**Phytates:** Fermentation activates phytase enzymes in the grain and helps to break down phytic acid. Also, some of the acids produced during fermentation might actually boost absorption of some minerals. **Lectins:** Fermentation allows beneficial bacteria to digest and convert many of the harmful substances, reducing their negative effect. But not all lectins are completely destroyed by these methods.
Adding vitamin C	Vitamin C appears strong enough to overcome phytic acid. In one study, adding 50 mg of vitamin C counteracted the phytic acid load of a meal. In another study, 80 mg of ascorbic acid (vitamin C) counteracted 25 mg of phytic acid.	
Milling and processing	Milling grains and removing the bran decreases phytic acid – but it also tends to remove many of the minerals! This is why we now have 'enriched' refined flours – but as we'll see below, this may be very misguided.	

Should we be eating gluten grains at all?

As I've mentioned the Paleo community argue that since humans did not evolve to tolerate grains, we should shun them altogether. But many traditional food advocates hold that grains cause digestive issues because we no longer prepare them by the traditional methods of soaking, fermenting and sprouting. Each of these methods not only substantially decreases the anti-nutrient content, but also makes the grain more digestible and nutritious.[17]

Whole grains vs milled flours

It's worth remembering that the carbohydrate content in all milled flour will be absorbed into our blood stream more quickly than would the whole grain (or legume, nut or seed) and will also tend to cause spikes in blood sugar more quickly. At the same time, these milled flours (and their products) won't necessarily be digested any more easily. Indeed, some gluten-containing grains (like barley, spelt and oats) seem to be better tolerated if cooked whole in a soup, stew, porridge or in pilaf rather than ground into flour, so it may be that the problem of gluten intolerance is partly due to the mechanical effects of flour in the gut, slowing down transit time and increasing the sensitivity of the intestinal wall to proteins such as gluten.

"My general rule of thumb is that if you can get your food to stick to the wall or ceiling, like pasta for example, then you probably want to avoid it."

- Todd Caldecott
Food as Medicine - The Theory & Practice of Food

'Enriched' flours - do they make us nutritionally wealthy?

Our preference for (and reliance on) refined, white enriched flours and their products in our standard Western diet may be a significant factor driving obesity.

We've seen that refined white flour and its products are nutritionally deficient. In the UK, USA and Canada, our reliance on these products has led to a policy and requirement for enrichment, pushed through by heavy lobbying by the food industry. The enrichments now most frequently added are thiamin, riboflavin, niacin, folate and iron. However, European countries like France and Italy do not enrich their white flours.

As far back as the 1920s, scientists already knew that when they fed rats pure, nutrition-less flours and refined grains as staples, the rats quickly lost their appetites and ate less of the product. However, by adding brewer's yeast, rich in B vitamins, the animals' appetites could quickly be increased to promote beneficial weight gain.

So, if animals were to rely on refined foods as staples, they would naturally lose their appetites; however, when researchers add vitamins to a synthetic, purified diet, it will significantly increase appetite and intake for that refined diet. Needless to say, farmers were soon adding small amounts of brewer's yeast to their cattle feed and unsurprisingly this was quickly picked up by the food industry.

Enrichment policies - do you smell a rat?

In his 2016 article *How Food Enrichment Promotes Obesity,* Richard Nikoley [18] describes a series of research papers published since 2010, linking food enrichment to the obesity epidemic and related metabolic diseases, including diabetes, leading him to conclude that excess vitamins may play a causal role in the increased prevalence of obesity. Results show that there are strong correlations between enrichment levels and obesity trends in developed countries; that developed countries which do not fortify have lower levels of obesity in its population (France or Italy, for example); and that obesity epidemics occur immediately after increases to enrichment levels. Nikoley points out:

> **"A single slice of enriched white bread now has as much appetite-stimulating B vitamins as a medium sweet potato and more riboflavin and niacin than a cup of beans. These enrichments are specifically designed to enable people to eat refined foods as staples, which are rapidly digested and lack the satiating fibre and phytonutrients that are found in whole grains and complex carbohydrates. Moreover a diet that lacks fermentable fibre promotes diet-induced adiposity."**

Beware imposters and 'faux' sourdough!

Despite on-going efforts by organisations like The Real Bread Campaign and other campaigners, there is still no legal definition of authentic sourdough bread. This means that the retail food industry (and too many local so-called 'traditional' bakeries) are producing commercial bread, to which dried, powdered sourdough starter has been added for flavour and are selling it to unsuspecting customers as the real deal and charging accordingly. Next time you read the bread label, just remember this: authentic sourdough bread has just THREE ingredients and a helper: flour, water, salt and time.

Yeasted breads: a caution

So far, we've not considered the subject of yeasted breads. Baker's yeast (related to brewer's yeast) comprises the strains of yeast commonly used as a rising agent in bread and bakery products (and in alcoholic fermentation). The yeasts convert the fermentable sugars present in the dough into carbon dioxide and ethanol - remember the distillery dairies described in the Milk chapter?

Baker's yeast is available in a number of different forms: creamed, compressed, active, dried, instant, rapid rise - the choice depends on the recipe in question, but they are largely interchangeable.

Traditionally, British bread was raised with 'barm' - the froth from the top of brewers' yeast - and it enjoyed an overnight, long fermentation. Back in the day, master bakers were also master brewers: many of them brewed their own distinctive barm. Now the baking industry relies on a toxic, chemically-driven industrial process to produce conventional baking yeasts which can perform reliably (and at speed) in mass production.

"... ammonia, ammonium salts and lyes, plus a variety of acids (including sulphuric acid), synthetic vitamins and growth substances. Conventional yeast requires several rinsing stages after fermentation, to remove unpleasant tastes and odours. The resulting wastewater is heavily contaminated and requires complex purification processing."

- John Downs

Why you should consider organic yeast - shipton-mill.com

This diagram details the stages of conventional yeast production compared with organic yeast production:

	Manufacture of Bioreal Organic Yeast	Manufacture of Conventional Yeast
Sugar source	Organic Grain	Molasses
Nitrogen source		Ammonia (NH_3) Ammonium Salts
pH Regulator	No pH level regulation	Acids (e.g. Sulphuric Acid) Lyes (e.g. Caustic Soda Lye)
Processing & Growth Substances	Sufficiently present in natural media	Synthetic Vitamins and Mineral Salts
Anti-foaming Agent	Organic Sunflower Oil	Synthetic Anti-foaming Agent
Rinsing	Unnecessary	Two Times
Waste Water	Raw material and other products	Disposal difficult

Taking a moment to consider all the steps involved in conventional yeast production gives yet another reason to choose organic when selecting your yeasted breads and bakery products.

Long-fermentation, as we've seen, is your friend when it comes to the digestibility (and flavour) of bread. With yeasted breads, speed is neither your friend nor does it do the bread any favours. For a gentle and inspiring rewind into French traditional bread-making techniques, make yourself a cuppa and enjoy Samuel Fomartz's account of his experience as an amateur baker apprentice with an artisan Paris boulanger.[19]

Ancient - or heritage - grains

Ancient grains include the original strains of wheat - einkorn, spelt, khorasan and emmer (aka farro) - and generally refers to grains that have remained true to their centuries-old original form. Ancient wheat grains have been found to have higher amounts of antioxidants, protein, vitamins and minerals, but lower amounts of gluten.

Higher gluten, higher starch modern wheat is less likely to be as easily digested, more likely to spike blood sugar and has been bred to withstand pesticides. It's worth remembering that ancient grains have different properties from those of modern wheat, so will perform quite differently in the kitchen; if you choose to cook with them, be patient and be prepared to experiment.

Alternatives to gluten and grains

There are now quite a few varieties of gluten and grain-free flours (almond, cassava, arrowroot, coconut, tiger nut, tapioca, amaranth, teff, plantain) available for those who wish to go gluten- or grain-free. You can successfully use these alternative options featured in the increasing number of gluten and grain-free cook books and recipes posted online. Google and a little patience are your friends.[20]

However, be aware that many of these alternatives can cause other problems for those with weakened or poor digestion; for example, almond flour can be a gut irritant in itself and the high fibre content of both almond and coconut flour will cause issues for some. Again, it's a case of proceeding with caution and listening to your body and, if you're really struggling, being prepared to take all grains out of your diet for a while.

Also, be aware that most corn (maize), although gluten-free, is now predominantly genetically-modified and contaminated with glyphosate (unless organic) and imported into the UK, usually as animal feed: a reminder here, that you are not only what you eat, but also what your animal eats. Always check the sources of corn flour and other corn products.[21]

While growing rice organically makes no difference to arsenic level, it will protect us from pesticides. However, if you're eating rice (grains, flours, milks or other rice products) regularly, it may be a good idea to get up to speed on a number of emerging concerns about the world's rice supply, especially the issue of arsenic contamination.[22]

Arsenic occurs naturally in soil and water, so small amounts do get into cereal crops. Because it's grown in flooded fields, it's easier for rice to absorb the arsenic, so it has many more times (10 - 20) arsenic than other cereal crops. Arsenic is classified as a 'Category 1 carcinogen' by the EU, which means that it's known to cause cancer in humans.

In his article, part of BBC Two's *Trust Me I'm a Doctor* series, Dr Michael Mosely explains that over 80% of the arsenic in rice can be reduced by careful preparation and cooking: experts advise us to soak rice overnight and then rinse it well several times, before cooking it in five parts water to the amount rice. A final rinse with boiling water is also recommended.

Dr Mosely advises additional caution where children are concerned. Rice products specifically destined for children are tightly controlled for arsenic, but rice cakes and cereals are not included in this category so can contain adult levels. He also points out that, while the UK Food Standards Agency advises that rice drinks should not be used as an alternative to milk for children under 5 years old, there is no legal obligation for producers to put this warning on the label.

When to limit or avoid wheat or grains

Increasingly, experts are advising those with allergies, asthma, eczema, skin conditions, leaky gut, food intolerances, IBS, IBD, coeliac, autoimmune, and arthritis to avoid wheat and/or grains and embark on various autoimmune protocols (for example, GAPS) in order to heal and seal their gut and restore a beneficial balance to their gut microbiome, before attempting, slowly, to resume them.

Back to the future of grains? Eating them safely

- ALWAYS buy organic grains/flour products
- Be cautious over enriched flours and flour products
- Consider swapping to ancient grains
- Make the effort to sprout, soak, or ferment grains
- Avoid gluten grains (or all grains) until digestive and/or autoimmune issues are resolved.

And try to support your local, authentic bakery or start making your own bread. Your baker, your community and your body will thank you.

"When we see community bakeries beginning to appear in a country like Britain where 95% of the loaves people eat are factory pap, we are right to feel hopeful.

If just one in every 35 of the 2.6 million unemployed people in Britain opted for good 'company' rather than the dole, we'd have bakers a-plenty to bring real bread to every community in the land."

- Andrew Whitely
breadmatters.com

REAL BREAD Recipes

MAKING THE 'MOTHER' STARTER

First, you'll need to make a 'mother' starter - this will take about 7 days at normal room temperature, but it may take a little longer if your kitchen is very cold.

You'll need:

10g flour
10g* filtered water

Day 1: Place the flour and water in a 2 litre Pyrex bowl, cover loosely with a clean tea towel and leave on kitchen counter 24 hours.

Day 2: Add another 10g flour + 10g filtered water, mix well, cover and leave on kitchen counter for 24 hours.

Day 3 - 6/7: Repeat as above, adding 10g flour + 10g filtered water each day.

Around day 6 there will be definite signs of life with bubbles appearing on the surface of the starter mix; this is the carbon dioxide produced by the microbes as they munch their way through the sugars in the flour.

When your mother starter is ready, it should look really lively and bubbly, if it doesn't then continue adding the flour + water and make sure your kitchen isn't too cold!

By day 7, you will have created 140g of lively, bubbly mother starter and you are ready to start making your sourdough loaves.

If you're not ready to bake straight away, cover and store the mother starter in the refrigerator until you're ready to start. The low temperature in the fridge will render the microbes dormant, so you'll need to 'refresh' the mother starter with fresh flour and water (as below), to enliven it before you bake.

When you are ready to bake, remove the mother starter from the refrigerator, take out the required quantity (see recipe below) and return the rest to the fridge. You'll need to repeat this step each time you bake.

** Although liquids are normally measured in millilitres, for traditional bakers, the convention is to use water weight so this is what I am using here.*

BAKER BRIDGE'S CLASSIC WHITE SOURDOUGH

The recipe makes 2 x 450g loaves (approximate weight)

What you'll need:

Mother starter mix: 10g (taken from the fridge)
Strong bread flour: 570g (+ extra for flouring surfaces & bannetons)
Filtered water: 345g
Sea salt: 8g (Maldon, crushed)

2 x 450g bannetons (dough proving baskets)
Or 2 x 450g loaf tins
Shallow baking tray
A thick oven cloth

What to do:

Morning 1: Refresh your mother starter (1)
Mother starter: Take 10g of mother starter from the fridge
Water: Add 20g
Strong bread flour: Add 20g
Total weight: 50g

- Mix together, cover and leave on the kitchen counter until the evening.

Evening 1: Refresh the starter (2)
Starter mix: You now have a total of 50g of starter (i.e. the total from above)
Water: Add 50g
Strong white bread flour: Add 50g
Total: 150g

- Mix together, cover and leave on the kitchen counter overnight. In the morning it should be very lively and frothy.

Morning 2: Mix the dough

Starter mix: Take 135g of starter mix from above (and add the leftover to replenish the mother starter in the fridge)
Strong white bread flour: Add 500g
Water: Add 275g
Sea salt: Add 8g
Total weight: 918g

1. Put the water into large bowl, add the starter mix, flour and salt in that order. This will stop the starter from sticking to the bowl and the salt from damaging the starter. Mix well with a wooden spoon until the dough comes together and the sides of the bowl are clean - you can use your hands toward the end.

2. Sprinkle bread flour onto a clean work surface and tip out the dough. Flour your hands and knead the dough, stretching and turning it to develop the gluten. Continue until the dough feels pliable and the surface develops a soft sheen - this will take 7-10mins. Form the dough into a rough ball.

3. Sprinkle 1 tablespoon of olive oil into the same bowl and place the dough-ball into the bowl, turning it until the surface is covered with a thin layer of oil - this will prevent the dough sticking to the bowl and stop a skin forming, which will impede it rising properly.

4. Cover the bowl with clean tea-towel, or a large plate and set aside to double in size (make sure your bowl is large enough!).

5. When the dough has doubled in size it's ready to be shaped and placed into the banneton or loaf tin. Depending on the ambient temperature, this can take 3-5 hours, perhaps a little longer in winter.

6. Scoop the dough ball out of the bowl and turn it onto a lightly floured surface. Divide the dough equally into two halves.

7. Flatten the dough down onto the work surface, as if to make a 'clock face'. Starting at 12 o'clock, pick up the edge of the dough (with one or two fingers and a thumb) and pull it towards the centre, pressing it down lightly. Continue around the clock, until you have a firm, round ball.

8. Repeat this process again - this will ensure that the dough traps air and will help the bread on its final rise.

9. Turn the dough over, so that the folds are face down on the work surface. Put your hands flat on the work surface, palms up. In a fluid motion, bring your hands together to cup and turn the dough. You are aiming to bring one hand towards and the other hand away from you, as you cup and turn the dough. This will create a tight ball with good surface tension, ensuring that the bread will rise well in the oven.

If using a banneton: Flour the banneton *really* well and place your dough ball, smooth side DOWN, so that the folds are UPPER-most. Flour the surface of the dough well, cover with another bowl or a well-floured tea towel and leave to double in size. Again, depending on the ambient temperature, this will take between 3-5 hours, perhaps a little longer in winter.

If using a loaf tin, oil the bottom and sides of the tin with olive oil and place the dough, smooth side UP and folded side DOWN. Flour the surface of the loaf and cover with well-floured tea towel and leave to rise as above.

When the dough is ready, place a small, shallow baking tray on the bottom of the oven and preheat the oven to 220°(Fan) or Gas Mark 9.

When the oven has reached required temperature, open the oven door carefully and CAREFULLY pour boiling water into the shallow baking tray and quickly close the oven door. This will create steam and help the crust to form well.

If using a banneton: Working quickly, tip the dough out onto a solid, lightly floured baking tray. With a very sharp knife (a serrated bread knife is good) make a firm cut across the top of the dough, pulling the knife toward you. This will enable 'oven-spring' and allow the loaf to rise really well.

Put the dough into the hot, steamy oven and bake for approximately 40 mins until the loaf is lightly and evenly browned - the exact baking time will depend on your oven and oven thermostat. To test if it is done, hold the loaf in a thick oven cloth and tap the bottom - it should sound hollow and dry. If it doesn't, return the loaf to the oven for a few more minutes.

If using a loaf tin: Leave the dough in the tin, slash the top as above and place in the oven. Bake for approximately 40 mins, until the loaf is lightly and evenly browned - the exact baking time will depend on your oven and oven thermostat. To test if it is done, carefully remove the loaf from the tin (use a thick oven cloth!) and tap the bottom - it should sound hollow. If it doesn't, return the loaf to the oven (without the tin) for a few more minutes.

Leave to cool on a wire rack and once cooled, slice, spread thickly with raw (unpasteurised) butter and enjoy!!

BAKER BRIDGE'S 5 SEEDED SPELT SOURDOUGH LOAF

Without a shadow of a doubt, this sourdough is a winner! No matter what else is on the menu, we always serve this to guests and there's *always* a fight to grab the last slice!

I can guarantee that it can't be beaten for flavour and texture, and the omega-rich seeds add a mighty nutritional punch. Crusty, malty and savoury, it pairs brilliantly with cheeses, cold meats, soups and stews.

The recipe makes 2 x 450g loaves (approximate weight)

What you'll need:

Mother starter mix: 10g (taken from the fridge)
Strong white bread flour: 335g (+ extra for flouring surfaces & bannetons)
Wholemeal spelt flour: 84g
Filtered water: 197g
Sea salt: 7g (Maldon, crushed)

Poppy seeds: 20g
Sunflower seeds: 20g
Pumpkin seeds: 20g
Golden linseeds: 20g
Sesame seeds: 20g
Boiling filter water: 100g

2 x 450g bannetons
Or 2 x 450g loaf tins
Shallow baking tray
A thick oven cloth

What to do:

Morning 1: Refresh your mother starter (1)
Mother starter: Take 10g of mother starter from the fridge
Water: Add 20g
Strong bread flour: Add 20g
Total weight: 50g

- Mix together, cover and leave on the kitchen counter until the evening.

Evening 1: Refresh the starter (2)
Morning starter mix: You now have a total of 50g of starter (i.e. the total from above)
Water: Add 50g
Strong bread flour: Add 50g
Total: 150g

- Mix together, cover and leave on the kitchen counter overnight. In the morning it should be very lively and frothy.

Evening 1: Make the 'soaker'
Poppy seeds: 20g
Sunflower seeds: 20g
Pumpkin seeds: 20g
Golden linseeds: 20g
Sesame seeds: 20g
Boiling filter water: 100g
Total soaker = 200g

- Mix together, cover and leave overnight to soak.

Morning 2: Mix the dough
Starter mix: Take 117g starter mix from above (and add the leftover to replenish the mother starter in the fridge)
Strong white bread flour: Add 335g
Wholemeal spelt flour: Add 84g
Water: Add 197g
Sea salt: Add 7g
Soaker: Add 200g
Total weight: 940g

1. Put the water into a large bowl, add the starter mix, flours, salt and starter, in that order. This will stop the starter from sticking to the bowl and the salt from damaging the starter. Mix well with a wooden spoon, making sure that the soaked seeds are evenly distributed. Mix until the dough comes together and the sides of the bowl are clean - you can use your hands towards the end.

2. Sprinkle bread flour onto a clean work surface and tip out the dough. Flour your hands and knead the dough, stretching and turning it to develop the gluten. Continue until the dough feels pliable and workable and the surface develops a soft sheen - this will take 7-10mins. Form the dough into a rough ball.

3. Sprinkle 1 tablespoon of olive oil into the same bowl and place the dough-ball into the bowl, turning it until the surface is covered with a thin layer of oil - this will prevent the dough sticking to the bowl and stop a skin forming, which will impede it rising properly.

4. Cover the bowl with clean tea-towel, or a large plate and set aside to double in size (make sure your bowl is large enough!).

5. When the dough has doubled in size it's ready to be shaped and placed into the banneton or loaf tin. Depending on the ambient temperature, this can take 3-5 hours, perhaps a little longer in winter.

6. Scoop the dough ball out of the bowl and turn it onto a lightly floured surface. If making two loaves, divide the dough equally into two halves.

7. Flatten the dough down onto the work surface, as if to make a 'clock face'. Starting at 12 o'clock, pick up the edge of the dough (with one or two fingers and a thumb) and pull it towards the centre, pressing it down lightly. Continue around the clock, until you have a firm, round ball.

8. Repeat this process again - this will ensure that the dough traps air and will help the bread on its final rise.

9. Turn the dough over, so that the folds are face down on the work surface. Put your hands flat on the work surface, palms up. In a fluid motion, bring your hands together to cup and turn the dough. You are aiming to bring one hand towards and the other hand away from you, as you cup and turn the dough. This will create a tight ball with good surface tension, ensuring that the bread will rise well in the oven.

If using a banneton: Flour the banneton *really* well and place your dough ball, smooth side DOWN, so that the folds are UPPER-most. Flour the surface of the dough well, cover with another bowl or a well-floured tea towel and leave to double in size. Again, depending on the ambient temperature, this will take between 3-5 hours, perhaps a little longer in a cold winter.

If using a loaf tin, oil the bottom and sides of the tin with olive oil and place the dough, smooth side UP and folded side DOWN. Flour the surface of the loaf and cover with well-floured tea towel and leave to rise as above.

When the dough is ready, place a small, shallow baking tray on the bottom of the oven and preheat the oven to 220°(Fan) or Gas Mark 9.

When the oven has reached required temperature, open the oven door carefully and CAREFULLY pour boiling water into the shallow baking tray and quickly close the oven door. This will create steam and help the crust to form well.

If using a banneton: Working quickly, tip the dough out onto a solid, lightly floured baking tray. With a very sharp knife (a serrated bread knife is good) make a firm cut across the top of the dough, pulling the knife toward you. This will enable 'oven-spring' and allow the loaf to rise really well.

Put the dough into the hot, steamy oven and bake for approximately 40 mins until the loaf is lightly and evenly browned - the exact baking time will depend on your oven and oven thermostat. To test if it is done, hold the loaf in a thick oven cloth and tap the bottom - it should sound hollow and dry. If it doesn't, return the loaf to the oven for a few more minutes.

If using a loaf tin: Leave the dough in the tin, slash the top as above and place in the oven. Bake for approximately 40 mins, until the loaf is lightly and evenly browned - the exact baking time will depend on your oven and oven thermostat. To test if it is done, carefully remove the loaf from the tin (use a thick oven cloth!) and tap the bottom - it should sound hollow. If it doesn't, return the loaf to the oven (without the tin) for a few more minutes.

Leave to cool on a wire rack and once cooled, slice, spread thickly with raw (unpasteurised) butter and enjoy!!

SOURDOUGH CRUMPETS (OR PIKELETS)

As you get into a routine of making deliciously digestible sourdough bread, over time you'll find yourself with a lot more starter than you can use. Don't throw it away: make crumpets or pikelets instead - they're easy, quick and a million miles away from any shop bought offerings.

The pikelet is said to originate from Wales, where it was known as *'bara piglydd'* and later anglicised to pikelet. Some call it the 'poor man's crumpet' as it was made free-form by those who couldn't afford the rings to make traditional crumpets. I tend to make pikelets as opposed to crumpets, which can be difficult to get out of the ring and, because pikelets are cooked free-form, they're thinner than crumpets so quicker to cook and are deliciously crispy at the edges… all good, I say.

We enjoy them for breakfast or brunch, buttered and topped with poached or scrambled eggs (smoked salmon optional) and served with a pile of well-seasoned buttered spinach and a couple of grilled tomatoes on the side. If I'm craving an afternoon snack (not often, but I sometimes do) then a couple of these beauties, drizzled with raw honey and a dusting of cinnamon (think blood sugar) and a cup of loose-leaf Earl Grey tea, really hits the spot.

What you'll need:

Coconut oil: 1-2 tablespoons (enough to oil your pan)
Sourdough starter: 270g
Sugar or honey: 1 tsp (or to taste)
Sea salt: Maldon, pinch
Bicarbonate of soda: ½ tsp

What to do:

1. Oil a heavy-based frying pan or griddle with a little oil and then place over a medium heat.
2. Add the sugar or honey and salt to the starter and whisk well.
3. When the pan or griddle is at a medium heat, add the bicarbonate of soda and whisk again.
4. Working quickly (the bicarb has a limited 'fizz' window) carefully drop a tablespoon of the batter onto the pan. You want the free-form crumpets to be around the circumference of a normal crumpet, but they are likely to be a little thinner.
5. Cook for a couple of minutes, until bubbles start to form on the uncooked surface of the pikelet, then flip over to cook the other side - aim for a light golden brown.

6. If using rings, oil them really well and set the rings onto the hot, oiled pan or griddle. Scoop the batter into the rings and proceed as above. Crumpets will be thicker and will take much longer for the bubbles to form on the uncooked surface, so watch that they don't burn, and they'll need a little longer when you've flipped them.

7. Butter, generously - and enjoy!

In the unlikely event that you have any left, cover them over and toast them later!

BRUSCHETTA & CANAPÉS

We love to make sourdough bruschetta and canapes to serve with drinks for guests - simple, quick and delicious! Add a green leaf and herb salad and you have a light lunch or supper.

For bruschetta: Lightly toast slices of Classic White Sourdough and rub with a cut clove of garlic while still warm. Drizzle with a little good quality extra virgin olive oil and top with your choice of toppings and drizzle with more olive oil:

- Diced tomatoes, torn mozzarella, fresh black pepper, basil leaves
- Finely diced Greek salad, dill
- Griddled courgettes, lemon juice, black pepper, mint
- Roasted red peppers, crumbled feta, stoned Kalamata olives,
- Smashed sardines, diced red onion, lemon juice, flat-leaf parsley.

For canapes: Lightly butter slices of 5-Seeded Spelt Sourdough, cut into quarters and top with your choice of toppings:

- Garlic labneh, chives, smoked salmon, black pepper
- Humus, finely grated carrot, flat leaf parsley
- Brie de Meaux with red onion marmalade
- Smoked mackerel paté with horseradish and red onion
- Chicken liver and garlic paté, cornichons.

CHAPTER SEVEN

IT'S IN YOUR BONES!

"Come to me all you who are weary and burdened and I will restore you."

- A. Boulanger

Did you know that the first restaurant in history (in 1765) was reputed to have been opened by a Frenchman - A. Boulanger - who wanted to provide a nourishing broth to the industrial workers of Paris? Boulanger believed so much in the power of soup that he's said to have put a sign above his establishment encouraging all to come in for sustenance:

'VENITE AD ME VOS QUI STOMACHO LABORATIS ET EGO RESTAURABO VOS'

The translation is in the quote above, and it's thought that Boulanger's sign launched the use of the term restaurant for food establishments.

And now, bone broth is trending; wherever you live, if you're 'hip' you drink bone broth and extol its virtues to anyone who'll listen. It seems that bone broth is the new coffee: we now have 'broth booths' and can readily buy it online – at a price!

What is 'bone broth'?

In essence, bone broth is a humble liquid - just bones and water, simmered for anywhere between two and 48 hours. As a culinary ingredient, it's indispensable to any chef (it's one of the first things we learned to make at Ballymaloe). With the addition of seasonings, it can be taken as it comes or by adding other ingredients (vegetables, herbs, spices), it can be used as the basis for delicious soups, stews, casseroles, curries and more.

Countless health experts are proclaiming the health and healing benefits of traditional broth and are encouraging us get into the habit of consuming it regularly. But is this just all 'brothy' hype, an old wives' tale put about by early French restaurateurs and our grannies? Or is bone broth seriously good medicine? Did Granny know best and is there any basis in science for her traditional food wisdom?

Healing broth - an old wives' tale or a universal folk-wisdom?

Bone broth certainly has history. Even before Boulanger, broths had been used for food and in healing remedies as far back as AD1000. Just about every culture on the planet has used their own version of bone broth as a healing remedy.

Chicken soup or broth - often hailed as 'Jewish penicillin' - has acquired a sterling reputation as a folk remedy for colds and 'flu and is prized by many cultures as go-to comfort food. Jewish people everywhere love their *'goldene yoich'*. In Poland, it's known as *'rosol z kury'*. Italians adore their *'fedelini in brodo'* and in Romania they ask for seconds of *'ciorba de pui'*. Mexicans spice theirs up in *'zopa di fideros'*, while Peruvians enjoy a *'caldo de gallina'*.

Broth: an ancient medicine

Traditional Chinese Medicine has long prized the healing *congee*, a well-cooked, rice-based porridge, often made with stock from chicken feet. It's earned its reputation as stock-on-steroids!

The centuries' old plant and food-based medicine of India, Ayurveda, has prescribed various versions of *kitchari* (a well-cooked broth of rice, mung beans, vegetables and spices) to countless generations for detoxing and restoring weak digestion.

And in the present day, there surely can't be many of us who don't love a good home-made broth. Have you ever wondered why home-made broth warms, comforts and makes us feel safe in a way that no shop-bought soup ever could?

I've been making bone broth therapeutically for several years (have you noticed how expensive it is to buy?) and I use it almost daily in all kinds of delicious ways, but I grew up with my Mum's version of bone broth. Here's my special memory of my mum's chicken soup...

Mum's Chicken Soup

It's early on a Sunday morning when I awake to the rich, comforting aroma of chicken and creep down the stairs. Mum's been busy in the kitchen since dawn, skimming the 'big pot' simmering gently on the stove. Inside sits a plump, glistening cockerel in an aromatic broth of onions, carrots, garlic, black pepper corns and bay leaves. It will sit there for two or three hours, slowly blipping away, leaching its chickeny goodness into the surrounding broth.

Clean white sheets cover every surface of the dining room. Over the sheets are draped huge circles of freshly rolled egg-yellow pasta dough. The circles will be floured, rolled up tightly and cut into thin noodles with a long sharp knife and left to dry in floury, coiled mounds: *fedelini* - 'little faithful ones.'

I settle on the bottom stair and shut my eyes with a warm glow of anticipation. I see the family arriving and gathering around the dining table, chatting and laughing. Mum brings in her best white, wide-rimmed soup plates filled with clear, golden 'brodo' - a perfectly seasoned, clear golden chicken broth ladled from the big pot. In the centre of each bowl, sits a generous nest of fedelini, topped with a sprinkle of pungent chopped parsley. We smile as we lift our spoons for Mum's Chicken Noodle Soup, a universal bowl of 'mother's love'.

Broth: TLC and the 'placebo effect'

One thing's for sure: home-made broth is laced with the 'TLC' factor. Made with love and compassion for the invalid, a broth (or a broth-based meal) is inherently healing. As we saw in the introductory chapter, Ayurvedic tradition counsels that food must be prepared mindfully and with good intentions, because the cook's energy is transmitted to the food. Shamanic traditions hold that we must cook with love to heal with food.

Modernists call this the 'placebo effect' and placebo, as it turns out, is mighty powerful medicine. Increasingly, our modern evidence-based practices are drawing on established and emerging science behind the placebo effect.

Dr David Hamilton, a British, former pharmaceutical research chemist working on developing drugs for cardiovascular disease and cancer, was so intrigued by how the placebo effect works that he changed his career to study the science behind it. He has devoted himself to exploring the effect of visualization, belief and positive thinking on the body, showing how our imagination and mental processes can stimulate our own defences and healing systems to combat disease, pain and illness. In stroke patients, for example, using the mind to visualise moving normally enables damaged areas of the brain to begin to regenerate.[1]

Elsewhere, Dr Lissa Rankin, a former US obstetrician and gynaecologist, has researched and documented the huge body of scientific evidence on the placebo effect and now encourages her patients to write their own prescriptions for healing. Marla, for example, in spite of a super-healthy diet and lifestyle, suffered from four different chronic health conditions. Marla's body was able to heal completely within three months of her leaving a stressful role as a carer and moving close to the sea.[2]

Dr Jo Marchant PhD, a UK medical science journalist, has tracked down the cutting-edge research and the scientists who are studying the effects of the mind on the body, looking at what the mind can really do, how it works and why - and how the latest findings can help patients and ourselves in our daily lives. She cites, for example, how patients who were hypnotised before surgery suffered fewer complications and recovered faster.

And she describes Marette, whose autoimmune lupus put her into heart failure. Marette's condition stabilised and began to improve after her physician 'conditioned' her body to respond to increasing doses of a strongly odoured but harmless drink, paired with decreasing doses of a highly toxic immunosuppressant drug.[3]

So, one way or another, it's looking like Granny got it right; her wisdom was based on generations of experience and of just doing what worked. Now, nutritional science is showing us why it worked, and it is exciting stuff.

Bone broth is a central plank in my own training and practice and I've seen compelling results for gut-related disorders, for arthritis and for skin conditions, as well as autoimmune disorders.[4]

Let's look at how healing happens when tradition meets science

What is the science telling us about the health-giving components of this humble liquid? Here are my top six picks of why broth is so hot:

1. Bone broth's collagen beats the sag

As we age, we all worry about dry and wrinkly skin, dry, flaky nails, thin wispy hair and saggy muscles. We worry about stiff, achy joints and digestive issues like reflux, IBS, IBD and more.

Women (and increasingly men) spend a fortune on face and body creams that contain the magic of collagen that will restore our youthful bloom and on hair and nail products which promise to strengthen, build and protect.

As far as the beauty industry is concerned, collagen is king. It's estimated that nutricosmetics like collagen containing creams will be worth a cool $7billon by 2020.[5]

And collagen is king - it's the most abundant protein in the body and one of the most studied in science. Collagen holds the body together by providing structure and supports strength and cushioning. It's crucial for fabulous hair, skin and nails (enter: the beauty industry) and it makes up bones, teeth, tendons, ligaments, joints and cartilage. It strengthens muscles, helps cell growth and supports the hollow organs of the digestive tract (your oesophagus, stomach, and small and large intestines).

Making bone broth breaks down the collagen into gelatin (a jelly-like substance) making it easily digested and absorbed by our body. Besides being good for hair, nails, skeletal and connective tissue, gelatin helps your digestion by lining the mucous membranes of your digestive tract, protecting and sealing them against damage from food or drinks. And if that wasn't enough, it increases the nutritional value of other foods that you eat with it. Indeed, there's an old wisdom that a small cup of broth should be consumed with every meal.

After the age of 20, our production of collagen declines by around 1% annually and stress and autoimmune conditions further reduce our ability to produce collagen.

2. Bone broth pre-digests proteins and other nutrients - so you don't have to

- Proteins (amino acids)

Proteins are made up of building blocks called amino acids. They're needed to make and repair every tissue and organ in our body. The amino acids key to collagen are glycine, proline and glutamine - glycine plays a critical role in fuelling the liver's detoxification processes.[6]

Glycine is used to make haemoglobin in the red blood cells that carry oxygen around your body (and give blood its red colour). It is also needed to produce bile salts and in the secretion of gastric acid to aid digestion.

Proline supports skin health - especially when paired with vitamin C.

Glutamine provides food for your intestinal lining and amazingly can actually regenerate it. And, when taken as a supplement on an empty stomach, it can help diarrhoea. So, move over Imodium!

- Minerals

When it comes to minerals, calcium tends to hog the limelight. But for sound bone and overall health, we need a full range of minerals - magnesium, potassium, sulphur, selenium, iron, phosphorus, zinc, copper and more - plentiful in bone broth and easily absorbable.

- Glycosaminoglycans (GAGs) - Hyaluronic acid

Hyaluronic acid is highly prized by the beauty industry and we pay dearly for products containing it. It's a glycosaminoglycan and provides lubrication and cushioning for skin, joints, muscles and eyes. Other well-known examples of GAGs are glucosamine and chondroitin sulphate - often taken as expensive supplements for joint health. Bone broth provides us a great source of these nutrients at very little cost.

- Healthy fats

Bone marrow, skin and pasture-fed fatty meats are chock-full of mood-satisfying and brain-health-supporting healthy fats. These healthy fats are crucial for carrying the fat-soluble vitamins A, D, E, and K into your body, and because they're so satisfying, they help keep your weight down. You could do worse than to opt for a cup of delicious, home-made bone broth over one of those fake, full-of who-knows-what processed meal replacements.

3. Bone broth is a seriously 'intelligent' food

Our ancestors always knew this wisdom and now modern nutritional science is showing us that when we eat a specific part of an animal, it nourishes that same part of our body.

- Smart nutrition for eyes

Did you know that fish stock - made with intact fish heads as well as other bones - yields optimum nutrition for our eyes? The tissue in the back of the eyeball contains the highest source of available vitamin A, known specifically to support healthy eyesight.[7]

Forget carrots - they contain only the pre-cursor to vitamin A, which our body then needs to convert to actual vitamin A and many of us (especially infants and older people) struggle to do this efficiently, if at all. If you have trouble with night vision, make fish head broths - great in fish soups and seafood risottos. For the very best source of vitamin A, see the chapter on Meat and Offal ... and eat more liver!

- Smart nutrition for kidney and adrenal function

Age-old wisdom from Traditional Chinese Medicine (TCM) tells us that bone broth nourishes our kidneys, supports our vital essence and builds blood.

In TCM, bone (and teeth) tissue relates to the kidney-adrenal system and therefore consuming bone broth will support kidney and adrenal function. Dr Catherine Shanahan (*Deep Nutrition: Why Your Genes Need Traditional Food*) suggests that bone broth may actually patch the holes in damaged kidney tissue which causes sub-optimal kidney function.

- Smart nutrition for bones and teeth

Bone broth contains the same minerals, in proper proportion, as our teeth. Calcium and phosphorous (the two main tooth minerals) make up around 65% of bone broth.

So when you notice that the bones in your broth are soft and yielding (after hours, even days of cooking), you can be sure that it's yielded all of its bone and tooth-nourishing minerals. And provided your diet has sufficient minerals, your saliva can re-mineralise your teeth and heal tooth decay and gum disease. Gum disease is the primary reason for adult tooth loss, so this is great news.

In fact, tooth decay and gum disease are related: both involve the deterioration of bone and connective tissue. If left untreated, gum disease breaks down the bone which acts as a foundation for teeth, and eventually, the teeth fall out.[8]

You might be thinking: why didn't my dentist tell me this!? Well, one reason (you may be able to guess at others) is that our modern diets are so impoverished in optimal minerals that the concept of tooth re-mineralisation is largely absent and not well-understood in our culture.[9]

4. Bone broth is a natural, beautifying flavour enhancer

No matter what it says on the label, any processed stock or bouillon will contain preservatives and processing chemicals which don't need to be listed on the label. Have you noticed that the flavour enhancer monosodium glutamate (MSG) is often found in stock cubes and a host of other processed foods? It's not the same as the naturally occurring glutamine in bone broth, rather it's an excitotoxin which messes with your body and particularly your brain.[10]

Making your own natural flavour enhancer (bone broth) delivers not only clean flavour, but health and beauty too.

5. Bone broth is budget, animal and planet-friendly

The (completely illogical) preference that we've developed for expensive choice cuts and lean meats has not only impoverished our health, their expense has also emptied our purses and spawned the growth of inhumane, intensive factory farms.

Back in Granny's day, we ate nose-to-tail. Not only were we healthier from eating all the parts of the animal and those nutritious slow-cooked and gelatinous cuts on the bone, but we ate more cheaply: a whole cow, for example, would feed a family for the year!

6. Bone broth is 'anti-stress'

The science here is a little tricky, but stick with me, as it's important to understand why we need to eat nose-to-tail.

Eat lean, fight mean? In our modern-day Western diet, we've developed a preference for eating high-protein, lean muscle meats; two of our favourites are steaks and chicken breast. We've come to believe (or been brain-washed?) that lean meat is healthiest, but here's the thing: eating large amounts of lean muscle meat stresses our body.

Here's the story:

Around 20% of the substance of our body is made of protein which plays a crucial role in almost every biological process in the body. Amino acids are the building blocks of protein and they make up a large proportion of our cells, muscles and tissues.

All lean muscle meats - like steak, chicken breast and our own muscles too - contain high levels of the amino-acid tryptophan. In turn, tryptophan is the key ingredient in making the neurotransmitter serotonin, involved in regulating a stable mood. Put simply, having sufficient serotonin has become associated with maintaining our mood and its deficiency is associated with depression.

However, as we've seen in the Meat chapter, having excess tryptophan and serotonin produces a broad range of harmful effects: inflammation, immuno-depression, fibrosis, neurological damage, cancer, bronchoconstriction, hypertension and impaired learning and generally the same changes seen in ageing. So, munching through copious steaks or chicken breasts will tip the scales in favour of excessive amino acids and will stress our body. Clearly, this is not good.

When we're under any kind of stress, our digestion slows or shuts down (a primal response, as our body prepares to 'run-from-the-bear') and we produce large amounts of cortisol, a catabolic hormone, which breaks down our own muscles to provide us with energy and material for cellular repair while we're running-from-the-bear. It's a sorry fact that so many of us live with chronic stress from our modern lifestyles and toxic environment.

When we regularly eat large amounts of muscle meats, even more cortisol is released as our body tries to break down the muscle protein and more tryptophan and serotonin is released.

This, together with the high circulating levels of tryptophan/serotonin from chronic lifestyle stress, eventually sets up a toxic cycle which suppresses our thyroid function - reducing the efficiency of every cell in our body; promoting leaky gut, muscle and joint pain; and ultimately decreases our ability to withstand stress.[11]

The message to take-home is this: eating a lot of lean protein regularly is stressful for our bodies, particularly if we are already struggling with the added burden of a stress-promoting lifestyle and stress-promoting health issues.

Enter our anti-stress 'hero': gelatin to the rescue!

The amino acid glycine found in abundance in gelatin contains no tryptophan and is anti-inflammatory and protective. Glycine has a variety of anti-stress actions throughout the body, promoting natural sleep, helping recovery from strokes and seizures, improving learning and memory and is generally anti-ageing.

> **"The range of injuries produced by an excess of tryptophan and serotonin seems to be prevented or corrected by a generous supply of glycine. Fibrosis, free radical damage, inflammation, cell death from ATP depletion or calcium overload, mitochondrial damage, diabetes, etc. can be prevented or alleviated by glycine."**

- Dr Ray Peat
Tryptophan, Serotonin & Ageing - raypeat.com

So, bone broth is an all-round nutritional big hitter and powerful medicine. Once again, good science is proving the case for our grannies' traditional food wisdom.

If all else fails, reach for grass-fed gelatin powder

Nutritionally, there's really no substitute for the complete amino acid profile found in a properly made bone broth. While making your own is obviously your first - and least expensive - option, there are now a number of excellent bone broths on the market and available online.

However, when life overtakes our best intentions and our budget is tight, rather than miss out on bone broth's amazing nutritional benefits, there is a food-based supplement available in the form of powdered gelatin.

We're all familiar with the powdered or sheet gelatin we use to make liquids gel for desserts and so on, but gelatin isn't just for jelly - although home-made jelly made with real, organic fruit is actually very good for you.

Grass-fed, powdered gelatin is a nutritious and effective supplement - and it's one of the very few I'd recommend. Although it doesn't have the complete amino-acid profile of bone broth, it does provide the non-inflammatory, protective amino acids that are missing from the lean muscle meat proteins that we're over-consuming.

There are two types of powdered gelatin:

Regular/traditional gelatin - this form of gelatin is tasteless and is soluble in hot water but it will set when cold. Use this to make jellies, desserts like panna cotta, marshmallows and gummy bears. However, too much too soon may give a digestive upset (see below).

Collagen hydrolysate - this form of gelatin is tasteless and doesn't set, so it's great for adding to any sweet or savoury, hot or cold liquids - you can add it to all drinks, soups, sauces, stews and casseroles. I personally use only grass-fed gelatin, easily available from online retailers.

How often and how much gelatin? Ideally, we need to consume gelatin every day for optimum health, either in the form of bone broth or powdered gelatin.

Those with a weak digestion would do better to start with a slow-cooked bone broth and gradually work up to a mixture of broth and collagen hydrolysate and avoid large amounts of regular gelatin.[12]

To aid the proper digestion of gelatin, it needs to be taken with a source of fats (such as coconut oil, ghee, or butter) and some carbohydrates (such as white rice) to stimulate strong digestive juices and properly utilise the protein.

Bone Broth vs Stock - what's the difference?

Some say stock; some say bone broth. It's confusing and does it matter? Actually, it does matter if you're looking to use broth therapeutically.

Culinary stock

Culinary stock is the foundation for flavour. Auguste Escoffier said:

> **"Indeed, stock is everything in cooking. Without it, nothing can be done."**

Culinary stock is basically meat stock, but the focus is on producing intense flavour rather than a healing medicine. Depending on the purpose of the stock, chefs will add all kinds of vegetables and aromatics herbs and spices.

Meat Stock

Meat stock is made with meat on the bone, with ligaments and gelatinous tissue still attached. It can be cooked without the addition of vegetables, but it's obviously going to be tastier with them. Meat stock needs to be short cooked (6-10 hours depending on whether it's chicken or beef) at a bare simmer.

Meat stock aids digestion by promoting the secretion of hydrochloric acid to break down proteins and is rich in gut-healing gelatin and in the anti-inflammatory amino acids proline and glycine.

This is particularly important for those following autoimmune diets or the GAPS Intro Diet[13], who need gut-healing meat stock - rather than bone broth - for reasons explained below.

Bone Broth

Bone broth, on the other hand, is longer cooked (often for more than 48 hours, and up to 72) at a bare simmer. Cider vinegar is added to help extract the minerals from the bones. It's also rich in gelatin and richer than meat stock in amino acids and minerals. It's also considered a milk replacement for those with lactose intolerance.

However, with longer cooking, glutamine and glutamic acid are produced. These free glutamates can cause digestive issues: provoking a die-off reaction in those with gut dysbiosis; exacerbating symptoms in those with compromised digestive systems (leaky gut, Crohn's disease); and provoking a neuro-toxic reaction in those who are sensitive to MSG and children on the autistic spectrum.

Unless digestion is strong, and no other symptoms are evident, it's better to start out with meat stock and transition to bone broth when the gut has healed sufficiently.

A word about the provenance of your bones

As we saw in the Soil chapter, the nutritional quality of our food depends entirely on the conditions under which is was raised, grown or produced. Like any other part of the animal, the health and nutritional value of the bones will reflect how the animal has been raised.

The quality of meat stocks and bone broths made from the bones of animals raised on diverse, organic or unsprayed pasture is a million miles away from those made from animals raised conventionally, where their feed is likely to be GM and contaminated with the pesticide glyphosate.

In fact, we'd do well to take heed of a recent study by Samsel and Seneff[14] on the inadvertent ingestion of glyphosate from bone broth and collagen supplements or foods. Their study confirmed that glyphosate accumulates in bones, ligaments and collagen and they discuss how glycine, the most prevalent amino acid in collagen, is likely to be replaced by glyphosate residues.

As we know, soya and corn provide the protein requirement in conventional animal feeds and the crops are desiccated with glyphosate pre-harvest. The authors conclude that this feature can explain the epidemic of allergies to foods that are likely to contain high amounts of glyphosate contamination, such as gluten, casein, soya and corn.

Bone broth, collagen supplements and collagen containing foods are widely available in health food stores and from online vendors and increasingly in supermarkets. Please do your research and source the best and cleanest quality you can, i.e. those products that have been fed only organic feed, are certified organic or 100% grass-fed.

How to store meat stock/bone broth

Always cool stock or broth as quickly as possible by placing your covered stock-pot in a sink of cold water. As soon as it's cool, decant the stock into clean, wide-necked, freezer-safe containers. The fat which rises to the top of the broth is useful for sealing the broth as it sets hard, but you can skim it off if you wish and save it for frying or roasting - it's delicious and healthy.

Fat-sealed stock/broth will keep in the fridge for a couple of weeks. Once the fat is disturbed or removed, the stock needs to be used within five to seven days. It will keep in the freezer for six months. To thaw, place the container in cold water until the frozen contents are loose enough to be popped into a saucepan. Bring up to the boil and simmer for a few minutes before use, skimming if necessary.

12 Cool Ways to Use Bone Broth

1. Drink it straight-up. Add plenty of salt, pepper, other seasonings, spices or herbs and drink a small cup with every meal.

2. Drink 'pimped up' bone broth (see the recipe section).

3. Use bone broth in soups. This must be the #1 use for bone broth and takes any soup to a new dimension.

4. Use bone broth in braises, casseroles, stews, ragù, chillies, curries and forget cubes, sachets, boxes or cans. If the recipe calls for liquid, reach for bone broth. And when re-heating, loosen up the consistency by adding more broth.

5. Use bone broth in gravy/sauces - just reduce the broth by boiling rapidly, season well and add arrowroot to thicken for a grain-free sauce.

6. Add bone broth to cream-based sauces - add up to half bone broth when making cream or cheese sauces.

7. Add bone broth to tomato-based sauces - instead of using chopped tomato or passata, dilute tomato purée or tomato paste with bone broth.

8. Cook your vegetables in bone broth - add broth, a little at a time, to steam-fry your veggies and infuse them with deliciousness.

9. Cook rice with broth instead of water. So delicious you'll want to make a meal of it.

10. Cook and mash potatoes, cauliflower, cauliflower 'rice' and other root veg. in, or with, bone broth (and use in place of milk if you're dairy-free).

11. Add bone broth to egg dishes - replace some (or all) of the water or milk with bone broth when scrambling eggs, making a quiche or frittata.

12. Soak in a bone broth bath at the end of a long day... while slurping a bowl of ramen noodles - just kidding!

Actually, it's true - 'Ramen baths' are big in Japan. The Japanese love bone broth - it's the basis of ramen noodle and other dishes - and it seems they're diving head first (almost literally!) into bone broth baths. A canny spa owner in Hakone, Japan believes it could catch on as fun treatment that exposes his customers, increasingly concerned with their skin, to tons and tons of collagen.[15]

BONE BROTH Recipes

CHICKEN STOCK & BONE BROTH

Chicken stock is short cooked (2-4 hours) and features the anti-inflammatory, gut-healing amino acids proline and glycine, and gelatin.

Chicken broth is longer cooked (often in excess of 48 hours and up to 72) with the aid of cider vinegar and, thanks to the longer cooking time, is rich in minerals and in gelatin - but it's also rich in 'free glutamates' which cause problems for gut sensitive and gut compromised individuals.

Unless digestion is strong - and no other symptoms are evident - it's better to start out with meat stock and transition to bone broth when the gut has healed sufficiently.

Supermarkets aren't the only ones with 'buy-one-get-one-free' offers: you can get double the value of your chicken bones and make both chicken *stock* and bone *broth*. When you've made and sieved your delicious chicken meat stock, you can pick the meat off the bones, put the bones back into the pan (adding a few more bones and more vegetables and a shot of apple cider vinegar, to help leach the minerals from the bones) and make your longer cooked chicken bone broth.

All kinds of chicken bones make stock:

- Raw bones and carcasses - cooked from raw
- For a richer flavour, roasted raw bones - roast uncovered for 20-30 mins
- Bones from carcasses saved from roast chicken (you can freeze them)
- A mixture of both - the more the merrier!

Therapeutic stocks and broth:

If you're making bone broth or meat stock as a gut healing remedy, it's best to cook the bones from raw. Adding a couple of chicken feet or a pig's foot is optional but will enrich the gelatin content of the stock or broth and ensure it gels up nicely.

What you'll need:

For Chicken Meat Stock (short-cooked):
Chicken: 1 kg (whole/thighs + meaty backs/carcass)
Whole chicken feet: 2-3 (optional, but packed with gelatin) OR 1 pig's foot (optional, but packed with gelatin)
White onion: 1 large (roughly chopped)
Carrots: 3-4 medium (peeled*, roughly chopped)
Celery: 3-4 sticks (roughly chopped)
Black peppercorns: 1 tbsp
Cloves: 6 (whole)
Garlic: 2 cloves (peeled, roughly bashed)
Fresh ginger: 3-6 cm (peeled, thinly sliced)
Parsley stalks: ½ handful
Filtered/mineral water: enough to cover the bones by about 5cm

For Chicken Bone Broth (long-cooked):
All picked bones & whole feet
Chicken bones: 1-2 kg**
White onion: 1 large (roughly chopped)
Carrots: 3-4 medium (peeled, roughly chopped)
Celery: 3-4 sticks (roughly chopped)
Black peppercorns: 1 tbsp
Cloves: 6 (whole)
Garlic: 2 cloves (peeled, roughly bashed)
Parsley stalks: 1 handful
Filtered/mineral water: enough to cover the bones by about 5cm
Organic apple cider vinegar: 3 tbsp

**Carrot skins can make the broth bitter.*
***Use the larger quantity if you have no bones from the meat stock.*

What to do:

For Chicken Meat Stock:

1. Put all the ingredients into a large stock pot, a large Dutch oven, or a slow cooker.

2. Slowly bring up just to the boil and simmer VERY slowly. Depending on the size of your whole chicken (if using), cook on the stove top on a low heat (the stock should just 'blip')

or in a low oven for 2 - 4 hours; or for 8 about hours in a slow cooker (following the appropriate instructions for yours).

3. Let the stock cool down and carefully strain the contents of the pan through a colander. Leave any chicken feet or pigs feet intact and pick the meat off the other bones. Set aside the meat and the bones/intact feet separately.

4. Gently take out the vegetables and set aside. Sieve the strained liquid stock through a fine mesh strainer - it's now ready to use.

5. Use the stock, meat and vegetables in a soup or recipe of your choice. If not using straight away, cool the stock to room temperature and transfer to convenient sized containers.

6. Refrigerate for up to 5 days or freeze for up to 6 months. Any fat which rises to the top can be used with the stock or skimmed off.

7. If you're going on to make Chicken Bone Broth, return the picked bones and any feet to the pan and proceed as below. If not, you can freeze them for a later batch of broth.

For Chicken Bone Broth:

1. Put all the ingredients into a large stock pot, a large Dutch Oven, or a slow cooker.

2. Slowly bring up just to the boil and simmer VERY slowly. Cook on the stove top on a low heat (the stock should just gently 'blip'); in a low oven; or a slow cooker for at least 48 and up to 72 hours (following the appropriate instructions for your slow cooker).

3. Follow the steps above for straining, sieving and storing your bone broth, discarding any solids.

BEEF MEAT STOCK & BEEF BONE BROTH

Beef stock is short cooked (6 - 10 hours) and is rich in the anti-inflammatory and gut-healing amino acids *proline* and *glycine* and in *gelatin*.

Beef broth (as with chicken broth) is longer cooked (48 and up to 72 hours) with the aid of cider vinegar and again, thanks to the longer cooking, is not only rich in minerals and in gelatin, but it's also rich in free glutamates, which cause problems for gut sensitive and gut compromised individuals.

Unless digestion is strong and no other symptoms are evident, it's better to start out with meat stock and transition to bone broth when the gut has healed sufficiently.

Again, you can get double the value of your beef bones and make both meat *stock* and bone *broth*. When you've made and sieved your delicious beef meat stock, you can pick the meat off the bones, put them (the bones) back into the pan, add a few more bones and more vegetables and a shot of apple cider vinegar (to help leach the minerals from the bones) and make your longer cooked beef bone broth!

Which beef bones to use? All kinds...

- Raw bones: meaty bones from rib, sirloin, brisket, shin and oxtail; marrow bones and knuckles, joints with cartilaginous and connective tissue attached
- Roasted raw bones: roast uncovered for 20-30 mins for a richer, darker stock
- Bones saved from previous roasts and braises: rib, sirloin, brisket, shin (you can freeze them)
- A mixture of everything: the more the merrier!

Size matters

Remember to ask your butcher (or farmer) to cut the bones up into pieces which will actually fit into your pot - or you'll find yourself outside wielding a hacksaw! Don't forget to add apple cider vinegar to the bone broth to help leach the minerals from the bones. Note the recipe doesn't call for salt - add this to your stock or broth when using it in a recipe.

Therapeutic stocks and broth:

If you're making bone broth or meat stock as a gut healing remedy, it's best to cook the bones from raw. Adding a couple of chicken feet or a pig's foot is optional and will enrich the gelatin content of the beef stock or broth and ensure it gels up nicely.

What you'll need:

For the Beef Meat Stock (Short-cooked)
Meat beef bones: 1 kg

Chicken feet: 2-3 (whole, trimmed - gelatin rich, helps stock to gel) OR Pig's Foot: 1 optional; gelatin rich, helps stock to gel)
White onion: 1 large (roughly chopped)
Carrots: 3-4 medium (peeled*, roughly chopped)
Celery: 3-4 sticks (roughly chopped)
Black pepper corns: 1 tablespoon (whole)
Cloves: 6 (whole)
Garlic: 2 cloves (peeled, smashed)
Parsley stalks: 1 handful
Filtered/mineral water: enough to cover the bones by about 5cm

For the Beef Bone Broth (Long-cooked):
Picked bones & whole feet (from above beef meat stock)
Beef bones of choice: 1-2 kgs.**
White onion: 1 large (prepared as for stock)
Medium carrots: 2-3 (prepared as for stock)
Celery: 3-4 sticks (prepared as for stock)
Black pepper corns: 1 tablespoon (whole)
Cloves: 6 (whole)
2 cloves garlic (prepared as for stock)
Parsley stalks: 1 handful
Filtered/mineral water: enough to cover the bones by about 5cm
Apple cider vinegar: 3 tablespoons

**Carrot peelings can make the broth/stock bitter*
***Use the larger quantity if you have no bones from the meat stock*

What to do:

Beef Meat Stock:

1. Put all the ingredients into a large stock pot, a large Dutch Oven, or a slow cooker.

2. Slowly bring up just to the boil and simmer VERY slowly. Cook on the stove top on a low heat (the stock should just 'blip'), or in a low oven for 6 - 10 hours; or for this equivalent in a slow cooker (following the appropriate instructions for yours).

3. Let the stock cool down and carefully strain the contents of the pan through a colander. Leave any chicken feet or pigs feet intact and pick the meat off the other bones and remove the marrow from any marrow bone. Set aside the meat and the bones/intact feet separately. Gently take out the vegetables and set aside.

4. Sieve the strained liquid stock through a fine mesh strainer - it's now ready to use.

5. Use the stock, meat and vegetables in a recipe of your choice. If not using straight away, cool the stock to room temperature and transfer to convenient sized containers. Refrigerate for up to 5 days or freeze for up to 6 months. Any fat which rises to the top can be used with the stock, or skimmed off and used for sautéing or roasting

6. If you're going on to make beef bone broth, return the picked bones and any feet to the pan and carry on as below. If not, you can freeze them for a later batch of bone broth.

Beef Bone Broth:

1. Put all the ingredients into a large stock pot, a large Dutch Oven, or a slow cooker.

2. slowly bring up just to the boil and simmer VERY slowly. Cook on the stove top on a low heat (the stock should just 'blip'); in a low oven; or in a slow cooker for at least another 48 hours and up to 72 hours, or this equivalent in a slow cooker (follow the appropriate instructions for your slow cooker).

3. Follow the steps above for straining, sieving and storing your bone broth, discarding any solids.

What to do next?

I've suggested 12 ways to enjoy your delicious, healing stocks and broths in Chapter Seven.

PROPER GRAVY - THE BONE BROTH WAY

What you'll need:

Ghee or organic, grass-fed butter: 2 tbsp
Yellow onions: 2 large (roughly chopped)
Garlic: 5 cloves (minced)
Fresh sage: 1 tbsp (minced)
Fresh thyme: 1 tbsp (minced)
Fresh rosemary: 1 tbsp (minced)
Red wine: 2 tbsp

Bone broth: 4 cups
Sea salt: ½ tsp (Maldon, to taste)
Freshly ground black pepper: ½ tsp (adjust to taste)

What to do:

1. Melt ghee or butter in a pot over medium heat and add onions. Cook for 15 minutes or until the onions begin to turn golden brown.

2. Add the garlic and herbs and sauté for a minute. Then add the red wine to deglaze the pan.

3. Add the bone broth and increase the heat to high. Once the mixture comes to a boil, reduce the heat to a simmer. Cover the pot and cook for 20-30 minutes, or until the mixture reduces by half.

4. Place the remaining sauce into a blender. Puree until smooth.

CHAPTER EIGHT

KEEP CALM and EAT YOUR FRUIT and VEG!

"The act of eating is very political. You buy from the right people, you support the right network of farmers and suppliers who care about the land and what they put in the food.

With vegetables, you have to be careful where they come from; you have to know the farmers and trust them. If you buy from the farmers' market, it's already been investigated."

- Alice Waters
American chef, restaurateur and author

Both vegetables and meat contribute to our optimum nutrition. In her book *Vegetarianism Explained*, Dr Natasha Campbell-McBride - neurologist, nutritionist, clinical practitioner, author and my Certified GAPS Practitioner teacher - has done an excellent job of explaining, very simply and clearly, why and how we humans, as omnivores, have evolved to eat whatever we could find in our immediate environment - both plant *and* animal foods.

Foods that build and foods that cleanse and heal

In line with evolutionary wisdom, Mother Nature has provided us with plant foods and animal foods; but we need to understand how these food groups work differently in the body.

Animal foods - meat, fish, eggs, dairy - are rich in proteins and fats and build the structural foundation of our body: our bones, brain, muscles, heart, and organs.

Plant-based foods are Mother Nature's pharmacy. They contain a rich source of a wide variety of nutrients, including vitamins, macro, micro and trace minerals, dietary fibre and important phytonutrients (protective plant chemicals). These nutrients work together to provide us with energy in the form of glucose, co-factors in the formation of vitamins and minerals (we get these from animal foods too) and fibre for healthy digestive and bowel function. They also help support our immune and cardiovascular systems. With their many medicinal properties, plants clean and detoxify our body and help protect us from chronic disease, especially when consumed raw and in juices*.

In addition, we are learning more and more about the nutritional power of traditional foods which may be novel to us in the West, like mushrooms, seaweeds, algae, bee propolis and honey and of course, fermented vegetables.

**However, before you rush off and start a juice detox, know that raw foods are difficult to digest and can cause issues for those with a weak digestion - so if you're drawn to this, do your research and read Dr Natasha's books before you start!*

Make some room for mushrooms

We're all familiar with the culinary use of mushrooms, but it's well worth dedicating a few words here to their important medicinal benefits. In fact, mushrooms aren't actually a vegetable, they're the fruiting body of fungi and are neither plant nor animal, but they are more closely related to humans than to plants. Fungi comprise a huge variety of organisms and it's estimated that there are around 140,000 species of known mushroom-bearing fungi across the globe and of these, around 2000 species are considered edible and/or medicinal.

Fungi absorb nutrition from other organisms and serve a critical role as ecological decomposers, supporting soil health and ecosystems. Fungi have been used for thousands of years in the culinary and health practices of Japanese and Traditional Chinese Medicine and were highly prized by the Ancient Egyptians. Nutritional research has only recently been getting to grips with the tremendous the health benefits of these incredibly diverse organisms and we're going to be hearing much more about them. Studies show that mushrooms not only provide us with key nutrients like protein, fibre, B vitamins, vitamin C, minerals and phytonutrients, but they also support our gut health, immune system and help us to reduce stress.

All varieties of edible organic mushrooms (such as button and portabellas) offer benefits, but it's the significant health benefits of Asian varieties like *shiitake, reishi* and *cordyceps* that has attracted most research. Specific varieties can support liver disorders, arthritic conditions and demonstrate anti-allergic, anti-inflammatory, anti-viral, anti-bacterial, and antioxidant and powerful anti-tumoural properties.[1]

Mushrooms are a great addition to omelettes, creamy sauces, Asian soups and in chicken casseroles.[2] A wide variety of fresh, dried and extracted mushroom products (like coffees, teas, cacaos and elixirs), together with a plethora of recipes, can all be found online.[3]

Lately, fruits and vegetables have been dragged into what has become a strongly polarised debate between diet gurus who, on one hand are aggressively demonising particular foods and those who vehemently believe that these same foods are the very ones we should all be eating.

Some 'experts', often of the low carb/high fat persuasion, insist that fruit and many varieties of vegetables are chock-full of those wicked carbohydrates and wreak havoc with our blood sugar, weight and our general health. *"Let's restrict or avoid them completely*!" they shriek.

Others insist that these very same foods form the basis of a healthy diet: *"We should all be eating more of them, or even eating them exclusively!"* comes the cry from the high carb/low fat, plant-based contingent.

Confusion reigns, but who is right? The answer could be neither or both. What and how much of these foods you should eat depends entirely on your metabolic needs and your skill in listening to your body.

> **"Any diet you follow is not set in stone, you have to adapt it for your unique body, for its unique daily needs … One day you may feel like only an apple for breakfast; but the next day you may enjoy a large cooked breakfast … At one meal, you were happy to eat some roasted pork, but at another meal you do not feel like eating meat and are much happier to eat vegetables and yoghurt."**

- Dr Natasha Campbell-McBride
Vegetarianism Explained

Dr Campbell-McBride firmly believes that Mother Nature, through human evolution, has given our body the wisdom to communicate its nutritional requirements through our senses of smell, taste and the desire for a particular food, and our sense of satisfaction after eating it - but we need to learn to listen. I wholeheartedly agree with Natasha - our bodies are far wiser than our muddled brains.

Here's what I believe to be at the root of arguments about fruits and vegetables:

Fruit and veg in context

In the West, we've earned the reputation of being over-fed but under-nourished and successive generations have come to subsist on convenient, refined carbohydrate and sugar-rich, ultra-processed, hyper-palatable 'fake' foods.

The food tech and manufacturing industry spend eye-watering amounts of money, expertise and effort in developing, manufacturing and marketing cheap, refined carb-cocktails, laden with every conceivable variety of refined sugar, industrial-grade salt, chemical additives, preservatives and flavourings. Physiologically, these fake foods need little or no effort to digest as they are ultra-processed; they're also manufactured to be hyper-palatable, making us want more by satisfying what has become known in the food industry as our 'bliss-point'. These same fake foods are then packaged attractively and cleverly promoted with trigger words like 'healthy,' 'natural' and 'free-from'.

Over time, these products have slowly eroded our innate ability to hear our body's wisdom and millions of us have developed a carbohydrate and sugar 'addiction' that has destroyed our innate ability to distinguish the smell, taste, desire and satisfaction of the real, whole, nutrient-dense foods that our body needs and craves.

These kinds of refined and highly-processed carbohydrates (like snack foods, white and brown breads and pasta, processed cereals, pastries, cakes and other products made with refined white flour, sweets and confectionery and sugar-sweetened beverages) are at best nutritionally impoverished and at worst, they're nutritionally worthless. Despite this, clever food technology design and smart marketing has meant that we now can't help over-consuming these worthless but extremely profitable products.

You well might ask what all this has to do with fruit and vegetables. They're healthy, surely?

Well, yes, and no. Food consumerism and global supply chains have given us ready access, at any time of year, to almost any variety of fruit and veg from any part of the world. So, not only have we got used to over-consuming the highly-refined and processed carbs and sugars described above, we've also forgotten that traditional, local fruit and vegetables were foods to be consumed in season when fully ripe, sweet and easy to digest.

Our once-abundant varieties of wholesome, indigenous, heritage fruit and vegetables have slowly been replaced by vast monocultures of conventionally grown fruit and veg. These have been selectively hybridised to be far sweeter that traditional varieties, in order to appeal to the increasingly 'sweet' tooth, nicely nurtured by our love of highly-refined and ultra-processed carbs. Clever, joined up thinking, eh?

Putting all these elements together, it's not difficult to see why some experts are pointing the finger at modern fruit and vegetable consumption - particularly those high in carbohydrates - for heaping yet more damage onto our already refined and ultra-processed, carb-loaded bodies.

Processed vs whole foods

There can no longer be any question that our over-consumption of highly refined and processed carbs and the enormous amount of hidden sugar - by every name - in processed foods, has displaced critical nutrients in our diet. At the same time, whole fruits and whole vegetables do have a very important place in the human diet.

The 'natural' food chain

In the Soil chapter, we saw how the sun's energy and photosynthesis acts on plants to provide plant-based nutrients for our herbivorous animal friends. Looking at the digestion of food through an evolutionary lens, herbivores and the ruminant animals that we commonly eat - cattle, sheep, goats - have evolved a complex and lengthy digestive system which, structurally and functionally, is able to masticate, digest and absorb the tough cellulose plant matter. Their gut bacteria then break down a large percentage of this carbohydrate content into short-chain fatty acids - saturated fats - which build and sustain their bodies. Imagine that - the main source of energy for herbivores is actually high fat!

In turn humans, in common with other predators (whether we like to be associated with this term or not!) have evolved a much shorter digestive apparatus, which is able to chew, digest, absorb and preferentially thrive, on animal foods and to use plant foods as an important but supplemental part of our diet.

The wisdom of eating with the seasons

Mother Nature has seen to it that our planet provides us with foods which will best nourish us for each and every season. Our job is to remember that we are a part of nature and we need to reconnect with her wisdom by listening to our body and learning to follow our intuition.

Just as there is no 'one-diet-fits-all' there are foods for different seasons - foods which yield their optimum nutritional potential when eaten in season. When we adjust our diet to each season, not only do we benefit from this potential, but our health-promoting digestive microbes dramatically change too!

Seasonal Fruit and Veg calendar

Each month's best:

January	Carrots, kale
February	Leeks, savoy cabbage
March	Spring greens, cabbage
April	Cauliflower
May	Asparagus, Jersey royal potatoes, rhubarb
June	Broad beans, strawberries, peas
July	Curly lettuce, cucumber, cherries
August	Cos lettuce, raspberries, plums
September	Courgettes, blackberries, runner beans
October	Cox's apples, sweetcorn
November	Red cabbage, potatoes
December	Brussels sprouts, white cabbage

The wisdom of ancient wisdom

Back in the day, our ancestors intuitively followed a diet to reflect the incoming - our forbearers just 'knew' what to do. But now, we tend to hang our dietary hooks on nutritional dogma, the latest trend, or a stoic belief in a single 'healthy' diet. We forget that, as smart as we think we are, we are an inextricable part of this planet and its natural cycles - and that goes for our food too.

To the old school - those with the benefit of traditional food wisdom and the followers of ancient life-sciences, like Ayurveda - this makes perfect sense:

"The concept of 'food as medicine' is rooted in our most ancient of healing traditions, including Greek, Indian and Chinese medicine. If we consider the anthropological evidence, it is very likely that our hunter-gatherer ancestors learned about medicinal herbs by observing wild animals deliberately eating certain plants in their diet as a way to treat different health issues. For all of nature and throughout the history of medicine there has never been any real separation between food and medicine."

- Todd Caldecott
The Theory & Practise of Food

The wisdom of eating organic fruit and veg

We saw in the Soil chapter how conventional farming and growing methods have all but destroyed the integrity and health of our soils, decimated soil microbial life and depleted the mineral and micronutrients available to us through our food. While research evidence on how this translates into the nutritional quality of our food and the impact of this on our health is far from abundant, it is beginning to come through.

The Pesticide Action Network analysed the School Fruit and Vegetable Scheme; their recent report *Food for Thought* (September 2017) had this to say:

> **"Children in England are being exposed to a cocktail of pesticide residues in the fresh produce they receive through the Department of Health's School Fruit and Vegetable Scheme (SFVS). These pesticides have documented potential to harm human health, especially the health of young children who are particularly vulnerable to their impacts.**
>
> **Residues of 123 different pesticides were found, some of which are linked to serious health problems such as cancer and disruption of the hormone system. In many cases, multiple residues were found on the produce. This is another area of serious concern as the scientific community has little understanding about the complex interaction of different chemicals in what is termed the 'cocktail' effect."**

The full report, together with summary tables showing the pesticide residues found in common varieties of fruits and vegetables, is available on their website.[4]

In 2018, researchers reported on a study of 325 women undergoing infertility treatment with assisted reproductive technology (ART). They found that intake of high-pesticide residue fruits and vegetables (FVs) was associated with a lower probability of live birth, while low-pesticide residue fruit and vegetable intake was not associated with this outcome. They concluded that:

> **"Higher consumption of high-pesticide residue FVs was associated with lower probabilities of pregnancy and live birth following infertility treatment with ART. These data suggest that dietary pesticide exposure within the range of typical human exposure may be associated with adverse reproductive consequences."**[5]

Research[6] carried out on historical changes in the mineral content of fruits and vegetables indicated a diminishing nutrient quality in food over the last 50 years. The comparison of the mineral content of 20 fruits and 20 vegetables grown in the 1930s and the 1980s - during the period of industrialisation of agriculture - showed statistically significant reductions of between 30% - 50% in mineral content. For example, calcium, magnesium, copper and sodium in vegetables and magnesium, iron, copper and potassium in fruit were all significantly depleted. The only mineral that showed no significant differences over this period was phosphorus.

Don Davis[7] reviewed the evidence for declining nutrients in fruits and vegetables and describes an 'agronomic dilution effect' - an inverse relationship between crop yield and mineral concentrations (the larger the crop yield, the lower the nutrient content). He found that, per 100g of increased carbohydrate yield, the nutrient content decreased due to the accompanying increased use of fertilisers. He also describes a *"genetic dilution"* where different high yield varieties of crops - like broccoli and grains - are grown side-by-side to directly compare nutrient quality. These studies have shown a consistently negative association between yield and concentrations of minerals and protein.

"In fruits, vegetables, and grains, usually 80% to 90% of the dry weight yield is carbohydrate. Thus, when breeders select for high yield, they are, in effect, selecting mostly for high carbohydrate with no assurance that dozens of other nutrients and thousands of phytochemicals will all increase in proportion to yield."

The wisdom of the 'Precautionary Principle'

It's not difficult to envisage the uphill struggle for independent research bodies and agencies working hard to influence legislation and to educate and protect us from the impact of these chemicals on or soil, our food and our health. These agencies argue for the 'Precautionary Principle':

"When an activity raises threats of harm to human health or the environment, precautionary measures should be taken even if some cause and effect relationships are not fully established scientifically."

The tide is slowly turning on widespread pesticide use, but for now it's very much up to us to adopt this principle and protect our health - and particularly our children's health - by sourcing organic whenever possible.

Sourcing organic: box schemes and farm gates

Anyone who has visited a local farmers' market in the UK will have noticed that prices are at a premium. These prices reflect not only the costs of production, but of transporting produce and down-time for the farmer or staff to sell at market. On top of this, there's the cost of hiring a stall for the day.

However, there are an increasing number of direct-to-customer national, regional and local organic box schemes and the Soil Association publish an organic food-finder of box schemes and farm gates. Google is your friend here.

Guy Watson of Riverford Organic Farm has won respect as a people's champion for the principles and benefits of growing organically and trading ethically:

> **"Many of us are inclined to believe that a natural diet is likely to be a healthy diet; that means eating less processed food with fewer additives and trying to stick to foods that we evolved to eat, and ideally growing them in as natural a way as possible.**
>
> **It is obvious to many (especially gardeners) that the way food is grown affects how it looks, feels, smells and tastes. Indeed, studies published in the British Journal of Nutrition conclusively show organic food to be different; simply put, you get more of the good stuff and less of the bad.**
>
> **Do listen to your intuition; mine firmly tells me that the closer we stay to the diet we evolved to eat, made up of (largely) plants and (small amounts of) animals, the healthier we will be. Better still if that food is raised in organic conditions, bringing the many benefits to wildlife, the soil and our environment that are intrinsic to this way of farming."**

Who can disagree with Guy and the saying "Mother Nature obeyed"?

Growing organic: allotments and neighbours

On every level, home-grown fruit and vegetables are beneficial for our health. They may look a little wobbly, but there is huge satisfaction in knowing that what-you-plant-is-what-you-get and the texture and flavour of the produce bears no resemblance to the all-too-often dull and tasteless offerings that we find in most high street shops.

Even with little space, it's well worth the effort and pleasure of growing your own - it really does incite a sense of achievement and pride to sit down to a plate of vegetables or fruit that you've sown, tended, harvested and brought to the table all by yourself. I've lost count of friends who've started small and then moved home for a bigger garden and perhaps even an allotment!

Books, blogs and videos with advice on what to grow, how to grow and when to grow are in plentiful supply. Again, Google is your friend and it's always worth putting up a local advert for a garden share.

One of the best blogs I've come across is by Nicky Kyle,[8] an ex-grower with 40 years' experience - commercially and as a home grower - of growing and cooking her own organic food.

She shares information and education with passion and sound practical advice:

"Whether you grow your own vegetables or if you buy them - the most important thing you need to know about maximising nutrients, first and foremost, is that they also have a circadian clock exactly like we do. This means they have light-sensitive cells in every part of the plant which tell them whether it's day or night! That light-sensitivity governs their internal circadian clock and all the biological functions which they perform at particular times of day or night.

This works in exactly the same way that our circadian clock governs our bodies. As a result - plants have a constant awareness of what time of day it is, just from sensing light. In other words - plants can tell the time - probably a lot more accurately than we can! Because of this ability - plants don't waste precious energy on producing their protective phytochemicals during the night.

They start to step up production of them a couple of hours before dawn - in anticipation of attacks by the hungry hordes of insects which will descend on them at daybreak for breakfast! That way the plants hope to repel them either by a nasty taste or unpleasant smell! How clever plants are and how beautifully Nature designed everything!

I hope you like getting up early! Don't wait until after work to go down to the allotment to pick your vegetables or run down the garden just before supper.

Get up a bit earlier in the morning instead. Then you can harvest them at the absolute peak of their super-nutritional best!"

Eating organic vegetables: cooked or raw?

Recently the number of experts, writers and bloggers applauding the benefits of a raw food diet has increased dramatically. There's no doubt that raw vegetables and fruit hold a rich potential for nutrition and most of us can benefit from eating some raw food, some of the time.

While a raw food diet might seem like a great idea, remember that our digestive system struggles to (and often can't) break down many kinds of raw food. And what doesn't get properly broken down doesn't get digested or absorbed.

For those with a strong digestive system this means loss of potential nutrients, but for those with a weak digestion or digestive disorders, eating raw foods can also bring digestive distress and worsen symptoms.

While we know that cooking depletes food nutrients, we need to look deeper than *just* nutritional value of certain foods and ask: "*Can humans digest and absorb this food?*", "*Are the nutrients in the food available in the raw state?*" and "*Does the food contain anti-nutrients?*"

However, one raw food which has been shown to be powerfully therapeutic is grated raw carrot salad, dressed with a little coconut oil and raw apple cider vinegar eaten daily. Not only does it taste good, this simple salad can play an important role in both male and female hormone balance. Acting as a natural antibiotic 'brush' in the gut, it helps to remove harmful toxins from the bowel.

It also helps to prevent the re-absorption of oestrogen; this is an important benefit, since today men and women face oestrogen dominance from exposure to stressful lifestyles which stimulate our body to produce excess oestrogen, from xenonestrogens (oestrogenic chemicals in our daily environment) and from dietary phytoestrogens (soya products).

These all throw our body's natural oestrogen production out of balance and increase our oestrogenic load. Oestrogen dominance underlies, or has been strongly linked to PMS, menopausal symptoms, hormonal acne, infertility, mood disorders, lack of muscle tone, erectile dysfunction 'man boobs', breast and prostate cancer.[9]

Plants are smarter than we are!

If we think that plants are just innocently waiting around to be eaten, we can think again - they're smart. Very smart.

Every plant has a complex chemical system that defends it against plant predators. Below ground, fungi and nematodes (little round worms) love to feed on plant roots and tubers; above ground, insects, birds and animals have their beady eyes on the plant's delicious stems, seeds, and leaves.

If a plant is to reproduce, then its seeds - which contain a high concentration of nutrients - need to have good protection. This protection is afforded by the hard shell which surrounds the seed and also by chemical anti-nutrients within it.

These anti-nutrients inhibit a predator's digestive enzymes and allow the seed to pass undigested through the predator's digestive tract… to live and grow another day.

"Many plants have evolved fruits that provide concentrated food for animals, and that serve to distribute the seeds widely, as when a bird eats a berry, and excretes the undigested seed at a great distance. If the fruit were poisonous, it wouldn't serve the plant's purpose so well.

In general, the plant's most intense toxins are in its seeds, and the fruits, when mature, generally contain practically no toxins.

Roots contain chemicals that inhibit microorganisms, but because they aren't easily accessible by grazing animals and insects, they don't contain the digestive inhibitors that are more concentrated in the above-ground organs of the plant."

- The Healthy Home Economist

As we'll see in the Fats chapter, when we ingest specific kinds of polyunsaturated fats contained in a plant's seeds - i.e. the vegetable and seed oils - the biological processes that depend upon the effective breakdown of protein are disrupted and our body's ability to produce thyroid hormones and remove blood clots is undermined.

However, the many plant toxins and metabolic inhibitors can be disabled by traditional methods of food preparation - soaking, sprouting and fermenting - and by cooking them well. Once again, our Granny knew best.

More difficult to digest:	Easier to digest:
• Leafy greens: spinach, lettuce, kale, rocket, watercress (G) • Whole peas • Green beans • Corn kernels • Bell peppers • Aubergines • Celery • Onions, shallots, leeks, spring onions garlic • Cabbage, bok choy, Brussels sprouts (G) • Broccoli (G) • Cauliflower (G)	• Carrots • Squashes • Starchy tubers: potatoes, sweet potatoes • Turnips • Parsnips • Celeriac • Beets • Plantains

Cooking - and soaking, sprouting and fermenting - foods is a way of pre-digesting them and in general, the more fibrous the food,[10] the better we are able to digest it if it is well-cooked.

Although al dente and stir-fried vegetables are popular, it's the well-cooked foods which release their nutrients most readily. Steaming well, roasting or adding vegetables to casseroles is an ideal way to preserve their nutrients.

However, some foods, like those marked with a 'G' in the table above, have been shown to be goitrogenic when they're eaten raw, or in excess, so are far better fermented or well-steamed and the cooking water discarded.

A goitrogen is a substance that suppresses the function of the thyroid gland, impacting on our metabolism and ability to use energy and can cause swelling of the thyroid gland in susceptible people.

I must admit to loving my vegetables al dente, but I now compromise by cooking them a little longer for the sake of my digestion and for better absorption of all those lovely organic nutrients.

Benefits of ripe, seasonal fruit

If you grow your own - or have access to a neighbour's produce - you'll know that ripe local fruit, in season, is a wonderful experience. No wonder Keats described autumn as a "*season of mists and mellow fruitfulness*."

In the UK, our fruit is in its prime in late summer/early autumn, when we're given the opportunity to enjoy an abundance of seasonal ripe, local fruits (and vegetables) rich in carbohydrate to fuel our energy needs, delivering quick, powerful, easily digested nutrition to our cells.

This seasonal carb-loading is an evolutionary and adaptive process; it peaks towards the end of September, when our wise bodies become naturally insulin-resistant and begin to divert excesses of carb-derived energy into fat storage, ready for a much slower winter burn.

Sadly, for advocates of the very low-carb approach, many fruits are pretty much off the menu.[11]

In common with cooked vegetables, cooked fruits - especially fibrous fruits - are often more easily digested than raw. A simple baked apple with a little cinnamon can be medicine to a distressed gut - the pectin in the skin, which helps (like gelatin) to heal the gut membrane, is made more available by cooking.

Five, Ten, Fifteen-a-day?

It depends on the individual - there can be no 'ideal' fruit and veg prescription for everyone. For some, even a couple of servings of whole fruit or veg a day, can cause digestive issues.

My advice is to go for colour, variety and listen to your body. If you feel fine on a gazillion portions, then go for it. If not, start slowly and gradually increase - let your body be your guide.

The table overleaf will help you make informed choices:

Introducing phytonutrients into your diet Begin with ONE serving (a cup or fist-full) of each colour every day. Build up to TWO servings of each colour every day.				
PURPLE	**RED**	**GREEN**	**WHITE**	**ORANGE**
Aubergines	Tomatoes	Spinach	Mushrooms	Sweet potatoes
Red cabbage	Radishes	Watercress	Parsnips	Squashes
Beets	Strawberries	Lettuce	Cauliflower	Corn
Black beans	Raspberries	Kale	Garlic	Carrots
Plums	Red apples	Collard greens	Onions	Oranges
Blueberries	Pomegranate	Green peppers	Turnips	Tangerines
Blackcurrants	Cranberries	Courgettes	Horseradish	Lemons
Blackberries	Cherries	Broccoli	White beans	Passionfruit
Figs	Guava	Brussels sprouts	Black-eyed peas	Apricots
Grapes		Green beans		Papaya
		Green tea		Cantaloupe melon

A final thought: to juice, or not to juice?

There's no doubt that juicing can be beneficial to health and with the right guidance, can be extremely therapeutic. However, consuming large amounts of raw 'green' juices or smoothies is not the best plan for most and certainly not for those with metabolic or digestive issues. Dr Campbell-McBride recommends that juices are made up from 50% ripe fruit and 50% vegetables. If you want to include green vegetables in your smoothie, consider steaming and cooling them, before you blend them.

In defence of fruit juice

At the risk of enraging critics, I'm compelled to include a (cautious) defence of fruit juice. Despite all the controversy over fruit juices, high-quality, organic, natural fruit juices (not made from concentrate) are a traditional, nutrient-dense food and have been unfairly demonised as sugar-laden, health-destroying poisons. In my eBook[12] *Demonised Drinks*, I devoted a chapter to explaining in detail why most of us should stop fearing orange juice and how we can enjoy its health benefits.

Without doubt, orange juice does contain a significant amount of sugar. One medium-sized navel orange contains 17.56 grams of total carbohydrates, which includes 11.9 grams of natural sugar. Sucrose (glucose + fructose) accounts for half of the total sugar. Another 23% of the total comes from glucose alone, while fructose alone represents 27 percent of the sugar in an orange.

For more information on sugars take a look at Appendix 1 - A Deeper Dive into Carbs. However, consuming adequate glucose helps us to manage the stress response that follows when our blood sugar gets too low and we have no dietary protein available, or when we significantly restrict - or completely avoid sugar.

In this situation, our wise body senses danger and our sympathetic nervous system fires stress hormones - adrenaline and cortisol - which act to restore sugar to our bloodstream, an adaptive response to protect us against the threat of hypo-glycaemia. Over time, chronic elevation of stress hormones can reach damaging levels and impact on thyroid and energy metabolism and on other areas of our health too.

By judiciously taking in some natural sugars through our diet, our body gets a message of safety and relaxes, allowing our parasympathetic nervous system to switch off the emergency response. Think about that cup of sweet tea we're offered when our body goes into shock, or the glucose drip which feeds us in hospital when we can't eat?

And remember that recent Czech study (2018) that we looked at in the Meat chapter? It found that one of the stronger negative associations between consumption of foods/food groups and death from cardiovascular disease was with fruits.

OJ - getting the real deal

When you buy commercial, industrially-produced juice - often passed off as 100% pure orange juice - remember that much of it is highly-processed from concentrate, pasteurised and is not organic, so it will lack the heat-sensitive, beneficial enzymes and vitamins that break down when exposed to the high temperatures of pasteurising; and it will also contain those unwanted chemical extras too.

Real, organic orange juice (like you'd juice at home) is a million miles away from this kind of product and raw, freshly-pressed organic juice will preserve the heat-sensitive enzymes and nutrients, like the precious vitamin C.

More reasons to drink fresh, organic orange juice:

- It provides minerals such as magnesium and potassium which are essential for blood sugar and insulin level regulation. Potassium gets sugar into the cell and lets us make use of it. Sometimes, when we crave sugar, we are actually craving potassium.

- One 250ml glass of fresh OJ provides about 15% of our daily requirements for potassium and significant amounts of folate (19%), B-6, thiamine, choline, and vitamin A. And it provides 207% of our recommended daily value of vitamin C.

- The vitamin C in fresh OJ increases our white blood cell count - which improves our immune system's function - and is critical for building collagen, which not only helps us to look younger, but supports a healthy digestive system, joints, strong bones and teeth and more.

- Fresh, raw, organic OJ is also rich in bioflavonoids, which are plant pigments that enhance the bio-availability of nutrients such as vitamin C, making fresh orange juice one of the best antioxidants we can consume.

- OJ helps our body eliminate harmful substances because it contains so many beneficial antioxidants, vitamins, minerals and enzymes which support our body's detoxification pathways.

- OJ supports our adrenals and thyroid from the nutrients it provides. Magnesium, potassium, vitamin C and glucose are essential in the production and conversion of the active form of thyroid hormone (T3). Without them, our thyroid can't keep up with our body's hormonal demands, and overall physiological stress is increased.

Two reasons to limit or avoid drinking orange juice:

1. Anyone who suspects - or knows - that they have problems with regulating blood sugar, struggles with obesity, metabolic syndrome, or pre/Type 1 or 2 diabetes will need to exercise caution and closely monitor their response to drinking fruit juices.

   That said, before rejecting them out of hand, a first step is to ditch ALL processed foods and drinks and get back on track with a whole-food, unprocessed diet and with careful management over time, nutritious fruit and fruit juices can be back on the menu.

2. Anyone with iron overload (more common than you'd think) or with a hereditary condition like hemochromatosis are best to limit or avoid drinking OJ near - or with - a red meat meal, as the juice acts to enhance iron absorption.

Final word: how to drink orange juice

- Always treat OJ as a FOOD and sip (don't guzzle!) it slowly or dilute it with non-fluoridated water
- Always choose a high-quality, organic juice that's not made from concentrate
- There is no real substitute for freshly-squeezed, organic juice, prepared at home, either with the help of a juicer or by hand - many organic box schemes now carry fruit for juicing
- If you have digestive issues with fibre, strain the freshly-squeezed juice, or choose high quality, no-bits varieties
- Add up to ¼ teaspoon of sea salt (you won't taste it and it brings out the juice's sweet notes) to aid hydration, regulate stress hormones and boost the liver's production of thyroid hormone
- Add a teaspoon or two of powdered gelatin (collagen hydrolysate) to OJ for added benefits and slow absorption
- To reap the benefits, drink OJ judiciously!

FRUIT and VEG Recipes

AVOCADO BONE BROTH

(Serves 1)

Forget coffee, everyone's 'pimping up' bone broth. Bone broth is trending everywhere as a 'forgotten' superfood. Indeed, a well-made bone broth (or meat stock) is not only an intensely flavoursome experience, it's a truly healing medicine. There's no vegetarian version of this as the whole point of it is in the broth.

What you'll need:

Bone broth: 250ml (chicken or beef)
Avocado: ½ (roughly chopped)
Organic coconut oil: 1 tsp
Organic, unsalted butter: 1 tbsp
Collagen hydrolysate: 1 tbsp (grass-fed)
Lemon juice: squeeze
Organic egg yolk: 1 (optional, but recommended)
Maldon salt: ½ tsp (or to taste))
Black pepper: pinch (freshly ground, to taste)

What to do:

1. Put all the dry ingredients into the bowl of a food processor (or you can use a blender) with a little of the bone broth and whizz until smooth.

2. Over a low heat, warm the bone broth and whisk in the avocado mixture and egg yolk, if using.

3. Heat until a comfortable drinking temperature, whisking well all the time.

4. Adjust seasoning to taste and enjoy yourself!

PEA & CORIANDER SOUP

(Serves 4)

This soup is quick, easy and absolutely delicious; it's one of Ballymaloe Cookery School's staples and it makes a lovely light summer starter soup and I often serve it before a fish course (like the Cod & Chorizo Stew you'll find in the Seafood chapter).

This soup is at its very best with a home-made chicken stock base, but for a vegetarian version, you can use a mineral stock or good quality low salt stock powder or cube.

What you'll need:

Frozen peas: 300g
Butter: 30g (unsalted)
Onion: 100g (finely diced)
Garlic: 2 cloves (smashed & finely chopped)
Finger chilli: 1 (green, finely chopped & deseed if liked)
Chicken stock: approx. 400 ml (home-made)
Fresh coriander: 2 tbsp (chopped)
Sea salt: Maldon - to taste
Ground black pepper: to taste
Sugar: to taste

What to do:

1. Bring the chicken stock up the boil (if frozen, do this slowly).

2. Melt the butter over a slow heat, add the onion, garlic and chilli and sweat for 5-6 mins until soft and translucent, but not coloured.

3. Add the peas and cover with 300ml of the hot stock. Bring everything slowly up to the boil and simmer for 5-8 mins with the lid OFF (this will help retain the vibrant green colour).

4. If not serving straight away, cool the soup and refrigerate until needed. Reheat slowly with the lid off.

5. Just before serving, add the coriander and liquidize. If the soup is thicker than desired add a little more boiling stock.

6. Season well with salt and pepper. Adding a little sugar will really bring out the taste.

Serve with a swirl of Greek yoghurt, a little fresh coriander sprinkled over the top and good bread or sourdough toasts.

TOMATO (& MUSHROOM) RAGÙ

(Serves 2-4)

This so-simple recipe will soon become a trusty 'go-to' in your culinary repertoire. It can turn its hand to a variety of dishes: a simple sauce for pasta, polenta, beans, pulses, or a medley of fresh, seasonal vegetables; a topping for pizza; or a delicious support for seafood, grilled, or roasted meats. Make the basic ragù in bulk and freeze in portions that suit you - I promise you'll never want to buy a processed tomato-based sauce again. EVER.

In season, I use fresh, peeled tomatoes (just cut a cross in the bottom, dunk them in boiling water for a minute or two and the skin will peel easily). Otherwise, I use good quality organic chopped tinned tomatoes - either way, since we're not in sun-blessed Italy or Sicily, a little cinnamon or dark brown sugar cuts the acidity of the tomatoes.

When the sauce is almost cooked (or on reheating it if frozen) you can get creative by adding a handful of mushrooms and/or finely sliced red peppers (just sauté them in a little olive oil or butter until soft) and/or stoned black olives per person and ramp up the volume Sicilian-style with freshly-grated ginger and/or finely-diced chilli.

What you'll need:

Celery: 2 sticks
Carrots: 2 medium (peeled)
Onions: 2 medium (peeled)
Olive or coconut oil: 2 tbsp
Garlic: 2 fat cloves (crushed and left to stand for 10 mins)
Tomatoes: 900g (peeled, chopped) or 2 x 400g tins chopped (good quality)
Tomato puree: 2 tbsp
Bay leaf: 1 (dried is fine)
Oregano: 2-3 medium sprigs (or 1 tsp dried)
Cinnamon: ½ tsp and/or 1 tsp dark brown sugar (to balance acidity)

Filtered water: 400ml (approx.)
Maldon salt and freshly ground black pepper: to taste
Basil: fresh handful (optional)

What to do:

1. Blitz or very finely chop the celery, carrots and onions. In a large saucepan, sauté them very gently in the oil, until well-softened and very lightly coloured.

2. Add the garlic, tomatoes, bay leaf, oregano, tomato purée, cinnamon/brown sugar, water, salt and freshly ground black pepper.

3. Mix well, cover with a lid and allow to simmer on a low heat for approximately 30 mins for fresh tomatoes or 1 hour if using tinned; stir frequently and lower the heat if the sauce is reducing too quickly, adding water as necessary to retain a thick (but not solid) consistency. Adjust the seasonings to taste as the sauce cooks.

4. Leave the sauce chunky or take out the bay leaf and oregano stalks and blend it to your preferred consistency. Add the torn basil just before serving.

The tomato ragù will keep well in the fridge for several days and (without the mushrooms/red peppers) it will freeze perfectly - just add in the vegetables and a little extra water and seasonings when re-heating.

BARE-NAKED BROCCOLI & FETA CRUSTLESS QUICHE

(Serves 3-4)

This is one of my favourite vegetarian recipes - I love crust-less quiches! They take minutes to prepare and are nutrient-dense. And they don't come simpler than this one: eggs, cheese and vegetables, bound together with Greek yoghurt.

This quiche makes a relaxed brunch or lunch dish, it's equally good served hot or cold. For supper, scatter sliced tomatoes and finely sliced red onions over crisp green leaves, add sweet potato wedges and you're done!

What you'll need:

Broccoli: 1 medium head (cut into small florets, stalk finely cut)
Red pepper: ½ medium (medium dice)
Organic, free-range eggs: 4 large (beaten)
Greek yoghurt: 2 tbsp
Milk: 125ml (full fat)
Garlic: ½ clove (crushed)
Sea salt: ½ tsp (Maldon)
Ground black pepper: ½ tsp
Extra virgin olive oil: 1 tbsp
Feta cheese: 80g (cut into small cubes)
Spring onions: 3 (with green stems, chopped small)

What to do:

1. In a steamer or a steamer basket set inside a saucepan, steam the broccoli and red pepper until they only just reach the 'al dente' stage - they'll continue to cook in the oven. You can also use a lidded wok over a high heat and 'steam-fry' by adding small amounts of water. Drain and set aside to cool.

2. Mix together the eggs, yoghurt, milk, garlic, salt and pepper until well combined.

3. Liberally oil an oven-proof dish with olive oil and arrange the broccoli and red peppers evenly in the dish. Scatter over the feta cheese and spring onions and pour the egg batter over, very gently pushing the contents down into the batter (they'll pop back up during cooking).

4. Bake at 160°C (Fan) Gas Mark 4 for about 40 mins, or until the quiche has risen and is golden and just set in the centre.

5. Let cool for a few minutes before slicing and serving. It will keep well (covered) in the refrigerator for 2-3 days.

SOUTH INDIAN RED PEPPER, SPINACH & CASHEW NUT CURRY

(Serves 2)

This fresh vegetarian curry - inspired by the flavours of Kerala in Southern India - isn't just super-delicious, it's also deeply nutritious and healing. It's rich in protein, good fats, vitamins and minerals; the ingredients are high in anti-inflammatories, and are anti-bacterial, anti-oxidant and immune system strengthening.

I like to serve with plain Basmati rice and a grated raw carrot, coconut and red chilli salad.

What you'll need:

Coconut oil: 40g
Onions: 125g (peeled)
Ginger: 20g (peeled)
Garlic: 2 fat cloves (peeled)
Maldon salt: ½ tsp
Ground coriander: 1 tbsp
Ground cumin: 1 tbsp
Ground turmeric: ¼ tsp
Chilli flakes: 1 tsp (or more, to taste)
Nigella (Kalonji) seeds: ½ tbsp
Chopped tomatoes: 75g
Coconut milk: 200ml (full fat)
Lime: ½ (zest & juice)
Unrefined sugar: ¼ tsp
Desiccated coconut: 30g (unsweetened, medium)
Red peppers: 150g (1cm dice)
Cashew nuts: 75g (lightly toasted in a dry fry pan)
Spinach: 1-2 large handfuls (washed, spun and roughly chopped)

What to do:

1. Chop the onions, ginger and garlic very finely, or pulse them in a food processor to the consistency of a rough paste.

2. Gently heat the coconut oil in a deep lidded sauté pan, or flame proof casserole and stir in the onion paste and salt. Cover and sauté very gently, without browning, for 10mins until the onions are translucent and well softened, stirring gently so the mixture doesn't catch.

3. Increase the heat and add the coriander, cumin, turmeric, nigella seed and chilli flakes and stir well. Add the tomatoes, coconut milk, lime zest and juice, sugar and the coconut flakes. Stir well, cover and simmer very gently for 20 mins.

4. Add the red peppers and simmer gently for a further 20 mins, stirring occasionally. Add the roasted cashew nuts and continue to cook for until the red peppers are tender but still hold their shape about 30 mins. Add the spinach and simmer for a further 1-2 mins, until just wilted down.

Serve and enjoy!

CHAPTER NINE

FAT: FRIEND OR FOE?

"Jack Sprat could eat no fat; his wife could eat no lean. And so betwixt them both, you see, they licked the platter clean."

- Traditional English nursery rhyme

Is fat our friend or our foe? Both - it depends on the fat and how it's consumed. It also depends on our bodies.

We need fat!

We get fats from a wide range of natural sources, like dairy, egg yolks, beef dripping, lard, coconut, avocado, olives and many varieties of nut and seed oils.

We simply cannot live, or function without eating fat. Fats (known as lipids) insulate us and protect our organs from trauma; they form our cell membranes (the semi-permeable layer that surrounds each and every cell); and they circulate in the blood, bringing energy to our cells and providing 60% of our energy when we're resting. Fats provide the cholesterol which helps to manufacture and balance our hormones and helps to transport fat-soluble vitamins A, D, E and K around our body to reach our cells.

Fats also provide important omega-3 and omega-6 fatty acids, which we aren't able to make ourselves, helping to reduce triglycerides and other fatty substances in our blood which protect our vision and nervous system and reduce inflammation.

In food, fats give us flavour, aroma and they slow down the digestion of other nutrients, helping to stabilise our blood sugar and keeping us feeling fuller for longer.

The simplest unit of fat is the fatty acid, organised into saturated fatty acids (SFAs) and unsaturated fatty acids (UFAs). The latter comprise both monounsaturated fatty acids (MUFAs) and polyunsaturated fatty acids (PUFAs). Fatty acids are made up of carbon and hydrogen molecules joined together in long groups, and are referred to as short, medium, long and very-long chain fatty acids. The table overleaf summarises the sources and benefits of fatty acids.

A fat's chain length impacts its melting point. Fats that are solid at room temperature (like butter and coconut oil) have a longer, more stable chain length and a higher melting point than those that are liquid at room temperature (like olive, fish, vegetable and seed oils).

There is also an important group of fatty acids which, as we shall see below, are NOT good news: trans-fatty acids. Trans-fats are a by-product of hydrogenation - a process where a hydrogen molecule is added to a polyunsaturated fat to make it more solid (saturated) and give it a smoother texture. These properties give margarine, vegetable spreads and a huge variety of processed foods (where these kinds of fats are prolific), a more appealing texture and extend their shelf life. This is good news for the food industry, but very bad news for us.

Good fats and bad fats - which is which?

We've all heard the terms 'good' fats and 'bad' fats. For decades, conventional dietary wisdom has demonised traditional saturated fats (butter, cream, egg yolks, beef dripping and coconut oil) on the basis that these 'bad' fats are not good for our hearts or our waistlines. Instead we're encouraged to eat polyunsaturated fats like margarine, spreads and vegetable and seed oils, on the basis that these 'good' fats are healthier for our hearts.

However, most foods are made up of some combination of saturated, monounsaturated and polyunsaturated fatty acids. Take eggs and beef, for example:

"39% of the fat in eggs is saturated, while 43% comes from monounsaturated fat, and 18% from polyunsaturated fat. Beef contains 55% saturated fat, 40% monounsaturated fat, and 4% polyunsaturated fat." [1]

Is it true that saturated fats clog our arteries and kill us, or it this yet another case of foods being unjustly demonised?

Fatty Acid	Name	Source	Helps
Saturated Fatty Acids (SFA)			
Short chain (SCFA)	Butyric acid Acetic acid	Butter, beef dripping, ghee, raw apple cider vinegar Probiotic foods High-fibre foods	Beneficial to gut bacteria and gastro-intestinal tract; supports immune system; lowers stress and inflammation
Medium chain (MCFA)	Lauric acid Caprylic acid	Coconut oil	Fuels muscles; supports immune system; reduces glucose and serum cholesterol; lower calorie; reduces appetite; increases fat-burning, helping weight loss; anti-oxidant, anti-microbial, anti-coagulant Monolaurin present in breast milk, helping immunity.
Long chain (LCFA)	Stearic acid Palmitic acid	Meat and dairy	Increases cholesterol healthily; adds structure and stability to cell membranes and hormones - but risks are associated with negative lifestyle factors.
Unsaturated fatty acids (UFA)			
Monounsaturated (MUFA)	Oleic acid Palmitoleic acid	Pastured pork, olive oil, avocados, canola/rapeseed, sesame seeds, almonds	In moderation, weight loss, risk factors for heart disease, cancer, inflammation and insulin resistance.
Polyunsaturated (PUFA)	**Omega-3** • Alpha-linoleic acid (ALA) • Eicosapentaenoic acid (EPA) • Docosahexaenoic acid (DHA) **Omega-6** • Linoleic acid (LA) • Arachidonic acid (AA) • Gamma-linoleic acid (GLA)	Wild-caught oily/fatty fish (sardines, mackerel, salmon), walnuts, eggs, flax seeds. Oils/seeds/nuts: sunflower, soya, corn, cottonseed, grapeseed, walnut, flax, hemp, sesame, pine, pumpkin, walnuts, almonds, cashew. Avocado, meats, dairy eggs yolks, seafood/plants	In **BALANCE**, omega-3: omega-6 fatty acids reduce triglycerides and cholesterol; support cell membranes, vision, nervous system; help modulate gene expression for inflammation, cardiovascular and chronic health conditions. In **EXCESS**, omega-6 fatty acids are pro-inflammatory. Most vegetable and seed oils contain large amount of omega-6 and little/no omega-3; modern commercial agricultural have increased the amount of omega-6 available in veg, eggs, fish and meat

Let's rewind... again

From 1958, the diet-heart hypothesis, developed by an American scientist Ancel Keys, has been held up to prove the case against saturated fats. This hypothesis infers that:

- saturated fat raises cholesterol in the blood
- cholesterol furs up the arteries causing atherosclerosis and heart disease over time.

In support of his hypothesis, Keys had examined the association between diet and cardiovascular disease in different countries. He presented data from his *Seven Countries Study* to show that countries with the highest fat consumption also had the highest levels of heart disease so Keys asserted that his data proved that eating saturated fat caused heart disease.

On this basis, the political players in the USA (Senator George McGovern's 1978 *Dietary Goals for The United States of America*) and companies with a vested interest in the results of Key's hypothesis, promoted a health policy that advised the public to shun traditional fats in favour of the new kids on the block - cheap, industrially-produced, polyunsaturated fats. These cheap new fats quickly became the darlings of the US food industry and were heavily marketed as the healthy option. Over the next 20 years many millions followed this advice not only in the USA but worldwide.

Only years later did it emerge that Keys had had 'cherry-picked' his data, leaving out countries where people ate a lot of fat (Holland and Norway, for example) but had low rates of heart disease, and those where heart disease rates were high (Chile) but fat consumption was low.

However political will, commercial interests and media support of the day prevailed to ensure that Keys' findings stood firm and were incorporated into recommendations for the public to eat less fat and cholesterol and to eat more complex carbohydrates from vegetables, fruits and grains.[2]

As a result, the low-fat, high-carbohydrate diet (LFHC) was born and public health authorities, doctors and dieticians all rejected a higher-fat diet rich in animal foods and embraced this diet with plenty of grains.

So, fat is our friend? Some say, "Yes!"

In one of the most respected reviews, Hooper[3] and colleagues undertook a meta-analysis of over 59,000 participants in 15 randomised controlled trials, performed by the Cochrane Collaboration - an independent organisation of scientists. These studies lasted for at least two years and found no statistically significant effects of reducing saturated fat, in regard to heart attacks, strokes or deaths from all-causes. Put simply, the results showed that people who reduced their saturated fat intake were just as likely to die, or get heart attacks or strokes, compared to those who ate more saturated fat.

Similarly, Schwab et al carried out a systematic review of over 600 studies which had looked at the effect of the amount and type of dietary fat on the risk for cardiovascular disease, Type 2 diabetes and cancer. Their analysis confirmed that saturated fat was not linked with an increased risk of heart disease, or an increased risk of Type 2 diabetes.[4]

Many randomised controlled trials have shown that saturated fat does not cause heart disease, and that a LFHC approach does not work for those it was predominantly meant to help - people with obesity and Type 2 diabetes. Indeed, the Public Health Collaboration in the UK was founded on this very premise and actively promotes a low-carb, high-fat (LCHF) diet for those with obesity and Type 2 diabetes and presents compelling evidence in support of it.[5]

It is true to say that over the years sound, independent science has found that reducing saturated fat has no effect on the risk of heart disease, or death and that replacing saturated fat with a diet high in refined carbs seems to increase the risk of heart disease.[6]

Others say: "Hang on... not so much!"

There are some risks associated with the consumption of one class of saturated fats: long-chain fatty acids found in meat and dairy (see the above table). These fats can be a problem for those who consume a high sugar diet, eat processed foods high in trans-fats and are exposing themselves to environmental toxins, such as smoking; diet and lifestyle changes would be an important step towards reducing these risks. However, for those with a relatively healthy diet and lifestyle these fats are not considered to be a problem.
But, before we get the idea that a high-fat diet is benign, healthful, or even superior, let's take a look at some astonishing material uncovered by researcher Denise Minger in a review of the clinical success of using a low-fat, high carbohydrate (LFHC) diet to treat a range of chronic health issues.

Minger wrote an extraordinary piece[7] entitled *In Defense of Low Fat: A Call for Some Evolution of Thought*, in which she systematically presented the case for reconsidering the health benefits of a low-fat diet:

> **"In the process of redeeming fat, we traded one form of oversimplified blame for another. And it's led to a brand-new wave of cherry genocide. We now dismiss high-carb populations in the same way we justified ignoring the**

high-fat ones. We snub decades of clinical success involving fat reduction (to the point where you might think such evidence doesn't even exist).

We deny the potential for low-fat diets to be anything other than a metabolic train wreck, ending in a smoking heap of shrapnel and insulin injections.

"Surely those low-fatters are starving all the time," we proclaim. "Surely they're making themselves diabetic! They might feel okay right now but won't those carby diets go all Cujo on them as the years progress...."

In Minger's review, her time-line precedes Ancel Keys' *Seven Countries Study* and McGovern's *Dietary Guidelines*, to detail the clinical success of doctors who had used a low-fat intake of 10% to treat a range of disorders.

She makes a crucial point in detailing how our definition of what constitutes a low-fat diet has changed significantly over the years and points out that more recent studies that have examined the negative impact of low-fat diets, have mostly used a fat intake of 30% of calories:

"When the USDA tells us to eat low fat, they mean 30% of calories. When the American Heart Association tells us to eat low fat, they mean 30% of calories. This number has been parroted far and wide across the Western world, drilled into our noggins and slapped with a skull-and-crossbones."

To support her argument, Minger details the work of Dr Walter Kempner, who in the 1930s very successfully used a low-fat diet of - wait for it - white rice, fruit and fruit juice and refined table sugar to treat those with renal failure, diabetes, heart disease and obesity.

She goes on to describe how Dr Lester Morrison successfully used low-fat diets to treat heart-disease during the 1940s, after noticing that deaths from heart disease and stroke dropped hand-in-hand with wartime food rationing, which curbed dietary fat.

And she also describes how Dr Roy Swank succeeded in treating multiple sclerosis (MS) patients with low-fat diets in 1948, after he noticed that MS rates were lower in in countries with a higher carbohydrate diet and that high MS rates dropped in countries during World War II, when fats were rationed.

Finally, she sets out how Nathan Pritikin reversed his own heart disease in 1958 with a low-fat diet, before later opening the Pritikin Longevity Centre[8] in 1978, where his programmes have successfully treated those with heart disease, cancers, diabetes and obesity

Carbs or fats?

So, should we favour carbs over fats? Or fats over carbs? It depends, Minger suggests:

> **"Something special happens at very high levels of fat intake (and very low levels of carbohydrate intake). That thing's called ketosis. It's where your body creates ketones to use when glucose is scarce, and where fat metabolism is optimised.**
>
> **Something equally special happens at very low levels of fat intake (and very high levels of carbohydrate intake). I'm not aware of a formal name for this, so I'm dubbing it carbosis until further notice. It's a state where insulin sensitivity dramatically improves, and where carbohydrate metabolism is optimised."**

In the middle, there is what Minger calls a confusing 'macronutrient swampland' of 'low-fat' studies, which use a standard (but not particularly low) definition of fat intake of 30% of calories:

> **"My goal here is to create a space where two very different dietary approaches can sit down for tea, respectfully coexist, and interact without any subsequent homicide investigations.**
>
> **In fact, I'll be arguing for a more panoramic view of nutrition where the success of both high-fat and low-fat diets are compatible, and maybe even make sense.**
>
> **It just requires zooming out farther than we're used to looking and acknowledging that our ever-rivalling communities could actually learn a lot from each other."**

- Denise Minger

I'd encourage to read Minger's piece for yourself but be warned it's a long one! For those who prefer to watch a video, take a look at her excellent presentation to the Icelandic Health Symposium (2017), available on You Tube.[9]

What should we take from all this?

Each and every one of us is 'bio-individual' meaning that while we share many similarities, nature has fashioned each of us as a unique human microcosm with highly individualized nutritional requirements. No one diet will suit all.

For those of us who are in reasonably good health, all macronutrients (proteins, fats and carbs) in the right balance for each individual, are important.

For those who have health issues like weight management, blood-sugar and/or insulin dysregulation, then a low-carb/high-fat (LCHF) diet may well help with symptom control in the short-term. However, in the longer term and depending on our individual's constitution, too few carbs may hinder our metabolic health (i.e. the ability to produce energy) and so keep us from healing. And for everyone, a low-fat/high-carb (LFHC) diet will certainly not be beneficial if we're consuming vast amounts of refined carbs from refined grains, flours, ultra-processed and fake foods.

But what about cholesterol - is it a friend or a foe?

I'll say this loud and clear: CHOLESTEROL IS OUR FRIEND, especially as we age and particularly for women. Here's why:

Cholesterol is critical - every single cell in the body depends on it, as does our digestive function, hormone production, brain, memory, bones and our vitamin D production. Without cholesterol, we would die. It's as simple as that.

Because it's life-critical, during sleep our body not only carries out repair and maintenance tasks, it actually makes cholesterol, in case we don't get enough from external sources like food.

Although we have come to call HDL (high density lipoprotein) 'good' cholesterol and LDL (low-density lipoprotein) 'bad' cholesterol, neither are actual cholesterol. These lipoproteins are vehicles whose role is to carry cholesterol and other substances around in the blood stream to destinations which perform our vital tasks.

It's significant that, despite his cherry-picking of data regarding saturated fats, even Ancel Keys exonerated cholesterol itself:

> **"There's no connection whatsoever between cholesterol in food and cholesterol in blood. And we've known that all along."**

Keys' 1950s studies saw his human subjects consume high levels of dietary cholesterol from eating animal foods (meat, fish, eggs, dairy) without any impact on blood cholesterol levels.

What does the research tell us?

Since Key's day, the debates and heated arguments have raged on among researchers and no doubt will continue to do so. To sum up the position to date, leading lipid researcher Dr Chris Masterjohn is of the view that: no one has clearly shown that foods with saturated fat raise the risk of heart disease; for most - but not all people - dietary cholesterol has no effect on blood cholesterol; the effect of foods is complex, and most people can eat a significant amount of saturated fat.[10]

Interestingly, researchers from Liverpool University (Penson, et al 2017) investigated the association of low and very low HDL at the start a study and subsequent incidents of all-cause mortality, death from malignant disease (i.e. cancer), and with fatal or non-fatal incident coronary heart disease. They found that very low HDL in women was significantly associated with cancer-related deaths.[11]

So, if you take away nothing else away, please just take this on board:

- LOW cholesterol is associated with HIGHER mortality
- HIGHER cholesterol is associated with LOWER mortality.

Especially for women. Read that again: ***especially for women***.

Polyunsaturated fats: should we be eating them at all?

Polyunsaturated fats (PUFAs) are liquid fats - vegetable oil, sunflower oil, nut oils and seed oils like rapeseed oil. These fats have been strongly promoted as heart-healthy by the media and by many nutrition professionals in the past few decades. However, some authorities have always argued that these PUFAs are in fact very harmful to our health and should be reduced or avoided:

Food-derived polyunsaturated fatty acids (PUFAs) play an important role in the development of all of the problems associated with aging - reduced immunity, insomnia, decreased learning ability, substitution of fat for muscle, susceptibility to tissue peroxidation and inflammation, growth of tumours, etc., and are probably involved in most other health problems, even in children. If research hadn't been guided by the economic interests of the seed oil industry, many of those problems would have been solved by now.

> **"At present, the most important issue is to recognise the dangers presented by the intrusion of corporate power into science, especially as it relates to nutrition and medicine, and to consider the implications of the known effects of the PUFA on all of our biological systems."**

- Dr Ray Peat [12]

While many of us, strongly encouraged by conventional health advice, have been using vegetable and sunflower oils, nut oils and more recently, rapeseed oil for cooking for many years, the unstable properties of these fats actually make them very unsuitable for cooking. Indeed, many authorities now explicitly caution against their use for cooking.

The molecular structure of PUFAs is unstable; these oils rapidly oxidise (think rust) and go rancid and toxic on exposure to light and heat (even at very low temperatures), promoting the development of free-radicals in the body, triggering inflammation and accelerating the ageing process.

The negative impact of excess and imbalanced PUFAs on the body is wide-ranging; they decrease the ability of the cell to produce energy and, as well as promoting ageing, they negatively impact thyroid function, interfere with digestive enzymes and are strongly implicated in the development of diabetes.[13]

Our body controls inflammation by balancing anti-inflammatory substances from omega-3 fats and pro-inflammatory substances from omega-6 fats (recall the discussion on omega-6 linoleic acid in eggs?) When we consume too many omega-6 fats, while not eating enough omega-3s, our diet becomes a source of systemic inflammation, which, if uncontrolled, can cause cardiovascular disease and the chronic degenerative illnesses associated with ageing. Increasingly, we are now seeing these conditions in much younger people.

However, while omega-6 fats are known for their pro-inflammatory properties, particularly arachidonic acid (AA) and linoleic acid (LA), not all omega-6 fats are pro-inflammatory. The omega-6 fat gamma-linolenic acid (GLA), made from linoleic acid, has powerful anti-inflammatory properties - but we only need a very small amount of it.[14]

Thanks to the now ubiquitous use of vegetable and seed oils in cooking, together with our consumption of industrially processed foods, grain-fed animal products, cheap damaged oils and pro-inflammatory omega-6 fatty acids, our consumption of PUFAs has gone through the roof, but our health has steadily declined. Many of the chronic, degenerative problems that plague us today can be traced back to our modern Western diet with its very high and pro-inflammatory PUFA content.

Trans-fats: cheap and highly dangerous

In 1901, the German chemist Wilhelm Normann discovered a process in which he was able to convert cheap, liquid vegetable oils (PUFAs) into solid shortenings, margarines and, ultimately, spreads.

This process - partial hydrogenation - causes a rearrangement of the hydrogen atoms in the fat molecule, moving one or more hydrogen atoms across to the other side of the molecule, causing the polyunsaturated fat molecule, which is normally bent or wavy, to straighten out. These straight molecules pack together easily, so they behave chemically like saturated fats - they are solid at room temperature and are stable for high-temperature cooking.[15]

The food processing industry quickly saw the value in using cheap, partially-hydrogenated fats rather than more expensive saturated animal fats, or tropical oils like coconut oil for baked goods and fried foods. Because these cheaper, longer-lasting products mimicked the traditional cooking fats of European and North American cuisines, many countries quickly (and gleefully) incorporated them into their food supplies.

However, no-one paid much attention to the potential health effects of these partially-hydrogenated or trans-fats (trans-unsaturated fatty acids) that were created as a by-product. It would be decades before scientists realised how deadly trans-fats really were.

When coronary heart disease began to emerge as epidemic in the West, doctors quickly threw the blame onto - yes, you got it - saturated fat and dietary cholesterol, naming butter and lard as key villains. Because margarines and vegetable shortenings were low in saturated fat and free from cholesterol, they were widely promoted as healthy alternatives.

By the mid-1970s, scientists had begun to report that trans-fats had adverse effects on arteries of pigs and Mary Enig of the University of Maryland tracked the correlation over time between increases in trans-fat intake and higher rates of coronary heart disease.[16]

During the 1980s researchers conducting the *Nurses' Health Study* cohort of over 100,000 women found that women with the highest intake of trans-fat had a 50% greater risk of hospitalisation or death due to coronary heart disease. Margarine, the primary source of trans-fat by 1980, was also associated with greater risk.[17]

By 2003, the evidence was compelling enough to require that trans-fats be declared on food labels in the US and by the end of that decade most manufacturers had stopped using them, with other countries quickly following suit. However it was only in 2015 that the US Food and Drug Administration finally determined that trans-fats (the primary dietary source of artificial trans-fat in processed foods) are not "*generally recognised as safe*" for use in human food.[18]

Trans-fatty acids have been increasingly implicated as contributing to cancer, heart disease, auto-immune disease, tendon and bone degeneration and problems with fertility and growth. Trans-fatty acids in partially hydrogenated vegetable oils are considered to be a major cause of Type 2 diabetes, characterised by high levels of both insulin and glucose in the blood, because they inhibit the insulin receptors in the cell membranes.[19]

Trans-fats: the sting in the tail

However, while food manufacturers have decreased the use of trans-fats, as ever they've left us with a crafty sting in the tail. Because food manufacturers are allowed to claim 'zero trans-fats' if the food contains 0.5g or less of trans-fats per serving, many foods that are touted as 'trans-fat free' can and do actually contain them. So, if we eat several servings per day of these (needless to say) processed foods, we can end up consuming quite a lot of trans-fats.

> **"Someone eating a whole bag of potato or corn chips will be taking in quite a bit of trans-fats. The serving size for Ritz crackers is one cracker."**

- Weston A. Price Foundation

And it doesn't stop there. Rather than reverting back to making good use of the saturated fats Mother Nature has provided, the food industry has come up with their own solution: a highly industrialised process called 'interesterification'.

In this process, which further rearranges fatty acids, the new re-formulated fat has different melting and baking qualities: 'improved' baking qualities (read: more volume in cakes) and a higher melting temperature.... does anyone remember the slogan *"It melts in your mouth, but not in your hand"*?

It should surprise no-one that these production methods also employ dangerous and highly toxic industrial solvents, alloys and enzymes.

"Whichever method is used, rest assured that this is a highly industrialised process involving heat that begins with oils that have already been subjected to a highly industrialised process. The resulting product may be trans-free, but it will still contain chemical residues, hexanes and many dangerous breakdown products full of free radicals."

- Mary Enig

While trans-fats are becoming less and less frequent in food production, we should also look out on the label for 'mono- and di-glycerides of fatty acids' (you'll find it in virtually all processed and baked goods) which are just one step away from trans-fats.

In a 2007 study, researchers recruited 30 volunteers to a study which compared trans-rich and interesterified fats with saturated fat, for their relative impact on blood lipids (fat) and plasma glucose. They found the subjects' insulin levels dropped 10% on the partially hydrogenated soybean oil diet. But they dropped more than twice as much on the interesterified fat diet, causing blood sugar to rise by an alarming 20%.[20] The interesterified blends were affecting the production of insulin by the pancreas (as in Type 1 diabetes), rather than the receptors for insulin in the cell membranes (as in Type 2 diabetes).

Potato crisps, anyone?

I had a passion for crisps, until I came across a piece[21] written in 2007 by Dennis Meizys who works with a US company Maryland Green Power, that converts used vegetable oil to bio-fuel:

"One manufacturer replied to my offer to purchase their used oil with the explanation that they hardly have any used oil left-over after the process. Tens of thousands of gallons come in, barely hundreds come out.

The reason? This manufacturer recycles the oil until it is entirely absorbed by the food. All that dirty oil eventually ends up in the potato chips themselves."

So, which fats for which purpose?

Traditional fats (like animal fats, coconut and olive oil) have been used in the human diet and in cooking since ancient times. Fat carries the flavour in our food - just think of the delicious fat that borders a steak or beef joint, or the varieties of flavoursome olive oils, from light and citrusy to rich and peppery. However, other fats like industrially-processed vegetable and rapeseed oils are newer (and most unwelcome) additions to our diet.

Most cooking fats contain a combination of saturated, mono- and poly-unsaturated fats. As a general rule, saturated fats are the best for cooking, while monounsaturated fats are suitable for light cooking. Polyunsaturated fats should never be cooked at all and you'd be well advised to avoid them altogether.

High-temperature cooking using traditional saturated fats	Mid/low-temperature cooking using 'raw' and traditional monounsaturated fats
Grass-fed* and finished beef suet, tallow or dripping	Lard and bacon fat from truly free-range pigs
Grass-fed and finished mutton tallow or dripping	Goose, duck and chicken fat from truly free-range, grass-fed birds
Unrefined coconut oil and cocoa butter	Butter from grass-fed and finished cow or goats (use raw)
Ghee (clarified butter) from grass-fed cows	Unrefined olive oil (use raw)
	Avocado oil (use raw)
	Macadamia/hazelnut/cashew nut oils (use raw)
** remember the discussion on grass vs grain-fed and finished meat in the Meat chapter?*	

Saturated fats stay solid at room temperature - their molecular structure makes them stable at high temperatures and they're less prone to oxidation. These traditional fats can be used for high- and low-temperature cooking. They can be eaten raw too: crusty sourdough bread spread with beef dripping and sprinkled with a little sea salt is a delicacy well worth trying - just ask Granny!

Monounsaturated fats are less stable at higher temperatures and more prone to oxidation, so are best heated more gently, or preferably eaten raw. Butter is a saturated fat, but its milk fats will burn at high temperatures and note that cooking with olive oil will destroy its valuable vitamin E.

That said, ghee from grass fed cows[22] and raw, extra virgin olive oil[23] - due to their very different, but complimentary nutritional profiles - are amongst the most nutrient-dense and healthiest fats on the planet.

Fats to avoid

- trans-fats and their 'derivatives'
- all vegetable and seed oils and most nut oils. Nuts, seeds and their oils contain high levels of PUFAs, although macadamia, hazelnuts and cashews are better nut choices due to their much lower levels
- sunflower oil; rapeseed/canola oil; corn oil; safflower oil; sesame oil; soybean oil; grapeseed oil; rice bran oil; cottonseed oil; flaxseed oil.

Industrially-produced seed and vegetable oils are highly-processed, refined products, cheap to produce. They're found everywhere in processed and packaged foods, take-away and restaurant foods and are a substantial ingredient in animal feed.

These oils are high in omega-6 pro-inflammatory fatty acids and one study, which looked at common vegetable oils on food shelves in the US market (soya and canola/rapeseed) discovered that they contained between 0.56 to 4.2% trans-fats, which are highly toxic.[24]

If you see any of these names on the label, choose another option.

Rapeseed oil is worth a special mention

On the face of it, rapeseed oil looks to tick all the health boxes: predominantly a monounsaturated fat, its omega-6 to omega-3 profile is balanced.

However, to extract the oil, the seeds need to undergo very harsh chemical treatment with the solvent hexane (made from crude oil) in a process which removes the toxic, bitter euric acid and produces the oil we see on supermarket shelves. Pure n-Hexane has an unpleasant odour, is highly flammable and its vapours can be explosive.

The major use of hexane is to extract vegetable oils from crops like rapeseed. Rapeseed oil is now everywhere in every kind of processed food and animal feeds and is frequently used to make butter 'spreadable'. Witnessing the process of how this so called 'healthy' oil is made (search online) should be enough to put you off it for life.

How to buy and store oils

If you do choose to consume PUFAs, I strongly suggest using them very sparingly and for dressings only. Always buy them in small batches and check the date. Oils should always be traditionally cold-pressed and then left in their natural, unrefined state and stored in dark glass bottles, away from light sources.

If they're expeller-pressed (extracted under friction and pressure) the heat created during processing damages the fragile oils. Exposure to light compounds this damage and, in consequence, damages your health.

A final word on fats

If you're confused and worried about fats, you're not alone - nutritional science in this area is contradictory and, in view of our bio-individuality (and as Denise Minger has shown) two opposing facts can be true at the same time.

Whether fat is your friend or not depends on the type of fat, how you use it, the current state of your health and the amount you consume. What is for sure is that our bodies need traditional, unprocessed healthy fats.

When in doubt, remember that Granny knew best. Stay with traditional fats and oils and use and consume them in moderation, as closely as possible to the way Mother Nature intended.

Let the chemists do their chemistry and let Mother Nature look after your health!

CHAPTER TEN

SEAFOOD… and EAT IT!

"A loaf of bread," the Walrus said, "is what we chiefly need:

pepper and vinegar besides are very good indeed —

now if you're ready, oysters dear, we can begin to feed."

- Lewis Carroll
The Walrus and the Carpenter

It was probably the zinc content in the oysters that sealed their fate - little did Carroll's innocents suspect that the Walrus and the Carpenter, who feasted upon them, were about to tuck into one of the best sources of zinc on the planet - one 6oz serving can provide the body with enough zinc for the entire week.

Oysters are a seafood superfood - not only are they fabulously high in zinc - an essential trace mineral needed for a healthy immune system, cell growth, wound healing, energy levels and hormonal function - but they are also rich in other key trace minerals like selenium, calcium, copper and iron, vitamins A, E, C and B12 and they're an excellent source of protein.

Why eat seafood anyway?

As I've just touched on above, seafoods (fish and shellfish) are high in many important nutrients and eating at least one serving of fish per week has been linked to reduced risk of heart attacks and strokes - two of the world's biggest killers. Additionally:

- fish consumption is linked to reducing the decline in brain function in old age
- people who eat fish regularly also have more grey matter in the brain centres that control memory and emotion
- the omega-3 fatty acids in fatty (oily) fish can be beneficial against depression

- eating fish has been linked to reduced risk of Type 1 diabetes and several other autoimmune diseases
- and those who eat more fish have a much lower risk of developing macular degeneration, a leading cause of vision impairment and blindness - especially as we age.[1]

White fish

White fish refers to any type of fish that has flaky white, light-flavoured meat, for example:

- cod, haddock, sea bass, pollack, coley, hake and whiting, plaice, sole, John Dory, halibut, flounder, turbot.

Whilst much is made of the health benefits of oily fish, white fish plays an important part in a nutritious diet. It's a great source of cellular-building, energy-giving and anti-ageing protein. It's also low in fat, so it's a good choice for anyone looking to manage or maintain their weight.

And that's not all that white fish does for us. With its high phosphorous content, it:

- protects our bones
- helps our bodies produce red blood cells via a rich source of vitamin B12
- fights inflammation via vitamin B6 and helps to reduce arthritic pain
- keeps our immune system strong via vitamin B3, helping us to recover from infections
- supports pregnancy to term, via vitamin B2. [2]

Oily fish

Oily fish - species like salmon, trout, sardines, tuna and mackerel - are rich in omega-3 fatty acids and vitamin D. Omega-3 fatty acids are important for growth and development, particularly docosahexaenoic acid (DHA) because it accumulates in the developing brain and in the developing eye.[3]

Research has shown[4] that consuming fish (and particularly oily fish) helps us in a variety of ways:

- genes that use fatty acids for energy are turned on (activated or up-regulated), while those that promote fat storage are turned off (deactivated or down-regulated). Fatty acids in fish help our cell membranes to remain sensitive to hormones and balance the release of steroids and stress hormones released from the adrenal glands.

- consuming oily fish can prevent inflammation and pain; it also helps our blood vessels to remain elastic and so control blood pressure and supports brain tissue and the function of our neurotransmitters, helping our mood and focus.

- expectant and nursing mothers are often advised to eat plenty of oily fish to make sure they get enough omega-3 fatty acids.

However, as we'll see below, some fish are high in mercury - which is linked to brain developmental problems - so pregnant women would do better to choose the oily fish that are low in the food chain (sardines and wild-caught salmon and trout) since they absorb less mercury

Fish eggs: a traditional 'superfood'

Fish eggs - or roe - are a traditional, sacred food. They were highly prized by traditional societies; the primitive peoples studied by Dr Weston A. Price valued key high-vitamin foods - fish eggs, shell fish, liver, bone marrow - for growing children and for men and women of childbearing age.[5]

For example, the natives of the Andes would travel hundreds of miles from their mountain villages down to the sea to procure dried roe to nourish women of childbearing age to ensure healthy and robust babies and children. Likewise, Eskimos also consumed roe - particularly from salmon - and again, the eggs were dried for nourishing pregnant women and for consumption during winter months.

One tablespoon of roe provides a similar dose of vitamin D as does a dose of the midday sun on the skin. The Weston A. Price Foundation's analysis showed a single tablespoon of roe contains approximately 17,000 international units of vitamin D, as well as A, K2, zinc, iodine, and omega-3 fatty acid DHA in ample amounts.[6]

Fish eggs come in a variety of sizes and colours. Traditionally, only the roe of the wild sturgeon from the Caspian Sea and Black Sea are referred to as 'caviar' and are prohibitively expensive, as well as featuring on the endangered species list.

Less costly - at least financially - is the large orange salmon roe that we see at sushi bars, Japanese restaurants and supermarkets: the keta roe from wild Alaskan salmon. Lumpfish - 'poor man's caviar' - is also widely available. Roe can be fresh or pasteurised (to preserve it) but be aware that the latter will have lost important nutrients, however, their intense flavour means they are excellent as a garnish, elevating even a simple plate of scrambled eggs to new heights.

Fish bones: nutritious and delicious

As we've seen, meat bones are an important source of nutrients and that also goes for fish bones. For all of us - but particularly for those with thyroid issues - fish broth, stock or soup, made with well-sourced fish heads and bones, is a chef's dream ingredient. It's also rich in iodine, thyroid-supporting follicles - around the eye and pharynx of the fish - and in fat-soluble vitamins.

Fish stock should be a regular part of a traditional diet, and unlike bone broth, is very quick to make. Use bones from non-oily fish, otherwise the odour of the stock is very strong, and the cooking will render the oils rancid.[7] Many fishmongers make and sell their own fish stock and will save fish bones for you or give you the bones from any whole fish you've asked to be filleted. It also freezes well.

Shellfish

Shellfish - oysters, mussels, clams, scallops, crab, lobster and prawns - were highly prized by traditional peoples. Dr Weston A. Price described how two warring tribes in New Guinea would regularly make peace in order to trade shellfish for sweet potatoes.

We now know why: shellfish are, nutritionally-speaking, uniquely dense. They spend their lives immersed in mineral-rich water and are excellent repositories for zinc, iodine, selenium and magnesium, along with A and B-vitamins (especially B12).

Equally important, when we eat shellfish, we usually eat the entire animal - muscle meat, digestive tissue and organ mass - all nicely wrapped up in a shell. We can also get these nutrients from land animals and some plants, but where else can we get them so conveniently?

Each species of shellfish offers us its own nutrient profile and ideally, shellfish need to be eaten very fresh and in season, as they are prone to rapid spoilage.[8] Although the cost of shellfish can be eye-watering, they are so nutrient-dense that consuming even a small amount reaps health benefits. Don't think of them as protein replacements, but as Mother Nature's finest food supplements.

Let's talk about prawns

We eat prawns mainly for their taste - prawns aren't powerfully nutrient-dense (compared with oysters and liver, for instance) but they're a good source of selenium, calcium and iodine and are rich in protein and some B vitamins and low in mercury. While they may taste amazing, prawns are now considered environmentally unfriendly. A once-traditional subsistence activity amongst Asian peoples, prawn farming was initially confined to small ponds within rice paddy fields, producing enough to feed a family, plus a little to sell at market.

Fast forward to 2007 and the Food and Agriculture Organisation (FAO) of the United Nations' Fisheries and Aquaculture Department reported that around 2.6 million tons of farmed prawns were in production every year, worth in excess of £5.7 billion!

Prawn farming is now another huge, intensive monoculture, bringing with it all the ecosystem-destroying practices and pollution issues that, as we'll see shortly, plague salmon farming in Scotland.

Most prawns consumed in the UK are imported frozen - farmed or wild-caught - from the Far East and South America, where harvesting wild farming prawns severely damages the ecosystem and intensive prawn farming pollutes the local environment and produces prawns which are highly susceptible to disease.

There are moves in the UK to establish less destructive methods - 'closed-loop' (re-circulating) systems which mimic the biological and physical processes used by nature to remove waste materials and to oxygenate and re-use the water. Some producers have won accreditation with the Marine Conservation Society for production and sustainability, and they now supply online.[9]

I love prawns, but for me the cost on every level is unacceptably high, so now they're a very occasional and well-sourced treat. Incidentally, always save, and freeze, if necessary, the heads and shells from the prawns to use in your fish stock; they lend colour and an intense flavour, forming the delicious base for fish soups, seafood risottos or paellas.

The woes of farmed fish

Prepare yourself for a distressing picture painted by Lynne Schweisfurth, a consultant for non-profits and a member of the Salmon Aquaculture Reform Network Scotland (SARNS). [10]

"Over 250 salmon farms operate throughout the west coast of Scotland and on the islands of Orkney and Shetland...mainly owned by Norwegian multinationals, some of them registered in tax havens.

The equivalent of approximately 700,000 fish, sit ominously on the surface of sea lochs and coastal waters, usually in symmetric arrangements of 12 cages, each 120 metres in diameter, like a silent occupation of visiting aliens.

The cages are connected by rubber tubing which deliver the feed containing toxic chemicals and antibiotics used to fight sea lice and other diseases."

- Lynne Schweisfurth

Some 45 sea lochs in Scotland have been contaminated by toxic pesticides (particularly emamectin benzoate) from fish farms. Each year, thousands of tonnes of fish farm effluent flows into the sea through open net cages, causing damage to sea life, birds and mammals - including humans.

Most distressingly, Scotland's wild salmon and sea trout stocks are in dangerous decline and in some rivers, they're close to extinction. This is because they are picking up parasitic infestation from swimming in close proximity to fish farms contaminated with high numbers of sea lice.

The farming industry has been using 'cleaner' fish - such as wrasse and lump sucker - to eat the lice off the salmon. These species are now being fished in vast numbers in the south of England and transported by lorry to Scotland. But this is making a desperate situation worse - by anticipating a rapid depletion of wild wrasse stocks, the industry has already begun to farm the wrasse, only to find they are also prone to disease, which they then transmit to the salmon!

"As the industry endeavours to stay one step ahead of nature, it is now looking to GMO plant-based feed for the many millions of fish it is breeding across the globe."

- Lynne Schweisfurth

In 1970, aquaculture (farmed fish) provided under 1kg of fish per person per year; by 2002 this had jumped to 6.4 kg and now, nearly half - 43% - of fish consumed globally are farmed. This may be good news for the fish farming industry, but environmentally it's a disaster.

The largest salmon farms hold about 1.3 million fish - nearly 22lbs per cubic yard. That's tight - tighter than battery cages on factory farms. Quite apart from the shocking husbandry practices dictated by a huge intensive monoculture[11], this results in massive overpopulation, excessive waste, germs, disease and over-reliance on medications.

The characteristic pink/red colour of wild salmon comes from a diet of krill, from which they get astaxanthin carotenoid pigment (farmed salmon are fed a synthetic version of the pigment).

About one third of the world's total fish catch goes towards fish meal/oil for farmed fish and other animals.

Salmon are a carnivorous species and industrial aquaculture has begun to incorporate by-products from land-based animals, such as poultry meal (intestines, eggs, blood), feather meal and manure. And as we have seen, some fats in the fish feed now come from GM vegetable oils, which can decrease the omega-3 content of fish.

The future of wild-caught fish

As if the woes of farmed fish weren't enough, the plight of wild fish is as worrying:

"Unless we fundamentally change the way we manage all the oceans' species together, as working ecosystems, then this century is the last century of wild seafood."

- Stephen Palumbi
Marine biologist, Stanford University

With 90% of world fish stocks fully or over-exploited from fishing - plus pressure from climate change and pollution - the future of wild fish is in a state of serious decline.

Whether it's fresh, frozen or canned, the Marine Stewardship Council is asking us to look out for its blue eco-label kite mark - which tells us that the fish was wild-caught. This helps to reduce the strain on certain species by demanding that our choice of fish comes from sustainably-managed stocks and is caught - or farmed - in a way that causes minimal damage to the marine environment and other wildlife.[12]

Wild.

What a word. What a place. Worth caring for? We think so!

Out here. Out past the hustle. Past the surf. Out past the bustle.

This is wild.

Wild is the headwind. The white cap. The bending light.

Wild is the calm before the swell. Before the storm.

And while only a brave few go into the wild, we all want what comes out.

Keep it wild. Choose the blue fish.

Fish and mercury: are fish safe to eat?

There is ongoing food safety concern over whether fish, and if so which, are contaminated with toxins, particularly mercury, and whether fish should be consumed at all by pregnant women or children. In his 2014 review, Chris Kresser[13] explains that studies of mercury exposure in fish consistently ignore the important role of selenium in preventing mercury toxicity. Mercury is harmful because it 'binds' to selenium, preventing it performing its vital roles in the brain - including motor function, memory, cognition and protecting us from neurodegenerative disorders such as Alzheimer's and Parkinson's disease.

Luckily, the vast majority of fish we consume have more selenium than mercury. Varieties to avoid, however, are shark, swordfish, tuna, tilefish and king mackerel, which contain more mercury than selenium. In summary, Kresser advises:

"There's no evidence that pregnant women or children (or anyone else) will be harmed by eating more than 12 ounces (340 g) of the most commonly consumed varieties of fish.

In fact, there's a lot of evidence that eating less than 12 ounces a week of fish could cause significant harm to both pregnant women and young children. Most pregnant women need to eat more fish, rather than less.

Fortunately, many of the most sustainable choices (e.g. sardines, anchovies, mackerel, wild-caught salmon, etc.) are also the fish that are highest in the beneficial long-chain omega-3 fats."

Fish and plastics: our ultimate insult to Mother Nature

In recent decades, our production of plastic material has increased tremendously and around 10% of these plastics end up in the oceans each year through sewage treatment plants, waste handling or simply from airborne plastic particles landing in the sea. As we have seen from appalling images in the media, plastics now make up 60-80% of the total marine debris and consumer outrage and pressure is gaining momentum. Debris from plastics affects almost 700 different marine species through ingestion and entanglement and is an alarming pollutant in aquatic environments.

However, few studies have researched the effects of the tiny plastic particles known as nanoplastics. Researchers at Lund University studied how nanoplastics may be transported through different organisms in the aquatic ecosystem, from algae to animal plankton to larger fish.

"Once in the aquatic environment, plastic material breaks up into smaller pieces through the action of sunlight, waves, living organisms in the water and by the water itself.

Eventually plastic material is broken down to nanoparticles which may be an even more potent threat since plastic nanoparticles are able to pass through biological barriers, penetrate tissues and accumulate in organs and affect behaviour and metabolism of organisms."

- Mattsson et al, 2017 [14]

The study showed that the uptake of nanoparticles was transferred via a bottom-up, three-level food chain: first by algae, then through zooplankton, continuing up the food chain and ultimately showing the effects on the brain physiology and behaviour of the top consumer - the fish itself.

Tommy Cedervall, one of the study's authors, commented that these effects were likely to considerably impact natural ecosystems, since *"top predators have a crucial impact on lower trophic levels and ecosystem functions."*

A trophic level is the position that an organism occupies in a food chain - what it eats and what eats it - so this is cold comfort indeed, given that man is THE top predator on the planet!

However, Cedervall says he does not dare draw the conclusion that plastic nanoparticles could accumulate in other tissues in fish and thus potentially be transmitted to humans through consumption, as he's *"very cautious about commenting on it."*

Fish and sustainability

"If we want our children to have fish, we'd better leave some for them."

- Ruth Reichl

The Marine Conservation Society (MCS) is the UK's leading charity for the protection of our seas, shores and wildlife. Their goal for responsible fisheries and aquaculture is to:

"Ensure there are more fish in healthier seas, improve the way wild fisheries and farms are managed and influence consumers and seafood businesses to be more responsible in their seafood buying choices."

The MCS online guide and app will help you choose seasonal, sustainable seafood and suggest cooking tips. They have produced a handy guide - *Buying Seasonal Fish* - for the best options in choosing fresh, wild-caught fish. Available online, it teaches us to avoid buying fish during breeding or spawning times and those below their mature size.

Where to buy

If you want spanking fresh fish, the supermarket fish counter is seldom your best source. An investigation in October 2017 revealed that supermarket fish can be up to nine days old - and previously frozen - by the time you buy it.[15]

I usually buy my fish from a champion 'wet' fishmonger; he's about 15 miles from my home, but it's well worth the journey for quality and cooking tips - he also runs a small fish cookery school. There are several excellent online suppliers for fresh, seasonal fish, from whom I also order (with some fish-loving friends to save on delivery costs). I've frequently used The Cornish Fishmonger, who has a great website and who sources fresh fish daily from the four quayside fish markets of Cornwall and South Devon.

Cooking fish - without the tears!

Less is definitely more when cooking fish - both oily and white fish take very little cooking, unless you want an unpalatable, dry result. White fish contains little fat, so will dry out very easily if cooked for too long.

Generally, it's better to cook white fish by steaming, poaching or pan-frying so most of the moisture and flavour is retained. My favourite method of cooking any fish is to pan-fry in plenty of butter, over a medium heat. I like to cook the fish skin-side-down for several minutes, to crisp the skin and allow the heat to penetrate about a third of the way into the flesh. With salmon, you can see the colour of the flesh change as it cooks. Then reduce the heat and turn the fish over for just a couple of minutes to cook through.

If you prefer your fish skinned, you can either poach it, or make a parcel from greaseproof paper and add a tablespoon of water to create some steam and then any seasoning or herbs. Seal the parcel loosely and bake it in a medium-hot oven for around 10 minutes, depending on the thickness of the fish. You can carefully undo the parcel to check if it is done. Be brave - DO NOT over-cook!

I no longer use aluminium foil for cooking; research has shown that small amounts of aluminium leach into food under high temperatures. I also avoid using foil to wrap acidic foods like tomatoes and citrus fruit, as the acids cause leaching. Aluminium deposits in the brain are implicated in Alzheimer's Disease and to a lesser extent, in inflammatory bowel disease; while the science isn't fully settled... I'd prefer to avoid it until further notice! [16]

Some final words on fish

Choosing and eating healthy, sustainable fish is becoming a minefield and there's no question that what we buy and how we source it has a big impact not only on the environment, but on our pockets, as well as our health. We are what we eat, digest and absorb - bear in mind those nanoplastics.

Here are my eco-friendly suggestions for enjoying healthy, happy fish:

- **buy your fish from a trusted and traditional fishmonger**. Seek their advice and consider less popular varieties of seafood - they'll be just as delicious and also much cheaper.

- **always buy fish in season** and from sustainable sources; always ask about the provenance of your fish and buy wild-caught fish whenever possible - choose the blue label fish.
- **avoid or limit consumption of farmed fish** to once a month - and please choose the blue eco-label kite mark label fish!
- **aim for one serving of white fish** each week and one serving of fish low in the food chain - sardines, wild caught salmon or trout - each week.
- **budget** to use shellfish as a powerful food supplement.

Finally, having cared about where you source your fish, please… DON'T OVER-COOK IT!!

SEAFOOD Recipes

FISH STOCK

Fumet (as the French call it) cannot be beaten for flavour and reinforces the flavours of seafood dishes, sauces and soups and is especially important in a good seafood risotto. And, unlike meat broths, fish stock is very quick - just 20 minutes or so cooking time.

There are four important things to remember about making fish stock:

- Source your fish well
- Don't use oily fish (the oils make the stock overwhelmingly pungent and they are damaged in the cooking process)
- Meticulously clean the bones, heads and gills as these can impart a bitter flavour and darken the stock
- Cook it very gently for best results.

You can make a simple stock with just water, fish bones and cider vinegar, but I like to flavour mine with aromatics. Depending on your final dish, you can use onions, leeks, garlic, celery fennel, parsley, tarragon, bay leaves, garlic, celery, ginger, fennel and carrot (omit carrot if you want a colourless stock). I don't season the stock as it cooks, as this can interfere with a particular recipe that I want to use it in.

Here's my recipe for a basic fish stock:

What you'll need:

Filtered water: 3 litres
Fish heads/bones: 1kg (or just heads of non-oily fish)
Apple cider vinegar: ¼ cup (raw, organic)
Garlic: 2 cloves (peeled, smashed)
Carrots: 2 medium (peeled, very thinly sliced)
Ginger: 1 thumb (peeled, very thinly sliced)
Celery: 1 stick (very thinly sliced)
Whole black peppercorns: 1 tsp

What to do:

1. Place the water and prepared fish heads/bones in a 4-litre stockpot, or equivalent.
2. Stir in the vinegar and bring the water up to a gentle boil.
3. As the water begins to boil, skim off any foam that rises to the surface with a slotted spoon (or a small strainer). It's very important to remove this foam as these impurities will impair the flavour of the stock.
4. When you've removed the foam, gently add in the rest of the ingredients
5. Reduce heat to a simmer for around 20 - 30 minutes.
6. Cool and then strain into containers; freeze what you will not use within one week.

SMOKED HADDOCK, SPINACH & CAULIFLOWER GRATIN

(Serves 2)

This deliciously unctuous dish will leave you planning to cook it again - soon! Topping the gratin with a lightly poached organic, free-range egg adds a powerful protein hit and a colourful, crisp salad on the side and a slice of crunchy sourdough toast rounds, balances this dish beautifully.

Remember that both smoked haddock and cheese are salty so season conservatively. Always try to source your fish from a traditional fishmonger who'll be pleased to give you tips and ideas for cooking different fish.

What you'll need:

New (or waxy) potatoes: 2 medium/4 small (scrubbed and cut into 1cm dice)
Cauliflower: ½ medium (divide into small florets & slice stem finely)
Sea salt: ½ tsp (Maldon and scant - the cheese will be salty)
Olive oil: I tbsp
Butter: 1 tbsp
Garlic: 1 fat clove (peeled & finely sliced)
Spinach: 250g (washed, well drained & roughly chopped)
Ground black pepper: ½ tsp
Spring onion: 2 large (finely sliced)

Dill: 1 tbsp (finely chopped)
Double cream: 200ml
Greek yoghurt: 200ml
Cornflour: 1 tsp (heaped)
Cheese: 200g (strong, coarsely grated)
Smoked haddock: 2 thick fillets (skinned, cut into 2cm chunks)
Eggs: 2 large

What to do:

1. Sprinkle the new potatoes with a little salt and set them to steam over boiling water; when still a little firm in the centre, add the cauliflower and continue to steam until just tender (about 10 mins).

2. Meanwhile, in a deep sauté pan melt the butter and olive oil and sauté the garlic and spinach over medium heat, until the spinach is just wilted.

3. Add the spring onions, dill, double cream, pepper and stir well. Stir in the cooked potatoes and cauliflower, breaking them up slightly with the back of a fork. Combine everything with the yoghurt, cornflour and half the cheese and gently stir in the (uncooked) smoked haddock chunks.

4. Transfer the mixture to an oven-proof dish, push the haddock down into the mixture and top with the rest of the grated cheese.

5. Bake the gratin in a hot oven at 190°C (Fan) or Gas Mark 7 for about 10 mins or so, until sizzling and finish under a hot grill.

To serve, top with a lightly poached egg and plenty of black pepper.

COD & CHORIZO STEW

(Serves 2)

This dish is such a treat - nutritious, delicious, really simple and looks stunning! If you can, try to source juicy, thick cod fillets from your local traditional fishmonger - you'll be amazed at the flavour and quality!

Serve with steamed broccoli and a slice of sourdough toast.

What you'll need:

For the stew:
Olive oil: 1 tbsp
Butter: 1 tbsp
Carrots: 1 medium (peeled, halved lengthways & thickly cut diagonally in 1cm slices)
Celery: 2 sticks (washed, trimmed & cut as above)
Small new potatoes: 6 (scrubbed & sliced thickly as above)
Onion: ½ small (peeled, halved lengthways & finely sliced)
Ginger: ¾ inch (peeled & cut into fine matchsticks)
Garlic: 2 medium cloves (peeled & finely sliced)
Sea salt: ¾ tsp (Maldon)
Ground black pepper: ½ tsp
Paprika: ¾ tsp
Black Kalamata olives: handful (stoned, halved)
Chopped tomatoes: 1 x 400g tin, drained & roughly cut (reserve juice)
Muscovado sugar: 1-2 tsp

For the Cod:
Cod: 2 x 200g (thick fillets, pin boned & skinned)
Seas salt: light sprinkling
Ground black pepper: light sprinkling
Butter: 1 tbsp
Olive oil: 2 tsp

To finish:
Flat-leaf parsley: handful (roughly chopped)
Ground black pepper: to taste
Lemon: 2 wedges

What to do:

1. Heat the oil and butter in a deep, lidded sauté pan. Over a medium heat, sauté the carrots, celery, new potatoes, onion, ginger and garlic, salt, pepper and paprika until beginning to soften.

2. Add the olives, drained tomatoes, muscovado sugar and enough of the juice to come half way up the top layer of vegetables, when everything is pushed gently down. Bring up to the boil, then reduce heat to a slow simmer and cover.

3. Simmer until all the vegetables are just tender (about 45 mins - but will depend on the variety and thickness of your potato slices). Turn the vegetables frequently and push them down into the sauce. Add a little more tomato juice if required (or a little fish stock if you have it).

4. When the vegetables are just tender, stir in the chopped parsley, reserving a little for finishing the dish.

5. Season the cod well. If your sauté pan is oven-proof, place the fillets side by side directly over the stew; if not, transfer the stew to an oven-proof dish first. Dot the fillets with butter and sprinkle with a good grinding of black pepper.

6. Place the pan or dish, uncovered, in a preheated oven 180º (Fan) or Gas Mark 6 for about 10 mins, or until the cod is beginning to flake, but still opaque. Be brave, or you'll overcook it! Cover the dish, turn off the oven and leave the oven door open for 5-6 minutes for the fish to continue to cook gently until perfectly done.

7. With a wide spatula, carefully lift the cod out from the stew, set onto a warmed tray and cover. Quickly divide the stew between warm, wide plates and top with the fish, ground black pepper and a little more parsley. Serve the lemon wedges at the side.

Get ahead:

- Stop when the vegetable stew is cooked, cool and refrigerate until later or overnight.
- When needed, bring the stew to room temperature, and re-heat until piping hot in the deep sauté pan.
- Continue with the recipe.

SIMPLY SARDINES: ON TOAST

(Serves 2)

This breakfast is deliciously healthy and sustaining and you can prepare the sardine paste the night before if you want to save time. We enjoy sardines on toast with a small glass good quality orange juice - the citrus cuts through the richness of the sardines!

Tinned, or canned sardines are healthful and always take the trouble to look for brands which are ethically-sourced and sustainably and preserve the fish in organic olive oil, or brine.

What you'll need:

Sardines: 2 x 120g tins (well-sourced, canned in brine)
Lemon juice: good squeeze, to taste
Sea salt: Maldon, to taste
Ground black pepper: to taste
Slices of toasted organic sourdough bread

What to do:

1. Roughly mash up the sardines, retaining the highly nutritious backbone. If (like me) you don't like the texture of the bones, just remove the backbones, press them down gently into a paste with the blade of a knife and mix back into the sardines. You'll never know!

2. Add lemon juice and season to taste.

3. Toast and butter the bread, top with the sardine paste, grab your OJ and tuck in!

For a luxe version, add in chopped hard-boiled eggs, or freshly chopped tomatoes and finely chopped dill, or top with a poached egg or two.

OTHER QUICK WAYS WITH SARDINES:

Sardine, Egg & Spring Onion Paté:
Hard boil the eggs, cool and roughly chop and mix everything together. Serve on organic sourdough or rye bread, organic oatcakes, or as a dip with apple slices, carrot and celery sticks.

Sardine and Potato Salad:
Create a version of sardines to your liking, add a little seasoned yoghurt, chopped mint or dill (or both) and stir through cooked, cooled and chopped new or sweet potatoes.

Linguine with Sardines, Tomato & Kalamata Olives:
Stone and roughly chop a handful of olives. Chop a couple of fresh tomatoes into a small dice, add in a couple of diced spring onions (including green parts), crush a clove of garlic and finely chop a small chilli (optional) and heat everything through in a frying pan with a little butter and olive oil.

Stir in roughly chopped sardines and heat gently. Season well and add a good squeeze of lemon juice. Toss through cooked linguine (loosening with extra olive oil) and sprinkle with chopped parsley. Try a beetroot, orange and mint green leaf salad on the side.

CHAPTER ELEVEN

CULTURED and FERMENTED FOODS

"Moving toward a more harmonious way of life and greater resilience requires our active participation. This means finding ways to become more aware of and connected to the other forms of life that are around us and that constitute our food -- plants and animals, as well as bacteria and fungi -- and to the resources, such as water, fuel, materials, tools, and transportation, upon which we depend."

- Sandor Katz
The Art of Fermentation

It all begins with our gut critters

The health of our soil and its microbes are inextricably linked to our health. In recent years, our knowledge of the human microbiome has exploded and, far from considering bacteria as a deadly enemy, we are now beginning to understand the fundamental role our gut flora - trillions of microscopic bacterial critters - play in determining our physical and emotional health.

"The more we learn with our modern scientific tools, the more we realise just how correct Hippocrates was: all diseases do begin in the gut! Science has discovered that about 90% of all cells and all genetic material of the human body belongs to the 2 -3 kilos of gut flora - a mixture of various beneficial microbes - which live inside our digestive tract.

So, in reality your body is just a shell, a 10%, providing a habitat for this mass of micro-creatures living inside you; and their role in your health and physiology is monumental.

Our modern world poses many dangers for human gut flora, and once it is damaged, the health of the whole body enters a downward slide towards disease."

- Dr Natasha Campbell-McBride MD
Gut & Psychology Syndrome

The human microbiome, gut flora and immune system

Our microbiome is made up of complex communities of micro-organisms. This micro-flora comprises bacteria, viruses and fungi, that populate our body-shell. The microbiome is crucial in building our immunity and determining our health. Microbes populate and look after our bodies top-to-tail, our skin, hair, eyes, noses, mouth under-arm/groin and digestive tract are all protected by their own microbiome.

There are plenty of jobs for which our gut bacteria are responsible:

- digesting food
- producing vitamins (particularly B and K vitamins)
- increasing nutrient absorption
- regulating hormones
- detoxing
- regulating intestinal pH
- improving bowel transit time
- crowding out invading pathogens
- repairing and protecting intestinal walls
- preventing yeast and fungal infections
- maintaining our immune system.

Clever little critters, aren't they? Our gut is the major player in maintaining the integrity of our immune system - 70 to 80% of which resides in our gut - so our gut lining forms the first line of immune defence.

Beneficial gut critters can and do influence inflammation and immune responses throughout the body. I have no room here for a full discussion, but there are many explanatory videos on the micro-biome, gut health, inflammation and immune function online.[1]

No, it's not all in your mind!

Based on years of work with people with mental health disorders, French psychiatrist Phillipe Pineal concluded in 1807 that:

> **"The primary seat of insanity generally is in the region of the stomach and intestines."**

Now, research evidence is emerging almost daily on the gut-brain axis - the inter-relationship and biochemical signalling between the brain and the gut - to illustrate the role that our gut flora plays in determining our mood, our emotional and mental health.

The gut-brain axis encompasses our two nervous systems: our central nervous system (CNS) which consists of the brain and spinal cord, and our enteric nervous system (ENS) of the gastrointestinal tract. These two systems are formed at the same time during foetal development and are created from the same tissues.

We are only just beginning to understand how the actual composition of our gut flora and its communication with the brain - via the vagus nerve which connects the gut to the brain - not only affects our physical health, but also has a significant impact on brain function and our mental/emotional states.

Gut-brain communication is a two-way street, but it's beginning to look as though our gut, not our brain, is in the driving seat, with many more connections running from gut to brain than the other way around.[2]

The idea that mental health issues are rooted in brain-chemical imbalances is slowly being displaced by science's understanding that it's our gut bacteria that produce the neurotransmitter serotonin, involved in mood control, depression and aggression.

It is worth noting that the greatest concentration of serotonin is found in your intestines and *not* in your brain.

As Dr Kelly Brogan argues in *A Mind of Your Own: The Truth About Depression and How Women Can Heal Their Bodies to Reclaim Their Lives*, this is why drugs like antidepressants, which raise serotonin levels in the brain, are ineffective in treating the root cause of depression and other mental illness, whereas a whole food, unprocessed diet and lifestyle changes can not only improve, but in fact reverse life-long conditions.

The gut-brain connection is now well-recognised as a basic tenet of physiology, medicine and behavioural science. There's no shortage of evidence of gastrointestinal involvement in a variety of neurological diseases and it's easy to see how the balance of gut bacteria can play a significant role in your psychology and behaviour. Mounting research is showing us that the bacterial colonies residing in the gut may in fact play key roles in:

- brain development
- behavioural and emotional problems
- anti-social behaviour, aggression, anxiety, depression
- ADHD, autism and more serious mental illness like schizophrenia.

Feeding our gut critters: pre- and pro-biotic foods

From cradle to grave, nourishing our gut flora is extremely important since, in every sense, we have two brains - one inside our skull and one in our gut and each needs nourishment with the right kinds of pro- and pre-biotic foods.

Pro-biotic foods

Fermented and cultured foods are teeming with live, probiotic lactic-acid producing bacteria and are an important source of support to our digestive health and proper immune function. The time-honoured, traditional process of fermentation pre-digests the food and makes nutrients more bio-available - i.e. the amount of a nutrient that is absorbed and utilized. Soaking and sprouting also achieves this.

Fermentation also generates additional nutrients, especially B vitamins, unique protective micro-nutrients not present in the raw ingredient, which help us to make use of the energy provided by our food. Fermentation can also help to detoxify anti-nutrients - those mineral-binding phytates and lectins in grains/legumes/seeds/nuts - and other food toxins, as well as helping to bio-degrade some pesticide residues on vegetables.

Pre-biotic foods

Quite simply, pre-biotic foods are the indigestible fibres that we eat, which feed our gut critters.

Pro-biotic foods include	Pre-biotic foods include
Dairy: raw milk and cream; fermented or cultured dairy (clabbered - soured - milk; yoghurt; labneh; cultured cream; kefir; cheeses)	**Vegetables:** asparagus; Jerusalem artichokes; chicory; leeks; onions. broccoli; Brussels sprouts; cabbage; cauliflower; collard greens; kale; radish
Vegetables: fermented vegetables - sauerkraut; kimchi; carrots; tempeh and miso (fermented soya) Just about all veg and fruits can be fermented	**Fruit;** organic bananas; berries
Others: raw honey; raw apple cider vinegar; kvass; kombucha tea (fermented sweet black tea); authentic sourdough bread; quality dark chocolate; and a variety of sausages and cured meat products	**Others:** oatmeal*; authentic sourdough bread* red wine; honey; maple syrup; apple cider vinegar; legumes*; beans (including green beans); nuts; peas; lentils

**Note: All grains and legumes contain anti-nutrients which interfere with digestion and block absorption of some nutrients. These foods are rendered more digestible if soaked for 1-2 days in an acid medium (lemon juice, vinegar or whey).*

'Cultured' vs 'Wild' Ferments

The term 'cultured' in relation to fermented foods relates to the fact that a starter - containing specific strains of lactic acid forming bacteria - is used to initiate the fermentation process. So, as we'll see in yoghurt-making, the milk is 'cultured' by adding a small amount of live probiotic yoghurt from a previous batch.

But the process of fermentation can happily proceed un-aided. The now old-fashioned clabbered (soured) milk which our grannies used to make is simply raw milk left out on a counter top, exposed to the ambient microbes in the environment. After a couple of days, the microbes have worked away on the milk, which then sours. This type of fermentation is known as 'wild' fermentation since it utilises the ambient bacteria all around us. It's this process that underlies traditional methods of fermenting vegetables and other foods where no starter culture is used.

Authentic sourdough bread-making utilises both methods. The wild fermentation of flour and water creates the starter, which is then added to fresh flour and water and left to slowly ferment as the microbes consume the sugars in the grain and producing carbon dioxide bubbles which make the dough rise. Clever little critters, aren't they?

Cultured Dairy: yoghurt, labneh & kefir

Cultured dairy foods have been around since about 10,000 BC and their pedigree is evident in almost all culinary traditions. The pharaohs reputedly feasted on them and to the ancient Assyrians, yoghurt was known as 'lebney' or 'life'.

Persian traditions believe that Abraham owed his longevity to eating yoghurt regularly and present-day Hindus offer and consume curds (cultured milk) - along with milk, sugar, ghee and honey - as gifts to the gods in their ancient ritual of Panchamitra (the Five Elixirs of Life).

In the early 1900s, the Russian-born bacteriologist Dr Illya Mechnikoff noted yoghurt was the key ingredient in the longevity-promoting diet of Bulgarian peasants in the Balkans, who had an average life expectancy of 87 years, despite extremely impoverished living conditions. Yoghurt remains a key part of the diet of the growing number of Bulgaria's centenarians.

The process of culturing - or lacto-fermenting - dairy produces lactic acid to break down the milk protein casein, one of the most difficult proteins to digest. It restores many of the enzymes which are destroyed during pasteurisation, but which we need to absorb calcium and other minerals.

One such enzyme is lactase, which helps us to digest the milk sugar lactose, so many who are lactose intolerant can tolerate lacto-fermented foods.

Research now shows that a regular diet of cultured dairy:

- lowers cholesterol
- protects against bone loss
- boosts the digestive tract with beneficial bacteria and lactic acid to keep pathogens at bay and support the immune system, thereby guarding against infectious illnesses
- enables us to fully digest our food.

Yoghurt: Mechnikoff's research led him to discover that the beneficial bacteria which ferments the milk remains 'live' throughout its passage through the intestine. The beneficial bacteria found in yoghurt help keep the digestive tract clean and provide food for the friendly bacteria found in a healthy gut; these transient bacteria pass right through and out of the digestive tract and with their antibiotic properties support intestinal equilibrium.

Our contemporary culture is finally catching on to this ancient food wisdom and yoghurt is credited with healing everything from gastrointestinal complaints to eczema.

Labneh: Labneh (aka labane, lebni, labne, or lebnah) originates in the Middle East. It's a simple, mild tasting 'yoghurt-cheese' made by straining yoghurt in a muslin cloth until most of the whey drips off, leaving a luxe creamy curd.

Like yoghurt, it's rich in beneficial bacteria and can be flavoured with either sweet or savoury ingredients and used as a dip or topping.

Kefir: Milk kefir is a cultured dairy food originally from the Caucuses - the region where Europe meets Asia. Like yoghurt, milk kefir has been traditionally prized as an elixir of long life and health - it's rich in beneficial bacteria, phosphorus, vitamin K, biotin and folic acid - nutrients that are essential to health and well-being.

Kefir is a SCOBY - a symbiotic colony of bacteria, fungi and yeasts (known as kefir 'grains', resembling tiny cauliflower florets).

Milk kefir contains a much wider range and different types of bacteria (as well as friendly yeasts) than those found in yoghurt. These bacteria are critical to the intestinal tract, helping to crowd out over-growths of pathogenetic (disease causing or promoting) bacteria and helping to restore a healthy equilibrium in the gut.

Kefiran: a single component of kefir - successfully protects beneficial bacteria from damage in the hostile environment of the digestive tract.

Benefits of Milk Kefir and Kefiran

Milk kefir - particularly from raw milk - is a powerful anti-inflammatory food and helps in combating gastrointestinal distress caused by infections from salmonella, E. coli, helicobacter pylori and clostridium difficile infection (and gastrointestinal discomfort and diarrhoea which often accompanies use of antibiotics.)

Kefir is powerful antimicrobial food, helping to limit the growth of pathogens while encouraging the proliferation of beneficial bacteria in the intestinal tract and exhibits anti-tumour effects.

Like other cultured dairy foods, it may play a role in the prevention of cancer. Cultured dairy foods have been found to play a role in the prevention and treatment of several cancers - notably breast, bladder and colon cancer. Milk kefir appears to be one of the most promising foods when it comes to cancer prevention.[3]

You'll find more detailed information about kefir online[4] and there are a number of Facebook forums devoted to all things fermented.

Gut health, healing and fermented foods

The food we eat and how we live impacts directly and indirectly on the integrity and health of our gut. Our gut lining is like a fine cheese cloth, designed to allow the tiny molecules from fully digested foods to pass through into our blood stream.

In a healthy gut, beneficial bacteria live alongside pathogenic microbes, keeping them in check. Our gut critters are very smart, but they're also very sensitive and are subject to a wide range of influences which displace the balance of our beneficial gut flora, to allow opportunistic bacteria and pathogens to proliferate. These influences include:

- eating a diet of low fibre, processed and fake foods
- chlorinated water
- baby milk formulas
- antibiotics (including antibiotics in food)
- medications (including the contraceptive pill)
- anti-microbial/anti-bacterial personal care, household and homeware products
- alcohol and nicotine
- environmental toxins
- stress and dysfunctional lifestyles.

The more we ingest or are exposed to the above, the more we set ourselves up for a vicious cycle of intestinal dysbiosis (unbalanced gut bacteria), inflammation and intestinal permeability (leaky gut) which allows undigested proteins to enter our blood stream. This cycle triggers constant immune system responses, which if left to progress, will develop into a full-blown autoimmune, degenerative or chronic disease.

It's worth remembering that persistent digestive symptoms and/or other difficult-to-resolve health issues are a strong indication that the gut needs to be 'healed and sealed' through addressing not only diet, but also lifestyle factors like sleep, stress, movement, relationships and environment.

There are several healing/autoimmune protocols which are beneficial. I was trained as Certified GAPS Practitioner by Dr Natasha Campbell-McBride, who has developed a comprehensive healing protocol specifically for healing chronic and autoimmune disorders, by treating the root cause: compromised gut health.

However, everybody is an individual and no single approach will suit everybody. A good practitioner will take a comprehensive health history and employ a wide range of evidence-based methods to find a personalised approach to suit their client's needs.

There's power in their punch!

Home-made probiotic foods are very powerful friends (particularly kefir and fermented vegetables), much more so than commercially produced products. Dr Joseph Mercola famously sent his sauerkraut off to a lab and reported the findings of probiotics saying:

> **"We had it analysed. We found in a 4-6 oz. serving of the fermented vegetables there were literally ten trillion bacteria."**

This means just 2oz (around 55g) of home-fermented sauerkraut contains more probiotics than 100 probiotic capsules - just work out the cost savings!

As a GAPS practitioner employing probiotic foods, I'd recommend that everyone considers consuming a variety of home-made fermented foods regularly, ringing the changes to enjoy the deliciously different flavours. Also, the juice from a vegetable or fruit ferment makes a healing and digestive tonic. But there are a few points of which you need to be aware:

- those with digestive issues who have loose stools may find that kefir is a better friend than sauerkraut or kimchi, while those who struggle to pass stools do better with sauerkrauts and other fermented vegetables.

- fermented foods are high in histamine, so those who experience histamine intolerance may not find them beneficial.

- fermented foods are very powerful and need to be introduced gradually. The probiotic bacteria will destroy and displace pathogenic bacteria in the digestive tract. This is a very good thing, but as the pathogens die, they will release a high level of toxins into the gut.

- those with severely compromised gut health may experience a 'Herxheimer' reaction (healing crisis, known as 'die off'). This can cause a wide range of symptoms from nausea, headache, fatigue, dizziness, bloating, gas, constipation or diarrhoea, to swollen glands, increased joint or muscle pain, chills, cold feeling in extremities, skin break-outs, body itchiness, hives or rashes, sweating, or raised temperature.

While all this sounds quite alarming and these symptoms are not at all pleasant, those who experience extreme symptoms are generally very severely compromised in their gut health and ultimately, the pathogens which are causing these symptoms need to exit the body for the gut to heal. An experienced practitioner will guide anyone undertaking a healing process to minimise die-off symptoms and reactions.

But, for all fermented food newbies, it's always wise to introduce probiotic foods gradually, not least because they are very tasty and it's very tempting to over-indulge. Go really slowly at first - maybe starting with a teaspoonful at a time - and gradually increase the amount over a period of months.

If you experience any of the above symptoms - usually loose stools - then ease back for a few days to an amount you can tolerate and then gradually increase the amounts again, working up to a good shot of daily kefir and perhaps a tablespoon of kimchi with each meal.

The idea is to incorporate fermented foods into your daily diet as a condiment - not a meal replacement!

A happy healthy gut makes a happy, healthy you, so... get fermenting!

CULTURED and FERMENTED Recipes

Culturing and fermenting foods is definitely a forgotten skill - but thankfully it's one which is finally seeing a slow renaissance. Although we have an increasing variety of commercial products available, nothing beats home-made!

Making Yoghurt

Home-made yoghurt rocks and is far cheaper, far more delicious and far more beneficial than anything you'll buy at any price. Good quality commercial, organic probiotic yoghurt is expensive and even top-quality brands contain thickening, emulsifying and stabilising ingredients. By making your own, not only can you control what goes into it, it's going to be spanking fresh and will contain the beneficial microbes present in your unique environment.

Most commonly, yoghurt is made with a thermophilic (heat loving) culture which contains the beneficial bacteria:

- lactobacillus bulgaricus
- streptococcus thermophilus.

You can find more information on yoghurt starters online.

Using raw milk: If you want to make a true raw milk yoghurt, you'll need a mesophillic starter (works at room temperature). Because the milk is not heated, it retains all the beneficial nutrients. The proteins also remain intact, resulting in a much thinner yoghurt - more like a thick drinking yoghurt and great to use in smoothies.

Heating raw milk denatures (changes) the milk proteins somewhat, but it yields a thicker, set yoghurt. Although heating impacts its nutritional value, gently heating raw milk to around 85 - 95°F is a far less damaging process than the methods that are used by industrial dairy processors to 'manufacture' yoghurt. So, whichever method you choose, it's still well worth starting with raw milk.

Using pasteurised milk: By culturing organic pasteurised milk with a thermophilic starter (heat loving) you can restore some of the valuable nutrients and probiotics. If you're using pasteurised milk, please cast your mind back to the Milk chapter and do your health a big favour by choosing organic full-fat, non-homogenised, pasture-fed milk.

TO MAKE YOGHURT

This recipe yields about 600ml of gorgeous, creamy, mild yoghurt.

What you'll need:

Organic whole (full-fat) milk: 800 ml
Organic, full-fat, natural 'live' yoghurt: 2-3 tbsp (e.g. Duchy or Yeo Valley)
A food thermometer (recommended)

What to do:

1. In a heavy-based, or non-stick saucepan, slowly heat the milk until it reaches 85°C. If you haven't got a food thermometer (get one!), stop heating the milk at the stage when it's simmering (just 'fizzing' but not actually bubbling, or boiling). Keep it 'fizzing' for 2-3 minutes. This step inhibits enzymes that retard subsequent fermentation.

2. If you're using good quality whole milk, a creamy skin will form on top; no worries - just whisk it into the milk. Take the pan off the heat and let the milk cool to around 43°C.

3. Note that the window of proper fermentation is between 42-44°C; any higher and the lactobacillus will be destroyed and the milk won't culture or set. As the temperature is raised up to 44°C, the rate of culture metabolism is higher, and the yoghurt is sweeter. Faster growth also prompts the yogurt to set faster.

4. When the milk has cooled (around 15 minutes) stir well and test the temperature. If you haven't got a food thermometer, put a very clean pinkie finger into the milk. If the milk has cooled enough for you to be able to keep your finger in it comfortably, it should be at the right temperature.

5. Put the plain yoghurt into a small bowl and add enough cooled milk to make a thin liquid. Add this mixture to the remainder of the milk and stir it in thoroughly.

6. Pour the mixture into spotlessly clean lidded glass containers (jars, a bowl, or a jug). Cover and leave the mixture to incubate in a warm place for at least 8 hours (or overnight).

7. You can use the oven on the 'defrost' setting, or set to 30-35°C. Or, use a cooler box in which you've placed two jars of freshly boiled water to raise the temperature. (I make my yoghurt in the evening and leave it in the oven overnight).

8. When set, allow to cool to room temperature and then refrigerate. It will keep well for at least a week.

9. To make the next batch of yoghurt, always keep back 2-3 tbsp from your present batch to 'inoculate' the new batch.

TO MAKE LABNEH

For an utterly sublime and healthy middle-eastern experience, simply strain yoghurt in a muslin-lined sieve to make a delicious soft creamy 'yoghurt-cheese' and season it to create a variety of delicious savoury and sweet spreads/dips/pâtés and toppings. Or you can preserve it in a good quality olive oil.

You can use either home-made or shop-bought yoghurt to make labneh. Be aware that home-made yoghurt is often less dense than its commercially-made cousin, so when strained, it will yield less solid matter and more whey.

What you'll need:

500ml of cold, fresh, full-fat yoghurt
A sieve
A piece of muslin/clean hanky
A bowl

What to do:

1. Line the clean sieve with a clean piece of muslin and set it over a small bowl. Tip the cold yoghurt into the sieve and cover.

2. Leave it to drain for several hours or overnight - the pale liquid that drains from the yoghurt is the 'whey'. The longer the yoghurt drips, the firmer the labneh will be. (If the weather is very warm, leave it to drain in the fridge).

3. Labneh will keep for at least a week in the fridge - just take out what you need and season or flavour it to taste!

4. By the 'whey'.... don't waste the whey - it's probiotic and protein-rich, helps digestion and contains trace minerals. You can use it in several ways:

- Add whey to your vegetable ferments to 'kick-start' the lacto-fermentation process
- Whey can be added to your smoothies or soups, stirred into a home-made curry, casserole, or a thick stew to loosen the gravy - it lends a silky texture
- You can make whey ice cubes for adding to cold drinks, or for using as above.

TO MAKE KEFIR

Making kefir is super easy! Simply put the kefir grains into milk, stir, wait overnight, strain, drink! However, there are as many subtle differences in the methods of various kefir-making as there are people making it - my method is really simple.

Kefir has thinner consistency than yoghurt. If you want a thicker kefir, refrigerate the unstrained grains in the milk for up to two days; the grains will continue to ferment, but at a slower rate.

You'll read many sources that caution never use any metal implements with kefir. I have used both a metallic and a nylon mesh strainer and have never had a problem, but always use a glass jar to make and store it.

What you'll need:

Live kefir grains*: 1-2 tbsp (1 tbsp of grains per 500ml milk)
Organic full-fat milk: 500ml - 1lt (raw, or non-homogenised)
Lidded glass jar: large enough for the milk + 5cm 'head-room'

**You can buy live kefir grains online.*

What to do:

1. Put the kefir grains into a thoroughly clean glass jar (JAR 1) and pour over the milk. Cover loosely with the lid.

2. Leave the jar on the counter for at least 24 and up to 48 hours. During this time the grains may rise to the top of the jar (they're loving the cream!) or the kefir may separate into curds and whey. All this is normal - give it a stir (with a wooden or nylon spoon) and continue fermenting until you like the flavour and thickness.

3. Strain the kefir into a clean jar (JAR 2) or jug, through a fine mesh strainer and refrigerate until needed.

4. If you want to make another batch of kefir right away: Rinse out JAR 1 and put the grains back into it and repeat the process.

5. If you don't want to make another batch just yet: Rinse our JAR 1, put the grains back into it and add enough water (not tap) to cover them by 5-6cm.

6. Refrigerate for up to a week before 'feeding' them again.

To ferment Kefir for a second time....

Fermenting kefir for a second time with flavourings produces a much mellower flavour by removing some of the sharp acidity. It also improves the kefir's bacterial content and reduces its lactose content.

A second fermentation period can range from six to 12 hours, depending on the temperature of your home and your taste preference - just keep it going until you like the taste!

You could try:

- Organic orange or other juices
- Vanilla with ground cinnamon
- Organic cocoa powder
- Organic citrus fruit peels
- Pumpkin pie spice
- Chopped fruit
- Garlic or onion for a savoury kefir dip or salad dressing

Use flavour additions that you can easily remove (citrus peels rather than zest, for example) from the kefir when the second fermentation period is complete - fruit juices, ground spices or cocoa powder obviously won't need to be removed.

Note that fruit additives are likely to make the kefir more carbonated. If you prefer not to have effervescent kefir, wait until after the kefir has been fermented a second time before adding them.

FERMENTED VEGETABLES

"Getting the vegetables submerged is the most critical factor for success in vegetable fermentation."

- Sandor Katz

There is now a lot of great information available online on how to ferment vegetables. My own inspiration comes from the simple philosophy of fermentation 'hero' Sandor Katz, probably the most knowledgeable expert in the West.

I like his really simple approach and reassurance that there really is no precise recipe for fermented vegetables. It really is a matter of courage, following the key principles below, experimenting with flavour combinations and exercising a little patience. I suggest making small batches at first and with experience, tweaking your ingredients and process to achieve the flavour and degree of acidity that pleases your palette.

You can't beat home-made ferments for their probiotic power, variety and taste and (low) cost. However, and it may sound obvious, if you're buying a commercial product, please make sure it's live and hasn't been pasteurised!

My basic process:

1. Chop: or grate your vegetables of choice.

2. Salt: Salt the chopped vegetables. Start off lightly and add more to achieve a slightly over-salted taste (otherwise the finished ferment will be bland) and pound or squeeze until the vegetables release their liquid.

3. Pack: the vegetables TIGHTLY into clean jar, so they are forced below the liquid that is released - getting and keeping the vegetables submerged is critical. Add a little filtered little water if necessary. Cover loosely with a lid or a piece of muslin.

4. Wait: taste frequently and move to cold storage when you like the taste.

**You can also add 1 - 2 tbsp of whey from your dripped yoghurt to kick-start the fermentation. This is optional and while whey will speed up the fermentation, using salt alone tends to retain the crispness of the vegetables.*

Other techniques include:

Dry salting: The salt is sprinkled on the vegetables. A rule of thumb is 1½-2 tsp of salt per 500g of veg. (Salt slows fermentation and enzyme activity and therefore prolongs preservation potential. Temperature also affects fermentation rates, so in the summer heat less salt is used to ensure slower fermentation).

Brining: The vegetables are submerged in a salt solution - useful for fermenting whole or larger chunks of vegetables.

Spicing: When the vegetables are nice and moist (through bruising or soaking), they can be further salted and spiced to taste, before being packed.

- **Common spices**: garlic*, ginger, onions, shallots, spring onions, chilli, juniper, dill, celery seeds, caraway seeds, turmeric, cumin seed, coriander seed and leaf, oregano, rosemary, thyme, mint, tarragon. As well as flavouring the ferment and adding nutritional benefits, many spices act as mould inhibitors.

**Don't panic if garlic cloves turn blue this is normal and only temporary.*

Surface Moulds and Yeasts: To prevent moulds the vegetables need to remain submerged below the surface liquid. However, don't panic - surface growth is common and normal; it needs to be removed, but it does not ruin your ferment. Simply scrape it off, together with the layer beneath, push the vegetables down further and add a little non-chlorinated water.

However, use your nose and 'gut' feeling...if your ferment looks and smells bad, start again.

BASIC KIMCHI

This is my favourite - I love its vibrant, ruby red colour and punchy flavour and versatility! For me, this is the queen of home-made ferments.

What you'll need:

Red cabbage: 1 large (finely shredded)
Red onions: 3 large (finely shredded)
Fresh ginger: 5 cm, or more to taste (peeled & sliced to fine match-sticks)
Red Jalapeños chillies: 3, or more to taste (with seeds, very finely sliced)
Garlic: 4 fat cloves (finely sliced)
Maldon salt (1 - 1.5 tablespoons - it should taste just a little too salty)
Whey: 1.5 tbsp (the liquid part from straining yoghurt - optional, but gets the ferment going)

What to do:

1. Put all the above into a large bowl and, if you have strong hands, scrunch and squeeze the veg to release the natural juices. Otherwise, bash everything down with the end of a rolling pin.

2. Then pack it as tightly as possible into a Kilner jar, pushing each layer down with the end of a ladle. Leave a couple centimetres 'collar' to allow the juices to bubble up as the vegetables ferment and top with filtered or still mineral water until the contents are just covered - make sure the contents are submerged.

3. Cover loosely and stand the jar on a plate, to save your counter from any juices bubbling over. Depending on the temperature of your kitchen, leave for one to two weeks to ferment.

4. Check daily that the kimchi remains submerged, pushing it down and adding a little more filtered water if needed.

5. When you like the flavour, transfer the jar to the fridge to prevent further fermentation. The kimchi will keep for months in the fridge - just pack down every time you take some out so the surface is covered with water to prevent mouldy growth.

SOME SUGGESTED INGREDIENTS & COMBINATIONS:

BASIC KIMCHI	Red, or red + white cabbage / red onions / salt / garlic / chillies peppers / ginger / radishes / celery
SAUERKRAUT	White cabbage / white onions / salt / garlic / caraway seeds / celery seeds / dill / whole black pepper / mustard seeds / turmeric
CARROT & GINGER PICKLE	Carrots / ginger / salt + optional white onion / celery / cumin / caraway / chilli
HOT RED PEPPER SALSA	Romano or bell peppers / white onions / spring onions / chilli / ginger

Fermenting vegetables in raw cider vinegar

Apple cider vinegar (ACV) is a prebiotic and naturally fermented food that supports and feeds the probiotics existing in the gut, contributing to a healthier environment in the body. Raw cider vinegar is both pre and pro biotic as it contains live cultures which help to alkalize the body and replenish the beneficial bacteria to crowd out yeasts. Taking a teaspoon of ACV in a little warm water before meals helps to increase stomach acid production to aid digestion - very helpful for those with weak digestion, or as we age.

For thousands of years raw garlic has been recognised and utilised not only for its flavour, but for its health benefits. However, eating raw garlic can also provide 'social' difficulties from breath odour, and side effects such a burning sensation in the mouth or stomach, heartburn and digestive upsets. Fermenting garlic in apple cider vinegar preserves it and helps to eliminate most of the complications from eating the garlic raw.

Fermenting fruit

Fruits can be fermented in the same way as vegetables, but due to their high sugar content, they will ferment much more quickly than vegetables. Depending on the room temperature, the ferment will be ready in 12-48 hours; leave it too long and you'll produce alcohol! Fruit ferments will last in your refrigerator for one to two months.

Fermented Fruit Juices

Freshly squeezed apples, oranges and lemons make fabulously refreshing and very healthy drinks

Ways to enjoy your ferments every day

4 ways with Yoghurt:

1. **For breakfast**: Overnight-soaked porridge, bircher muesli, cooked or fresh fruit compote or pancakes can be topped generously with a creamy dollop and given a drizzle of honey, a scattering of toasted flaked almonds and a good dusting of cinnamon. I also grate some fresh ginger into the yoghurt and let it sit for a while before serving. Cinnamon helps blood sugar regulation and both cinnamon and ginger taste good and are anti-inflammatory.

2. **In an ultra-luxe smoothie**: The night before I want an awesome protein and omega hit, I soak a heaped tablespoon of finely ground flax seeds and another of ground almonds in half a cup of yoghurt. The next morning, I blitz this mix with fresh soft, or stewed fruit and enough raw milk (or coconut milk) to make up generous glassful. The addition of a very fresh organic egg yolk to the food processor sends the protein content into overdrive and will keep me going for hours!

3. **In yoghurt 'mayonnaise'**: I whisk together a couple of tablespoons of yoghurt with a little olive oil, a teaspoon of Dijon mustard (or grain mustard) and an egg yolk - then add a drop of apple cider vinegar, or a teaspoon of lemon juice and season to taste.

   Yoghurt mayonnaise is great with just about anything: Try experimenting by adding finely chopped tarragon (great with chicken or eggs); a teaspoon of horseradish sauce (great with smoked mackerel); very finely diced spring onions and plenty of pepper (great with baked potatoes); or finely chopped fresh mint (great with spicy Indian chicken/lamb skewers). The possibilities are endless, and the taste experience is always delicious!

4. **In a marinade**: Yoghurt's acidity makes it a deliciously natural tenderiser for meat. I mix it with crushed garlic, black pepper, finely chopped mint and lemon juice for a simple marinade for lamb skewers.

3 ways with Labneh:

1. **A savoury dip or topping**: Add sea salt and ground black pepper and your choice of crushed garlic; finely diced herbs, chives, spring onions, red onions, sweet peppers, cornichons.

2. **Preserved labneh**: Roll small walnut-sized nuggets of labneh and place on a clean tray in the fridge to dry for 24 hours (you can add seasonings or herbs to the labneh before rolling). Place the balls in a jar of good quality extra virgin olive oil (you can add sprigs of herbs and whole peppercorns to the oil). It keeps well in the fridge for a couple of months.

3. **A sweet treat**: Serve it drizzled with honey, a-top a fruit compote. Flavour it with finely chopped crystallised stem-ginger and shredded mint and sit a quenelle inside halved, roast peaches. Add a little fresh ginger juice and sweeten with a little raw honey, unrefined cane sugar for a fabulously healthy topping for carrot cake.

5 ways with Kefir:

1. Whisk into to dips.

2. Use as a basis for salad dressings.

3. Incorporate into smoothies.

4. Blend with pureed fruit.

5. Add other flavourings in a second fermentation.

9 ways with Fermented Vegetables & Fruits:

1. **As a small side to your meal**: serve a small portion of fermented vegetables or fruit.

2. **Add to green salads**: chop and scatter the veggies over green leaves vegetables.

3. **Add to a pasta / rice / grain / tuna / egg / bean salad**: chop the vegetables and toss through.

4. **Add fermented fruits** and their juices to your smoothies.

5. **As a sauce or topping**: use fruits as a topping or puree for a sauce for pancakes, ice cream, yogurt.

6. **In a wrap or sandwich**: with cold cuts and cheeses.

7. **As a dip**: fermented salsas make a great dip and pair well with chilli and atop yoghurt as a condiment for curry.

8. **As a condiment**: almost any homemade condiment can be fermented for extra probiotic goodness: ketchups, mustards and mayonnaise can all be fermented within a couple of days.

9. **In vinaigrettes and salad dressings**: use the juice from a ferment to flavour dressings.

Enjoy cultured and fermented foods in your daily, remember they're a condiment, not a meal replacement and your body will thank you!

CHAPTER TWELVE

SALT

"Our physical inner world was born of the sea and we carry the saltiness of the ocean inside us."

- James DiNicolantonio
The Salt Fix [1]

Sodium chloride - aka salt - makes up 90% of the mineral content of the world's oceans and we find the same the percentage in our blood, but in a lesser concentration (sea water is five times as salty as our blood). We find salt in rainwater, rock salt and salt-licks - naturally occurring areas where animals can go to lick essential mineral nutrients from salts and other minerals deposits. This important white crystal is found everywhere in Nature.

Throughout our human history we've valued, prized and eulogised salt. Homer called it a "*divine substance*"; Plato claimed it was "*near to the Gods*"; and Roman soldiers were actually paid a 'salarium' - money set aside for purchasing salt.

Until the beginning of the last century, salt retained its pre-eminence as one of the most sought-after commodities, even making its way into common language: that dependable friend we call "*the salt of the earth*"? The hard-working person who is "*worth their salt*"?

In food, salt also helps slow the growth of bacteria and has been used as a natural preservative and mould inhibitor throughout history.

Salt - the food wisdom

There can't be a chef worth their salt (sorry!) on this planet who doesn't know that what separates good food from great food is salt. One piece of cooking advice every chef will give you is that food needs seasoning. How often have you heard top chefs in TV cookery shows implore the contestants to "*Taste, taste, taste*!"?

Salt suppresses bitterness, enhances sweet and savoury flavours and has a remarkable alchemy to ramp-up the flavour stakes, from barely detectable to.... WHAM! BAM! BOOM!

No more bitterness...

Did you know that coffee aficionados add an undetectable pinch to their grounds before brewing? And have you noticed that a salty olive is the perfect accompaniment to the bitter, liquorice finish of wines such as Valpolicella? It's not just foodie-ness - sodium ions tone down bitter responses on the tongue.

Much more sweetness...

Salt will also bring out sweetness - and savoury - in a dish. If a food has both bitter and sweet notes (grapefruit, for instance), salt will dampen down the bitter notes and turn up the sweet taste. It's the same with fresh orange juice - it actually tastes sweeter with a pinch of salt.

Ramped-up aroma...

Salt magnifies the natural aromas in food by changing its taste profile. It seems:

> **"We have 'learned synergies' between tastes and smells. The smell of peanut butter goes with salt, strawberry and vanilla are associated with sugar, and so on. (Salting will) "not only change the flavour profile by suppressing bitter, thereby bringing out sweet more.**
>
> **The sweet will go with the fruit flavours and maybe enhance or synergise with the fruit flavours."**

- Paul Breslin
Rutgers University

In addition, when a liquid surface is salted, for example on a melon or grapefruit, a process called 'salting out' occurs. The salt effectively changes the vapour pressure, drawing out more of the volatile molecules that give rise to the aroma.[2]

Yep, salt is pretty smart and prized by cooks throughout history and across every culture.

Salt nay-sayers

Chefs love salt, but not everyone agrees:

"Salt puts up our blood pressure. Raised blood pressure (hypertension) is the major factor which causes strokes, heart failure and heart attacks, the leading causes of death and disability in the UK.

There is also increasing evidence of a link between high salt intake and stomach cancer, osteoporosis, obesity, kidney stones, kidney disease and vascular dementia and water retention. Salt can also exacerbate the symptoms of asthma, Ménière's disease and diabetes."

- UK Action on Salt [3]

My goodness! With this sort of press, who in their right minds would want add salt to anything?

In recent years, salt has been taking the rap for a whole variety of serious health conditions. Is this justified, or is salt another victim of poor and misunderstood science - or no science at all? Jason Fung, a leading nephrologist with a special interest in Type 2 diabetes, wrote recently:[4]

"Our belief in the benefits of low salt consumption are largely based on mis-information and myth-information."

Let's get clear on 'salt'

Although people tend to use the terms 'salt' and 'sodium' interchangeably, they are different:

Sodium is a pure mineral, found naturally in the earth and in our environment, bound up in minerals and rock and is a vital nutrient to the human body. Sodium is found in a variety of whole foods such as fruits, vegetables, natural sea salt and in soil. However, our biggest dietary source of sodium is from salt.

Salt (as we know it) is actually sodium chloride - 40% sodium and 60% chloride - and is harvested by two methods: from salt mines, or by evaporating sea or mineral-rich water. There are a several different varieties (common table salt, pink Himalayan salt and natural sea salt) and some contain traces of calcium, potassium, iron and zinc.

Is all salt created equal? Absolutely not!

Unrefined salts (such as Himalayan salt and salt harvested from the sea) contains a broad spectrum of trace elements, often in the same balance as found in human blood. These trace elements include magnesium and potassium.

Getting enough magnesium and potassium into our diet helps the body to metabolise the sodium itself and to work synergistically with it, regulating water balance and nerve and muscle impulses.

Refined, industrial-grade table salt, however, is very heavily processed. Mined from underground salt mines, it reaches the table stripped of all its minerals and trace elements (except for sodium and chloride) and subjected to anti-caking agents (chemical additives, such as sodium ferricyanide, which prevent the salt from clumping) and, in some cases is iodised (enriched with iodine).

Around 93% of refined salt goes to industries, which require chemically pure sodium chloride to make explosives, chlorine gas, baking soda, fertilisers and plastics. The remaining 7% ends up in our food.

"Table salt is an acidic, inorganic substance; this means the body cannot break the chemical bonds to utilise the sodium and it is not easily excreted from the body.

This leads to various health issues, is responsible for 100,000 deaths each year, and contributes to the 'Sodium is bad' mentality."

- Natural News, 2011 [5]

Mmm... industrial leftovers anyone?

Iodised table salt was introduced after the World Health Assembly adopted the concept of adding iodine to salt for human and livestock consumption in 1995.

The aim was to eliminate iodine deficiency disease (and related disorders such as goitre, cretinism, myxedema) in adults and neurological disorders in children. As a result, countries around the world routinely require all salt (apart from kosher) to contain added iodine.

However, not everyone quite so keen on this practice:

> **"The addition of iodine to table salt is a real problem and makes the 'simple' table salt so many of us rely on little more than a poison...**
>
> **The problem is that iodising salt is a crude form of prevention more appropriate for those living in conditions of famine. People eating a relatively well-balanced diet are not at risk of iodine deficiency because iodine is widely available in sea fish, shellfish, eggs, cereal grains, legumes and dairy products from cows fed with iodised salt. Certain food additives also contain iodine.**
>
> **But there are also hidden sources of iodine that mean most of us get too much. These include cough expectorants, antiseptics, certain drugs such as sulphonamide, lithium, dopamine, steroids, aspirin and certain heart and anti-diabetic drugs. Natural supplements such as kelp and seaweed also contain high levels of iodine."**

- The Ecologist [6]

Iodised salt and thyroid disorders

The recommendation for iodine is currently 150mcg per day - easy to achieve if you consider that just ¼ teaspoon of iodised salt contains 115mcg - 77% of the recommended daily allowance. We need iodine to regulate our metabolism and produce hormones and our thyroid is a major player in this task. About 75% of our body's iodine is stored in the thyroid gland - too much iodine and levels of these hormones can become dangerously unbalanced, leading to metabolic as well as immune disorders.

"In Galicia, in northwest Spain, where iodised salt is mandatory, there is an abnormally high incidence of hyperthyroidism (an overactive thyroid), particularly among women.

In Japan and the US, where intake of iodised salt is highest, the problems of too much iodine are responsible for health problems such as including thyroiditis (inflammation of the thyroid) and hyperthyroidism, which can produce, among other symptoms, increased heart rate and blood pressure, abnormal heart rhythms (arrhythmias), excessive sweating, hand tremors (shakiness), nervousness and anxiety, and difficulty sleeping (insomnia)."

- The Ecologist

Hypothyroid sufferers also develop hyponatremia (low salt levels). They lose sodium rapidly in urine, so need to take in more salt to maintain sufficiency. But iodised salt only further compounds the problem and increases the risk of iodine toxicity.

What does independent science tell us about salt and our health?

From anthropological research, we know that salt was rarely, if ever, added to hunter-gatherer and Paleolithic diets. Therefore, it would seem sensible to assume that limiting salt in the diet would mimic our ancestors' diet beneficially.

However, the evidence is mounting to the contrary; from the remains of the early humans who roamed the non-coastal areas of East Africa 1-2 million years ago, it looks like they enjoyed a diet of abundant tiger nuts and grass hoppers, both extremely high in salt. Our ancestors also ate 'nose-to-tail' and organ meats and blood are both high in salt.

Independent science, recently reviewed by Dr James DiNicolantonio - a leading cardiovascular research scientist - shows us that salt may be one solution to, rather than a cause of, our chronic disease crisis. In his book *The Salt Fix - Why the Experts Got it All Wrong and How Eating More Might Save Your Life*, he argues that a low-salt diet may actually lead to serious health issues and higher death rates, particularly in conditions like heart disease and diabetes.

Sodium - the 'youth' mineral

Organic sodium is known as the 'youth' mineral because it is associated with youthful limbs and flexible joints. Sodium is essential for absorbing calcium and also helps magnesium absorption which reduces inflammation and cramping. Salt increases the metabolic rate and heat in the body and helps thyroid function by suppressing stress hormones. It aids gastric secretions, helps digestion and bile production, relieves constipation, supports the function of our brain, kidneys, liver, lymphatic system, blood, spleen and improves insulin sensitivity.

Unlike table salt, excess organic sodium is easily excreted from the body.

"Sodium's organic alkalinity helps neutralise acids that result from stressful lifestyles and poor nutrition. Without adequate amounts of sodium, the body will take minerals from its reserves, including the bones, to neutralise acidity."

- Natural News, 2011

Salt and blood pressure

Salt's primary role is to help maintain blood pressure and volume in the blood. Sodium is critical to cellular function and metabolism and is a component in the fluid around our cells, acting as an important electrolyte in the body. It maintains our blood volume so that sufficient blood can reach our capillaries (our smallest blood vessels) and thus maintain normal cellular metabolism, nerve transmission and muscle function.

Sodium is involved in increasing blood pressure, but in most cases, it's not *the* reason blood pressure increases - it's just one element in a complex and tightly controlled process. Key to this process is a self-regulating, auto-correcting salt 'thermostat' - the renin-angiotensin-aldosterone system (RAAS) - an extremely sensitive hormonal system, which controls blood pressure and water balance in the body and is largely responsible for our salt cravings.

The RAAS switches on to hold onto salt when our blood pressure is too low, or we're stressed out, or if we don't take in enough salt. It's our body's adaptive response to prevailing conditions and its mechanics help our body work hard to hold onto and use what we have.

Salt retention and increased blood pressure occurs when we over-stress our bodies and our RAAS doesn't turn off. Although salt is found at the scene of the blood pressure 'crime', it didn't pull the trigger.

In his paper *Salt, energy, metabolic rate and longevity*, Dr Ray Peat[7] summarises a range of large scale, long-term studies that do not support the 'conventional' wisdom on salt - quite to the contrary:

- in one large study, which followed 3000 people over a period of four years, Alderman et al reported a clear increase in mortality in the individuals who ate less salt. An extra few grams of salt per day was associated with a 36% reduction in coronary events - i.e. these people lived longer and had fewer heart attacks.

- in a later study which followed more than 11,000 people over a 22-year period, Alderman et al reported that those who ate more salt had a lower death rate.

- in pre-eclampsia (high blood pressure during pregnancy) Shanklin & Hodin showed that the addition of salt has been known to stabilize the condition: could it be that salt may be acting as an 'anti-stress' weapon against the very condition it's supposed to cause?

Overall, research data suggests that a diet high in minerals such as potassium, magnesium and calcium may help in reducing high blood pressure. Yet another reason to care how you source your food.

Not enough salt?

If animals become sodium-deficient they will seek out salty food and often consume far more sodium than needed to restore homeostasis - think of 'salt-licks' provided by farmers.

Every one of our cells contains and is bathed in water. Sodium is an electrolyte and helps to regulate the amount of water in and around our cells. If true sodium deficiency occurs in humans, we experience symptoms of hyponatremia a condition where the concentration of sodium in the blood is abnormally low. Several factors, from drinking too much water to an underlying medical condition can cause the sodium to become diluted and can lead to a variety of mild to serious health problems, such as brain swelling, coma, congestive heart failure, cardiovascular collapse following acute blood loss and impaired cardiovascular responses of our sympathetic nervous system in stress.

For athletes, especially those participating in endurance sports, salt restriction is potentially dangerous. Hyponatremia can result from salt lost through the skin from sweating and can produce both mild symptoms (nausea and lethargy) and more severe manifestations, such as cerebral oedema, pulmonary oedema, and even death. Hyponatremia is common in the elderly, especially in those with acute illnesses.

Menopause and ageing both are associated with weakening bones. The Women's Health Initiative (a large, long-term population study of postmenopausal women focused on ways to prevent heart disease, breast and colorectal cancer and osteoporosis) collected fracture data on all 70,000 women included in their assessment and bone mineral density studies (an indicator of bone strength) on about 4,400.

The study[8] found that high salt intake was not a major adverse factor in bone health and showed association between a higher salt diet and stronger bones, including higher bone mineral density throughout the body and fewer hip fractures.

Low-salt diets are also bad news for those with Type 2 diabetes. One of our body's ways of retaining sodium is to increase insulin, which helps the kidneys retain sodium. Low salt intake is associated with an immediate onset of insulin resistance (a precursor to Type 2 diabetes) to stop cells taking up insulin.

For those with Type 2, low salt intake is associated with a higher death rate from cardiovascular disease and with death from all causes.

So, in one way or another, it looks like sodium restriction puts us all at increased risk of serious health consequences. Our salt cravings may be telling us something important.

Too much salt?

While most of us can rely on an innate 'salt-appetite' to guide us and our taste buds will soon tell us when we've had enough, some of us do need to take care…

- **Impaired renal function**: some people with high blood pressure have inherited salt sensitivity, a condition thought to be due to impaired sodium transport in the kidney. These folks are more sensitive to fluctuations in dietary salt and may benefit from reducing intake.

  However, salt sensitivity is dose-dependent, and it decreases when dietary potassium is increased. So these folks may benefit from including ample potassium-rich foods in their diet, rather than drastically reducing sodium. That said, people with chronic renal disease and impaired renal function may have more difficult excreting excess sodium and therefore may need to restrict their salt intake.

- **Kidney stones and calcium excretion**: those who are prone to kidney stones may need to reduce their salt intake, as high sodium intake leads to a higher level of calcium excretion in the urine - people who consumed the highest levels of sodium tended to have the greatest urinary calcium excretion. Higher calcium excretion may lead to kidney stone formation, particularly if insufficient fluids are consumed.

How much salt?

Most adults consume around 8-10g of salt (approx. 2 teaspoons) daily without even realising it. If you consume processed foods like bread, breakfast cereals and pastry products, you'll be getting as much as 70% of your dietary intake just from these.[9]

Salt recommendations vary and are based on age, gender, physical activity, and health conditions. Chris Kresser[10] suggests that the data supports an intake of 1.5 to 3.5 teaspoons of salt, per day. Those who are active or sweat more should go for the upper end and while there may be some conditions where moderate salt restriction is warranted, for the majority of healthy individuals, adding salt according to taste will provide an appropriate level of sodium in the diet.

Verdict on salt

It's definitely the victim of misplaced blame. Given the clear importance of salt to our good health, how much of a surprise can it be that its traditional (and irreplaceable) culinary use serves to enhance our experience of real, whole food cooked from scratch? After all, why would Mother Nature not want us to enjoy what she has provided?

But just compare the aroma, flavour and the whole experience of delicious home-cooked dishes with the food industry's 'offerings' which line supermarket shelves, fast food outlets and, sadly, most restaurants. This nutritionally worthless, fake food is pumped up with vast quantities of industrial salt to make these miserable products palatable!

Some simple tips for using salt

- DO heal with food - Mother Nature always provides and our food is our best medicine.

- DO try to manage blood pressure naturally - be aware of any dietary calcium/magnesium/potassium deficiencies and include more mineral rich whole foods in your weekly diet.

- DO pay attention to salt cravings (during pregnancy, the menstrual cycle, after hard exercise and night cravings) as these are a sign your body needs more, not less salt.

- DO use natural sources of sodium, like sea vegetables, fish, shellfish, and meat, plus certain plants such as beets, carrots, celery, spinach, and turnips.

- DO ditch all processed and ultra-processed foods - NOW. They're packed with refined, industrial salt, a common flavour enhancer and preservative 'hidden' in huge quantities and then masked, in just about every packaged and processed food on the market. It's also ubiquitous in most restaurant food, which nowadays comprises mainly of processed foods that are formulated and prepared especially for the catering industry.

- DON'T use salt substitutes (low-sodium table salt alternatives marketed to reduce the risk of high blood pressure and cardiovascular disease) - many contain potassium chloride, which for those with chronic kidney disease or taking some anti-hypertensive medications, may result in hyperkalaemia- a potentially fatal potassium overload.

- DO use salt at home - we need its many benefits to manage our blood pressure and stress response and to keep our metabolism high.

- DON'T use refined, industrial table salt. Need I say more? And DON'T choose Dead Sea salt (due to its high bromide content)

- DO choose unrefined sea salt. In the UK, there are three sources of locally produced salt: Maldon Salt is made from sea water from the River Blackwater in Essex; Cornish Sea Salt is harvested from water from ocean around the Cornish coast; and the Welsh Halen Môn is made from water drawn from the Menai Straits. Unrefined Celtic sea salt harvested off the shores of Brittany (known as sel de gris and the top quality sel de Guérande)) is also available in the UK. All claim to retain high levels of trace elements.

  As a point of interest, Himalayan salt, mined in Pakistan, takes its characteristic pink colour from iron oxide deposits. The characteristic grey colour of sel de gris from Guérande and depth of flavour comes from the dense clay which lines the salt marshes where it's harvested. Probably the most highly prized salts of all (reserved for 'finishing' dishes at the table) is Fleur de Sel de Guérande, delicately harvested from the very top white layers of the salt marshes of the Guérande. Each of these unrefined salts have their fans and their critics and choice depends on flavour and cost, but all are a much better choice than common table or cooking salts.

- DO treat unrefined salt as a powerful supplement and use it mindfully.

- DO increase salt intake slowly and make sure to exclude all processed foods before increasing it. Allow your taste buds to regulate your intake - they're wiser than you are!

Salt has been revered as a primordial condiment, part of this earth for billions of years. Its history grows richer as generations of food wisdom and emerging science appreciate its importance to our health and to our food:

"Let there be work, bread, water and salt for all."

- Nelson Mandela

CHAPTER THIRTEEN

SUGAR

"If you want to understand Western history, you have to understand sugar. And vice versa. Because sugar's not just something sweet: over the centuries it's been a medicine, a spice, a symbol of royalty, and an instrument of disease, addiction, and oppression."

- Saveur

Sugar has been part of human culture for a long, long time. As long ago as 8000 BC Archaeological evidence shows us that sugarcane was produced by the inhabitants of New Guinea, who gradually exported their knowledge across the southern hemisphere. As early as 300 BC, sugar had come to Europe as 'honey powder' during the reign of Alexander the Great. But it was the Muslim countries of the Middle East and Asia, which adopted sugar production during the Arab Agricultural Revolution in the 9th and 10th century, enabling European countries to gain access to this very expensive 'gold'.

The establishment of numerous sugar plantations in Central America during the 1500s intensified the trading of African peoples as slaves to supply labour to the burgeoning sugar industry in the Americas. By the 18th century, sugar (mostly as sugar beet) had become a highly popular and very much cheaper ingredient. From that time and up to the present day, it has become an indispensable element in our diet - appearing everywhere in beverages, preserves and confectionary. And, as we shall see, sugar (often in the form of cheap, refined high-fructose corn syrup) has become a major ingredient in processed foods today.[1]

Pure, white and deadly?

Refined white sugar has been portrayed as 'pure, white and deadly' by many nutritionists and people in the medical profession. But actually, is it?

Compare this:

"The 'No Sugar' movement - is leading a global fightback and warning that our sweet habit is completely out of control, leaving a nasty taste in the mouth of the body public. Sugar, whether added to food by you or the manufacturer, is the greatest threat to human health, bar none, they say.

And unless we wise up and quit *en masse*, we don't just risk personal obesity and disease, but national bankruptcy and collapse, as the toll our ill health takes on our countries' economies threatens to destabilise the modern world."

- Daily Telegraph (2014)

It all began in the 1950s, when Professor John Yudkin - quite rightly - didn't accept the idea that eating saturated fat was the cause of high blood levels of triglycerides and cholesterol. However, he didn't question the associated theory of the day: that lipids (fats) in the blood caused atherosclerosis and heart disease.

Instead, Yudkin argued that it was sugar, especially the fructose component of sucrose (table sugar), rather than dietary fat, that caused the high blood lipids seen in people from affluent countries. He specifically blamed the chemical effect of the fructose component because, he argued, the nutrients that were removed when refining white flour and white sugar were insignificant in the diet. Yudkin's ideas were wholly rejected by the medical establishment of his day, however, more recent interest in Yudkin's work, has converted many, including contemporary clinicians, to Yudkin's view that sugar is a 'demonic' food.

These views have become influential and have essentially grown into a cult. As we have seen, sugar has become the new 'saturated fat' - that sweet, addictive poison singularly responsible for fuelling the obesity epidemic and causing every kind of illness. As we saw in the opening quote, every day we are implored to cut sugar, quit sugar and put an end to sugar altogether.

And contrast this:

Dr Chris Masterjohn, a leading nutritional science researcher, writer and teacher writes in his paper, *Sugar is the ultimate antioxidant and insulin will make you younger: Appreciating a few poorly-recognised but critical contributions of carbohydrate*: [2]

"As we move forward, we need to frame our discussions of glucose as a nutrient and insulin as a protective hormone whose protective functions are being lost in obesity and diabetes. With this framework, we may be able to shake off the old rhetoric about fats without redirecting it toward carbohydrate as the new nutritional boogeyman.

Then we can look freely at the buffet of dietary tools at our disposal and study with a clearer collective mind how to maximally reap their benefits in a way that is tailored to each of us as an individual."

It looks like more rational, independent science is finally beginning to understand that too little can be just as bad as too much; that the dosage of sugar and insulin are very important; and that, in the right amounts for each one of us, both are supportive of a healthy metabolism.[3]

What do I actually mean by 'sugar'?

Primarily, what I mean by 'sugar' is that which we find in whole foods, like fresh, whole ripe and exotic fruits, fresh unadulterated fruit juices, honey, maple syrup and molasses.

However, when you consider that maple syrup, molasses and 'unrefined' sugars are actually quite highly processed in order to be consumed, it somewhat blurs the distinction between these and other 'refined' sugars - like table sugar! Please don't faint.

What I most certainly DON'T mean by 'sugar' is the plethora of refined and manufactured sugars and sugar substitutes found extensively in ultra-processed foods. Just consider the number of ways the food industry has come up with to disguise the excessive sugar content in their offerings:

Beet sugar, blackstrap molasses, brown sugar, cane sugar, caramel, carob syrup, castor sugar, coconut sugar, date sugar, demerara sugar, evaporated cane juice, fruit juice concentrate, golden sugar, golden syrup, grape sugar, honey icing sugar, invert sugar, jaggery, maple syrup, molasses, muscovado sugar, raw sugar, sorghum syrup, sucanat, treacle sugar, yellow sugar, barley malt, brown rice syrup, corn syrup, corn syrup solids, fructose, high fructose corn syrup, dextrin, dextrose, diastatic malt, ethyl maltol, galactose, glucose, glucose solids, lactose, malt syrup, maltodextrin, maltose, rice syrup.

Next time you shop, just take a good look at the label and count how many of the above versions of sugar are included in the ingredients. Then pause for serious thought before proceeding to buy, since not only are these various forms of sugar used in excess, but the majority are highly refined substances; few are found in nature.

Our body cannot recognise these man-made, chemical manipulations and it will not thank you for consuming them. Remember 'garbage-in, garbage-out'?

Craving sugar: our bodies are wiser than we are

We humans are 'hard-wired' to desire sweetness over a tart or bitter taste and it's something we retain from cradle to grave. Throughout our evolution, we have sought out sweet foods - like fruits and honey - and sugar 'cravings' are often a message our wise body is giving us to help us not only to survive, but to thrive:

"Any craving is a good starting point, because we have several biological mechanisms for correcting specific nutritional deficiencies.

When something is interfering with your ability to use sugar, you crave it because if you don't eat it you will waste protein to make it."

- Dr Ray Peat

So, we should let our taste - our body's innate wisdom - be our guide. If you're craving sugar relentlessly, it's a clear sign that your body is asking for more energy - so feed it with a few more carbohydrate-based foods like milk, fruit, fresh fruit juices and root vegetables.

But do not feed the craving with ultra-processed, hyper-palatable foods packed with damaging fake sugars: those cloying snack bars, grain-based 'energy' bars, cereals, cheap chocolate bars, commercial breads, cakes, muffins, biscuits and sweets.

Just about every commercial drink you can think of - alcoholic or not - contains excessive amounts of various of cheap and fake sugars. These are the very foods that derail our natural appetite for sweet foods and our body's ability to control our blood sugar and have us left over-fed but under-nourished.

As a traditional, nutrient-dense diet gradually provides our body with its requisite level of nutrition, your natural taste mechanisms will be restored, and sugar cravings will reduce until… they go away!

But what about candida, cancer and diabetes?

Candida: the prevailing wisdom is that sugar feeds candida, but candida overgrowth is a sign that your body is out of its natural balance and lacks the requisite nutrients to support proper function. Eliminating real and natural sugar will eliminate the symptoms, but it doesn't address the root issue - the failure of the metabolic and digestive function to control yeast overgrowth. Root causes are resolved with optimum nutrition diet and lifestyle changes.

Cancer: here, the theory[4] is that a ketogenic diet - in which virtually all carbohydrates and sugars are eliminated, forcing the body to burn ketones bodies (fats) rather than carbohydrates (sugars) and thereby starves the cancer of its primary food source - is highly disputed.

The late Dr Nicholas Gonzalez, considered to be the world's most experienced and influential medical doctor in treating many aggressive and advanced forms of cancer with highly personalised nutritional interventions, researched exhaustively[5] the efficacy of the ketogenic diet as a regimen and wrote an eight-part series on the history - and failure - of the ketogenic diet for cancer.

Naturopathic practitioners believe that all disease results from two root causes: deficiency and toxicity. If your diet comprises refined, fake, processed sugar combined with highly processed, nutritional-empty foods your body will be malnourished. In this context, it can be seen how it is the displacement of nutrient-dense foods by nutritionally-empty, synthetic and toxic foods which increases cancer risk, not the consumption of sugars from whole foods.

Diabetes: here, an argument is made[6] that a low carbohydrate/high fat (thus low-sugar) diet, or even nutritional ketosis - where the body burns fat, not glucose for energy - is a universal panacea especially for weight gain, obesity and diabetes. And, indeed we are seeing evidence to support this.

But, let's just bring back to mind Denise Minger's comprehensive review *In Defense of Low Fat: A Call for Some Evolution of Thought* from the Fats Chapter, in which she systematically presents the case for reconsidering the therapeutic health benefits of a high carbohydrate/low fat diet (thus high sugar), detailing the clinical successes of Dr Walter Kempner and other physicians, who successfully treated people with diabetes (and obesity, heart disease and renal failure) with white rice, fruit and fruit juice and refined table sugar.

Once again, we see that historical and emerging science is giving us the same simple, but challenging message: no 'one size diet' fits all!

Can we use sugar intelligently?

Yes! It's difficult to over-consume sugar if you cook from scratch, unless you regularly eat vast quantities of home-made cakes and treats or drink countless cups of tea with two sugars. Just try eating piles of sugar straight off the spoon - I'll bet you'll find it difficult to manage even a teaspoonful. Think of sugar as a condiment to your food and, like fruit juices, enjoy them judiciously and at home. Favour sugars from ripe, whole tropical fruits, seasonal fruits, berries and starches from root vegetables.

Just remember that most fruits are digested quickly and higher up in the digestive tract, whereas proteins - like meat and fish - take much longer and are digested lower down. So, unless your digestion is strong, eat fruit before a protein meal and it won't hang around to start fermenting while your body is digesting the protein!

Honey - especially raw honey where the enzymes and rich nutrients remain intact - is a good sugar source as well, but for some it may be allergenic. Similarly, experiment with judicious use of real maple syrup and molasses. My father-in-law - a WW2 Latvian émigré - used to swear by his morning cup of molasses in hot water!

And drink your milk! I favour live, raw milk that's straight from the cow, but if you can't source it then go for organic, pasteurised, non-homogenised milk. Many clients I've worked with have benefited from a little sugar - honey, maple syrup, molasses or even a little refined sugar of choice - in a milky bedtime drink!

Always eat your sugars with proteins and fats, to slow down the absorption of sugar into your blood stream - this is especially important if you have blood sugar regulation issues.

In the face of the significant health issues (particularly obesity and diabetes) facing the developed world today, any defence of sugar will be seen as controversial. However, I would maintain that most of us, with judicial use can enjoy the nutritional benefits of whole fruits and by intelligently limiting our natural love for all things sweet, we can still enjoy an occasional, traditional, home-made treat.

But first, we must wholly resist the manipulative seduction of industrially produced, ultra-processed, sugar laden fake-foods.

CHAPTER FOURTEEN

HERBS and SPICES

"As my kitchen will attest, I'm an herb and spice enthusiast. My cooking tends not to be subtle, and I'm always looking for interesting flavours that will stand out in a dish."

- Sarah Hope

Like Sarah, I too am a herb and spice enthusiast. The difference that the addition of a herb or a sprinkle of spice can make to an otherwise routine dish is astonishing. For me, herbs - and especially spices - conjure up taste memories of home. My parents were from northern and southern Europe and lived in Persia, India and Africa before settling in the UK. Mum's culinary repertoire transported us around the globe with her inspired use of herbs and spices.

Get creative and sprinkle a little fresh dill over your buttery boiled potatoes, add a pinch of cinnamon to your stewed apples or finely chop a little tarragon into a creamy sauce to serve with your salmon fishcakes.

Help your digestion by cooking your cabbage, cauliflower or broccoli with a teaspoon of caraway seeds - or add them to your rye bread. Rub your chicken with a mixture of salt, black pepper, paprika and olive oil for a delicious bronze glaze and adding fresh basil and oregano to your ragù will make your taste buds sing with joy.

Melt a pat of parsley and garlic butter onto your pan-fried fish; suspend a neatly tied bouquet-garni - a few parsley stalks, a sprig of thyme, a bay leaf and a stalk of celery - in your slow-cooked stew; stew apples with a couple of rose geranium leaves; or simply grate a thumb of fresh ginger into that rhubarb you're about to poach.

It's all so, so good!

Go on a voyage of discovery and transport yourself around the world with the masalas of India or the herb and spice blends of cuisines from China, North Africa, the Americas, northern Europe and the Mediterranean. Visit a different country with every meal, learn about their culture and culinary traditions and enrich your understanding of your own world by understanding theirs.

In what seems to be an increasingly disconnected and polarised world, where our idea of safety and belonging centres on seeking out social groups that make us the most comfortable, the sociologist Dr Brene Brown[1] entreats us to "*Hold hands. With strangers.*" to find true belonging in our shared humanity.

Can you think of any better way to open the door to our shared humanity than by seeking to understand each other through the food we eat? Neither can I.

Why not drink your herbs and spices in an infusion of apple mint or lemon verbena leaves and enjoy a clean refreshing tea? Alternatively, add some turmeric or ground coriander to your milky bedtime drink for a soothing, anti-inflammatory and healing end to your busy, stressful day.

It's hard to think of a more traditional food than a herb or a spice. There are a gazillion ways to enhance everyday life with these culinary magicians that have been prized throughout history, not only by cooks all over the planet, but also by the wisdom of traditional medicine.

Thankfully, modern science is exploring and uncovering the richness of these health-promoting and healing benefits for our body.

Herbs vs Spices

The essential difference between herbs and spices lies with the part of the plant they originate from. A herb is the leafy, fragrant, aromatic part of a plant; it can be used fresh or dried for seasoning or flavouring food, for fragrances and as a natural medicine. But beware - not all herbs are edible.

Any other element of the plant is usually considered to be a spice, including the dried bark, roots, stem, flowers, fruit, berries or seeds. A plant can be host to both a herb and a spice at the same time, like cilantro and coriander. Cilantro is the aromatic leaf of the plant, while coriander is the seed or root that comes from that same plant.

Unlike herbs, all spices are edible. Of the scores of herbs and spices that might fill up our kitchen cupboards, relatively few originate in the Western hemisphere - most of them coming from a wide variety of other climactic regions across the globe and are associated with traditional cultural cuisines:

French/English	thyme, tarragon, marjoram, fennel, leek, chervil, parsley, sage, salt
Mediterranean	garlic, basil, rosemary, oregano, black pepper, bay leaf, salt
East European	coriander, caraway, dill, thyme, marjoram, garlic, paprika, bay leaf, salt
Persian	leek, parsley, basil, mint, garlic, coriander, fenugreek, cumin, salt
Indian	cumin, black mustard, coriander, cardamom, cinnamon, black pepper, clove, nutmeg, saffron, ginger, curry leaf, turmeric, ajwain, fenugreek, hing, pink salt
Thai	ginger, Thai basil, garlic, soy sauce, lemongrass (or lemon), galangal, fish sauce, red chilli, coconut, peanut
Chinese	black bean (douchi), garlic, ginger, sesame oil, soy sauce, fish sauce, star anise, Szechuan pepper, cinnamon, clove
Japanese	tamarind, miso, ginger, shisho, seaweed, sesame seed, rice vinegar, umeboshi
Mexican	dried or smoked chilli (e.g. chipotle), garlic, oregano, thyme, coriander, cumin, cinnamon, nutmeg

A key figure in the Ancestral Health movement, organic chemist Dr Mathieu Lalonde[2] compared the nutrient density of meat, vegetables, herbs and spices, fruits, nuts and seeds to that of grains and legumes. He found herbs and spices second only to organ meats - the food most prized by traditional peoples since the beginning of culture.

SPICES - the physician's friend

"Wars were fought over them, kingdoms were lost because of them, and new lands were discovered in search of them. In ancient times and for centuries to follow, spices were often more precious than gold.

But before they were money, spices were medicines."

- Bharah B. Aggarwal

Originating in India, Indonesia and other parts of south and south-east Asia, spices were imported to eastern Mediterranean countries like Syria and Egypt. By the 17th century, spice trading made the Dutch East India Company the richest corporation in the world. By the 18th century, the global colonial endeavours of the Spanish, Portuguese, Dutch, French and the British put spices amongst the most important - and profitable - commodities in world trade.

From prehistoric times right up to the 19th century, when synthetic drugs were developed, herbs and spices were the basis for nearly all medicinal therapy. Thankfully, modern science is exploring and uncovering the power of their 'therapeutic' health-promoting and healing benefits for our body - rich in vitamins, minerals and phytochemicals.

Spices are rich in phytonutrients - powerfully anti-oxidant plant compounds that disarm free-radicals which damage cells causing illness and ageing. They're also highly anti-inflammatory, helping to combat the inflammatory processes that underlie modern chronic and degenerative diseases - like cardiovascular disease, Type 2 diabetes, autoimmune disorders, Alzheimer's, Parkinson's and cancer.

As if that wasn't enough, a spice's pungent aroma gives us a clue not only to its depth of flavour, but also to its underlying concentrated volatile oil compounds. Many of these powerfully healing phytonutrients are unique to spices and aren't found in other plants - curcumin in turmeric; piperine in black pepper; gingerol in ginger; capsaicin in chilli peppers; and rosemarinic acid in rosemary.

Studies show us that populations around the globe whose diet is rich in spices have much lower rates of diseases like cancer, Alzheimer's and heart disease.

And it doesn't stop there. Many spices:

- are anti-microbial and fight infections
- strengthen our immune system
- help our digestion and regulate our blood sugar
- boost our metabolic rate
- ease our pain and relax our body and mind.

Science is showing us that spices are loaded with medicinal properties[3] - even more so than herbs, vegetables and fruits. You might wonder if traditional food wisdom is putting a new spin on our 'five-a-day'? Now there's a thought…

Storing and using spices

Whole spices will keep their flavour and potency much longer than ground spices or herbs. The moment a spice - or a herb - is ground, its surface area is exposed to oxygen, releasing volatile compounds. Ready-ground spices lose their potency much faster, so it's best to buy spices whole and store in glass containers, away from heat, light and air and grind them as you need them.

Spices can withstand long cooking times and are enhanced by dry-roasting before being added early in the cooking process or tempering in hot oil and adding at the end of cooking to punctuate flavour.

HERBS - the culinary alchemists

Tribal cultures have used wild and cultivated herbs as medicines and foods for thousands of years. The ancient Chinese, Indians, Egyptians, Babylonians, Greeks, Romans and Native Americans were all herbalists. Herbs are mentioned the first chapter of the Bible and throughout its text.

Egyptian schools of herbalists have existed since 3000 BC and evidence of early herb gardens in Europe dates back to the Middle Ages. Throughout this period, herbalism was the preserve of the monasteries of Britain and mainland Europe, which also served as medical schools.

Monks copied and translated many of the works of physicians, surgeons and apothecaries such as Hippocrates, Dioscorides, and Galen. The monasteries' *physick* gardens were abundant with the most common and useful medicinal herbs, serving as basic training grounds for the next generation of physicians, monks and indeed laymen.

Later, when the printing press enabled these writings to be mass-produced and made accessible to the people, readers were able to gather the herbs and use them in the prescribed manner and dosage to treat illnesses and disorders.

In herbal medicine, the active properties of herbs are extracted with water, fat and alcohol to make powerful tinctures, teas, decoctions, medicated oils and are still the mainstay of Ayurveda and Traditional Chinese Medicine; having experienced both, I can attest to their efficacy.

In the kitchen, fresh herbs will add a transformational magic to your cooking, bringing brightness, depth and interest to the appearance of any dish. Both fresh and dried herbs can be used in a myriad of ways in infusions, dressings, salads, marinades or added to stocks, stews, soups, stir-fries or ferments.

And we get all this flavour from some of the most nutrient-dense (by weight) plants on the planet.

Storing and using herbs

Herbs - fresh or dried - are more delicate in flavour and constitution than spices and fresh herbs are at their most aromatic just before they flower, after which they become less potent and tougher. However, the herb flowers are delicious in salads and garnishes.

Stronger herbs - sage, thyme, rosemary, oregano - are better used in cooking, while more delicate ones - flat-leaf parsley, mint, tarragon, dill, chives, basil and marjoram - can be added to salads, dressings, dips and sauces or used as a garnish for soups or casseroles.

In some dishes, like pesto or salads, fresh herbs are preferable. When using dried herbs, it is often better to add them towards the end of cooking to maximize their flavour.

Growing herbs

Here in the UK, we are so privileged to have Jekka's Herb Farm and Herbetum near Bristol, where Jekka McVicar grows some 600 varieties of organic herbs, over half of which are culinary. From small beginnings, Jekka's passion has seen her herb patch grow into a world-renowned centre to ensure that the history, culinary and medicinal uses of herbs are not lost for future generations.

Treat yourself to a guided visit, workshop or open day and you'll be inspired, educated and hooked on herbs forever. You'll also come home with pots and pots of herbs to start your own herb garden!

You can also visit the National Herb Centre in Oxfordshire, where you can see and buy a wide selection of culinary and traditional herbs.

Growing your own

There's no question that it's better, cheaper and much healthier to grow your own herbs. They aren't difficult to grow and what you grow is what you get - no added ingredients.

If you're starting a herb garden, think 'location, location, location' and put your herbs as near to your kitchen door as possible. Believe me, the prospect of a trudge down the garden in the rain - or having to rush down to your perfectly-manicured (but distant!) raised beds at the last minute - will prove a major deterrent to your enjoyment.

So, create a herb space near your back door, on a balcony or even a window sill. If outdoors, invest in some wooden boxes or frost-free pots, stock them with the herbs you will use the most and you're ready to snip your herb of choice whenever you need it.

Prepare your patch, bed or containers carefully - herbs, more than any other plant, need well-drained soil. Boxes and pots dry out more quickly than free beds, so water and feed them regularly with organic plant food - herbs are thirsty and hungry - and protect them from frosts. They'll serve your kitchen very well.

Most herbs are perennial and hardy - bay, rosemary, sage, thyme and lemon verbena - but others are annual - like mint, chives, chervil and lemon balm. Tender herbs like basil are native to warmer, drier climates so don't expect to be able to make home-grown pesto in December!

There are many excellent sources of online information on how to get started and succeed at growing herbs. There will also be numerous local courses and workshops you can book yourself onto.

Commercially-grown herbs

When buying commercially-grown herbs and spices, be aware that most non-organic ones found on supermarket shelves will have been irradiated - quite literally been exposed to radiation - and heat-treated to such an extent that the nutrients will have been negatively affected. This process is ostensibly to kill bacteria, but it also destroys the natural enzymes and vitamins found in the untreated product.

In addition, many of the preservatives used can be harmful to our health. For example, sodium benzoate - an anti-fungal and anti-bacterial agent - is used in many commercial spices. It raises the acidity levels in the herbs and spices to prevent microbes and fungi from growing in them. But, if the product is not used, over time this chemical can turn into benzene, which is carcinogenic.

The good news is that more supermarkets are stocking dried organic herbs and spices and more suppliers of organic fresh and dried herbs and organic spices are appearing online. And if you're planning to visit India - or know anyone who is - be sure to take an extra case for the spices you'll want to bring back. You won't be sorry.

Preserving herbs

Once harvested, herbs rapidly begin to lose their pungency and nutrients, so if you grow your own, always pick them as you need them. Back in the day, before global supply chains and bio-tech, our grandparents and theirs relied on time-honoured food preservation skills to see themselves and their communities through the long winter months, when fresh foods were scare or unavailable.

But whether bought or home-grown, a little goes a long way with herbs, so there will always be surplus at the end of the growing season.

In the refrigerator - fresh herbs will last well over a week. Swish them in a bowl of cold, filtered water to remove any grit and spin them in a salad spinner. Store in a sealed container, lined with a little damp, non-toxic kitchen paper.

In the freezer - using a method I discovered online, I've found the best way to freeze herbs is to cover chopped herbs in olive oil - superior for preserving the flavour - either in ice cube trays or by spreading the chopped herbs and oil mixture in thin layer in a shallow baking-tray lined with parchment paper and open-freeze the herbs.

As soon as they are frozen, divide the herb sheet into useable portions and store them between squares of parchment paper, in a freezer-proof container. Either way, frozen herbs are quick and convenient - simply take out what you need, when you need it. This method is ideal for dropping into soups, sauces, stews and gravies.

By the way, whole fresh chillies can be frozen very successfully; my neighbour is a chilli addict and grows several varieties and way too many of each, so they get passed over the fence each summer! I open-freeze them and then store them in a freezer-proof container.

When I want a heat in a dish, I take out a chilli and slice it very finely with a sharp kitchen knife; the high-water content means they soften just enough to slice without risking finger-loss! For the risk-averse, a fine cheese grater works well. If I don't need the whole chilli, the rest just goes back into the freezer for next time.

In oil - submerging foods in oil excludes the air and preserves the contents, as well as flavouring the oil. Oil-preserved herbs are best used within a couple of months, but many will last much longer before their flavour diminishes.

Herbs like rosemary, marjoram, oregano, thyme leaves, sage and basil all work well preserved in oil, or as a flavoured oil. By the way, fresh or even dried chillies and roasted garlic oil work well too. Herbs like tarragon and dill work better preserved in vinegar.

Harvest organic herbs - the healthiest and most aromatic - just before they flower. Make sure the herbs are clean and dry - I wash mine only if they look dusty or gritty. Pour a little extra virgin olive oil into a very clean small kilner or jam jar. Push the herbs - and any spices of choice - into the oil, packing them tightly.

Make sure all the herbs are completely submerged and covered with at least 1cm of oil at the top of the jar, or they will spoil. At Ballymaloe, we learned the trick of placing the jar in the fridge until the oil had solidified and then topping up with a little more oil to ensure the contents were submerged.

Experiment by combining your favourite herbs and spices. For example, an oil flavoured with chilli flakes, roasted garlic, black pepper and oregano makes a delicious basting oil for roast chicken or barbecued pork. Stored in a cold place or the fridge, these tasty preserves will last for a couple of months, sometimes longer.

In vinegar - the acid acts to keep pathogenic bacteria at bay and vinegar preserves tend to keep longer than those in oil. The vinegar preserves the herb and the herbs flavour the vinegar. Tarragon, dill, basil, thyme, rosemary, oregano and mint all work well - just put a few good, clean sprigs of your herb into a bottle of good-quality vinegar. Depending on taste, you can use raw apple cider vinegar - and get the probiotic benefits - or a wine vinegar for a milder taste.

By the way, herb and fruit vinegars - particularly berries - diluted with filtered or sparkling water, make refreshing drinks and help your digestion. A small glass, at room temperature, taken with a meal will both hydrate your digestive system and promote stomach acid, which diminishes with age!

Drying - drying removes the moisture from foods, starves the micro-organisms which rely on it to survive and is one of the oldest methods of preserving foods. Dried herbs are never as potent as fresh herbs, but except for parsley and chives, most herbs can be dried successfully.

Pick the herbs just before they flower, check for dirt and grit and tie them loosely into small bunches. Hang the bunches somewhere warm and dry, but not in direct sunlight. Or, if you're going to make a habit of drying as a method of food preservation, you can invest in and use a food dehydrator.

When the herbs are dry enough to crumble - after three days or so - store them away from strong light, in airtight containers.

Amongst over 700 recipes for traditional foods, Darina Allen's book *Forgotten Skills of Cooking* has a huge variety of ideas on growing and using herbs in all kinds of delicious ways; I thoroughly recommend it.

To describe all the culinary uses for - and the myriad medicinal benefits of - herbs and spices would take a book of several volumes, and a discussion of these techniques and applications is beyond the scope of this book. If you're interested in learning more about using herbal oils as natural medicine, I'd recommend researching the applications of therapeutic essential oils - I've provided some references at the end of the book and on my website.

My own herb garden

Here, I'll share the culinary herbs that I like to grow and how I use them in the kitchen. I'll also share the contents of my spice cupboard, together with a 'flavour', if you will, of research-validated[3] health benefits.

Basil - this delicate, but pungent herb loves warmth and a gentle hand - its delicate leaves bruise and discolour easily. It will sit happily for ages on a warm windowsill or outdoors in a pot in mild weather, if kept just moist. Basil has a huge affinity with tomatoes any-which-way, but always add it at the end of the cooking time to preserve its colour and pungency. And of course, any classic pesto recipe will have to include basil. At the end of its life, the stalks can be used to flavour home-made tomato sauces.

Marjoram and Oregano - these two are cousins and can be used interchangeably and I grow both for use in different dishes. If I want a softer flavour, I choose marjoram - the less pungent of the two. This pairing is classic in Italian, Sicilian, Greek and Mexican dishes. I use them in ragù, with the addition of chilli in spicy tomato sauces, in meat or vegetable chillies, or as a marinade for grilled or barbecued meats and fish. These are robust herbs and need to be added at the beginning of the cooking time to allow the flavours to develop.

Parsley - I grow both curly and flat-leaf parsley, using flat-leaf for adding flavour at the end of cooking and curly in a parsley sauce, or to sprinkle as a garnish. I add it to egg dishes, salads, tabbouleh, garlic mushrooms (with cream, for sourdough toast or omelettes), most soups, a white sauce for grilled fish or a fish pie, to fish stew, steamed mussels - along with a little cream - or to serve with a poached bacon joint.

Rosemary - it always feels comforting to have rosemary growing in the garden. For me, its strong pungent stems always speak to "home". A classic with roast lamb, rosemary is also great in a fruity lamb tagine, with slow-roast chicken and a tasty addition to roast potatoes.

Sage - while it's not a herb I use often, I love the soft, velvety texture of sage leaves and can't resist growing it! For me, sage comes into its own in a golden sage butter to pour over filled pasta, like pumpkin or butternut squash ravioli.

Thyme - I grow lemon thyme for its mild, gentle aroma and the flavour and add it to soups. I also like to put several sprigs, along with half a lemon, some onion slices and a few black peppercorns, inside a chicken when I'm roasting it and use more with parsley to make a separate stuffing.

Mint - I dot cooked vegetables - potatoes, carrots, peas, green beans - with mint butter (butter helps with vitamin absorption) and it brings an extra fresh zing to yoghurts and cultured cream dips. Mint is also good with cucumber, grated carrot or grated beetroot. Apple mint tea is a must as a refreshing pick-me up, or an after-dinner digestive - so attractively green!

Chives - finely-chopped chives enliven egg, potato and cheese dishes, or make a lovely dip stirred into yoghurt or cultured cream, or as a garnish for fish dishes or thick soups. Their beautiful mauve flowers are deliciously punchy when broken apart and sprinkled over salads or a dish of egg mayonnaise.

The spice in *my* life

Black peppercorns:

As medicine - rich in curative piperine, Indian black pepper is considered superior to other varieties. Used as curative for many thousands of years by ancient Ayurveda, research has shown us that piperine powerfully stimulates our metabolism by kick-starting digestion and speeding up food transit time through the bowel. Black pepper has been shown to improve the absorption of turmeric, the metabolism of medications, support cancer prevention and treatment, ease arthritis, improve brain function and help hypertension and cardiovascular disease.

In the kitchen - next to salt, black pepper is our most abundantly used spice. Black peppercorns are considered the 'king' of spices; green, white and pink are all variations of the peppercorn bud at various stages of maturation. Indispensable in the kitchen, black pepper is a key element in spice blends in any cuisine which favours a gustatory 'bite' to any dish, including sweet fruits like strawberries, pears and even cheeses love a couple of twists of black pepper.

Ginger:

As medicine - traditional healers have reached for ginger to treat all kinds of nausea for thousands of years. Now science is showing us that its many properties (anti-oxidant, anti-inflammatory, anti-bacterial) are also effective against arthritis, asthmas, digestive distress cardio-vascular disease and cancer, and it also helps cholesterol and triglyceride regulation.

In the kitchen - I use ginger in: porridge, most pork-based dishes, all ethnic dishes, Asian salads and dressings, poached rhubarb/pears/peaches, stuffed baked apples, basmati rice and rice puddings, cultured cream, labneh toppings and dessert sauces, home-made ice cream, smoothies and teas.

Except when baking, I use it fresh - finely grated, thinly sliced or julienned and squeeze out the juice from the strands for smoothies and icings.

Garlic:

As medicine - apart from its legendary use to repel evil spirits, consuming garlic is associated with a decreased incidence of all age-related chronic diseases - particularly cardiovascular diseases, but also cancer, diabetes, prostrate disorders, colds and flu. The most potent properties of garlic come from its raw state where the alliinase is intact, but many find raw garlic very difficult to digest.

To retain some benefit in cooking, smash, cut or press the garlic at least 10-15 minutes before adding it to the dish. Adding garlic late in the cooking process retains its pungency and many more of its health properties.

In the kitchen - everything tastes better with garlic: marinades, soups, casseroles, sauces, pesto, dips, spice blends, stir-fries, butters, dressings and oils. Make little pockets in your slow-cooked lamb joint and push garlic slithers into the slits. Or roast a whole garlic bulb alongside your lemony thyme roast chicken - delicious!

Turmeric:

As medicine - once disparaged as 'poor man's saffron', turmeric turns out to be India's gold. A daily staple in Indian homes for centuries, science is showing us repeatedly that turmeric's active ingredient - curcumin - is able to protect and improve our health on just about every level.

Traditional medicines have lauded turmeric with scores of healing actions and now, many thousands of studies have provided evidence that the combination of curcumin's powerful anti-oxidative and anti-inflammatory abilities is as at least effective as pharmaceuticals, with no unwanted side effects. Always use with fat or a little black pepper for proper absorption.

Turmeric's potential for treating cancer, pollutants and toxins, Alzheimer's and Parkinson's disease, arthritis, bowel disease, skin conditions, cardiovascular disease (and more) is truly exciting.

In the kitchen: I use turmeric wherever possible: soups, casseroles, gravies, tomato sauces, savoury rice dishes, spice blends and rubs. It goes into chocolate smoothies and hot chocolate drinks. And of course, I'll be making a soothing Turmeric Latté, a traditional Ayurvedic 'golden' milk - see the recipe below - to end this day and welcome in a restorative, healing night's sleep.

Cinnamon:

As medicine - cinnamon is famed for its ability to control blood sugar, making it of great value to those with insulin resistance, diabetes and metabolic syndrome. It also has a track record for helping regulate high blood pressure, cardiovascular disease and yeast infections.

In the kitchen - I always add a little cinnamon to high-carbohydrate or sweet dishes like porridge, basmati rice and rice puddings, cooked fruits, dairy-based desserts and chocolate drinks and I love the depth it gives in a spice blend for chicken and beef dishes.

Chilli:

As medicine - chilli's fiery healer is capsaicin and the hotter the better as far as its therapeutic properties are concerned. Chillies contain a plethora of anti-oxidant vitamins and sound research has shown us its efficacy as a powerful pain-killer (ironic, if you've ever rubbed your eye after slicing a chilli!), a fat burner, a heart helper, a digestive and diabetic friend and a cancer foe.

In the kitchen - fresh or dried, chilli is a background spice, which sets the scene for spice blends - adding it alone does nothing for any dish. There are a wide variety of chillies from all over the world - India, Africa, Asia, the Caribbean and the Americas - and each cuisine has its own distinctive flavour notes and heat rating.

The heat is in the membrane and seeds, so you can regulate how hot you want your dish to be by excluding some or all of these. I rarely use ready ground chilli powder, preferring to use fresh or frozen chilli from my neighbour's garden.

Caraway:

As medicine - traditionally used in bread and cakes - or offered post-meal - caraway seeds are well-known for their supportive digestive properties. Caraway contains carvone which relaxes spasms in the digestive tract, easing post-meal problems. Studies have also shown it to be a useful aid to controlling blood sugar. But there's more - its over 50 compounds have been noted in research studies for cancer, combatting E. coli, managing cholesterol and triglycerides, easing constipation and for treating tuberculosis.

In the kitchen - I use caraway in breads (especially sourdough rye), loaf-style cakes, home-made sauerkrauts and fermented vegetables, cooked carrots, broccoli, cabbage, leeks, in goulash-style stews and I sometimes add it when cooking apples for a crumble or pie.

Coriander:

As medicine - coriander seed is known for soothing stomach and digestive ailments and we now have positive research outcomes for IBS, spasms, bloating, chronic constipation, inflammatory skin conditions, cholesterol regulation, diabetes, yeast infections, lead poisoning and liver disease, particularly non-alcoholic fatty liver disease (NAFLD).* It's also effective in treating insomnia - where it has been identified as a powerful sedative and muscle relaxant.

**Do you recall reading about glyphosate ingestion as causal in NAFLD in the Soil chapter?*

In the kitchen - a key spice in blends from many cuisines, coriander can flavour both sweet and savoury dishes. I use it liberally in ethnic dishes, in chorizo-style pork dishes alongside smoked paprika, as a flavouring for coffee and regularly add it to my evening Turmeric Latté.

Cumin:

As medicine - diabetes researchers have shown cumin to be equal to anti-diabetes drugs in its ability to reduce high cholesterol, triglycerides and to delay cataract development, a common risk for those with diabetes.

In the kitchen - a kitchen staple in cuisines all over the globe, I use it with slow-cooked foods along with cinnamon, for a north African-style flavour, in curry blends and in Mexican chilli dishes. I also make a glaze for roasting vegetables with ground cumin, olive or coconut oil, salt and pepper, sometimes adding dried chilli flakes for an extra kick.

Black Cumin:

As medicine - scholars, scribes, prophets and research scientists have all hailed black cumin as a potential cure-all. In addition to thymoquinone (an active compound unique to black cumin), researchers have uncovered over 100 compounds in black cumin important to our health and they're not finished yet.

We know that black cumin - also known as nigella or kalonji seed - boosts immunity, protects the heart, fights cancer, calms asthma and allergies and research suggests it can help with pain and inflammation, stomach and digestive disorders, multiple sclerosis and various skin conditions.

In the kitchen - I use nigella seed in chutneys, slow-cooked lamb dishes and curry dishes and cook it into basmati rice to accompany curries. Adding a little turmeric to the rice gives an additional health boost and depth of flavour; and the golden yellow and black combo looks stunning on the plate.

We are truly blessed with the variety of herbs and spices available to us today. Not only do they enhance the flavour of our food… they truly are food-as-medicine!

So, take on board the Spice Girls' good advice and bring a world of flavour right into your kitchen:

"Colours of the world… Spice up your life!

Every boy and every girl… Spice up your life!

People of the world… Spice up your life!"

HERBS and SPICES Recipes

PESTO

Fresh, home-made pesto is on another level and much lower in salt than shop-bought offerings. Known as *pistou* in France, classic pesto originates from Genoa in Italy and is simply made from pine nuts blended with fresh basil, parmesan (or pecorino) cheese, garlic and olive oil.

Walnuts can also be used in place of pine nuts; and a variety of herbs such as parsley, mint, tarragon, coriander, watercress and wild garlic, chervil, sun-dried tomatoes, grilled red peppers can also be used, making it incredibly versatile and deliciously health addition to rice and grain salads, fish, chicken, steamed or roast vegetables, potato dishes, eggs, soups and stews, or to simply to spread on bruschetta.

PARSLEY PESTO

(Serves 2-4)

What you'll need:

Flat leaf parsley leaves: 30g (no stalks - freeze these for flavouring stocks & soups)
Garlic: 1-2 cloves, crushed
Parmesan: 40g (finely grated)
Pine nuts: 30g
Extra virgin olive oil: 75ml
Sea salt: Maldon (to taste)

What to do:

1. Simply put all the ingredients, except the oil and salt into the food processer and blitz for a couple of seconds or use a large pestle and mortar to pound the ingredients into a paste.

2. Add the oil and little salt, blitz or pound again and season to taste. The pesto will keep well in the fridge.

SALSA VERDE

This vibrant, punchy 'green sauce' is a summer-time classic for just about any meat, fish and vegetable dish. Again, a selection of the softer green herbs can be used, but the woody ones like rosemary and thyme tend to dominate in flavour.

What you'll need:

Garlic: 1 clove (peeled & roughly chopped)
Flat-leaf parsley: small bunch, no stalks
Basil: small bunch
Mint: small bunch of mint, no stalks
Anchovies: 2
Capers: 2 tsp
French mustard: 1 tsp
Lemon juice: a few drops (to taste)
Sugar: ½ tsp (to taste)
Sea salt: Maldon, pinch (to taste)
Freshly ground black pepper: to taste
Extra virgin olive oil: 2 tbsp

What to do:

1. On a wooden board, smash the garlic down with the back of a wide-bladed knife and then finely chop it and the herbs together.

2. Add the anchovies and capers and continue chopping until everything is well combined.

3. Transfer the ingredients to a small bowl and add the mustard, lemon juice, sugar, salt and pepper and mix well.

4. Stir in the olive oil a little at a time, until the salsa is thick and glossy. Taste and adjust seasonings.

CHIMICHURRI

(Serves 4-6)

Originating from Uruguay and Argentina chimichurri is the one of the best accompaniments to any barbecued or grilled meats. It can also be used a marinade for grilled meat, brushed or spooned onto meat as it cooks, or onto the cooked surface of meat as it rests.

What you'll need:

Garlic: 1 clove (peeled, smashed and finely chopped)
Spring onion: 1 tbsp finely very finely chopped
White wine vinegar: 1 tbsp
Dried chilli flakes: 1 pinch (to taste)
Fresh coriander: 2 tbsp, chopped
Fresh parsley: 2 tbsp, chopped
Lime: juice of ½
Extra Virgin Olive Oil: 100ml
Salt and freshly ground black pepper: to taste

What to do:

Simply combine all the ingredients in a bowl and season to taste with salt and pepper.

HOME-MADE GARAM MASALA

What you'll need:

Cardamom seeds: 1 tbsp (if you can't buy the seeds then buy cardamom pods and shell them yourself)
Black peppercorns: 1 tsp
Black cumin seeds: 1 tsp (or regular cumin seeds if black seeds aren't available)
Whole cloves: 1 tsp
Whole nutmeg: ⅓ (you can break up a whole nutmeg by placing it on a cloth and bashing it with a meat mallet or rolling pin)
Cinnamon: a medium stick - about 5-8cm - broken up into 3 or 4 pieces

What to do:

1. Put all the ingredients in a clean coffee grinder or other spice grinder and grind as finely as possible.

2. Store in a tightly lidded jar, away from heat and sunlight and use as needed.

AU REVOIR et BONNE CHANCE!

Well, we've come a long way and covered a lot of ground in this book - I hope I've made it an enjoyable and enlightening journey. In *Once Upon a Cook*, we've:

- **reflected** on how many of us face a constant battle with fatigue, overwhelm, persistent weight gain, ill health and chronic health conditions, how and why our modern food and lifestyle choices are not supporting our health and how far we have become disconnected from traditional foods and food producers and time-honoured cooking methods

- **considered** how the myriad and conflicting advice on health, lifestyle, food and nutrition is frequently founded on poor research, at best inconclusive, and often plain wrong

- **reviewed** how generations of damage to our soils are causing many of the health issues we face today. We saw how microbes impact our immune system and our gut microbiome, and how monoculture and intensive farming's use of chemical fertilisers and pesticides are causing wide-scale damage to our food supply, our ecosystems and ultimately our planet. We considered the future of farming and how small-scale, organic agriculture can keep up with demand and feed the world with healthy, nutrient-dense food

- **applauded** the humble egg - one of Mother Nature's 'perfect' foods. We examined the nutritional value of eggs, the provenance of a variety of eggs on the market and why free-range and organic is so important to our health - as well as that of the hens

- **learned why** meat is a treat (and why offal isn't awful) and looked at how and why red meats have become demonised. We learned how increased demand and supply has led to a sharp decline in the quality and nutritional value of meat, animal welfare standards and an unsustainable environment. We considered the importance of sourcing high quality, organic meat and poultry, why the nutrients found in organic, pastured animals are superior and why offal (e.g. liver, heart, kidneys) is pre-eminent in a nutrient-dense diet

- **followed** the story of why and how milk has gone from its role as a prized food and an important medicine, to its current demonised status. We looked how milk's downfall began with American urbanisation and distillery dairies and continued with damage caused by the pasteurisation and homogenisation processes. We emphasised how truly organic, unpasteurised milk is in a different league nutritionally to the product we find in our supermarkets today

- **outed** mass-produced imposter breads and learned how these are a world away from the wholesome traditional bread our grandparents enjoyed. We discussed the nature of the wheat we now consume and how hybridised wheat, the impact of GM farming practices and mass production has rendered much of what we call 'bread' nutritionally bankrupt and for many of us, a potential health risk

- **marvelled** at gelatin-rich bone broths and stocks, and their centuries' long pedigree in all diets and every culture throughout history and we learned about the vital role broths and stocks play in a healthy, nutritionally-complete diet

- **assessed** the contribution of fruit and vegetables to a balanced diet and considered why whole fruit and vegetables are important. We looked at the trend towards eating more raw vegetables and the impact this has on our metabolism. We've discussed the growing trend towards plant-based eating and veganism, as well as the damage being caused by GM and intensive fruit and vegetable production

- **dismissed** the myths demonising traditional (saturated) fats and learned which fats are vital to our diet and which fats are best for cooking. We questioned the flawed conclusions of research and how it influenced conventional wisdom and advice dietary fats and cholesterol and we outed the real demons of the piece - trans and polyunsaturated fats

- **dived deep** into the important contribution of fish and seafood to optimum nutrition and looked at white fish, oily fish and shellfish, as well as fish bones and fish roe. We looked at how we can source and enjoy seafood sustainably

- **emphasised** how cultured and fermented foods have supported human health throughout history and took a closer look at how pre- and pro-biotic foods, cultured dairy and cultured and wild ferments promote a healthy gut microbiome, to underpin every aspect of our health

- **dispelled** salt myths which have unfairly and misleadingly portrayed salt as a food demon, considered why salt plays a critical part in optimum health and examined the relationship between salt and blood pressure, cardiovascular disease and diabetes

- **calmly considered** how sugar has become Public Enemy No.1 and how and why our body's natural craving for sweeteners has been high-jacked by modern food technologies to crave far more sugar than we can handle from highly refined, ultra-processed foods and beverages. We reviewed some of the implications of dietary sugar for cancer, diabetes and other chronic illness

- **learned** about the important contribution of herbs and spices to our diets for flavouring and for nutrition, summarised which ones to use when and discussed simple methods for growing, buying and storing herbs and spices.

In calling on you to reclaim your kitchen and take back your health, my aim has been to encourage you to care deeply where your food comes from and how it's produced.

In reading this book, I hope that it has succeeded in inspiring you to go back to the future of food and put the nourishing, traditional foods that kept generations of our grandparents healthy, right back where they belong - on *your* table!

I hope too, that I've left you a much better informed, more conscious and discerning consumer - equipped to ask questions, make demands and to make much better food choices, for much better health.

I would love to hear from you at any time, so please feel free to drop me a line at izabella@izabellanatrins.com and let me know what you think and how you're getting on!

IZABELLA NATRINS - FOOD | HEALTH | LIFESTYLE

Izabella Natrins - Food | Health | Lifestyle is an information and education website for holistic health and well-being. My original and curated articles and free resources help my readers to understand and keep abreast of quality research on how nutrition and lifestyle impacts health.

Focusing on how a strong metabolism is critical for a healthy mind and body, readers learn how eating a metabolically supportive diet; restoring restful sleep; reducing stress; taking regular breaks in nature to move our bodies; fostering inner and outer connectedness, finding true purpose and creating a supportive home environment work synergistically to create truly holistic health and well-being.

NUTRITION and LIFESTYLE HEALTH COACHING

Many of us have niggling health issues and want to tackle them before they get out of hand, but we don't know where to start in order to feel more in control and less overwhelmed.

Many more of us struggle on alone with stubborn weight gain and yo-yo dieting; with stress or poor sleep; with gut and digestive issues; or with hormonal or infertility problems.

Too many of us have a diagnosed, chronic, or degenerative health condition and need highly personalized and intensive support but don't know where to turn.

Nutrition and lifestyle health coaching can make the difference between wishing your health was better and creating better health. Health coaching isn't about diagnosing symptoms or treating diseases, nor is it about telling you what you should do.

It's about working with a skilled and sensitive mentor, coach and ally to identify your health goals and priorities. It's about creating specific, realistic and achievable steps to improve your health and well-being and keeping you motivated and accountable in the process.

Ultimately, health coaching is about equipping you to get into the driving seat to develop the knowledge, skills and confidence to manage your own health and well-being.

Femergy@40 Coaching Programmes for Women at Midlife

For women, midlife is pivotal and the start of a journey of new and exciting discoveries about who we are and how we want to live. It's a time of fundamental change and it's absolutely the time to embrace our wisdom, share our gifts with confidence and step forward with courage to make our contribution. And to make the rest of your life the best of your life.

But if we're honest, how often does it feel like this…?

🖤 I want to feel better, but I'm simply overwhelmed. My body keeps whispering "please, slow down", but I keep on going and going...

🖤 I want to nip my niggling health issues in the bud - I'm sleeping badly, run out of energy and am tired all the time. I have unexplained aches and pains, a permanently fuzzy head and difficulty in concentrating. I feel my body is urging me to "please, listen"...

🖤 I've been struggling for too long with multiple health issues - an intestinal or digestive disorder, an autoimmune condition, miserable hormonal dysfunction, infertility, a thyroid problem. I'm pre or T2diabetic with distressing weight-gain or obesity. My body's crying out: "Help. Me. Now."

After 30 years in the health space, I know that women at midlife need a supportive ally to stand beside them as they grow and transition into a new phase filled with purpose and limitless potential - but all too often they struggle just to keep going.

I've put together my own experience with supporting women with leading edge research and practise from top experts in functional and integrative medicine and holistic healthcare, to offer structured health coaching programmes to meet a range of needs and preferences.

Whatever your starting point and whether you'd rather work 1:1 or as part of an online community, visit:

izabellanatrins.com/coaching

and book a 30-Minute Health Consultation with me to discover how nutrition and lifestyle coaching can help you feel and live better.

APPENDIX 1

A DEEPER DIVE INTO CARBS

Despite the current backlash against carbs that is gripping diet gurus, the media and perhaps you too, dietary carbohydrates have a rightful place in the context of a whole food, varied, nutrient-dense and metabolically-supportive (energy-rich) diet. As we have seen, dietary carbohydrates comprise sugars, starches and fibre and these provide our bodies with energy to use - and store - for fuelling our cells. They provide structure; feed beneficial gut bacteria; bulk out our stool; and support our immune, digestive and cardiovascular systems. To appreciate the role of carbohydrates in health - and how they can support or derail it - we need to understand a little more about them.

Our cells' most important job is to create the energy we need to fuel every process in the body to meet the daily demands we put upon our bodies. The rate and efficiency of this process - our metabolism - is fuelled by sugar in the form of glucose, our body's primary and preferred source of fuel. Carbohydrates are made up of units of simple sugar called saccharides.

In the diagram below, I've set out the main classes of carbohydrates:

CARBOHYDRATES			
Free sugars		**Complex carbohydrates**	
Monosaccharides (1 sugar molecule)	**Disaccharides** (2 sugar molecules)	**Polysaccharides** (Many sugar molecules)	
↓	↓	↓	↓
GLUCOSE (Basic sugar)	**SUCROSE** (Table sugar: glucose + fructose)	**STARCHES**	**FIBRE**
↓	↓	Pectin	Cellulose
FRUCTOSE (Fruit sugar)	**LACTOSE** (Milk sugar: glucose + galactose)	Amylopectin	Hemi-cellulose
↓	↓	Amylose	Gums
GALACTOSE (Builds lactose)	**MALTOSE** (Starch/grain sugar: glucose + glucose)	Glycogen (Storage form of glucose)	

Glucose is a carbohydrate in its purest and simplest form. Derived from plant photosynthesis, glucose is the basis of all cellular respiration and all life. As a monosaccharide, glucose requires no digestion to break it down, so it can deliver energy to the cells very quickly and efficiently, increasing metabolism and supporting the thyroid to do its job of regulating every cell and bodily system. This is especially useful for the young, old and sick.

Sugar is a critical nutrient in feeding very premature babies, or those with neo-natal hypoglycaemia via glucose drips, when they're too small or too sick to feed from breast milk (initially high in the milk sugar lactose and water). Glucose drips are also used for anyone who is very weak, has lost a lot of blood through severe injury or major surgery, or who does not have the energy (or is unable to) to eat or digest food.

Simple sugars are particularly useful for those with digestive difficulties, since the more complex the carbohydrate – for example, grains - the more digestive strength is required. Indeed, glucose is a particularly important source of energy and too little can be just as bad as too much; in fact, if we don't get it, our body resorts to breaking down our muscles and fat stores to make glucose.

Starches and fibre

As you can see from the diagram, starches are a more complex form of sugars - polysaccharides. These complex carbohydrates take longer to break down and to properly digest than their simpler cousins. They're not as fast and efficient as free sugars for energy production, but they are more sustaining and they're a key source of fibre in our diet.

Fibre is an important carbohydrate which isn't (or is only partly) broken down and different kinds of fibre play important roles in the body: delaying glucose absorption; creating a supportive environment and food for our gut bacteria; fermenting resistant starch to produce the cancer-protective short-chain fatty acid butyrate; supporting our immune and cardiovascular systems; regulating and aiding cholesterol and toxin removal; supporting elimination and bulking out our stool. In our Western processed diets, we modern humans consume a tiny fraction of the fibre that our ancestors chomped down on daily!

Many different types of foods contain both simple and complex carbohydrates. It needs to be said up-front that the effects of carbohydrate in our body - and its impact on our health - depends on the type of carbohydrate and the person who is eating it; no 'one-carb' fits all! Ultimately, our body needs to break down all carbohydrates into simpler sugars like glucose, which can be more readily used for energy.

Whole, unprocessed carbs like whole grains (not milled flours), starchy roots, shoots, tubers (parsnips, turnips, swedes, beets, carrots, white and sweet potatoes, cassava, etc.), leafy green vegetables, whole fruits, legumes and dairy products are rich in natural sugars, unrefined, unprocessed starches and in fibre. In general, all are healthful, and these nutrient-dense foods play a proper part in an energy-rich diet.

However, the bulk of the starches we commonly consume in our processed Western diet come from a plethora of convenience foods and are derived from highly-refined and processed grains, like bread, pasta and other milled flour and bakery products, breakfast cereals, oats and rice. Not only do these processed foods contain hidden sugars, the kinds of starches they contain can cause a myriad of health problems: from the lack of traditional methods of preparation that make grains more digestible, to the way that modern agriculture has manipulated and adulterated and otherwise ruined them, to the way that the food industry has processed them.

In food processing, some or all of the natural fibre is removed, so our body is very easily able to break down the carbohydrates into a simpler form of sugar and to digest and absorb it into the blood stream quickly. Unless we're an athlete in training, or we expend a vast amount of physical energy in other ways, our over-consumption of refined and ultra-processed carbohydrates delivers far more energy than we actually need. What our body can't use for energy straight away, it stores for later use as glycogen in our liver and muscles.

Our body also has trouble dealing with the peaks and troughs in blood sugar levels provoked by refined and ultra-processed carbohydrates, paving the way for insulin dysregulation and triggering a hunger-craving-eating cycle for more high-carb and sugary foods, in a futile bid to satisfy our energy requirements. There is no doubt that our modern, ultra-processed diet (and lifestyle) has left us over-fed, under-nourished and falling prey to conditions like obesity, Type 2 diabetes and a host of other chronic disorders.[1]

But do we actually need carbs?

Evolution has 'wired' us to favour a sweet taste. Researchers argue that back in the day, our ancestors gorged on high-carb autumnal fruits which enabled them to build up the extra fat stores they would need to survive the winter months, when other foods may be scare. During this time, their bodies would convert this stored fat to back into glucose to use as energy.

However, the whole issue of whether carbohydrate is a necessary nutrient, is one which has been and continues to be, at the centre of heated arguments amongst respected experts on both sides of the debate. For example, some argue that carbohydrates are critical to metabolic health and to supporting thyroid function (our energy thermostat) and should constitute a major part of every meal.[2]

On the other hand, others hold that carbohydrate over-consumption in itself is responsible for obesity and Type 2 diabetes (and a host of other conditions) and argue that we should avoid it, or even cut it out completely, as in the ketogenic diet and derive our energy largely or only, from fats, since, in the absence of dietary glucose, our liver breaks down fats (and proteins) to use for energy (a process called gluconeogenesis).

This view is rooted in the ancestral diet movement, which is based largely on fats and proteins with few, seasonal carbs and fruit sugars.[3]

However, carb advocates retort that it's precisely because maintaining a sufficient supply of dietary glucose is so important, that our body has the capacity to convert fats and proteins for energy. When we go on a diet that severely restricts calories, or on low-carb diets, our carbohydrate intake can be depleted to the point of provoking an energetically expensive, inefficient process of breaking down both fat and proteins to make glucose.

On this view, when protein is scavenged for energy long-term, it puts the body into a stress mode - raising cortisol and adrenaline - and protein is not available to build muscle. It's also not available to support efficient metabolism, synthesize antibodies or perform any of its many life-sustaining roles.

Very low-carbohydrate diets put extra stress on the liver by forcing it to assist with manufacturing glucose from fats and proteins. Long term, the sharp reduction in the consumption of plant-based foods associated with many, but not all low carbohydrate diets, can also result in low fibre intake, lead to constipation and bowel issues and increase the risk of digestive cancers and cardiovascular disease. The reduction of fruit, vegetables, legume and whole grain consumption can result in inadequate phytonutrient, antioxidant, vitamin C and potassium intake.[4]

Low-carb impact on thyroid health

Our liver stores glucose in the form of glycogen and our body needs a steady supply of sugar to keep those glycogen stores topped up. The thyroid hormone (thyroxine or T4) produced by the thyroid gland needs to be converted from its inactive state (as thyroxine) to its active state (triiodothyronine or T3).

Our body judges, in part by our carbohydrate intake, whether we have enough energy to make this conversion and decides to make less T3 when we are depleted in carbohydrate. It's this T3 which actually fuels our metabolism, so without adequate glucose our metabolism - and thus our ability to create energy - is under-powered. A low metabolic rate and low energy production is a common feature of ageing and most degenerative diseases.

Personalised Nutrition

While whole, unrefined carbohydrates have a place in a metabolically supportive diet, emerging science is showing us that no dogmatic approach to consuming carbohydrates can fit all.

Each one of us processes starches, sugars and fibre differently and some of us tolerate some forms better than others. Some of us feel well on any and all forms of carbs. For others with conditions like obesity, pre-diabetes, Type 1 and 2 diabetes, metabolic syndrome or autoimmune disease, different kinds of carbs will provoke an unstable unhealthy elevation in blood sugar and insulin production, such that our consumption of carbs may need to be closely managed.

Recent research in the growing field of Personalised Nutrition is informing us how an individual's diet can be monitored and managed to get the energy benefits of carbohydrate consumption but avoid its pitfalls.[5]

But should we fear fructose?

Fructose - perhaps even more than glucose - has become demonised and we're now implored not to drink fruit juices and to limit our fruit consumption.[6,7]

In my eBook *Demonised Drinks*, I devoted a chapter to why most of us should stop fearing orange juice and use it judiciously as a valuable nutrient rather than avoid it as an unhealthy beverage. Let me highlight just some of its nutritional benefits:

- the sugars in orange juice come in three different forms (sucrose, glucose and fructose), all of which our body ultimately breaks down into glucose to fuel our energy needs. While orange juice contains a significant amount of sugar, it also provides minerals such as magnesium and potassium which, as nature would have it, are essential for blood sugar and insulin level regulation.

- magnesium in orange juice is also vital for cellular metabolism and the production of the energy (known as adenosine triphosphate or ATP) that our body needs to carry out all of its functions. Just one 250ml glass of fresh OJ provides about 15% of our daily requirements for potassium, significant amounts of folate (19%), B-6, thiamine, choline, and vitamin A.

  We also get 207% of our recommended daily value of vitamin C in one glass - a major antioxidant which also increases our white blood cell count to improve the immune system's function and helps us to assimilate collagen - which, as we saw in the Bone Broth

Chapter, not only helps us to look younger, but supports a healthy digestive system, joints, strong bones and teeth and more!

- Orange juice also supports our adrenal and thyroid glands from the nutrients it provides: Magnesium, potassium, vitamin C and glucose are essential in the production and conversion of the active form of thyroid hormone T3. Without these nutrients, our thyroid can't keep up with your body's hormonal demands, and overall physiological stress is increased.

By judiciously taking in some natural sugars through our diet (like whole fruits and freshly squeezed juices) our body gets a message of 'nutritional' safety - that all is well, that it can turn off its inflammatory stress response and go ahead with producing sufficient energy to fuel a healthy metabolism.

However...

As I discussed in the Fruit and Veg chapter, freshly squeezed, organic orange juice (like you'd juice at home) is a million miles away from the fake, industrially-produced juice, passed off as 100% pure orange juice! Raw, freshly pressed organic juice will contain more heat-sensitive nutrients like vitamin C and beneficial enzymes that break down when exposed to the high temperatures of pasteurising and processing. When you buy commercial juice, remember that most of it is pasteurised and is not organic so will contain high levels of both pesticide residues and added sugars.

Anyone who knows (or suspects) that they have problems with regulating blood sugar, struggles with obesity, metabolic syndrome, or pre/Type 1 or 2 diabetes will need to exercise caution and closely monitor their response to drinking fruit juices. That said, before rejecting juices completely out of hand, a first step is to ditch all processed foods and drinks (including anything with the label of 'fruit drink', as these hide frightening amounts of sugars). Over time and with careful management, by getting back on track with a whole-food, unprocessed diet nutritious fruit and fruit juices could be back on the menu.

So, do we need carbs?

I say yes... and no! Depending on our state of health, what we want to achieve with dietary adjustments, our lifestyle and energy needs, our ability to store and use glycogen and the quality of the carbs we consume, they can be great for us, or they can give us grief.

It's worth remembering that much dietary research draws information from studying sick people, who have a stressed metabolism and do not metabolise carbohydrates or sugar well. Consider this plea from Dr Chris Masterjohn, a leading a leading nutritional science researcher, writer and teacher:

"We need to frame our discussions of glucose as a nutrient and insulin as a protective hormone whose protective functions are being lost in obesity and diabetes." [8]

Personally, I'm not ready to throw the carb and sugar babies out with the bathwater - just yet!

APPENDIX 2

CHEMICALS, OUR FOOD, OUR HEALTH and OUR ENVIRONMENT

Fertilisers: progress at what cost?

We humans are made up of four essential elements: hydrogen, oxygen, carbon and nitrogen. Without any one of these elements we cannot survive.

Three of these four elements are abundant and easily obtained: hydrogen comes from the water we drink; oxygen from the air we breathe; and carbon from eating plants, or from eating animals that ate the plants. Carbon is also in the air and is converted by green plants via photosynthesis.

Getting our nitrogen fix, however, is less straightforward. Although nitrogen makes up around 80% of the atmosphere, it's in a form that is unavailable to us. It needs to be in a fixed form - and this is where soil becomes important.

We get our nitrogen from eating plants, or animals raised on nitrogen-rich soil.

Soil nutrients

We've seen how soil microbes play their part in our health, but the soil itself is a living entity and needs feeding to remain healthy and fertile. Soil must contain three main macronutrients to support healthy plant growth:

- **nitrogen** - for leaf growth
- **phosphorus** - for the development of roots, flowers, seeds, fruit
- **potassium** - for strong stem growth, movement of water in plants, promotion of flowering and fruiting.

Of these, nitrogen is the most important nutrient but agricultural crops like corn, wheat, barley, potatoes or rice deplete nitrogen from the soil and unless it's replenished, the soil becomes infertile.

Until the early 1900s, farmers used three traditional methods of enriching soil nitrogen. They:

- used natural fertilisers made from decaying plants or animal manure
- 'fixed' the nitrogen into the soil with crop rotation - by planting legumes (like chickpeas, alfalfa, peas, soybeans or clover) which harbour good bacteria in their roots, which take nitrogen from the air and convert it into ammonia in the soil
- waited for lightning to strike! Seriously, this can also 'fix' nitrogen from the air.

Commercial fertilisers

Because of the perceived need to feed growing global populations and - more importantly - the promise of huge profits for the German chemical company BASF, a smart German chemist changed the whole story...

Nitrogen fertilisers - in 1909, Fritz Haber succeeded in by-passing nature and taking nitrogen from the air to create ammonia - a perfect synthetic fertiliser. Today, around 130 million tons of nitrogen are removed from the air to spread across the earth as fertiliser, and around half the world's population have come to depend on nitrogen-based fertilisers for the production of their food.

Phosphate and potassium fertilisers - the industry went on to devise ways of producing phosphate fertiliser and today a huge variety of single, compound and micro-nutrient fertilisers are available to farmers, and as we'll see below, nitrate and phosphate additives are ubiquitous in our food and drinks.

What has been the impact of commercial fertiliser use?

While Mother Nature has seen to it that her soils are receptive to natural fertilisers, she's not at all happy with our meddling. Consider the following:

Nitrogen pollution -

The largest nitrogen-producing plant in the USA consumes a million dollars' worth of natural gas, boils 30,000 tons of water from a local river into steam and produces 5,000 tons of ammonia daily - which is 2 million tons a year!

Every day, these 5,000 tons of ammonia are loaded onto railcars, placed onto barges, floated down the Mississippi river and sprinkled onto corn and wheat fields across the land. But only about a third of nitrogen contained in ammonia and layered onto crop fields, ends up in crops. Nearly half washes away into streams and leeches into groundwater.

Every year, the Gulf of Mexico receives 1.5 million tons of such nitrogen, causing:

> **"... an overgrowth of algae that clouds the water and chokes off oxygen and sunlight to other species, like fish and molluscs. Algal overgrowth has killed streams, lakes, and coastal ecosystems across the northern hemisphere. And it's not just the fish that are dying. The birds that eat the fish are dying, too.**
>
> **Synthetic nitrogen pollution isn't limited to the waters; it's also entered the air and come back to earth as acid rain, further damaging lakes, streams, and forests as well as the animals that depend on them.**
>
> **These problems will only worsen. Synthetic fertiliser, a process that has given so many people their lives ... has probably started the clock on their eventual destruction."** [1]

- Pandora's Lab: *Seven Stories of Science Gone Wrong*

Depleted food nutrients

Mike Ursy, founder of Southland Organics in the USA - and a passionate champion of sustainable agriculture - has this to say: [2]

> **"An incredible interaction and activity exists with plants and microbes and other organisms and the environment. It is almost laughable to think that one can throw three elements in the form of synthetic chemicals onto the soil and say: Now I have balanced the mineral and biological and ion and pH and microbial content of the soil.**
>
> **The exact opposite occurs. Microbes are destroyed or inhibited in their balance when synthetics arrive. This stresses the plant, making the plant deficient in nutrients. Stressed plants attract diseases and pests. That is nature's way of handling the sick. Then, because the plant has bugs or a fungus, someone comes along with a chemical pesticide or fungicide in order to try to remedy the situation.**
>
> **This all translates to the foods which we eat. With naturally grown foods, you do not have to worry about pesticides or herbicides, but probably the best**

benefit of organic foods is their nutritional content. The difference can be dramatic. This includes livestock and poultry which are fed naturally grown grasses and food. Nutritional content is markedly different.

As a culture, we are becoming more and more nutritionally deficient and filled with toxic residues as an indirect result of synthetic fertilisers. This stresses the body making it more prone to health problems. In other words, synthetic fertilisers can dramatically diminish the nutritional value of foods."

Neurotoxic drinking water: phosphate and fluoride

This harmful waste is in many parts of the UK and the USA. The fluoride added to our drinking water - hexafluorosilicic acid - is a neurotoxic waste product from the phosphate fertiliser industry, which means it has the potential to cause serious damage to nerve tissue. It has been - and remains to this day - one of the largest environmental and public health liabilities of the phosphate industry.

"They call them 'wet scrubbers' - the pollution control devices used by the phosphate industry to capture fluoride gases produced in the production of commercial fertiliser. In the past, when the industry let these gases escape, vegetation became scorched, crops destroyed and cattle crippled.

After being captured in the scrubbers, the fluoride acid (hydrofluorosilicic acid), a hazardous waste, is barrelled up and sold, unrefined, to communities across the country. Communities add hydrofluorosilicic acid to the WATER SUPPLIES as the primary fluoride chemical for water fluoridation.

Even if you don't live in a fluoridated area, you'll get it through cereal, soda, juice, beer and any other processed food and drink manufactured with fluoridated water." [3]

As far back as 1983, Rebecca Hanmer, the Deputy Assistant Administrator for Water at the US Environmental Protection Agency (EPA) expressed this view:

> **"By recovering by-product fluorosilicic acid from fertiliser manufacturing, water and air pollution are minimized, and water authorities have a low-cost source of fluoride available to them."**

However, not everyone agreed. Dr J. William Hirzy, the then-senior vice-president of EPA Headquarters Union noted:

> **"If this stuff gets out into the air, it's a pollutant; if it gets into the river, it's a pollutant; if it gets into the lake, it's a pollutant; but if it goes right into your drinking water system, it's NOT a pollutant? That's amazing… There's got to be a better way to manage this stuff."**

'Glow in the dark' uranium

If that's not enough, what's to be done with an unavoidable by-product of the phosphate mining industry - radioactive uranium - which also leaches into water supplies from wastewater ponds? As we know, radioactive material is commonly associated with increased incidences of cancer and this association has indeed been found among workers in the phosphate industry in the United States.[4]

> **"…. because phosphate and uranium were laid down at the same time and in the same place by the same geological processes millions of years ago. They go together. Mine phosphate, you get uranium."**

More worrying for larger populations is the risk of contamination from leakages and overspills from gypsum stacks which hold the toxic soup of waste products from phosphate mining. Highly acidic wastewater ponds are littered with toxic contaminants, including fluoride, arsenic, cadmium, chromium, lead, mercury and the various decay-products of uranium.[4]

> **"Ponds full of 1.5 billion gallons of acid and three mountains of radioactive waste mean you just can't shut off the machinery and turn out the lights."**

Such activity may currently only exist on the other side of 'The Pond' but the world is getting smaller every day.

Water fluoridation and our health

The use of fluoride began in the 1940s in the US, when community water supplies were routinely fluoridated, ostensibly to prevent dental cavities. Acceptance of this measure by the World Health Organisation meant it was soon adopted worldwide. Currently, around 6 million people in the UK receive drinking water with added fluoride.

Is fluoridation mass medication?

Water fluoridation has always been, and will surely remain, a hugely controversial public health measure. Although artificial water fluoridation is promoted as a 'medicine' for preventing tooth decay, not one fluoridating country actually defines it as a medicine, nor is it subject to the strict pharmaceutical regulations in any of the countries which implement fluoridation. Indeed, within the European Union, the only regulation in place for hexafluorosilicic acid is where it is used as an industrial product.

Ongoing safety concerns have led many countries to abandon this toxic intervention and public opinion in the non-fluoridated areas within the UK consistently resists attempts to mandate fluoridation.

Dental and skeletal fluorosis

One of the key concerns about water fluoridation has always been the uncontrolled ingestion of fluoride from drinking water. Since the 1980s, numerous studies have shown that adults and children (and size really does matter here) are exceeding agreed limits, contributing to a rapid rise in dental fluorosis (where teeth become mottled and discoloured), the first sign of fluoride toxicity.

When you consider that the intensity of fluoride's adverse effects on bones and teeth is amplified by calcium deficiency, magnesium deficiency and malnutrition - all of which are features of our modern impoverished soils and nutritionally depleted 'Westernised' diet - the picture is bleak.

In areas of heavy fluoridation (like India, where over half of groundwater sources have fluoride above recommended levels), or with chronic exposure to large doses of fluoride (common in workers in fertiliser industries), skeletal fluorosis (a chronic, crippling, metabolic bone disease) is endemic.[5]

Low IQ

As of June 2018, *"53 studies have found that elevated fluoride exposure is associated with reduced IQ in humans... based on IQ examinations of over 15,000 children, providing compelling evidence that fluoride exposure during the early years of life can damage a child's developing brain.... After reviewing 27 of the human IQ studies, a team of Harvard scientists concluded that fluoride's effect on the young brain should now be a "high research priority."* children.[6]

Hypothyroidism

International studies have shown that fluoride ingestion is associated with clinical and sub-clinical hypothyroidism. A 2015 study[7] of UK general practitioners' patients found that higher levels of fluoride predict hypothyroidism:

> **"We found that practices located in the West Midlands (a wholly fluoridated area) are nearly twice as likely to report high hypothyroidism prevalence in comparison to Greater Manchester (a non-fluoridated area)."**

Fluoride binds to iodine receptor sites, preventing iodine uptake by the body. Iodine is crucial for the production of thyroid hormone, which drives the efficiency of metabolism and general health. Since every cell in the body has receptors for thyroid hormone, it's not difficult to see how fluoride impacts human health.

Cancer

Population-based studies also strongly suggest that chronic fluoride ingestion is a possible cause of uterine and bladder cancer. Unsurprisingly, researchers concluded:[8]

"Fluoride has modest benefit in terms of reduction of dental caries but significant costs in relation to cognitive impairment, hypothyroidism, dental and skeletal fluorosis, enzyme and electrolyte derangement, and uterine cancer."

For information on fluoride in your local water, most UK companies have an online facility where you can use your postcode to check the water in your area. If not, there may be a local action group you can contact for information and advice.

Action on fluoride: what can YOU do?

Boiling your water will not rid it of fluoride and your body will ingest fluoride via showers and baths (together with inhaling chlorine - another proven thyroid hormone disruptor to add into the mix).[9]

If your tap water is fluoridated, my strong recommendation is to install a water filter. Most will filter chlorine, but make sure to source one that filters fluoride. If your budget is tight, consider a counter-top filter, plus a bath or shower filter. But if your budget will allow, consider a whole-house water filter, many of which can be relocated if you move home.[10,11]

Even if you don't have fluoridated water, still consider fitting a chorine filter to your bath taps and shower head to help thyroid and skin conditions.

But please look out - fluoride is everywhere!

Before we leave this subject, bear in mind that significant fluoride exposure comes from toothpaste and fluoride dental treatment gels, most processed foods, US grape juice and wines, tea (especially processed tea products), non-stick pans, pharmaceuticals and mechanically de-boned chicken products.[12]

Food additives - phosphates, nitrates and nitrites

Phosphates

Phosphorous-based products are used in fertilisers, industrial and domestic detergents, baking powders, toothpastes, pharmaceuticals, personal care products, skin care and cosmetics and water softeners.[13]

But phosphorous, in the form of phosphate additives, is also added to our food and beverages. Phosphate additives act as emulsifiers* in cheese and canned soups; enhance flavour and moistness in processed deli meats (like bacon and ham), poultry and other meats. It is also in frozen foods, cereals and baked goods, as well as in sodas and prepared iced tea mixes.

**Emulsifiers bring and keep together substances that would otherwise separate into layers - like oil and vinegar in a salad dressing.*

Our intake of phosphate additives in fast foods and processed foods alone has doubled since the 1990s and many grocery items contain up to 10 different phosphate formulations. However, if a food naturally contains phosphorus, it doesn't need to be labelled and where it is added, the amount need not be detailed.

Phosphorous is naturally found in dairy, nuts, eggs and poultry and is crucial for our bone health, to enable our bodies to produce protein and to store energy. We absorb around 50% of this naturally occurring, life sustaining phosphorous, but we absorb a whacking 90% of phosphate additives!

This means we are consuming way more phosphorous than we need to. Does it matter?

The scientific literature says it does. The need for people with kidney disease to limit phosphate intake has long been established, but researchers have also found associations between high phosphorous intake and/or higher blood phosphate concentrations in the general population.

High-normal levels of blood phosphate are linked to a higher risk of cardiovascular disease and hardening of the arteries - even in healthy young men - and predict heart attacks. Research has also linked higher intakes of phosphorous to a negative impact on bone health.[14]

Recently, the Environmental Working Group (EWG, a consumer safety organisation in the US) joined the Kidney Foundation in expressing concerns about phosphate food safety and listed the additives on its Dirty Dozen guide to food additives.[15]

Nitrates vs Nitrites

Preserving meat with salt cures goes back to ancient times, with sodium chloride being the primary curing ingredient. Today, sodium nitrite has become the primary salt and antioxidant, giving meats like bacon and ham their characteristic pink colour and flavour, preventing spoilage and blocking the growth of botulism-causing bacteria.

Food producers in the 1900s discovered that when sodium nitrate interacts with bacteria in meat, it converts to sodium nitrite. However, today's commercial manufacturers skip this time-honoured bacterial conversion and just add synthetic sodium nitrite directly to cured meats. A pause for thought... perhaps Granny knew best?

After being linked to both gastrointestinal cancer and heart disease, bacon and other processed meats containing nitrates and nitrites made the EWG's list of dangerous food additives in the US - however a series of subsequent research papers have questioned and discredited these findings.[16]

A plus for nitrates?

Despite all the bad press, research actually shows that a diet rich in nitrates can actually improve cardiovascular health.[17]

Nitrates may also reduce the risk of stroke by thinning and widening blood vessels and lowering blood pressure.[18]

In fact, cured meats account for a very small percentage of our nitrate intake. Plants pick up nitrates from the soil, water and nitrogen in the atmosphere and when we eat them, our mouth bacteria convert them to nitrites, which are absorbed and stored by our cells and subsequently converted to nitric oxide, a beneficial compound that relaxes blood vessels and increases blood flow.[19]

Most of the food sources of nitrites are from vegetables, particularly from celery, leafy greens, beets, leeks, cabbage and fennel.

Confused? My personal takeaway from all this is that sourcing bacon, ham, sausages and other cured meats from traditionally-reared animals and consuming them sensibly is far more important than rushing to buy nitrate- or nitrite-free products.

A well-sourced, traditional English breakfast (or Irish, Scottish or Welsh for that matter!) has a rightful place in a nutritious, well-balanced diet... as have a wide variety of fresh, organic vegetables!

Pesticides, fungicides and herbicides

Herbicides and fungicides are both forms of pesticide, toxic chemicals which indiscriminately kill plant pests, fungi and other plant matter. Since the 1940s, the UK has been stimulating the growth of plants with chemical fertilisers and the side effects have caused huge increases in

> **"fungal diseases, pests and weeds - which we've suppressed with fungicides, pesticides and herbicides."** [20]

We've already seen how the integrity of our planetary soil - and the life that it supports, including its microbial life - is fundamental to our health. The last thing we need is to destroy it, but this is exactly what's happening when we apply pesticides.

Let's consider for a moment the sanity of this situation. We're applying chemical fertilisers to enrich the soil, yet they are causing disease. And then we're using different chemicals to suppress these diseases? Madness!

Does it matter?

You bet it does! The science is clearly showing that these 'systemic' chemicals remain both in and on the surface of the food products that reach our tables. Whether fruit, veg or animal (where grazing pastures and feed crops have been sprayed), they cannot simply be 'washed off.' [21]

Guy Watson, CEO of Riverford Organic Farm is clear about why he doesn't use pesticides:

> **"147 pesticides I was assured were safe in the 1970s, based on the "best science available" at the time, have subsequently been banned, as risks to users, the environment or the public have emerged. The "best science available" was proven wrong, and history suggests that regulation has repeatedly underestimated the risks posed by pesticides. Yet the underlying assumptions used in assessing the toxicity of pesticides have not changed."**

His is not a lone voice. The Soil Association is campaigning hard - on our behalf - to reduce or remove pesticides from our soil and our food.

"Our food system is killing itself. Perfectly. The past 70 years of pesticide overuse have seen a catastrophic decline in farming's natural life support systems - the bees, bugs and rivers - but each step has taken a generation to notice." [22]

Indeed, the United Nations in its 2017 Report of the Special Rapporteur[23] on the right to food have gone on record to state that *"people and the environment are still being failed in terms of protection from hazardous pesticides."*

Consider these findings from the report:

- hazardous pesticides impose substantial costs and have catastrophic impacts on the environment, human health and society as a whole
- reliance on hazardous pesticides is a short-term solution that undermines the rights to adequate food and health for present and future generations
- the assertion promoted by the agrochemical industry that pesticides are necessary to achieve food security is not only inaccurate, but dangerously misleading
- agro-ecology is capable of delivering sufficient yields to feed the entire world population and ensure that they are adequately nourished
- the pesticide industry's efforts to influence policymakers and regulators have obstructed reforms and paralysed global pesticide restrictions globally.

So, can there be any doubt about the persistent, growing and increasingly urgent call to action to reduce, or completely cease the use of common pesticides? To see why, let's take a closer look at three specific pesticides that are used extensively in the UK.

1. Organophosphates

Organophosphates, developed as chemical weapons(!) in Germany in in 1940s, have become a primary chemical weapon against agricultural pests, killing insects by disrupting their brain and nervous system.

Today, they are widely used as solvents, plasticizers and industrial lubricants in gearboxes, hydraulics and automotive engines. Also, due to their properties as 'nerve agents', organophosphates continue to be the basis of many insecticides and herbicides used in agriculture and are commonly used on a wide variety of crops, fruits and plants.

However, we know that even at low levels they are highly toxic to the brain and nervous system of animals - and humans too.

Our farmers bear the brunt

In 2012, a major study was conducted by research psychologists from the University College London and the Open University. The team gathered data from well-designed studies, undertaken over the previous 20 years, to carry out a meta-analysis to determine whether long-term exposure to low levels of organophosphates in occupational settings (many of them sheep farmers using the chemicals in sheep dips) had neurotoxic effects.[24]

They found a significant association between low-level organophosphate exposure and impaired cognitive function: independent analysis found that 13 out of 16 studies had shown evidence of neurological problems following long-term exposure - the health problems reported included poor memory, reduced reaction time, attention disorders and diminished ability to solve complex problems.[25]

Our children bear the brunt

If organophosphates are damaging adults, consider their effect on child health. Several studies have suggested that chronic low-level exposure has serious health consequences prenatally, and also for infants and for young children.

A 2010 study looked at Mexican-American children living in agricultural regions of California. They found that prenatal and early childhood exposure to organophosphates can increase the risks of neurological disorders such as attention-deficit/hyperactivity disorder (ADHD), suggesting that low levels of chronic exposure - which is considered safe - could functionally decrease the neurological capacity of children.[26]

Long-term studies have examined the impacts of exposure of a specific organophosphate (chlorpyrifos) on children's brain development, finding that virtually any level of exposure can adversely affect their IQ.

> **"Scientists studying the effects of prenatal exposure to pesticides on the cognitive abilities of children have come to a troubling conclusion: whether pregnant mothers are exposed to organophosphate pesticides in California fields or New York apartments, the chemicals appear to impair their children's mental abilities."** [27]

Other scientists have found that prenatal chlorpyrifos exposure can physically alter the development areas of the brain that control behaviour, emotion, language and memory.[28]

Even our daily bread bears the brunt

Pesticide Action Network UK used government data to analyse the pesticide residues in both supermarket 'own-brand' loaves and leading brand-name loaves. It found that 63% of the loaves analysed in 2013 contained traces of at least one pesticide and that contamination has run at these levels for at least a decade.

The report showed that two in every three loaves of bread sold in the UK contain pesticide residues and 25% contained residues of more than one pesticide.

The most frequently detected pesticide was glyphosate, a common weed killer - you'll read much more about this below. The next most common were chlormequat, a plant growth regulator used on cereal crops, plants and vegetables and malathion, an organophosphate insecticide.[29]

Given the evidence that chronic, low level exposure to organophosphates is toxic to adults and children, it surely beggars belief that we find it in our daily bread!

2. Neonicotinoids

The UK has been the world's biggest user of neonicotinoids, a powerful class of systemic pesticide widely used in intensive agricultural operations. These chemicals destroy pollinators - bees, butterflies, moths, ants, flower beetles - and as evidence now indicates, may also affect human health.

Thankfully, the EU banned the outdoor use of three major neonicotinoids in April 2018, so for the time being, we in the UK and our bees, have a reprieve. However, in the context of the current political climate in Europe, and in light of the USA's reversal of their ban on the use these chemicals, we in the UK have every reason to be cautious and remain vigilant for the future.

The alarming decline of honeybees and bumblebees has long been attributed to neonicotinoid usage. New research is showing that the extinction rates for wild bee populations are far higher where neonicotinoid is used to spray oilseed rape fields: up to 85% of UK oil seed rape crops are sprayed with neonicotinoids.[30]

The birds and the bees?

An important study from the Netherlands in 2014 shows that bird populations fall sharply in those areas where neonicotinoid pollution is highest. (Note: unlike the Netherlands, the UK does not monitor neonicotinoid pollution, despite being the world's highest user.)

At least 95% of neonicotinoids that are applied to crops end up in the wider environment, killing the insects the birds rely on for food, particularly when raising their chicks: starlings, tree sparrows and swallows appear to be most affected. Even when examining other factors which might account for the birds' decline, the Dutch researchers found that high pollution by one specific neonicotinoid was by far the largest factor.[31]

Why should we care? Although many of us are concerned with environmental and ecological damage that our modern industries wreak upon the planet, we need to remember that we are human organisms and are also a part of the environment. Consider this:

"Highly toxic substances that kill insects lead to declines in things that eat insects. This work flags up the point that this isn't just about bees, it is about everything.

When hundreds or thousands of species or insect are being wiped out, it's going to have impacts on bats, shrews, hedgehogs, you name it. It is pretty good evidence of wholesale damage to the environment."

- Dr David Goulson[32]

Let's be clear: we cannot take ourselves out of nature's equation. We are an intrinsic part of it and wholly dependent upon it.

The European Food Safety Authority has ruled that three specific neonicotinoid insecticides are an unacceptable danger to bees and despite pressure from the rest of Europe to restrict their use, both the UK and Germany are resisting. You may wonder if it's merely a coincidence that the two major manufacturers of these agrochemicals are located in… the UK and Germany respectively? [33]

3. The 'g' word: glyphosate

You're probably familiar with the weed killer *Roundup*? You'll certainly have seen it in gardening stores and may even have some in your shed or garage. Roundup is the trade name for glyphosate, a broad-spectrum, systemic herbicide, the most widely-used on the planet.

Conventional farmers (and growers, park keepers, allotment holders and home gardeners all over the world) were converted to glyphosate in the 1970s by its parent company - Monsanto - to clear their fields of weeds before crops emerge in the spring. Glyphosate is also used to desiccate crops shortly before they're harvested to make the timing more controllable.

In the UK, for example, summers are wet and crops may ripen unevenly, so farmers can better time their harvest. 78% of oilseed rape - used to satisfy the protein requirement in animal feed, in processed foods and in the now trendy 'gourmet' cooking and dressing oils - is desiccated with glyphosate before harvest in the UK.

"Glyphosate kills parts of the crop that haven't ripened evenly and dries the crop. This allows combine harvesters to move more quickly and cover more ground during harvest and may reduce drying costs. But applying glyphosate so close to harvest makes the likelihood of finding residues in food even higher." [34]

Glyphosate in our food

There's now absolutely no doubt that glyphosate is in the food chain, but is it a problem and should we worry?

Yes, it is. And yes, we should.

Concerns about the dangers of glyphosate are long-standing among the scientific community, and there have long been concerns that glyphosate is an endocrine (hormone) disrupter which can cause cancerous tumours, birth defects and other developmental disorders.

If it is the case - as many scientists argue - that there is no safe lower level for human consumption, it's important to understand that studies on the impact of glyphosate have, until relatively recently, been limited and of short duration. However, studies are now emerging to support a global consensus on the impact of glyphosate-based herbicides on human, plant and soil health.[35]

In the summer of 2016, bowing to widespread industry pressure, the European Commission agreed to re-license the use of glyphosate for a further 18 months, resisting the intense pressure from industry lobbyists who were seeking a further 15-year renewal. While a definitive decision on glyphosate licensing is yet to be reached by member states… the clock is running out for the chemical industry.

Let us hope that those agencies representing good science and our interests - the Pesticide Action Network UK, for instance, or the European Citizens Initiative - succeed in their campaign on behalf of our health, the environment and the planet.[36]

In the meantime, I strongly recommend reading the Glyphosate Monograph, produced by the Pesticide Action Network UK. This is a comprehensive new review of the science setting out the adverse impact of glyphosate and glyphosate-based herbicides on our health and our environment.[37]

Glyphosate and cancer

The World Health Organisation International Agency for Research on Cancer[38] has already concluded that glyphosate is a "*probable carcinogen*." Their decision provoked subsequent accusations of selective editing[39] but the outcome of recent landmark cancer litigation in the USA has validated and upheld the concerns of independent science.[40]

Glyphosate and our gut microbes

Glyphosate works by interrupting a metabolic function in plants' cells called the shikimate pathway. When this path is interrupted, the plants die. Human cells don't have a shikimate pathway, so pro-glyphosate researchers believed - and still argue - that exposure to glyphosate would be harmless.

However, Dr Stephanie Seneff (a senior research scientist at the Massachusetts Institute of Technology) has shown that our millions of gut bacteria do have a shikimate pathway: glyphosate knocks out this pathway and wrecks our gut integrity, causing nutritional deficiencies and allowing toxins to flood our now compromised immune system:

> **"Scientists have now linked glyphosate to autism ... gastrointestinal issues such as inflammatory bowel disease, chronic diarrhoea, colitis and Crohn's disease, obesity, cardiovascular disease, depression, cancer, cachexia, Alzheimer's disease, Parkinson's disease, multiple sclerosis, and ALS, among others."** [41]

Glyphosate and liver disease

More recently, a peer-reviewed study published in January 2017 and led by Dr Michael Antoniou at King's College London, has found that weed killers like Roundup cause non-alcoholic fatty liver disease (NAFLD) at very low doses, thousands of times below levels permitted by regulators worldwide.[42]

NAFLD can cause fatigue, weakness, weight loss, loss of appetite, nausea, abdominal pain, spider-like blood vessels, yellowing of the skin and eyes (jaundice), itching, fluid build-up and swelling of the legs and abdomen and mental confusion.

This research provides the first evidence of a clear causative link between consumption of glyphosate - at levels that are found in the real world - and serious disease. We shouldn't be surprised to find it's not the only causative link.

Pesticide 'cocktails' anyone?

Some pesticides interact with each other and increase their toxicity - the so-called 'cocktail effect'. Let's take lettuce, for example. There are 122 registered pesticides which can be used when growing lettuces in the UK. Of those:

- 20 are fungicides
- 45 are herbicides
- 57 are insecticides

amongst these are fungicides that are classified as carcinogens, developmental or reproductive toxins, suspected endocrine disruptors and potential groundwater contaminants, and insecticides classified as carcinogens, neurotoxins and suspected endocrine disruptors.

Fungicides are applied to the soil even before sowing, so if the lettuce is grown under cover, two to three applications of fungicides could be used, as well as an insecticide.

And because lettuces - and soft fruits, for example - are considered high-value crops, farmers will often use pesticides prophylactically to ward off pest damage even before any appears.[43]

Into the mouths of babes

The Pesticide Action Network (PAN UK) carried out a detailed data analysis of foods provided over the last 12 years to young children, through the Department of Health's School Fruit and Vegetable Scheme (SFVS).

Their analysis showed unacceptable levels of pesticides to be present in the food provided through the SFVS. Residues of 123 different pesticides were found, some of which are linked to serious health problems such as cancer and disruption of the hormone system.

In many cases, multiple residues were found on the produce - a serious concern in the scientific community, who admit to having little understanding about the complex interaction of different chemicals in what is termed the 'cocktail' effect.

PAN UK assert that, for just an extra 1p per day, all the core produce given out by the SFVS could be switched to organic.[44]

Genetic Modification

The issue of GMOs (genetically-modified organisms) and GE (genetic engineering) is, and will remain, highly controversial. Those in favour argue that we need powerful GM technologies to feed the world's growing population, combat intractable diseases and save the planet. Those against argue that GM technology is at best poorly researched, under-tested and unproven and at worst, it will ultimately destroy the planet.

GMOs and nature

GMOs are plants or animals that have undergone a process where scientists alter their genes with DNA from different species of living organisms, bacteria or viruses to get certain desired traits, such as resistance to disease or tolerance for pesticides.

Farmers have always manipulated plants - and animals through selective breeding - to achieve traits such as improved taste, increased yield, resilience or disease resistance. But this kind of breeding still relies on the natural reproductive processes of the organisms, whereas genetic engineering involves the addition of foreign genes which would not occur in nature.

GMOs and our environment

In a winner-takes-all strategy, the major biotech and agrichemical companies have developed genetically-engineered seeds which produce crops with built-in immunity to the pesticides that these same companies also produce.

With aggressive - and often sinister - marketing methods, biotech companies have seduced farmers all over the world with empty promises of increased yields and have:

- neatly tied them into contracts which require farmers to purchase GE seeds
- made it illegal for farmers to retain and use their own seeds
- worked to ensure they have purchased huge amounts of extra chemical pesticides.

Monsanto's 'Roundup-ready' crops, for example, are genetically engineered to resist the herbicide itself, so that farmers can destroy weeds without killing their revenue stream.

But nature is resilient and has retaliated by spawning Roundup-resistant weeds, leading farmers to apply greater and greater doses of the chemical or even resort to more toxic methods to battle back the super weeds. And so, it goes on.

GMOs and our food

GMOs are already present in 60 to 70% of food on US supermarket shelves and several common ingredients like corn starch and soy protein are predominantly derived from GM crops.[45]

Fortunately, in the UK, public opinion on GM technology has - up to now - been resistant to accepting GMOs, as has the rest of Europe. However, as the shape of our political and economic relationship with the world - and our trading partners - changes, we can't be sure this will continue to be the case going forward.

GMOs and animal feeds

The move to conventional, intensive farming practices - which took livestock off pasture and a natural, varied, grass-based diet to rear them on an unnatural, almost entirely grain-based diet - presented farmers with the problem of how to provide sufficient protein. Today, the protein needs of intensively-reared livestock are sourced largely from high-protein pulses (soya) and oilseeds (oilseed rape).

However, around 80% of the world's soya is genetically modified. In the United States, Brazil and Argentina - the three largest producers of soya - approximately 93%, 92% and 100% of their respective soybean crops in 2013 were GM.

Because UK consumers have remained consistently sceptical of GM technology and have resisted GM foods, retailers have been forced to remove products that contain GM ingredients from their shelves. However, there is no requirement to label GM-fed animal products, so apart from all-organic meat, organic dairy and organically-farmed fish, the majority of animal products produced and sold in the UK are fed on at least some GM feed.

Producers and retailers in the UK argue that supplies of GM-free feed cannot be guaranteed and that the costs are prohibitive. This is not the case with major French and German retailers, who are successfully able to maintain the promise that their supply chains will remain GM-free.

Over a million tons of GM crops are imported each year to feed the majority of non-organically raised livestock which produce our chicken, egg, pork, bacon, milk and cheese products. So, not only are UK consumers being kept in the dark[46] by retailers and producers about the fact that we are inadvertently consuming GM food, but also the supermarkets' reliance on GM animal feed is leading to huge environmental costs that occur all along the supply chain.

Chemicals, it would seem, are no friend to our food, our health or our environment. As the Pesticide Action Network points out:

> **"Over the last few decades many pesticides have been and gone. Despite claims of being a magic fix for farmers, without any side-effects, each pesticide is eventually shown to have detrimental effects to our health or the environment and subsequently banned or replaced with another."**

"Replacing highly hazardous pesticides with less hazardous pesticides is necessary and overdue but not a sustainable solution, as many pesticides initially considered relatively 'benign' are later found to pose very serious health and environmental risks."

- As stated in a report to the Human Rights Council by the Special Rapporteur on the right to food [47]

Chemical contamination of our soils and crops now mean we must extend the cautionary wisdom 'We are what we eat' to 'We are what our meat eats'.

APPENDIX 3

A DEEPER DIVE INTO 'GOOD' vs 'BAD' SCIENCE

According to the Merriam-Webster Dictionary, the word 'science' is derived from the Latin word 'scientia' - knowledge based on data that is demonstrable and reproducible. We can think about science as a systematic and logical approach to discovering how things in the universe work and the body of knowledge accumulated through these discoveries. Science aims for measurable results through testing and analysis, based on fact, not opinion or preferences. The process of science is designed to challenge ideas through research.

But despite the very best of human endeavour, science it appears, has problems - let's take eating red meat as our example.

1. Observational research studies

Most of the studies which have provided the data to influence thinking in the field of nutritional science are so-called 'observational studies', which find associations between two or more variables. Observational studies are useful to generate a hypothesis to inform formulation of a theory, but they cannot test the theory itself. Associations can only be descriptive, not explanatory, and cannot prove a causation.

Good science holds to an important maxim "*correlation doesn't prove causation*" which is often glossed over (or worse, completely ignored) by poor science when interpreting, reporting and disseminating research findings. This means that, just because there is a relationship (a correlation) between two variables (say between red meat and cardiovascular disease), it cannot prove that one causes the other, and because correlations are two-way, it could just as easily be argued that having heart disease causes you to eat red meat.

2. 'Healthy user' bias in research studies

One of the biggest problems with observational studies on red meat is the 'healthy user' bias. People who eat less red meat (influenced by years of demonisation in the press) are also more likely to eat less of other foods which are unhealthy (processed foods, trans-fats, vegetable cooking oils, etc.) and are more likely to engage in healthier lifestyle choices (for instance, not smoking, limiting alcohol and exercising regularly).

On the other hand, those that eat more red meat also tend to smoke and drink more, eat fewer fresh vegetables and fruits and exercise less.

3. Validity of data collection

Food Frequency Questionnaires are a popular (but problematic) way to gather data about dietary intake, often relying on participants to recall what they've eaten, often going back months or even years. I'm not sure about you, but sometimes I can't even remember what I had for breakfast, never mind last Thursday's dinner!

4. Controlling for 'confounding' variables

Many research studies also fail to consider 'confounding' variables. These variables may be one or more factors, such as smoking, stress, alcohol consumption, income, ethnicity or potentially something else like exercise, socio-economic status or social connection, any of which may impact a research variable to account for or confound the results.

For example, smoking, stress, alcohol consumption and lack of exercise have all been shown to be strongly associated with increased risk of cardiovascular disease, so unless each of these associations have been statistically 'controlled for' when analysing research data, any conclusion that red-meat is the culprit cannot be valid.

Also, when it comes to drawing conclusions about increased risk of cardiovascular disease, diabetes and death from eating meat, we need to make sure we're not comparing apples with pears! Very few studies distinguish between processed and unprocessed meat, or a grass-fed steak from a fast-food burger.

Yet, whether or how the meat was processed (and what it was eaten with) can have vastly different effects upon health.

The only way to establish cause and effect is to perform randomized controlled trials.

5. The 'Gold Standard' Randomized Controlled Trials (RCTs)

A randomized controlled trial (RCT) is considered the gold standard of 'good' science. In an RCT, people are randomly placed (i.e. not deliberately selected) into different groups, to receive one or more interventions. One group provides the comparison or 'control' - this could be a standard practice, a placebo or no intervention at all.

For example, one group eats Diet A, while the other eats Diet B and researchers then follow each group to see which diet is more likely to lead to a particular outcome.

Yet, as of May 2016, there has been no large, long-term RCT which has specifically examined red meat and/or compared conventionally raised with organic, grass-fed meat! Indeed, in May 2016 a study published in the Journal of the American Osteopathic Association[1] reviewed six previous studies which had evaluated the effects of meat and vegetarian diets on mortality had to conclude by admitting that:

"limitations exist in these studies, for example the lack of large, long-term randomised controlled trials."

A 'crisis' in science?

Taking a broader lens, we see in today's 'science' a lack of reproducibility of research results; problems with or lack of governance; the use of questionable research evidence to inform policy making; covert (and blatant) interference from vested commercial interests; and, not least, falling public trust in the integrity of individuals and institutions. Many commentators are increasingly (and rightly) concerned and vocal and are reaching a consensus that there is indeed a crisis in science.

As a prime example, remember Ancel Keys' *Seven Nations* study from the Fats chapter? His flawed and manipulated data identified a correlation between a diet high in animal fats and heart disease which was taken up by political interests, setting the stage for decades of dietary advice by the medical profession and governments.

Subsequently the study[2] was discredited, but not before many millions of us were caught in the 'low-fat trap' and trustingly followed the new healthy eating advice… that we now know to be so detrimental to our health.

In a swingeing attack on the validity of nutritional epidemiology, which relies heavily on observational evidence based on prospective cohort studies, eminent Stanford University professor Dr John Ioannidis argued that: [3]

- study authors frequently misrepresent association for causation
- researchers wrongly assume the things that people eat most (e.g. carbohydrates, fats) have the greatest influence on outcomes such as heart disease, cancer or death
- meta-analyses become nothing more than *"weighted averages of expert opinions"*
- relatively uncommon contaminants, pesticides and carcinogenic by-products from over-cooking red meat may be influential but are generally ignored
- all of the variation between one (healthy) cohort and another (diseased) may represent *"almost exclusively the magnitude of the cumulative biases in this type of research, with extensive residual confounding and selective reporting"*
- in large prospective studies, inherent variability between individuals resulting from genetic and environmental factors, renders the average perceived responses from average cohorts irrelevant
- findings are not only often misinterpreted by the authors themselves, but they are misrepresented further by the media.

Houston, it seems science has big problems and sadly, they aren't going to be easily resolved. The crisis in science, however, provides us with very good reason to pay more attention to what works.

Time-honoured, traditional food wisdom

Conventional wisdom holds that our ancestors lived much shorter lives than we do today, due to epidemics of acute, communicable infectious (rather than chronic) diseases, injuries and accidents and indeed, these perils were significant from infancy to early teens. However, researchers who have studied present-day hunter-gather tribes have found that if people survived childhood then, they like us, could expect to live some 80 years - despite poor hygiene and the lack of food security, medical care and technological innovations available today.[4]

An important factor that can account for our ancestors' longevity, is that if people survived childhood, they didn't have contend with the epidemics of chronic, non-communicable diseases that plague us now.

This brings us back full circle to the first chapter of this book - Nourishing Deeply - and to Dr Weston A. Price's research and accounts of the diet and resilient good health of traditional peoples in his tome *Nutrition and Physical Degeneration.*

Dr Price's early work, supported by sound (but buried) science and by new and emerging science, served to demonstrate that what works are the time-honoured, traditional foods that kept generations of our ancestors healthy long before we had the benefit of - and the problems with - nutritional 'science'!

Granny knew best.

RESOURCES

To access hyperlinks for the resources, links and references found below please visit:

onceuponacook.izabellanatrins.com/references

Amazon Affiliate links Disclosure

Some of the links below are Amazon Affiliate links which means that, at NO extra cost to you, I may receive a small commission if you click through and complete a purchase.

Useful websites & resources

Abel & Cole:
Abel and Cole are an organic UK-wide veg box delivery scheme, established for over 30 years. **www.abelandcole.co.uk**

Big Barn:
Big Barn's mission is to reverse the mass production of food and control of the food market by big business and food retailers. Their online portal reconnects consumers with local farmers and producers directly, or through local retailers, to encourage local trade and give farmers a much better deal and consumers fresher, cheaper, accountable food. **www.bigbarn.co.uk**

Farmdrop:
Farmdrop provides local farm-to-table foods and fresh fish for consumers in the London, Bristol and Bath areas via online deliveries. **www.farmdrop.com**

Fordhall Organic Farm:
Fordhall Organic Farm, in Market Drayton, Shropshire has a wonderful back-story and is now owned by a charitable community-benefit society on behalf of 8000 community shareholders.

Fordhall sells a wide variety of its 100% grass-fed beef, lamb and Gloucester Old Spot pork products on-line and from its farm shop. The farm is open to the public year-round as an enjoyable educational and community resource. **www.fordhallfarm.com**

Happerley Provenance:
Happerley work on behalf of the whole UK food industry and all consumers to develop and implement a means to secure provenance honesty and transparency. Their aim is to enable the consumer to track the journey of their food, while creating a level playing field for all food businesses to validate and protect the provenance value of their food production. **www.happerley.co.uk**

Nourished Kitchen: *How to render lard*. Available online: ***http://nourishedkitchen.com/how-to-render-lard***. Accessed 14.12.2018

Pasturefed Livestock Association.:
With over a 1000 producer-members, the PFLA promotes the unique quality of produce raised exclusively on pasture, and the wider environmental and animal welfare benefits that pastured livestock systems represent. **www.pastureforlife.org**

Raw Milk Suppliers:
Simkin Solutions maintain a list of raw milk / unpasteurised milk suppliers in the UK and Ireland. **www.rawmilk.simkin.co.uk**

Riverford Organic Farmers:
Riverford is an employee ownership trust organic farm and UK-wide organic veg box delivery company based in Devon, England, but with sister farms in three locations and delivery hubs around the country. **www.riverford.co.uk**

Shipton Mill:
Shipton Mill produces a wide variety of speciality and organic flours, using both traditional grain and traditional methods and deliver online. **www.shipton-mill.com**

Smallholder Range:
Smallholders are a family owned, national company with four generations of experience, providing well-balanced feeds designed for animals being raised more naturally. They make making natural feed without, artificial growth promoters or artificial yolk pigments. **www.smallholderfeed.co.uk/products/layers/natural-free-range-layers-pellets**

Sustain - The Alliance for Better Food and Farming:
Sustain fulfils its aims is through running a wide variety of projects and campaigns to improve food and farming, for example:

- The Real Bread Campaign
- Food Co-ops
- Food Waste
- Food Poverty

- Better Hospital Food
- Children's Food Campaign

www.sustainweb.org

Vintage Tradition Tallow Balm:
Whole body natural skincare. **www.vintagetradition.com/how-to-make-tallow-balm-at-home.php**

Weston A Price Foundation:
The Weston A. Price Foundation (WAPF) is an education and research foundation and an information resource on nutrition and health. It works to provide scientific validation of traditional foods like grains, dairy foods, meat, salt, fat, sauces, sweets and nightshade vegetables. **www.westonaprice.org**

Wholefoods Online UK:
Whole Foods Online is an international health food supplier, based in North East Kent. Wholefoods deliver natural and organic wholefoods, and related healthy living products, directly to homes and businesses across Europe. **www.buywholefoodsonline.co.uk**

Useful books

Allen D (2009). *Forgotten Skills of Cooking*. Kyle Cathie Ltd. (Amazon)

Blythman J (2015). *Swallow This: Serving Up the Food Industry's Darkest Secrets*. Harper Collins (Amazon)

Campbell C (2016). *The China Study Expanded*. BenBella Books (Amazon)

But see also: Minger Denise (2010). *The China Study: Fact or Fallacy*. Available online: https://deniseminger.com/2010/07/07/the-china-study-fact-or-fallac/ Accessed 14.12.2018

Campbell McBride N (2018). *Put Your Heart in Your Mouth - Natural Treatment for Atherosclerosis, Angina, Heart Attack, High Blood Pressure, Stroke, Arrhythmia, Peripheral Vascular Disease*. Paperback. Medinform Publishing (Amazon)

Fallon S (2009): *Nourishing Traditions: The Cookbook That Challenges Politically Correct Nutrition and the Diet Dictocrats*. New Trends Publishing (Amazon)

Gedgaudas N (2011). *Primal Body, Primal Mind*. Healing Arts Press (Amazon)

Lawrence F (2013). *Not on the Label: What Really Goes into the Food on Your Plate.* Penguin (Amazon)

Pollan M (2014). *Cooked: A Natural History of Transformation.* Penguin (Amazon)

Salatin Joel (2005). *Holy Cows and Hog Heaven: The Food Buyer's Guide to Farm Friendly Food.* Polyface Inc. (Amazon)

Shanahan Catherine MD (2017). *Why Your Genes Need Traditional Foods.* St. Martin's Press (Amazon)

Weston A Price (1997). *Nutrition and Physical Degeneration.* Keats Pub Inc. (Amazon)

REFERENCES

Welcome

(1) Natrins I (2017). *Are You a Dieting Casualty? IzabellaNatrins.Com*. Available online: *https://www.izabellanatrins.com/are-you-a-dieting-casualty-stop-dieting-and-start-eating*. Accessed 14.12.2018

(2) Tribole E (2012). *Dieting Increases Your Risk of Gaining More Weight. Intuitive Eating Pros®*. Available online: *https://www.intuitiveeating.org/warning-dieting-increases-your-risk-of-gaining-more-weight-an-update/*. Accessed 14.12.2018

(3) Shanahan C MD (2017). *Why Your Genes Need Traditional Foods*. St. Martin's Press (Amazon)

(4) Price Weston A (1997). *Nutrition and Physical Degeneration*. Keats Pub Inc. (Amazon)

(5) Gerson G. The Gerson Institute. Website: *http://gerson.org/gerpress/*

(6) Breast Cancer UK. Website. *http://www.breastcanceruk.org.uk/*

Chapter One - Nourishing Traditionally for Better Energy, Vitality and Health

Barnes B (1990). *Hypothyroidism: The Unsuspected Illness*. Harper & Collins (Amazon)

Blaser M (2015). *Missing Microbes - How Killing Bacteria Creates Modern Plagues*. Oneworld Publications (Amazon)

Dr Kelly Brogan Website. *http://kellybroganmd.com/*

Caldecott T: *Ayurveda, Herbal Medicine, Nutrition* (Amazon) & Website: *https://www.toddcaldecott.com/*

Campbell McBride N (2010). *Gut and Psychology Syndrome*. Medinform Publishing (Amazon)

Cordain L. *The Paleo Diet.com* Website: *http://thepaleodiet.com/dr-loren-cordain/*

Dr John Doulliard: *Proving Ancient Wisdom with Modern Science: Natural Health & Ayurved*a. Website: *http://lifespa.com/*

Fallon S (2000). *Ancient Dietary Wisdom for Tomorrow's Children*. Weston A Price Foundation. Available online: *https://www.westonaprice.org/health-topics/traditional-diets/ancient-dietary-wisdom-for-tomorrows-children/*. Accessed 14.12.2018

Fallon S & Enig M (2009). *Nourishing Traditions - The Cookbook That Challenges Politically Correct Nutrition & The Diet Dictocrats*. New Trends Publishing (Amazon)

Jaminet P & Jaminet S-C (2013). *The Perfect Health Diet*. Scribner Book Company (Amazon) & Website: *http://perfecthealthdiet.com/*

Knight R & Buhler B (2015). *Follow Your Gut: How the Bacteria in Your Stomach Steer Your Health, Mood and More*. Simon & Schuster UK (Amazon)

Kresser C (2014). *The Paleo Cure. Little, Brown Spark* (Amazon) & Website: *https://chriskresser.com/*

Chris Masterjohn PhD. Website: *https://chrismasterjohnphd.com/*

Dr Ray Peat Website: *http://raypeat.com/articles/*

Pottenger F.M. (2nd 1995). *Pottenger's Cats - A Study in Nutrition*. CABI Publishing (Amazon)

Price Pottenger Nutritional Foundation: Website: *https://price-pottenger.org/*

Price Weston A (1997). *Nutrition and Physical Degeneration*. Keats Pub Inc. (Amazon)

Professor Tim Spector. Website: *http://britishgut.org/*

Spector T (2016). *The Diet Myth - The Real Science Behind What We Eat*. Orion Publishing Group (Amazon)

Weston A. Price Foundation: Website: *http://www.westonaprice.org/*

Chapter Two - It Begins (and Ends) in the Soil

(1) Soil Association. *Let's Commit to Protecting Our Climate and Increasing Soil Carbon Globally.* Available online: *https://www.soilassociation.org/news/2017/let-s-commit-to-protecting-our-climate-and-increasing-soil-carbon-globally/*. Accessed 14.12.2018

(2) Wakeford T (2002). *Liaisons of Life P: From Hornworts to Hippos, How the Unassuming Microbe Has Driven Evolution.* J Wiley & Sons (Amazon)

(3) Robinson R (2017). *Why the Gut Microbiome Is Crucial for Your Health. Healthline.* Available online: *https://www.healthline.com/nutrition/gut-microbiome-and-health*. Accessed 14.12.2018

(4) Hirsch R (2016). *The Human Microbiome: The Germs That Keep You Healthy*. Twenty-First Century Books. (Amazon)

(5) Proal AD et al (2013). *The human microbiome and autoimmunity. Current opinion in rheumatology 2013 Mar;25(2):234-40*. Available online: *https://www.ncbi.nlm.nih.gov/pubmed/23370376*. Accessed 14.12.2018

(6) Appropedia. *Conventional Farming*. Available online: *http://www.appropedia.org/Conventional_farming*. Accessed 14.12.2018

(7) Regenerative.Com. *6 Problems with Monoculture Farming*. Available online: *https://www.regenerative.com/magazine/six-problems-monoculture-farming/*. Accessed 14.12.2018

(8) McKenzie R et al (2012): Neurobehavioral problems following low-level exposure to organophosphate pesticides: a systematic and meta-analytic review. *Journal of Critical Reviews in Toxicology Volume 43, 2013*. Available online: *http://www.tandfonline.com/doi/abs/10.3109/10408444.2012.738645*. Accessed 14.12.2018

(9) Levitt T (2012). Pesticide used by UK farmers is linked to brain damage. *The Ecologist*. Available online: *https://theecologist.org/2012/dec/14/pesticide-used-uk-farmers-linked-long-term-brain-damage*. Accessed 14.12.2018

(10) Marks A (2010): Organophosphate Pesticide Exposure and Attention in Young Mexican-American Children: The CHAMACOS Study. *Environmental Health Perspectives 2010 Dec; 118(12): 1768-1774*. Available online: *https://www.ncbi.nlm.nih.gov/pmc/articles/PMC3002198/*. Accessed 14.12.2018

(11) PAN UK Glyphosate Monographs: California to list glyphosate as a carcinogen. *Chemical & Engineering News Volume 95 Issue 27*. Available online: http://cen.acs.org/articles/95/i27/California-list-glyphosate-carcinogen.html. Accessed 14.12.2018

(12) Stevens R (2018): Does Monsanto's Roundup Cause Cancer? Trial Highlights -The Difficulty of Proving A Link. *Common Health 2018*. Available online: http://www.wbur.org/commonhealth/2018/08/07/does-roundup-cause-cancer. Accessed: 14.12.2018

(13) Mesnage R et at (2017). *Multiomics reveal non-alcoholic fatty liver disease in rats following chronic exposure to an ultra-low dose of Roundup herbicide*. King's College London. Available online: https://kclpure.kcl.ac.uk/portal/en/publications/multiomics-reveal-nonalcoholic-fatty-liver-disease-in-rats-following-chronic-exposure-to-an-ultralow-dose-of-roundup-herbicide(402ec9bb-c1fd-457f-aa87-4a89b60663ff).html. Accessed 14.12.2018

(14) Pesticide Action Network (2017). *Food for Thought*. Available online: http://www.pan-uk.org/food-for-thought/. Accessed 14.12.2018

(15) Beyond GM (2018): *Good Food Makes Everything Better*. Available online: https://beyond-gm.org/wp-content/uploads/2015/12/GMO.pdf. Accessed 14.12.2018

(16) Soil Association (2018). *Organic Animal Welfare: The very highest animal welfare standards*. Available online: https://www.soilassociation.org/organic-living/why-organic/better-for-animals/. Accessed 14.12.2018

(17) Grossman E (2017): *Can Organic Foods Prevent a Public Health Crisis? Civil Eats*. Available online: http://civileats.com/2017/03/08/can-organic-food-prevent-a-public-health-crisis. Accessed 14.12.2018

(18) Soil Association (2016) *Ground-breaking new study finds clear nutritional differences between organic and non-organic milk and meat*. Available online: https://www.soilassociation.org/media-centre/press-releases/ground-breaking-new-study-finds-clear-nutritional-differences-between-organic-and-non-organic-milk-and-meat/ Accessed 14.12.2018

19) Pasture for Life. http://www.pastureforlife.org/. Accessed 14.12.2018

(20) Harvey G. *Pasture Promise* TV Video. Available online: http://www.pasturepromise.tv/introductory-video.html. Accessed 14.12.2018

(21) Lechenet M et al (2017). *Reducing Pesticide Use while preserving crop productivity and profitability on arable farms*. Available online:

https://www.theguardian.com/environment/2017/apr/06/farms-could-slash-pesticide-use-without-losses-research-reveals?CMP=share_btn_tw. Accessed 14.12.2018

(22) Carlisle L (2017). *Mapping the Benefits of Farm Biodiversity. Civil Eats*. Available online: https://civileats.com/2017/04/03/mapping-the-benefits-of-farm-biodiversity/. Accessed 14.12.2018

(23) as (22) above - Carlisle, L (2017). *Mapping the Benefits of Farm Biodiversity. Civil Eats.* Available online: http://civileats.com/2017/04/03/mapping-the-benefits-of-farm-biodiversity Accessed 14.12.18

(24) Ponisio C et al (2015). *Diversification practices reduce organic to conventional yield gap Proceeding of the Royal Society B: Biological Sciences*. Available online: http://rspb.royalsocietypublishing.org/content/282/1799/20141396. Accessed 14.12.2018

(25) Waste and Resources Action Programme (2016/7). *Estimates of Food Surplus and Waste Arisings in the UK*. Available online: http://www.wrap.org.uk/sites/files/wrap/Estimates_%20in_the_UK_Jan17.pdf. Accessed 14.12.2018

(26) Montgomery D (2017). *How to feed the world? The answer lies in healthy soils*. The Ecologist. Available online: http://www.theecologist.org/blogs_and_comments/commentators/2988847/how_to_feed_the_world_the_answer_lies_in_healthy_soils.html. Accessed 14.12.2018

(27) By David R. Montgomery, The Conversation on April 5, 2017. Available online: https://www.scientificamerican.com/article/3-big-myths-about-modern-agriculture1/

(28) as (27) above - Montgomery D (2017). 3 *Big Myths about Modern Agriculture*. Scientific American. Available online: https://www.scientificamerican.com/article/3-big-myths-about-modern-agriculture1/. Accessed 14.12.2018

(29) Savory A (2013). *How to green the world's deserts and reverse climate change* (TED Talk Video). Available online: https://youtu.be/vpTHi7O66pI. Accessed 14.12.2018

(30) as (29) above - The Savory Institute (2017). *Regenerative Agriculture Reaches a Tipping Point.* Available online: https://www.savory.global/news/regenerative-agriculture-reaches-a-tipping-point/. Accessed 14.12.2018

(31) Swartz J (2013). *Cows Save the Planet: And Other Improbable Ways of Restoring Soil to Heal the Earth*. Chelsea Green Publishing (Amazon)

(32) Rodgers D (2017). *The Ecological and Morals Arguments for Raising Animals to Eat* with Joel Salatin. Sustainable Dish Podcast Episode 31. Available online: https://sustainabledish.com/podcasts/sustainable-dish-episode-031-ecological-morals-arguments-raising-animals-eat. Accessed 14.12.2018

(33) as 30 above - Chris Kerston - *Regenerative agriculture reaches a tipping point* - www.savory.global

(34) Kumar S (2013). *Soil Soul Society: A New Trinity for Our Time*. Ivy Press (Amazon)

Chapter Three - Eggs!

(1) World's Healthiest Foods: *Eggs: Pasture Raised*. Available online: http://www.whfoods.com/genpage.php?tname=foodspice&dbid=92. Accessed 14.12.2018

(2) Gedgaudas N. *Vitamin A Under Attack Down Under*. Available online: http://www.primalbody-primalmind.com/vitamin-a-under-attack-down-under/. Accessed 14.12.2018

(3) Walsh B (2018). *Vitamin D supplements. Are yours helping or hurting you?* Precision Nutrition: Available online: http://www.precisionnutrition.com/stop-vitamin-d. Accessed 14.12.2018

(4) Natrins I (2017/18). https://www.izabellanatrins.com/women-track-vitamin-d/ Accessed 14.12.2018

(5) Ravnskov U (2015). *People with high cholesterol live the longest. The Cholesterol Myths.* Available online: http://www.ravnskov.nu/2015/12/27/myth-9/. Accessed 14.12.2018

(6) Greenblatt J (2011). *Low Cholesterol and Its Psychological Effects*. Psychology Today. Available online: https://www.psychologytoday.com/blog/the-breakthrough-depression-solution/201106/low-cholesterol-and-its-psychological-effects. Accessed 14.12.2018

(7) World's Healthiest Foods (2018). *Choline*. Available online: http://www.whfoods.com/genpage.php?tname=nutrient&dbid=50. Accessed 14.12.2018

(8) Taffs F (2016). *How Free Range is Your Free-Range Egg?* British Hen Welfare Trust: http://www.bhwt.org.uk/free-range-free-range-egg/. Accessed 14.12.2018

(9) Karsten H et al (2010): *Vitamins A, E and fatty acid composition of the eggs of caged hens and pastured hens. Renewable Agriculture and Food Systems. Volume 25 Issue* 1. Available online: https://www.cambridge.org/core/journals/renewable-agriculture-and-food-systems/article/div-

classtitlevitamins-a-e-and-fatty-acid-composition-of-the-eggs-of-caged-hens-and-pastured-hensdiv/552BA04E5A9E3CD7E49E405B339ECA32. Accessed 14.12.2018

(10) Kresser C (2010). *How too much omega-6 and not enough omega-3 is making us sick.* Available online: https://chriskresser.com/how-too-much-omega-6-and-not-enough-omega-3-is-making-us-sick/. Accessed 14.12.2018

(11) Guyenet S & Carlson S (2015). *Increase in Adipose Tissue Linoleic Acid of US Adults in the Last Half Century. Advances in Nutrition 2015 Nov; 6(6): 660-664.* Available online: https://www.ncbi.nlm.nih.gov/pmc/articles/PMC4642429. Accessed 14.12.2018

(12) Simopoulos A (2006). Evolutionary aspects of diet, the omega-6/omega-3 ratio and genetic variation: nutritional implications for chronic diseases. *Biomedicine & Pharmacotherapy, Volume 60, Issue 9, Nov 2006.* Available online: https://www.sciencedirect.com/science/article/abs/pii/S0753332206002435. Accessed 14.12.2018

(13) DiNicolantonio J & O'Keefe J (2018). *Omega-6 vegetable oils as a driver of coronary heart disease: the oxidized linoleic acid hypothesis*. Open Heart 2018. Available online: https://openheart.bmj.com/content/openhrt/5/2/e000898.full.pdf. Accessed 14.12.2018

(14) Evenepoel J et al (1998). Digestibility of cooked and raw egg protein in humans. *Journal of Nutrition Oct;128(10):1716-22.* Available online: https://www.ncbi.nlm.nih.gov/pubmed/9772141. Accessed 14.12.2018

(15) World's Healthiest Foods (2018). *What are the pros and cons of raw eggs*? Available online: http://www.whfoods.com/genpage.php?tname=george&dbid=347. Accessed 14.12.2018

Chapter Four - Meat is a Treat (and Offal isn't Awful)

(1) Weston A Price Foundations. https://www.westonaprice.org/health-topics/soy-alert/myths-truths-about-soy/. Accessed 14.12.2018

(2) NHS UK (2015). *Antibiotic Use in Farming Threatens Human Health*. Available online: http://www.nhs.uk/news/2015/12December/Pages/Antibiotic-use-in-farm-animals-threatens-human-health.aspx. Accessed 14.12.2018

(3) Lymbery P (2015): *Farmageddon: The True Cost of Cheap Meat*. Bloomsbury (Amazon)

(4) Harvey G (2008): *We Want Real Food*. Constable & Robinson Ltd. (Amazon)

(5) Battaglia R. et al (2015): Health Risks Associated with Meat Consumption: A Review of Epidemiological Studies. *International Journal of Vitamin and Nutritional Research. 2015;85(1-2):70-8* Available online: https://www.ncbi.nlm.nih.gov/pubmed/26780279. Accessed 14.12.2018

(6) Kresser C (2009). *Where's the beef?* Chris Kresser.Com. Available online: https://chriskresser.com/wheres-the-beef. Accessed 14.12.2018

(7) Kresser C (June 2016). *Is Organic Meat Better?* Chris Kresser.Com. Available online: https://chriskresser.com/is-organic-meat-better/. Accessed 14.12.2018

(8) Peat R PhD. *Tryptophan, serotonin and ageing*. Ray Peat.Com. Available online: http://raypeat.com/articles/aging/tryptophan-serotonin-aging.shtml. Accessed 14.12.2018

(9) Kresser C (2015). Red Meat and Cancer - *Again! Will it Ever Stop?* Chris Kresser.Com. Available online: https://chriskresser.com/red-meat-cancer-again-will-it-ever-stop/. Accessed 14.12.2018

(10) Rea D et al (2018). Microbiota effects on cancer: from risks to therapies. Oncotarget. 2018 Apr 3; 9(25): 17915-17927. Available online: https://www.ncbi.nlm.nih.gov/pubmed/29707157. Accessed 14.12.2018

(11) Grasgruber P (2018). *Global Correlates of Cardiovascular Risk: A Comparison of 158 Countries. Nutrients. 2018 Mar 26;10(4)*. Available online: https://www.ncbi.nlm.nih.gov/pubmed/29587470. Accessed 14.12.2018

(12) Harcombe Z. PhD (2018). *Carbohydrates and Cardiovascular Disease*. Available online: http://www.zoeharcombe.com/2018/04/carbohydrates-cardiovascular-disease/. Accessed 14.12.2018

(13) Tang et al (2011). *Nitrite and nitrate: cardiovascular risk-benefit and metabolic effect. Current Opinion in Lipidology 2011 Feb; 22(1):11-5*. Available online: https://www.ncbi.nlm.nih.gov/m/pubmed/21102328/. Accessed 14.12.2018

(14) Mercola J (2013). *The Health Benefits of Consuming Organ Meats*. Mercola.Com Available online: https://articles.mercola.com/sites/articles/archive/2013/12/30/eating-organ-meats.aspx. Accessed 14.12.2018

Chapter Five - The Rise and Fall of Milk

(1) Weston A. Price (2010). *Nutrition and Physical Degeneration*. Benediction Classics (Amazon)

(2) Edwards R (2018). 9 *Myths of Pasteurization (or Homogenization) + Better Options*. Dr Axe.Com. Available online: *https://draxe.com/9-myths-of-pasteurization-or-homogenization-better-options/*. Accessed 14.12.2018

(3) Raw Milk Facts.Com. *http://www.raw-milk-facts.com/index.html*. Accessed 14.12.2018

(4) as (2) above - Axe J (2018). *9 Myths of Pasteurization (or Homogenization) + Better Options*. DrAxe.Com. Available online: *https://draxe.com/9-myths-of-pasteurization-or-homogenization-better-options/*. Accessed 14.12.2018

(5) Fassa P (2017). *Meta-Analysis Study: Whole Fat Dairy Healthy, Saturated Fats Myth Exposed*. Health Impact News. Available online: *http://healthimpactnews.com/2017/meta-analysis-study-whole-fat-dairy-healthy-saturated-fats-myth-exposed*. Accessed 14.12.2018

(6) Harvey G. *Pasture Promise*. TV Website: *http://www.pasturepromise.tv*. Accessed 14.12.2018

(7) Peat R. PhD. *Milk in context: allergies, ecology, and some myths*. Available online: *http://raypeat.com/articles/articles/milk.shtml*. Accessed 14.12.2018

(8) Hook & Sons Ltd*: Raw Milk*. Available online: *http://www.hookandson.co.uk/RawMilk/*. Accessed 14.12.2018

(9) Kresser C (2013). *Why Grass-Fed Trumps Grain Fed*. Chris Kresser.Com. Available online: *https://chriskresser.com/why-grass-fed-trumps-grain-fed/*. Accessed 14.12.2018

(10) UCL. *Lactase Persistence*. Available online: *https://www.ucl.ac.uk/mace-lab/gallery/lactase*. Accessed 14.12.2018

(11) Gerbault P, et al. Evolution of lactase persistence: an example of human niche construction. *Philos Trans R Soc Lond B Biol Sci. 2011 Mar 27; 366(1566): 863-877*. Available online: *https://www.ncbi.nlm.nih.gov/pmc/articles/PMC3048992/*. Accessed 14.12.2018

(12) Crow C NTP. *Why you're sensitive to dairy (lactose intolerance) and what to do about it*. Available online*: http://butternutrition.com/5-reasons-why-youre-sensitive-to-dairy-what-to-do-about-it/*. Accessed 14.12.2018

(13) McGruther J. *I drink real milk: fresh, raw, local and full of fat.* Available online: https://nourishedkitchen.com/drink-raw-milk/. Accessed 14.12.2018

(14) Jaminet P. *Lactose Intolerance (2010): Often A Result of 'Silent' Wheat-Derived Bowel Disease.* Available online: http://perfecthealthdiet.com/2010/07/lactose-intolerance-often-a-result-of-silent-wheat-derived-bowel-disease/. Accessed 14.12.2018

(15) as (7) above - Peat R PhD (2011). *Milk in context: allergies, ecology, and some myths.* Available online: http://raypeat.com/articles/articles/milk.shtml. Accessed 14.12.2018

(16) University of Minnesota Extension. *The ruminant digestive system.* Available online: http://www.extension.umn.edu/agriculture/dairy/feed-and-nutrition/feeding-the-dairy-herd/ruminant-anatomy-and-physiology.html. Accessed 14.12.2018

(17) Raw Milk Suppliers (UK). http://rawmilk.simkin.co.uk

(18) Weston A Price Foundation. *Milk: It Does a Body Good*? Available online: https://www.westonaprice.org/health-topics/making-it-practical/milk-it-does-a-body-good/ Accessed 14.12.2018

(19) Alterman T (2008). *How Do I Pasteurize Raw Milk at Home?* Available online: http://www.motherearthnews.com/real-food/pasteurize-raw-milk-at-home. Accessed 14.12.2018

(20) Allergy UK. *Types of Food Allergy.* Available online: https://www.allergyuk.org/food-allergy-or-food-intolerance/food-allergy-or-food-intolerance. Accessed 14.12.2018

Chapter Six - Give Us Back our Daily Bread

(1) Gunnars K (2014). *Why Modern Wheat is Worse than Older Wheat.* Available online: https://www.healthline.com/nutrition/modern-wheat-health-nightmare. Accessed 14.12.2018

(2) van den Broeck H et al (2010). *Presence of celiac disease epitopes in modern and old hexaploid wheat varieties: wheat breeding may have contributed to increased prevalence of celiac disease. Theor Appl Genet. 2010 Nov; 121(8): 1527-1539.* Available online: https://www.ncbi.nlm.nih.gov/pmc/articles/PMC2963738/. Accessed 14.12.2018

(3) as (1) above - Gunnars K. *Why Modern Wheat is Worse than Older Wheat.* Available online: https://www.healthline.com/nutrition/modern-wheat-health-nightmare. Accessed 14.12.2018

(4) Whitely A (2006). *The poisonous truth about our daily bread.* Available online: https://www.theguardian.com/commentisfree/2006/sep/17/comment.food. Accessed 14.12.2018

(5) Samsel A & Seneff S (2013). Glyphosate, pathways to modern diseases II: Celiac sprue and gluten intolerance. *Interdisciplinary Toxicology. 2013 Dec; 6(4): 159-184.* Available online: https://www.ncbi.nlm.nih.gov/pmc/articles/PMC3945755/. Accessed 14.12.2018

(6) Stevens R (2018). *Does Monsanto's Roundup Cause Cancer? Trial Highlights -The Difficulty of Proving A Link.* Common Health 2018. Available online: http://www.wbur.org/commonhealth/2018/08/07/does-roundup-cause-cancer. Accessed: 14/12/2018

(7) Rothamsted Research. *Cereal Transformation.* Available online: https://www.rothamsted.ac.uk/cereal-transformation. Accessed 14.12.2018

(8) Serena G et al (2015). *The Role of Gluten in Celiac Disease and Type 1 Diabetes. Nutrients. 2015 Sep; 7(9): 7143-7162.* Available online: https://www.ncbi.nlm.nih.gov/pmc/articles/PMC4586524/. Accessed 14.12.2018

(9) Greco L. et al (2011): Safety for patients with celiac disease of baked goods made of wheat flour hydrolyzed during food processing. *Clinical Gastroenterology and Hepatology 9 (1):2 4-9.* Available online: https://www.ncbi.nlm.nih.gov/pubmed/20951830. Accessed 14.12.2018

(10) Kesser C (2016). *3 Reasons Gluten Intolerance May Be More Serious Than Celiac Disease.* Available online: https://kresserinstitute.com/3-reasons-gluten-intolerance-may-serious-celiac-disease/. Accessed 14.12.2018

(11) O'Bryan T (2015). *Why going gluten-free and doing an Elimination Diet is so important.* Available online: https://www.youtube.com/watch?v=7urLipUwtDY. Accessed 14.12.2018

(12) The Patient Celiac (2013). *The Gluten Contamination Elimination Diet (Summary of Dr. Fasano's Recent Paper)* Celiac.Com. Available online: https://www.celiac.com/gluten-free/blogs/entry/1780-the-gluten-contamination-elimination-diet-summary-of-dr-fasanos-recent-paper/. Accessed 14.12.2018

(13) Cordain L (1999). Cereal Grains: Humanity's Double-Edged Sword. Evolutionary Aspects of Nutrition and Health. *Diet, Exercise, Genetics and Chronic Disease.*
World Review of Nutrition and Dietetics. Basel, Karger, 1999, vol 84, pp 19-73. Available online: https://pdfs.semanticscholar.org/ba07/b6e9f3cb6e77239d0e81de9aee8173595403.pdf. Accessed 14.12.2018

(14) Young et al (2000). *Type 2 diabetes mellitus in Canada's First Nations: status of an epidemic in progress. CMAJ. 2000 Sep 5; 163(5): 561-566.* Available online: https://www.ncbi.nlm.nih.gov/pmc/articles/PMC80466/. Accessed 14/12/2018

(15) Andrews R (2018). *Phytates and phytic acid.* Precision Nutrition.Com. Available online: http://www.precisionnutrition.com/all-about-phytates-phytic-acid. Accessed 14.12.2018

(16) Kresser C (2014). *Are Legumes 'Paleo'? And Does it Really Matter?* Chris Kresser.Com. Available online: https://chriskresser.com/are-legumes-paleo/. Accessed 14.12.2018

(17) Adams R (2018). *All about lectins.* Precision Nutrition.Com. Available online: https://www.precisionnutrition.com/all-about-lectins. Accessed 14.12.2018

(18) Nikoley R (2016). *How food enrichment promotes obesity.* Available online: https://medium.com/@rnikoley/how-food-enrichment-promotes-obesity-275989cb03b7. Accessed 14.12.2018

(19) Fromartz S (2012). *Time to Rise: Learning the Secret of Paris Boulangeries.* Afar.Com. Available at: https://www.afar.com/magazine/time-to-rise. Accessed 14.12.2018

(20) The Gluten Free Society. *Grain Free Flours.* Available online: https://www.glutenfreesociety.org/flours-grain-free/. Accessed 14.12.2018

(21) Gene Watch. *GM Crops and Foods in Britain and Europe.* Available online: http://www.genewatch.org/sub-568547. Accessed 14.12.2018

(22) Gluten Free Society*: Is rice safe as a gluten-free alternative.* Available online: https://www.glutenfreesociety.org/dangers-eating-rice-gluten-free-diet/. Accessed 14.12.2018

Chapter Seven - It's in Your Bones

(1) Hamilton D (2018). *How Your Mind Can Heal Your Body.* Hay House (Amazon)

(2) Rankin L (2013). *Mind Over Medicine - Scientific Proof You Can Heal Yourself.* Hay House UK. (Amazon)

(3) Marchant J PhD (2016): *CURE: A Journey into the Science of Mind Over Body.* Canongate Books (Amazon)

(4) Campbell McBride N (2010). *Gut and Psychology Syndrome.* Medinform Publishing (Amazon)

(5) Global Industry Analysts Inc (2018). *Increasing Emphasis on Oral Supplements for Maintaining and Enhancing Physical Appearance to Drive Growth in the Nutricosmetics Market*. Available online: https://www.strategyr.com/MarketResearch/Nutricosmetics_Market_Trends.asp. Accessed 14.12.2018

(6) Natrins I (2017). *De-Tox? Or Not-To-Tox? Get off the Detox Treadmill - forever!* (Amazon)

(7) Finn M: *The Whole Fish. How Adventurous Eating of Seafood Can Make You Healthier, Sexier, and Help Save the Ocean*. Kindle. (Amazon)

(8) Revak W (2018). *Peridontal Problems? Bone Broth Key to Your Recovery*. The Healthy Home Economist.Com. Available online: http://www.thehealthyhomeeconomist.com/periodontal-problems-bone-broth-key-to-your-recovery/. Accessed 14.12.2018

(9) Nagel R (2010): *Cure Tooth Decay: Heal and Prevent Cavities with Nutrition*. Create Space (Amazon)

(10) Daniel K PhD (2018). *Bone Broth and MSG: What You Need to Know*. Available online: http://www.thehealthyhomeeconomist.com/bone-broth-msg-what-you-need-to-know/. Accessed 14.12.2018

(11) Peat R PhD (2018). *Tryptophan, serotonin and ageing*. RayPeat.Com. Available online: http://raypeat.com/articles/aging/tryptophan-serotonin-aging.shtml. Accessed 14.12.2018

(12) Peat R PhD (2018). *Gelatin, stress, longevity*. Available online: http://raypeat.com/articles/articles/gelatin.shtml. Accessed 14.12.2018

(13) Campbell McBride N (2010). *Gut and Psychology Syndrome*. Medinform (Amazon)

(14) Seneff S (2017). *Glyphosate in Collage*n. Weston A Price Foundation. Available online: https://www.westonaprice.org/health-topics/environmental-toxins/glyphosate-in-collagen/. Accessed 14.12.2018

(15) Crowly C (2015). *Japan's Ramen Baths are Peak Bone Broth*. Available online: http://www.grubstreet.com/2015/06/ramen-baths-japan.html#. Accessed 14.12.2018

Chapter Eight - Keep Calm and Eat Your Fruit & Veg!

(1) Isokauppila T (2017). *Healing Mushrooms A Practical and Culinary Guide to Using Mushrooms for Whole Body Health*. Avery (Amazon)

(2) Epicurious. *Fourteen types of mushrooms and their uses*. Epicurious. Available online: *https://www.epicurious.com/ingredients/how-to-buy-and-store-different-types-of-mushrooms-recipes-article*. Accessed 14.12.2018

(3) Four Sigmatic Website: *https://us.foursigmatic.com/blog*. Accessed 14.12.2018

(4) Pesticide Action Network (2018). *Food for Thought*. Available online: *http://www.pan-uk.org/food-for-thought*. Accessed 14.12.2018

(5) Yu-Han Chiu et al (2018). *Association Between Pesticide Residue Intake from Consumption of Fruits and Vegetables and Pregnancy Outcomes Among Women Undergoing Infertility Treatment With Assisted Reproductive Technology. JAMA Internal Medicine. 2018;178(1):17-26*. Available online: *https://jamanetwork.com/journals/jamainternalmedicine/article-abstract/2659557?inf_contact_key=1fea38a6cf31fdaddd72cb6bfd9d5954a915ad02a889bee95449b05961992c8d*. Accessed 14.12.2018

(6) Mayer A-M (1997). *Historical changes in the mineral content of fruits and vegetables*. British Food Journal, Vol. 99 Issue: 6, pp.207-211. Available online: *https://doi.org/10.1108/00070709710181540*. Accessed 14.12.2018

(7) Davis D (2008). *Declining Fruit and Vegetable Nutrient Composition: What Is the Evidence?* Available online: *http://hortsci.ashspublications.org/content/44/1/15.full*. Accessed 14.12.2018

(8) Nicky Kyle Gardening Blog. *http://www.nickykylegardening.com*

(9) Functional Performance Systems (2018): *Ray Peat PhD on The Benefits of the Raw Carrot*. Available online: *http://www.functionalps.com/blog/2012/09/28/ray-peat-phd-on-the-benefits-of-the-raw-carrot/*. Accessed 14.12.2018

(10) Kresser C (2012). *Got digestive problems? Take it easy on the veggies*. Available online: *https://chriskresser.com/got-digestive-problems-take-it-easy-on-the-veggies/*. Accessed 14/12/2018

(11) Minger D Wild and Ancient Fruit: *Is it really small, bitter and low in sugar?* Available online: https://deniseminger.com/2011/05/31/wild-and-ancient-fruit. Accessed 14.12.2018

(12) Natrins I (2017). *Get Healthy with These 'Demonised' Energy Drinks.* Available online: https://gallery.mailchimp.com/ca994cbbd0ab46bfa5b89186f/files/d6391495-0153-4877-a701-4af2a320f186/DD_eBook_NEW.01.pdf. Accessed 14.12.2018

Chapter Nine - Fat: Friend or Foe?

(1) Precision Nutrition. *Encyclopedia of Food - Fats.* Precision Nutrition. Available online: https://www.precisionnutrition.com/encyclopedia/food/fats. Accessed 14.12.2018

(2) Select Committee on Nutrition and Human Needs (1977). *Dietary Goals for the United States.* Available online: http://zerodisease.com/archive/Dietary_Goals_For_The_United_States.pdf. Accessed 14.12.2018

(3) Hooper L et al (2015). *Reduction in saturated fat intake for cardiovascular disease. The Cochrane Database Systematic Reviews 2015 Jun 10;(6):CD011737.* Available online: https://www.ncbi.nlm.nih.gov/pubmed/26068959. Accessed 14.12.2018

(4) Schwab U et al (2014). *Effect of the amount and type of dietary fat on risk factors for cardiovascular diseases, and risk of developing type 2 diabetes, cardiovascular diseases, and cancer: a systematic review.* Food and Nutrition Research, 2014: 58. Available online: https://www.ncbi.nlm.nih.gov/pmc/articles/PMC4095759. Accessed 14.12.2018

(5) PHC (2018). *Meta-Analyses Comparing Low-Carb to Low-Fat Diets. Public Health Collaboration.* Available online: https://phcuk.org/rcts/. Accessed 14.12.2018

(6) DiNicolantonio J (2014). *The cardiometabolic consequences of replacing saturated fats with carbohydrates or Ω-6 polyunsaturated fats: Do the dietary guidelines have it wrong?* Openheart, BMJ Journals Vol 1 Issue 1. Available online: https://openheart.bmj.com/content/1/1/e000032. Accessed 14/12/2018

(7) Minger D (2015). *In Defense of Low Fat.* Denise Minger.Com. Available online: *https://deniseminger.com/2015/10/06/in-defense-of-low-fat-a-call-for-some-evolution-of-thought-part-1/*. Accessed 14.12.2018

(8) Pritkin Longevity Centre. https://www.pritikin.com/home-the-basics/about-pritikin/38-nathan-pritikin.html. Accessed 14.12.2018

(9) Denise Minger (2017). *In Defense of Low Fat. Icelandic Health Symposium 2017*. Available online: https://youtu.be/qBBtQ4QwWxg. Accessed 14.12.2018

(10) Masterjohn C PhD (2018). *Personal correspondence*. 23.10.2018

(11) Penson P (2017). *Associations between cardiovascular disease, cancer and very low hdl cholesterol in the reasons for geographical and racial differences in stroke (REGARDS) study*. European Heart Journal Volume 38. Available online: https://academic.oup.com/eurheartj/article/38/suppl_1/ehx504.3104/4089554. Accessed 14.12.2018

(12) Peat R PhD (2006-16). *Suitable Fats, Unsuitable Fats: Issues in Nutrition*. Available online: http://raypeat.com/articles/articles/unsuitablefats.shtml. Accessed 14.12.2018

(13) Kresser C (2010). *How too much omega-6 and not enough omega-3 is making us sick*. Chris Kresser.Com. Available online: https://chriskresser.com/how-too-much-omega-6-and-not-enough-omega-3-is-making-us-sick/. Accessed 14.12.2018

(14) DiNicolantonio, J (2018). *Anti-Inflammatory Effects of Gamma-Linolenic Acid (GLA)*. Life Extension Magazine. Available online: https://www.lifeextension.com/Magazine/2018/9/Extinguish-Fires-of-Chronic-Inflammation/Page-01. Accessed 14.12.2018

(15) Weston A Price Foundation (2012). *Trans Fats in the Food Supply*. Weston A Price Foundation. Available online: https://www.westonaprice.org/health-topics/know-your-fats/trans-fats-in-the-food-supply/. Accessed 14.12.2018

(16) Enig M PhD (2008). *Interestification*. Weston A Price Foundation. Available online: https://www.westonaprice.org/health-topics/know-your-fats/interesterification/. Accessed 14.12.2018

(17) Curtis C (2016). *How the Nurses' Health Study Helped Americans Take the Trans Fat Out. American Journal of Public Health. 2016 September; 106(9): 1537-1539*. Available online: https://www.ncbi.nlm.nih.gov/pmc/articles/PMC4981820/. Accessed 14.12.2018

(18) US Food and Drug Administration (2015). Final Determination Regarding Partially Hydrogenated Oils (Removing Trans Fat). Available online: https://www.fda.gov/Food/IngredientsPackagingLabeling/FoodAdditivesIngredients/ucm449162.htm. Accessed 14.12.2018

(19) Weston A Price Foundation (2012). *Trans Fats in the Food Supply*. Weston A Price Foundation. Available at: https://www.westonaprice.org/health-topics/know-your-fats/trans-fats-in-the-food-supply/. Accessed 14.12.2018

(20) Sundram K et al (2007). *Stearic acid-rich interesterified fat and trans-rich fat raise the LDL/HDL ratio and plasma glucose relative to palm olein in humans*. Nutrition and Metabolism (London). Available online: https://www.ncbi.nlm.nih.gov/pmc/articles/PMC1783656. Accessed 14.12.2018

(21) Meizys D (2007). *If You Eat French Fries or Potato Chips, This Will Stop You*. Mercola.Com. Available online:
https://blogs.mercola.com/sites/vitalvotes/archive/2007/01/23/More-Reasons-to-Avoid-Potato-Chips.aspx. Accessed 14.12.2018

(22) Natrins I (2018). *7 Reasons to Use Ghee*. Izabella Natrins.Com. Available online: https://www.izabellanatrins.com/7-reasons-to-use-ghee/. Accessed 14.12.2018

(23) Joseph M (2018). *Extra Virgin Olive Oil: The World's Healthiest Fat?* Nutrition Advance. Available online: https://www.nutritionadvance.com/extra-virgin-olive-oil. Accessed 14.12.2018

(24) O'Keefe et al (1994). *Levels of Trans Geometrical Isomers of Essential Fatty Acids in Some Unhydrogenated U.S. Vegetable Oils*. Journal of Food Lipids. Available online: https://onlinelibrary.wiley.com/doi/abs/10.1111/j.1745-4522.1994.tb00244.x. Accessed 14.12.2018

Chapter Ten - Seafood - and Eat It!

(1) Leech J (2015). *11 Health Benefits of Eating Fish*. Healthline.Com 24.05.2018. Available online: https://www.healthline.com/nutrition/11-health-benefits-of-fish#section3. Accessed 14.12.2018

(2) Nikitenko N (2018). *Top Ten White Fish Benefits*. Global Seafoods.Com. Available online: https://globalseafoods.com/blogs/news/white-fish-benefits. Accessed 14.12.2018

(3) as above (1) - Leech J (2015). *11 Health Benefits of Eating Fish*. Healthline.Com. Available online:
https://www.healthline.com/nutrition/11-health-benefits-of-fish#section3. Accessed 14.12.2018

(4) Adams R (2018). *All About Eating Seafood*. PrecisionNutrition.Com. Available online: https://www.precisionnutrition.com/all-about-eating-seafood. Accessed 14.12.2018

(5) Price Weston A (2003). *Nutrition and Physical Degeneration. 6th Edition*. The Price Pottenger Nutrition Foundation (Amazon)

(6) Allbritton J (2010). *Sacred Foods for Exceptionally Healthy Babies … and parents, too!* Weston A Price Foundation. Available online: https://www.westonaprice.org/health-topics/childrens-health/sacred-foods-for-exceptionally-healthy-babies-and-parents-too/. Accessed 14.12.2018

(7) Pope S (2018). *Fish Stock: The Healthiest and Best Bone Broth*. The Healthy Home Economist. Available online: https://www.thehealthyhomeeconomist.com/healthiest-and-best-bone-broth. Accessed 14.12.2018

(8) Sisson M (2011). *A Guide to Crustaceans, Bivalves and Molluscs, or Why You Should Be Eating Exoskeleton-Bearing Aquatic Invertebrates*. Mark's Daily Apple. Available online: https://www.marksdailyapple.com/types-of-shellfish. Accessed 14.12.2018

(9) FloGrow Fresh (2018). *Fresh British Prawns*. Available online: http://flogrosystems.com/. Accessed 14.12.2018

(10) Schweisfurth L (2018). *The tragic demise of Scotland's salmon. Sustainable Food Trust: Chemicals in Agriculture, Farming 22.03.2018*. Available online: http://sustainablefoodtrust.org/articles/the-tragic-demise-of-scotlands-salmon/. Accessed: 14.12.2018

(11) as above (4) - Adams R (2018). *All About Eating Seafood*. PrecisionNutrition.Com. Available online: https://www.precisionnutrition.com/all-about-eating-seafood. Accessed 14.12.2018

(12) The Marine Stewardship Council. Website: https://www.mcsuk.org/. Accessed 14.12.2018

(13) Kresser C (2014). *5 Reasons Why Concerns About Mercury in Fish Are Misguided*. Chris Kresser.Com. Available online: https://chriskresser.com/5-reasons-why-concerns-about-mercury-in-fish-are-misguided/. Accessed 14.12.2018

(14) Mattsson K. et al (2017). *Brain damage and behavioural disorders in fish induced by plastic nanoparticles delivered through the food chain*. Nature.Com. Scientific Reports Volume 7, Article number: 11452 (2017). Available online: https://www.nature.com/articles/s41598-017-10813-0. Accessed 14.12.2018

(15) FIS European Union (2017). *How fresh is the fish sold at supermarkets?* FIS.Com Available online: http://www.fis.com/fis/worldnews/worldnews.asp?monthyear=10-2017&day=2&id=94008&l=e&country=0&special=&ndb=1&df=0. Accessed 14.12.2018

(16) West H (2017). *Is it safe to use aluminium foil in cooking?* Available online: https://www.healthline.com/nutrition/aluminum-foil-cooking#section2. Accessed 14.12.2018

Chapter Eleven - Cultured and Fermented Foods

(1) National Public Radio (NPR*). The Invisible Universe of the Human Micro-biome*. Available online: *https://www.youtube.com/watch?v=5DTrENdWvvM*. Accessed 14.12.2018

(2) Monteiro-Haig M (2017). *The gut as a key player in neuroscience.* Available online: *https://www.thescienceofpsychotherapy.com/the-gut-as-a-key-player-in-neuroscience/*. Accessed 14.12.2018

(3) Sharifi M et al (2017). *Kefir: a powerful probiotic with anticancer properties*. Medical Oncology. 34. 10.1007/s12032-017-1044-9. Available online: *https://www.ncbi.nlm.nih.gov/pubmed/28956261*. Accessed 14.12.2018

(4) Cultures for Health. *Composition of Milk Kefir Grains: Bacteria & Yeasts*. Available online: http://www.culturesforhealth.com/milk-kefir-grains-composition-bacteria-yeast. Accessed 14.12.2018

Chapter Twelve - Salt

(1) DiNicolantonio J (2017). *The Salt Fix: Why the Experts Got it All Wrong and How Eating More Might Save Your Life*. Piatkus (Amazon)

(2) Fleming A (2014). *How the experts use salt in their cooking - and why*. The Guardian.Com. Available online: *https://www.theguardian.com/lifeandstyle/2014/jan/28/experts-use-salt-in-cooking-why*. Accessed 14.12.2018

(3) Action on Salt. *Why Eat Less Salt*. Available online: *http://www.actiononsalt.org.uk/less/health/*. Accessed 14.12.2018

(4) Fung J (2018). *The Salt Scam*. Medium 2018. Available online: *https://medium.com/@drjasonfung/the-salt-scam-1973d73dccd*. Accessed 14.12.2018

(5) Heimer M (2011). *Ditch the table salt, not the sodium*. Natural News.Com. Available online: *https://www.naturalnews.com/031608_table_salt_sodium.html.* Accessed 14.12.2018

(6) Thomas P (2009). *What type of salt is best?* Available online: https://theecologist.org/2009/may/01/what-type-salt-best. Accessed 14.12.2018

(7) Peat R PhD (2018). *Salt, energy, metabolic rate, and longevity*. Available online: http://raypeat.com/articles/articles/salt.shtml. Accessed 14.12.2018

(8) Carbone L et al (2016). *Salt intake appears to have little impact on bone health in menopausal women*. Science Daily (2016). Sodium Intake and Osteoporosis. Findings from the Women's Health Initiative. The Journal of Clinical Endocrinology & Metabolism, 2016; jc.2015-4017 Available online: https://www.sciencedaily.com/releases/2016/02/160225140420.htm. Accessed 14.12.2018

(9) Cardiosmart.org (2017). *The bulk of US salt intake comes from processed foods.* Available online: https://www.cardiosmart.org/News-and-Events/2017/06/The-Bulk-of-US-Salt-Intake-Comes-From-Processed-Foods. Accessed 14.12.2018

(10) Kresser C (2012*). Shaking Up the Salt Myth: Healthy Salt Recommendations*. Chris Kresser.Com. Available online: http://chriskresser.com/shaking-up-the-salt-myth-healthy-salt-recommendations/. Accessed 14.12.2018

Chapter Thirteen - Sugar

(1) Timeline of Sugar. Available online: http://www.sugarhistory.net/who-made-sugar/sugar-timeline/. Accessed 14.12.2018

(2) Masterjohn C PhD (2016). *Sugar is the Ultimate Antioxidant and Insulin will Make You Younger*. Available online: https://chrismasterjohnphd.com/2016/05/30/sugar-is-ultimate-antioxidant-and. Accessed 14.12.2018

(3) Dan@CowsEatGrass (2016). *Sugar Feeds Thyroid*. Available online: https://cowseatgrass.org/2016/02/12/sugar-feeds-thyroid/. Accessed 14.12.2018

(4) Seyfried T et al (2016). *The restricted ketogenic diet: an alternative treatment strategy for glioblastoma multiforme*. Available online: https://pdfs.semanticscholar.org/07ae/50a642ecd6b865daf7d87b30da31fe04d411.pdf. Accessed 14.12.2018

(5) Gonzalez N. *Dr. Gonzalez Dismantles the Ketogenic Diet for Cancer*. Available online: http://www.chrisbeatcancer.com/dr-gonzalez-dismantles-ketogenic-diet-for-cancer/. Accessed 14.12.2018

(6) Eenfeldt A MD (2019). *A low-carb diet for beginners*. Available online: *https://www.dietdoctor.com/low-carb*. Accessed 02.01.2019

Chapter Fourteen - Herbs and Spices

(1) Brown B (2017). *Braving the Wilderness: The Quest for True Belonging and the Courage to Stand Alone*. Vermilion (Amazon)

(2) Lalonde M (2012). *Nutrient Density: Sticking to the Essentials.* Ancestral Health Symposium 2012. Available online: *https://youtu.be/HwbY12qZcF4*. Accessed 14.12.2018

(3) Aggarwal B & Yost D (2011). *Healing Spices*. Sterling (Amazon)

Appendix 1 - A Deeper Dive into Carbs

(1) Monteiro C et al (2018). *Household availability of ultra-processed foods and obesity in nineteen European countries*. Public Health Nutrition. Access Volume 21, Issue 1 (Ultra Processed Foods) January 2018. Available online: https://doi.org/10.1017/S1368980017001379. Accessed 14.12.2018

(2) Peat R. PhD. *Sugar Issues*. RayPeat.Com. Available online: *http://raypeat.com/articles/articles/sugar-issues.shtml*. Accessed 14.12.2018

(3) Eenfeldt A MD (2019). *A low-carb diet for beginners*. Available online: *https://www.dietdoctor.com/low-carb*. Accessed 02.01.2019

(4) as (2) above - Peat R. PhD. *Sugar Issues*. RayPeat.Com. Available online: *http://raypeat.com/articles/articles/sugar-issues.shtml*. Accessed 14.12.2018

(5) Wolff R. (2017). *Wired to Eat: How to Rewire Your Appetite and Lose Weight for Good*. Vermillion. (Amazon)

(6) Yudkin J (2016). *Pure White and Deadly: How Sugar Is Killing Us and What We Can Do to Stop It.* Paperback Penguin Life. (Amazon)

(7) Lustig R (2014). *Fat Chance: The Hidden Truth About Sugar, Obesity and Disease*. Fourth Estate Ltd. (Amazon)

(8) Masterjohn C (2016). *Sugar is the ultimate antioxidant and insulin will make you younger: Appreciating a few poorly recognized but critical contributions of carbohydrate.* Available online: https://chrismasterjohnphd.com/2016/05/30/sugar-is-ultimate-antioxidant-and/. Accessed 14.12.2018

Further reading:

An introduction to Nutrition (v.1.0). Chapter 4: Carbohydrates. Available online: https://2012books.lardbucket.org/books/an-introduction-to-nutrition/s08-carbohydrates.html Accessed 14.12.2018

Gunnars K (2016). *Good Carbs, Bad Carbs: How to Make the Right Choice.* Healthline.Com. Available online: https://www.healthline.com/nutrition/good-carbs-bad-carbs. Accessed 14.12.2018

Appendix 2 - Chemicals, Our Food, Our Health and Our Environment

(1) Offit P (2017). *Fertiliser has saved billions of lives, but it also has a dark side. Excerpt: Pandora's Lab: Seven Stories of Science Gone Wrong*. Popular Science.Com. Available https://www.popsci.com/fertiliser-nitrogen#page-2. Accessed 14.12.2018

(2) Mike Ursy (2009). *The Health Effects of Synthetic Fertiliser*. Southland Organics. Available online: https://www.southlandorganics.com/blogs/news/17982096-health-effects-of-synthetic-fertiliser. Accessed 14.12.2018

(3) Connett M (2003). *The Phosphate Fertiliser Industry: An environmental overview - Fluoride* Alert.Org. Available online: http://fluoridealert.org/articles/phosphate01/. Accessed 14.12.2018

(4) as (3) above - *The Phosphate Fertiliser Industry: An environmental overview* - Fluoride Alert.Org - http://fluoridealert.org/articles/phosphate01/. Accessed 14.12.2018

(5) WHO (2018). Water Sanitation Hygiene: Water Related Diseases - Fluorosis. World Health Organisation. Available online: http://www.who.int/water_sanitation_health/diseases-risks/diseases/fluorosis/en/. Accessed 14.12.2018

(6) Connett M & Blank T (2016). *Fluoride & IQ: The 53 Studies*. Fluoride Alert.Org. Available online: http://fluoridealert.org/studies/brain01/. Accessed 14.12.2018

(7) Peckham S et al (2015). *Are fluoride levels in drinking water associated with hypothyroidism prevalence in England? A large observational study of GP practice data and fluoride levels in drinking water*. Journal of Epidemiology and Community Health.
Available online: https://news.kent.ac.uk/app/uploads/2015/02/Flouride-research.pdf. Accessed 14.12.2018

(8) Peckham S et al (2014). *Water Fluoridation: A Critical Review of the Physiological Effects of Ingested Fluoride as a Public Health Intervention*. The Scientific World Journal Volume 2014, Article ID 293019. Available online: https://www.hindawi.com/journals/tswj/2014/293019/. Accessed 14.12.2018

(9) Cates T (2016). *Your Skin, Your Health and Autoimmune Disease with Dr. Tom O'Bryan*. The Spa Dr Podcast.Com. Available online: http://thespadr.com/skin-health-autoimmune-disease-dr-tom-obryan/. Accessed 14.12.2018

(10) Berkey Water Filters. https://berkey-waterfilters.co.uk

(11) Osmio Water Filters. https://www.osmiowater.co.uk

(12) Fluoride Action Network (2012). *Top 10 Ways to Reduce Fluoride Exposure*. FluorideAlert.Org. Available online. http://fluoridealert.org/content/top_ten/. Accessed 14.12.2018

(13) *Phosphate Facts. Uses and Applications*. PhosphateFacts.Org. Available online: http://phosphatesfacts.org/uses-applications/. Accessed 14.12.2018

(14) Brissette C (2017). *Why phosphate additives will be the next taboo ingredient*. The Washington Post. Available online:
https://www.washingtonpost.com/lifestyle/wellness/why-phosphate-additives-will-be-the-next-taboo-ingredient/2017/03/29/7dd3247a-02cf-11e7-b1e9-a05d3c21f7cf_story.html?utm_term=.cd09d8bbb97c. Accessed 14.12.2018

(15) Baida B (2015). *Flavour enhancing ingredient carries risk for some*. WebMD.Com. Available online: http://www.webmd.com/news/breaking-news/food-additives/20150723/phosphates-food?page=3. Accessed 14.12.2018

(16) Kresser C (2012). *The Nitrate and Nitrite Myth: Another Reason Not to Fear Bacon*. Chris Kresser.Com. Available online: https://chriskresser.com/the-nitrate-and-nitrite-myth-another-reason-not-to-fear-bacon/. Accessed 14.12.2018

(17) Machha A & Schechter A (2011). *Dietary nitrite and nitrate: a review of potential mechanisms of cardiovascular benefits*. European Journal of Nutrition. 2011 Aug; 50(5): 293-303. Available online: https://www.ncbi.nlm.nih.gov/pmc/articles/PMC3489477/. Accessed 14.12.2018

(18) d'El-Rei J et Al (2016). *Beneficial Effects of Dietary Nitrate on Endothelial Function and Blood Pressure Levels*. International Journal of Hypertension 2016: 6791519.2016. Available online: https://www.ncbi.nlm.nih.gov/pmc/articles/PMC4819099/. Accessed 14.12.2018

(19) Praderio C (2015). Nitrites & Nitrates - *Are They Harmful or Actually Healthful?* Prevention.Com. Available online: http://www.prevention.com/food/healthy-eating-tips/nitrites-and-nitrates. Accessed 14.12.2018

(20) Holden P (2016). *Good Nutrition begins in the Soil*. The Sustainable Food Trust. Available online: http://sustainablefoodtrust.org/articles/good-nutrition-begins-soil/. Accessed 14.12.2018

(21) Watson G (2017). *Systemic Pesticides and Dubious Progress*. Riverford Organic Farmers. Available online: https://blog.riverford.co.uk/2017/03/31/guys-news-systemic-pesticides-dubious-progress/. Accessed 14.12.2018

(22) The Soil Association. *Pesticides*. Available online: https://www.soilassociation.org/media/8060/pesticides.pdf. Accessed 14.12.2018

(23) Pesticide Action Network (2017). *New United Nations Report on Pesticides in Food*. Available online: http://www.pan-uk.org/new-united-nations-report-pesticides-food. Accessed 14.12.2018

(24) McKenzie R et al (2012). *Neurobehavioral problems following low-level exposure to organophosphate pesticides: a systematic and meta-analytic review*. Critical Reviews in Toxicology Volume 43, 2013 Issue 1. Available online: http://www.tandfonline.com/doi/abs/10.3109/10408444.2012.738645. Accessed 14.12.2018

(25) Levitt T (2012). *Pesticide used by UK farmers is linked to brain damage*. The Ecologist. Available online: http://www.theecologist.org/News/news_analysis/1727905/pesticide_used_by_uk_farmers_is_linked_to_longterm_brain_damage.html. Accessed 14.12.2018

(26) Marks A (2010). *Organophosphate Pesticide Exposure and Attention in Young Mexican-American Children: The CHAMACOS Study*. Environmental Health Perspectives 2010 Dec; 118(12): 1768-1774. Available online: https://www.ncbi.nlm.nih.gov/pmc/articles/PMC3002198/. Accessed 14.12.2018

(27) Grossman E (2011). *From Fields to Inner City, Pesticides Affect Children's IQ*. Yale Environment 360. Available online: https://e360.yale.edu/features/from_the_fields_to_inner_city_pesticides_affect_childrens_iq. Accessed 14.12.2018

(28) Rauh V et al (2012). *Prenatal Exposure to Insecticide Chlorpyrifos Linked to Alterations in Brain Structure and Cognition*. Public Health Now. Mailman School of Public Health, University of Columbia. Available online: https://www.mailman.columbia.edu/public-health-now/news/prenatal-exposure-insecticide-chlorpyrifos-linked-alterations-brain-structure. Accessed 14.12.2018

(29) Carrington D (2014). *Over 60% of breads sold in the UK contain pesticide residues, tests show.* Available online: https://www.theguardian.com/environment/2014/jul/17/pesticide-residue-breads-uk-crops. Accessed 14.12.2018

(30) Mercola J (2016). Study: *Pesticides Are Creating Pollination Problems and Killing Bees.* Available online: http://articles.mercola.com/sites/articles/archive/2016/08/30/neonicotinoid-pesticides-bee-decline.aspx. Accessed 14.12.2018

(31) Hallmann C et al: *Declines in insectivorous birds are associated with high neonicotinoid concentrations.* Nature volume 511, pages 341-343. Available online: http://www.nature.com/nature/journal/v511/n7509/full/nature13531.html. Accessed 14.12.2018

(32) Carrington F (2014). *Neonicotinoids linked to recent fall in farmland bird numbers.* Dr David Goulson, University of Sussex quoted in The Guardian.Com. Available online: https://www.theguardian.com/environment/2014/jul/09/neonicotinoids-farmland-birds?CMP=twt_gu. Accessed 14.12.2018

(33) Watson G (2017). *Neonicotinoids and Bees - Again*. Riverford Organic Farmers. Available online: https://www.riverford.co.uk/neonicotinoids-and-bees-again. Accessed 14.12.2018

(34) Soil Association (2018). *What is glyphosate?* Available online: https://www.soilassociation.org/our-campaigns/not-in-our-bread/what-is-glyphosate/. Accessed 14.12.2018

(35) GM Free Cymru (2015). *Monsanto & EPA knew of glyphosate cancer link in 1981*. The Ecologist. Available online: https://theecologist.org/2015/jul/07/monsanto-and-epa-knew-glyphosate-cancer-link-1981. Accessed 14.12.2018

(36) Pesticide Action Network UK. *Glyphosate*. Available online: http://www.pan-uk.org/glyphosate/. Accessed 14.12.2018

(37) Pesticide Action Network UK (2016): *The Glyphosate Monograph. A comprehensive new review of the science documenting the adverse health and environmental impacts of glyphosate and glyphosate-based herbicides*. Available online: http://issuu.com/pan-uk/docs/glyphosate_monograph_complete?e=28041656/43997864. Accessed 14.12.2018

(38) World Health Organisation (2015). *IARC Monographs Volume 112: evaluation of five organophosphate insecticides and herbicides*. International Agency for Research on Cancer. Available online: http://www.iarc.fr/en/media-centre/iarcnews/pdf/MonographVolume112.pdf. Accessed 14.12.2018

(39) World Health Organisation (2017). *IARC rejects false claims in Reuters article ("In glyphosate review, WHO cancer agency edited out "non-carcinogenic" findings")*. International Agency for Research on Cancer. Available online: https://www.iarc.fr/wp-content/uploads/2018/07/IARC_Response_Reuters_October2017.pdf. Accessed 14.12.2018

(40) Stevens R (2018*): Does Monsanto's Roundup Cause Cancer? Trial Highlights -The Difficulty of Proving A Link*. Common Health 2018. Available online: http://www.wbur.org/commonhealth/2018/08/07/does-roundup-cause-cancer. Accessed: 14.12.2018

(41) Smith J & Seneff S (2013). *Health Dangers of Roundup (glyphosate) Herbicide*. Institute for Responsible Technology. Available online. https://www.youtube.com/watch?v=h_AHLDXF5aw&feature=youtu.be. Accessed 14.12.2018

(42) Mesnage R et al (2017). *Multiomics reveal non-alcoholic fatty liver disease in rats following chronic exposure to an ultra-low dose of Roundup herbicide*. Kings College London. Available online: https://kclpure.kcl.ac.uk/portal/en/publications/multiomics-reveal-nonalcoholic-fatty-liver-disease-in-rats-following-chronic-exposure-to-an-ultralow-dose-of-roundup-herbicide(402ec9bb-c1fd-457f-aa87-4a89b60663ff).html. Accessed 14.12.2018

(43) Mole N (2011). *Consumers and farm workers at risk from toxic pesticides sprayed on salad.* The Ecologist Available online: http://www.theecologist.org/blogs_and_comments/commentators/other_comments/1035098/consumers_and_farm_workers_at_risk_from_toxic_pesticides_sprayed_on_salad.html. Accessed 14.12.2018

(44) Pesticide Action Network (2017). *Food for Thought*. Available online: http://www.pan-uk.org/food-for-thought/. Accessed 14.12.2018

(45) Caldwell M (2013). *5 Surprising Genetically Modified Foods*. Available online: http://www.motherjones.com/environment/2013/08/what-are-gmos-and-why-should-i-care. Accessed 14.12.2018

(46) The Soil Association (2015). *GM… It's no chicken feed*. Available online: https://www.soilassociation.org/blogs/2015/January/gmits-no-chicken-feed. Accessed 14.12.2018

(47) Pesticide Action Network (2108*). Key Issues*. Available online: http://www.pan-uk.org/key-issues/. Accessed 14.12.2018

Appendix 3 - A Deeper Dive into Good vs Bad Science

(1) Fields H et al (2016). *Is Meat Killing Us?* The Journal of the American Osteopathic Association, May 2016, Vol. 116, 296-300. Available online: http://jaoa.org/article.aspx?articleid=2517494. Accessed 14.12.2018

(2) Saltelliab A & Funtowicza S (2017). *What is science's crisis really about?* Science Direct. Futures Volume 91, August 2017, Pages 5-11. Available online: https://www.sciencedirect.com/science/article/pii/S0016328717301969. Accessed 14.12.2018

(3) Ioannidis J (2018). *The Challenge of Reforming Nutritional Epidemiologic Research*. Journal of the American Medical Association 2018;320(10):969-9702018. Available online. https://jamanetwork.com/journals/jama/fullarticle/2698337. Accessed 14.12.2018

(4) Holloway A (2014). *Ancient Origins*. Available online: https://www.ancient-origins.net/news-evolution-human-origins/life-expectancy-myth-and-why-many-ancient-humans-lived-long-077889. Accessed 14.12.2018

36899829R00219

Printed in Poland
by Amazon Fulfillment
Poland Sp. z o.o., Wrocław